Battle for the Ballot

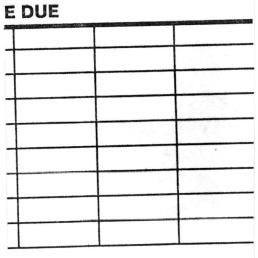

BATTLE FOR THE BALLOT

Essays on Woman Suffrage in Utah

1870–1896

Carol Cornwall Madsen
Editor

Utah State University Press
Logan, Utah
1997

Utah State University Press
Logan, Utah 84322-7800

Typeset in TEX by the Bartlett Press
Cover design by Michelle Sellers
Cover illustrations: Rocky Mountain Woman Suffrage Covention (1895) and
close-up of Susan B. Anthony. *Courtesy of Archives, Historical Department, Church of
Jesus Christ of Latter-day Saints.*

The paper in this book is acid free

Library of Congress Cataloging-in-Publication Data

Battle for the ballot : essays on woman suffrage in Utah, 1870–1896 /
    Carol Cornwall Madsen, editor.
        p.   cm.
    Includes bibliographical references (p.) and index.
    ISBN 0–87421–222–7 (cloth : acid-free paper).—ISBN
0–87421–223–5 (pbk.: acid-free paper)
    1. Women—Suffrage—Utah—History. I. Madsen, Carol Cornwall,
    1930–   .
    JK1911.U8B37   1997
    324.6'23'09792—dc21   96–51229
                                                              CIP

Contents

Foreword

Kathryn L. MacKay

Carol Cornwall Madsen has gathered up or excerpted from the significant studies of woman suffrage in Utah. Some were written contemporary to the battles for the ballot. Most are from research during the last twenty-some years. This collection thus demonstrates the richness of recent scholarship. Such work draws from the research on women and their experiences and expressions that has been a dynamic of the second-wave women's movement since it emerged from the civil rights struggle of the 1960s and 1970s. These writings also reflect the new Mormon scholarship that was stimulated by the newly opened Latter-day Saint (LDS) Church archives and by fresh interest in the lives of ordinary Mormons, a part of the national move to social and cultural, "bottoms-up" studies that informed many scholarly disciplines after World War II.

It is not surprising that Dr. Madsen has taken up this task. Those two dynamics shaped her own scholarly career. She joined many women in going back to college in the 1970s after rearing her children. She worked for a time at the then newly established Women's Resource Center at the University of Utah; helped organize the Utah Woman's History Association, serving as its president; and wrote a Ph.D. dissertation on Emmeline B. Wells, editor of the *Woman's Exponent* and one of the Mormon links to the national suffrage movement in the nineteenth century. As she undertook her university studies, Dr. Madsen also began working for the LDS Church history department under

Leonard J. Arrington and so contributed to a flurry of fresh, solidly researched texts on LDS women's organizations, Utah gender laws and politics, and lives of elite and ordinary Mormon women.

Battle for the Ballot arrives in the wake of two anniversaries. The seventy-fifth anniversary of the Nineteenth Amendment to the Constitution, which extended suffrage to women nationwide, was in 1995. Nineteen ninety-six was the centennial of Utah's statehood and constitution, which included woman suffrage. The lag between these recently celebrated events raises anew key questions: Why, if the ideology and the organizational energy for woman suffrage came out of the East, did the actuality of woman suffrage emerge in the West? And why Utah? Why woman suffrage among the Mormons? Why this expansion of democracy in a hierarchical theocracy? Why this status of individuated citizenship for women in a society marked by male ecclesiastical privilege and polygyny?

Woman suffrage in the West began with discussions in Washington Territory in the 1850s. (Washington extended suffrage to women in 1883, then revoked it in 1887.) Legislation passed by the Wyoming territorial assembly in 1869 allowed women to vote and to run for and hold public office, and Wyoming entered the union in 1890 with woman suffrage a part of its constitution. Idaho became a state in 1890, and a referendum passed in 1896 to amend woman suffrage to the state constitution. Colorado became a state in 1876; a referendum on woman suffrage in 1877 failed, but a second in 1893 passed. Woman suffrage was passed by the Utah territorial legislature in 1870 and again in 1896. Some fourteen years later these four states had been joined by seven others—all of them (including Kansas, where woman suffrage first had been put to a direct vote in 1867) west of the Mississippi.

Recent efforts to explain this phenomenon of woman suffrage in the West began with Alan P. Grimes in his 1967 *The Puritan Ethic and Woman Suffrage.* His strained analysis concluded that the movement for woman suffrage in the West was part of that region's "Puritan revival," which sought to purify American politics. Persons supporting suffrage supposed women would "clean-up" politics as they also fought for prohibition of liquor consumption, immigration restrictions, and laws limiting child labor. Grimes's analysis suffers because he did not adequately consider that the "Puritan" tradition was one of race, class, and gender hierarchy, not democratic egalitarianism, and failed to note, as Beverly Beeton has pointed out, that the 1869–1870 woman suffrage measures passed without accompanying "purifying" efforts.

Beeton maintained in her 1976 dissertation (published in 1986 as *Women Vote in the West: The Woman Suffrage Movement, 1869–1896)* that not only had Grimes erred but ideological motives for woman suffrage were less significant than expedient ones—such as attracting settlers and investors to the West, embarrassing political opponents, and recruiting eastern suffragists' support for statehood bids—and racist ones, such as pitting white women against Hispanics and new immigrants. She also noted in "How the West was Won for Woman Suffrage" (her chapter in *One Woman, One Vote, Rediscovering the Woman Suffrage Movement*, edited by Marjorie Spruill Wheeler for the 1995 anniversary) that woman suffrage in the West may have also derived from the process of forming new governments, which forced persons to think about and debate issues of who should be allowed the vote and hence to consider experimenting with expanded suffrage.

That argument might be extended by considering the work of the new Western historians, such as Richard White, who maintain that the West is distinguished as a region by the depth and breadth of federal government involvement—in land takings by Anglo-Americans, in economic development of the area, in the very settlement patterns of natives and intruders alike. It may be that, because the federal government had the power to set the terms of territorial and state organization, experimentation with woman suffrage in the West occurred to whatever degree arguments for experimentation persuaded the federal law makers. Certainly there was no groundswell of support for woman suffrage from Anglo settlers—women or men—in Wyoming or Utah during the 1860s. That support came from easterners whose motives were as varied as their backgrounds.

Few scholars are willing to explain woman suffrage in the West through a Turnerian notion that an indigenous strain of Western democracy engendered it. Sandra L. Myres's 1982 *Westering Women and the Frontier Experience, 1800–1915* is sufficiently anchored in the theories of Frederick Jackson Turner for her to suggest that the concept of innovation "both common and necessary to the frontier" might explain the "diffusion" of woman suffrage in the West. However, that suggestion has not been sustained by the new Western scholarship. Her observation, however, that "most women's suffrage and feminist historians have almost entirely ignored the West" remains surprisingly correct.

There are still very few studies of woman suffrage in the West at the state level. For example, no one has yet expanded into a book-length publication the work begun by Wyoming historian T. A. Larson on woman suffrage in Wyoming and Idaho (*Pacific Northwest Quarterly* [April 1965] and *Idaho's Yesterdays* [Spring 1972]). That there is such a dearth of state studies makes this collection of writings focused on Utah all the more significant. And Utah woman suffrage had such an intriguing history.

Woman suffrage in Utah got enmeshed in struggles over "reconstructing" Mormon Utah by forcing its theocracy to conform with the republican democracy of the rest of the United States. The struggle paralleled the more intense post-Civil War effort to reconstruct the race/class hierarchy of the South into a more egalitarian, participatory democracy. Questions about who was privileged to participate in making public policy and the extent or limits of that participation were aspects of the discourse about Utah and the South at the national level.

It is an interesting irony that support for Mormon women's promotion of suffrage came from the more radical National Woman Suffrage Association (NWSA) headed by Elizabeth Cady Stanton and Susan B. Anthony and not from the American Woman Suffrage Association (AWSA) led by Lucy Stone and others. The two groups were split over strategy: the NWSA concentrated on a national suffrage amendment; the AWSA was inclined to concentrate on state-by-state enfranchisement. The groups were split over other issues as well. Stanton and Anthony were willing to form alliances with all sorts of people: third political party adherents, members of the National Labor Union, the notorious Victoria Woodhull, and Mormon women who practiced or supported plural marriage as a matter of religious faith, a practice which the Supreme Court characterized in 1877 as "offensive to the public morals."

In their seeming commitment to the ideals of "true womanhood," in their acceptance of a theologically sustained gender hierarchy, Mormon women might be expected to find more compatibility with the philosophies of the AWSA, whose leaders preferred to work within what Anne Firor Scott and Andrew MacKay Scott called in *One Half the People: The Fight for Woman Suffrage* (1975) "the framework of gentility." It is more problematic than that. Like other Victorian women working in homosocial networks to better their communities and women's lives—work intensified by Mormon commitments to do whatever it took to build a literal "Zion" in Utah—many Mormon women became politically and publicly active and closely connected to national suffrage efforts. It was the leaders of NWSA who invited the Mormon women to participate in its conventions; it was with those leaders the Mormon women held an enduring affiliation. Whether suffrage work also convinced some of these Mormon women to join Stanton and Anthony in questioning gender hierarchy remains speculative. This book will enable readers to join in the speculation.

Acknowledgments

This volume emerged from many discussions I had with four friends and colleagues as we prepared a readers' theatre on woman suffrage in Utah for presentation during the centennial celebration of Utah statehood in 1996. Kathryn L. MacKay of Weber State University, Jean Bickmore White, professor emeritus of Weber State University, Jill Mulvay Derr of the Joseph Fielding Smith Institute for Church History at Brigham Young University, and Georgia Yardley Barker of the Utah League of Women Voters provided inspiration for this collection. Until a full history of woman suffrage in Utah is written, this volume will provide an overview from a variety of perspectives of this fascinating period in Utah history.

Appreciation for permission to include their essays is extended to contributing authors Lola Van Wagenen of Charlotte, Vermont; Maureen Ursenbach Beecher of Brigham Young University; Thomas G. Alexander of Brigham Young University; Beverly Beeton of the University of Alaska, Anchorage; Joan Iversen of Maryland, New York; Sherilyn Bennion of Humboldt State University; Gary L. and Carol B. Bunker of Brigham Young University and Provo, Utah; Lisa Bryner Bohman of Magna, Utah; Linda Thatcher of the Utah State Historical Society; and to Jean White, Jill Derr, and Kathryn MacKay. Appreciation is also extended to the previous publishers of the essays and to the Historical Department of the Church of

Jesus Christ of Latter-day Saints and the Utah State Historical Society for permission to use the photographs included in the volume.

I also appreciate the cooperation and support of my colleagues at the Smith Institute for Church History at Brigham Young University and the invaluable assistance given to me by our executive secretary Marilyn R. Parks, who prepared the manuscript, and typists Marlise Paxman and Sariah Wilson. I am also especially grateful for the excellent suggestions made by readers of the manuscript, particularly Kathryn MacKay, whose knowledge and insights I greatly value.

A special commendation is reserved for those women of the past who remained true to their convictions and undaunted in their struggle for equal rights despite public ridicule, formidable opposition, and worst of all, indifference. Theirs was a bloodless crusade to gain for women the political independence and civil rights that a revolution and a civil war had earned for men. Theirs is a story worth telling.

Introduction

Carol Cornwall Madsen

When the delegates to the Utah constitutional convention voted to include woman suffrage in the new state constitution in 1895, their momentous decision represented more than six years of intense grass-roots lobbying by Utah women. It also reflected several centuries of recorded discontent of women who felt excluded from the dynamics of public life.[1] By the end of the eighteenth century, their complaints acquired form and context as notions of natural law, human rights, and individual liberty came to inform public discourse.[2]

As these philosophical ideas gained sufficient political currency to foment rebellion against monarchical power, women saw rhetorical and political parallels to their own social disfranchisement. Adopting the enlightenment vision of human rights, early feminists employed the rhetoric of revolution for their own struggle for emancipation.[3] Treatises on women's rights, such as Mary Wollstonecraft's *A Vindication of the Rights of Women* published in England in 1792, preceded organized action, which slowly developed as women cautiously adapted to the new role of social activist.[4]

The steps between social theory and social activism, however, were daunting to most women. When John Adams failed to act on his wife Abigail's stirring appeal to "Remember the Ladies" in framing a constitution for the new nation, women did not "foment the rebellion" she had promised if they were excluded.[5] Soon thereafter, another "revolutionary" woman, Judith

Sargent Murray, also lamented the social disabilities of women, using the press as her outlet. But she wrote under a pseudonym, and she too did not go beyond the pen as her tool for social change.[6]

A few earnest women took a bolder step when they joined the lecture circuit. Not many women would have either desired or dared to speak in public on any issue in antebellum America. Angelina and Sarah Grimké, however, were among the few exceptions and used the public platform in the abolitionist cause.[7] They learned firsthand that the humanitarian nature of this movement and their eloquence in speaking for it could not offset the overwhelmingly negative response to such "unwomanly" behavior. Publicly defending their right as women to engage in public action, such as abolitionism, brought them only more ridicule and denunciation, but it also kindled a spirit of activism in other socially conscious women.

Finally, in 1848, a group of women prompted less by theories of equality than by their own experience with inequality, decided on a women's rights meeting.[8] Hopeful of using collective action to remove the legal, political, and social constraints on women, a number of these activists, all experienced abolitionists, temperance workers, or lobbyists, organized the first women's rights convention. The place was Seneca Falls, New York; the time, July 1848. The event brought three hundred men and women together for the two-day meeting of speeches and debate on woman's civil status. The Declaration of Independence provided the model for the convention's written demand for social justice. The author of the "Declaration of Sentiments," Elizabeth Cady Stanton, listed women's wide-ranging grievances, noting the loss of legal rights for women when they married, the restricted opportunities women had for education, and the limited fields of employment available to them. The Declaration decried their subordination in the churches as well as in the state and denounced the double moral code that condemned women for "moral delinquencies" but tolerated the same infractions in men.[9] The document was revolutionary in its complaints against society and in its sweeping resolutions for change, especially a bid for what was then the most radical of demands—the right to vote. No doubt emboldened by the favorable response of the New York assembly four months earlier to women's petitions for control of the property they brought to marriage,[10] the planners of the Seneca Falls convention understood that the common law, on which American jurisprudence rested, reinforced traditional views of women's dependency, and until women gained an independent legal identity, all other civil rights would be largely ineffectual. The movements for political and legal rights thus paralleled each other, and by 1920 when the Nineteenth Amendment, granting the vote to women, became law, all states had some form of a married woman's property act.

Antebellum America saw a proliferation of women's rights conventions following the Seneca Falls meeting. Since many of the earliest suffragists were also abolitionists, it was not surprising that they saw women's social disfranchisement as analogous to that of the slave and often employed abolitionist rhetoric in their feminist discourse. They also established a quid pro quo agreement with those male abolitionists who were sympathetic to their cause, enjoying male support for women's rights in exchange for the continuing presence of women in the abolitionist movement.[11]

The Civil War temporarily halted the movement for women's rights, but at its close leaders of the movement expected a joint effort with their abolitionist co-workers to secure civil rights for both former slaves and women. Male abolitionists, however, chose to defer the campaign to secure the ballot for women and focus on the civil rights of black men. A number of women suffragists agreed to this plan of action. This disassembling of a formerly strong coalition of social activists spawned two separate suffrage associations.[12] One group, calling itself the American Woman Suffrage Association, founded by Lucy Stone, Henry Blackwell, Thomas Higgenson, and Julia Ward Howe, had as its first president Henry Ward Beecher. It declined to press Congress to include women in the proposed Fifteenth Amendment enfranchising black men, fearful that the addition would jeopardize its passage. The Association was characterized by its "single issue" philosophy, its focus on supporting state referenda on woman suffrage, its courting of male support, and its exclusive position on membership. That is, it eschewed association with supportive but "unsavory" individuals or groups who advocated extreme social ideas, such as individuals like Victoria Woodhull and her sister Tennessee Claflin, whose unorthodox life styles and promotion of "free love" were anathema to the suffragists and mainstream Americans.[13]

The other group of suffragists, calling itself the National Woman Suffrage Association, was organized by Elizabeth Cady Stanton and Susan B. Anthony. This group continued to press for inclusion of women in the Fifteenth Amendment, finding allies in Senator Samuel Pomeroy of Kansas, who submitted a proposal to the Senate for an amendment enfranchising both blacks and women, and Representative George W. Julian, who championed a Sixteenth Amendment enfranchising women when the Fifteenth Amendment passed without including them. Amending the constitution thereafter became the focus of the National Association's drive for political parity. The

National Association earned the reputation of being more radical than the American because it welcomed anyone, including Mormon polygamists who supported woman suffrage, though disclaiming any endorsement of their other social views or practices. It also broadened its scope to include economic and social reform, organizing female industrial workers, advocating greater employment opportunities for women and improved health practices, and abolishing the so-called double standard of morality for men and women.[14]

For more than twenty years, the woman's rights movement was thus divided. Rather than weakening the movement, however, as some historians have maintained, recent studies argue that the division actually strengthened it, broadening the base of constituents and targeting both state and national legislative assemblies. Finally, in 1890 the two associations put their differences aside and reunited under the banner of the National American Woman Suffrage Association, a union which enabled them, despite many setbacks, to gradually swell their base of support sufficiently enough to convince Congress and American voters to pass the Nineteenth Amendment in 1920.[15] Their combined strength had become vital in combating a well-organized and supported anti-suffrage movement. Suffragists, according to historian Gerda Lerner, "consistently underestimated its [the counter-movement's] scope and significance and did not engage with its basic paradox, that it was a movement by women against women."[16]

While women argued for emancipation in the vocabulary of human rights, they did not intend to submerge the prevailing concept of female distinctiveness. Indeed, it was the absence of the female component in the existing social order, they claimed, that handicapped society from functioning at its full potential. They argued for equality from the premise that just laws should be guarantors of the inalienable rights of *all* citizens, but also that such rights carried concomitant social responsibilities, an obligation with which they were already familiar. For half a century or more, women had been serving their communities through benevolent, religious, and reform societies. Broader legal and political rights, they reasoned, could only facilitate their social usefulness.[17] Moreover, female moral authority, expressed in the moral caretaking adopted by women's reform organizations throughout the nineteenth century, gave these women social power before they had access to political channels, and social activists maximized this distinctive mode of civic participation as much as they could; they also recognized its limitations. Access to formal sources of power would necessarily change the nature of how women related to society but not the perspective or the values they would bring to it.

For some women, the woman's movement implied less a battle for social power and more a struggle for broader experience and usefulness. For them, and Elizabeth Cady Stanton and many of her co-workers in the National were certainly among the number, the movement was philosophically driven more by the belief in the dignity and value of the individual and the right of each to reach his or her highest potential than by ambition for social or political status.[18] With a common origin and a common destiny, they argued, women and men should have the same opportunity for maximum development and use of their faculties. An early American feminist, Margaret Fuller, voiced this theory of emancipation. "What woman needs," she explained in 1845, "is not as a woman to act or rule, but as a nature to grow, as an intellect to discern, as a soul to live freely, and unimpeded to unfold such powers as were given her when we left our common home."[19] These women believed that a woman's movement was necessary to break through the social barriers that had so long precluded their reaching the destiny designed for them. Merely staking a claim in the existing social order was ancillary to this fundamental ideal. They envisioned a society in which men and women worked as partners in developing their individual talents and abilities and using these gifts to benefit society. When the energy of the movement centered on the vote, especially in its final years before success, this vision of a social transformation tended to diminish in the single-minded drive for political equality though suffragists continued to claim the personal and social value of women's enfranchisement.[20]

If the power of the ballot in women's hands was unable to live up to its claims, its symbolic value was indisputable and promised a direct relationship between women and the state. Besides the psychological power it conferred, the sense of being recognized as distinct and equal members of the body politic, enfranchisement gave women an individuality as independent citizens, conveying an identity distinct from that of daughter, wife, or mother.[21] As voters, they demonstrated their consent to being governed, a cornerstone of republicanism, and had a voice in selecting those who would govern them as well as a connection to the formation of those laws under which they lived. Moreover, the vote represented the culmination of many other civil rights women had championed since, by the time the Nineteenth Amendment passed, several of the educational, legal, and professional goals of the woman's movement had been achieved in some measure.[22]

While national suffragists took different paths to win the vote for women, battling against entrenched legal and political systems in the long-established states, two western territories surprised the nation by enfranchising their women.[23] In December 1869, Wyoming's territorial assembly voted to permit its one thousand voting-age women not only to vote but to hold office. Utah followed in February 1870; its legislative assembly gave its far more numerous women the right to vote, with the distinction of voting before Wyoming women in a municipal election held two days after their enfranchisement. The disparate female population in the two territories made Utah, with 17,179 newly enfranchised citizens, the first major locus of woman suffrage in the United States. Such an event baffled the nation. Nothing seemed more anomalous than enfranchised Mormon women, popularly imaged as the "dupes" and "slaves" of tyrannical leaders.

But there were more than its large number of women voters and the curiosity factor that made the issue of woman suffrage in Utah pivotal. While claims to the rights of citizenship and promises of women's unique civic contribution permeated the self-congratulatory stance of Utah residents, other social elements affected the meaning of "woman's rights" in Utah. Though woman suffrage was always a complex social issue, pitting tradition and notions of propriety and stability of the social order against concepts of individual freedom and democracy, giving the ballot to Utah women involved even more complicated questions.

Historians have long theorized the reasons why the West in general and Utah in particular extended the vote to women so far in advance of the eastern states, which had cradled the quest for equal rights since 1848 (see the foreword). It is clear from even the limited number of currently extant studies of individual western states and territories that no single explanation applies equally to each area or wholly explains Utah. At a time when religious denominations were among the most avid anti-suffragists, the anomaly of a conservative religious community, as Utah was in 1870, advancing the cause of woman suffrage is the more intriguing. Mormon women, however, had from earliest times, enjoyed the religious franchise and had voted on civic matters as well for a brief period before Utah became a territory. Thus, extending the vote to the political arena was not as inexplicable as it might have seemed. Utah experienced other unique circumstances as well, all of which played a part in moving its all-Mormon territorial legislature to grant the vote to women in 1870. Certainly the national discussion of female suffrage and the proposals made in Congress and the press to "experiment" with woman suffrage in the territories did not escape notice in Utah. The urging by Utah's delegate to Congress, William Hooper, to consider suffrage as an antidote to the disparagement of Mormon women and a means of gaining them at least some measure of favor with the highly visible and vocal eastern suffragists also found sympathetic listeners.

Perhaps more pressing were internal developments signalled by the completion of the transcontinental railroad in 1869, which presaged a growing non-Mormon population in Utah, and the emergence of the New Movement, initiated by a schismatic group of Mormons who embraced the egalitarian tenets of spiritualism and promoted open economic policies in opposition to the closed economic system increasingly advanced by Mormon Church leader Brigham Young. Some contemporary observers argued that losing some of Mormonism's brightest and most successful businessmen and professionals may have prompted Brigham Young to strengthen the Church's internal control of the territory against further oppositional factions.

Finally, when Wyoming territory granted the vote to women, leading out in this radical departure from traditional politics, Utah seemed less anomalous in doing so two months later. Moreover, about the same time, after several earlier attempts, an anti-polygamy bill finally passed the House of Representatives. Passage of this highly punitive bill, introduced by Illinois Representative Shelby M. Cullom, may have spurred Church leaders to try to win support against the bill in the Senate by granting Utah women the vote, hopefully offsetting claims of their subjugation. That Mormon women would use the ballot to outlaw polygamy, as many Easterners hoped, was never a serious consideration in Utah. Later bills targeted the repeal of woman suffrage as part of their measures to abolish polygamy.

An intricate political triangle emerged when woman suffrage became inextricably linked to polygamy and statehood.[24] The issue focused on the question of the preeminence of church or the state and the extent to which citizens were required or willing to consent to being governed by the law of the land if it conflicted with the "higher law" of religious commitment.

Federal attempts to outlaw polygamy had begun in 1862 with the Morrill Act prohibiting bigamy but providing no effective enforcement measures.[25] The Cullom Bill of 1869–70 was designed to remedy this deficiency. Before any anti-polygamy bills were made law, however, it was deemed necessary to test the constitutionality of plural marriage in the United States Supreme Court. The court ruled in 1879 that while religious *beliefs* may be protected by the First Amendment, the unconventional religious *practice* of plural marriage did not warrant that protection. Several more enforcement measures, based on the provisions of the Cullom Bill were proposed before Congress passed the Edmunds Act in 1882 which prosecuted polygamists and withdrew most of their civil rights, including the franchise. An even more punitory measure, the 1887 Edmunds-Tucker Act, confiscated the financial holdings of the Church exceeding $50,000 and revoked the voting rights of all Utah women, among other debilitating measures.[26]

Not only did the issue of polygamy polarize Utah and the federal government; it was one of the principal divisive issues among suffragists, both local and national. In 1872, only two years after receiving the vote, a number of non-Mormon and lapsed-Mormon suffragists in Utah shifted their focus from defending suffrage to abolishing polygamy. Fearful that Utah would become a state with polygamy intact, they fervently opposed the fourth attempt at statehood during that year and joined the public voices calling for the repeal of woman suffrage in Utah in order to weaken the political prop for polygamy.[27] But national suffragists were unwilling to relinquish this important suffrage stronghold and attempted to separate the issues of polygamy and suffrage in proposed congressional legislation.[28] Capitalizing on this national support, Mormon Church leaders sent two women to Washington in 1879 on a twofold mission: one, to carry a memorial to President and Mrs. Hayes to use their influence to protect the religious rights of the Mormon people and two, to make personal contact with national suffrage leaders.[29] Emmeline B. Wells, editor of the LDS women's publication, the *Woman's Exponent*, and Zina Young Williams, a daughter of Brigham Young, were the choice of LDS leaders to represent Mormon women in Washington.

They were not successful in winning the support of the President and Mrs. Hayes, especially after the Supreme Court ruling on the Reynolds Case, issued just weeks before. The Supreme Court decision opened the way for passage of the Edmunds and Edmunds-Tucker Acts which in turn led to the 1890 Manifesto, issued by LDS Church President Wilford Woodruff, advising church members to abide by the law of the land.[30] In 1887, just three months after the Edmunds-Tucker Act was passed, Utah made a sixth attempt at statehood. Included in its proposed constitution was a clause providing for the complete separation of church and state and the prohibition of polygamy.[31] While this concession did not move Congress to accept Utah's bid for statehood nor lessen the effect of the Edmunds-Tucker Act, it encouraged women to begin to lay the groundwork for reclaiming the vote. Though many anti-polygamists were still hesitant to jump on the suffrage bandwagon, even after the Manifesto was issued three years later,[32] the local movement enjoyed the support of several prominent non-Mormon Utah women. They were themselves leaders or wives of prominent men in the non-Mormon community and more sanguine about an amiable and productive coexistence with Mormons in the new state.[33] The Territorial Woman Suffrage Association of Utah was officially organized in January 1889 with Margaret N. Caine, wife of Utah's delegate to Congress, as president. Over the next six years the organization used local newspapers, including the Mormon *Woman's Exponent*, the lecture platform, women's organizational networks, and grass-roots lobbying to win support for suffrage. Their success brought Utah into the union in 1896 as the third state granting women political equality.

Utah claimed other distinctions relating to women's rights besides the early franchise for women. Utah women, and especially Latter-day Saint women, had access to legal rights and judicial remedy unavailable to many American women in the nineteenth century. Suspicious of a legal system that had denied Mormons due process and equal justice, Mormon legislators established a judiciary that gave broad powers to local probate courts often administered by Mormon bishops and other ecclesiastical leaders.[34] This system allowed Mormons to avoid the federally appointed, and often hostile, district court judges and to bring their suits before more sympathetic adjudicators. Moreover, the Mormon legislative assembly nullified the common law (which made bigamy a crime) and empowered the courts to set their own precedents in judging the cases coming before them.[35] This measure, in effect, removed the heavy legal restraints on married women and permitted them many of the same rights as single women. In addition, an 1852 statute actually eliminated the need for lawyers, providing for the right of any responsible person to represent himself or *herself*.[36] Thus, Utah attempted to free itself from the constraints of the common law (but only until 1874 when it was determined to be in force after a series of Supreme Court decisions) and essentially opened its courts to women in the role of advocate.[37]

Divorce, another woman's issue, was easily accessible to all women in Utah through both the Mormon ecclesiastical courts and the civil courts, both of which were governed by a liberal divorce policy.[38] No plural wife (whose marriage was extra-legal) wishing a divorce was denied one through the ecclesiastical court system, and first—or legal—wives could find similar remedy in the probate or district courts. Only when Utah became a "divorce mill" for Eastern lawyers following completion of the transcontinental railroad in 1869 did the legislative assembly reluctantly tighten the requirements for divorce in 1878.[39] Plural wives, however, retained easy access to ecclesiastical divorce through Church courts.

Property laws also underwent modification to fit the peculiar circumstances in Utah. The common law denied married women control of the property they brought to marriage or their earnings, but the need for plural wives to supplement family income or to maintain their own households and to have an equal claim on their deceased husband's estate contributed to the rejection of the common law in Utah. In 1872, Utah passed a Married Persons Property Act, formally giving married women property rights which they had informally enjoyed before.[40]

Many unusual historical strands created the unique story of woman suffrage in Utah. The essays in this volume are attempts to examine each of those strands and explain their place in fashioning the complex historical pattern created in Utah by woman's quest for political equality.

The story of woman suffrage in Utah, as told in the following pages, unfolds in two parts. The first begins in 1870 when the Utah legislative assembly extended the franchise to women only to see it rescinded seventeen years later by the anti-polygamy Edmunds-Tucker Act. The second part begins two years after that when Utah women organized to regain their voting rights upon statehood in 1896.

All accounts of woman suffrage in the United States must begin with the six-volume history written by Susan B. Anthony, Elizabeth Cady Stanton, Matilda Joslyn Gage, and Ida Husted Harper.[41] As principal players in the suffrage movement in the United States, Anthony and Stanton demonstrated their historical consciousness with the decision to create a written record of the long, intensive, emotion-laden struggle for political equality. Elizabeth Stanton first conceived the idea of a history following the 1848 Seneca Falls meeting and worked at it sporadically through the next decade. In 1855 Susan B. Anthony followed her father's suggestion to collect newspaper articles and documents relating to the movement, all of which proved to be invaluable when the serious writing actually began.[42] Lucretia Mott, co-planner of the Seneca Falls convention, persistently urged such a project. No consistent effort was made, however, until after the 1876 centennial celebration of American independence which underscored the value of such a history. That year Elizabeth Stanton, Susan B. Anthony, and Matilda Joslyn Gage, editor of the *National Citizen and Ballot Box* and close associate of Stanton's, formed a partnership "for the purpose of preparing and editing a history of the woman suffrage movement." Stanton and Gage agreed to prepare and write the history while Anthony was to secure a publisher.[43]

Work actually began four years later at Elizabeth Stanton's home in Tenafly, New Jersey. After six months of work the first volume, covering events to 1860, was completed. It was published in May 1881. Subsequent volumes followed on a regular basis. Anthony bought out the partnership interests of Gage and Stanton and enlisted the assistance of Ida Husted Harper, an Indiana journalist, who completed the history after the death of Anthony in 1906.

The two extracts from *The History of Woman Suffrage* included in this volume are reports from Utah written by two ardent Utah suffragists, Emmeline B. Wells and Susa Young Gates. The first, by Wells, appears in volume four of the *History* and presents the story of woman suffrage in Utah from the first granting of suffrage to Utah women in 1870 to the end of the century, four years after statehood. It is a positive, well-organized, and complimentary account of a very complex and eventful period. It makes only a veiled reference to the Mormon-Gentile conflict that dominated those years or to the many local and federal efforts to disfranchise Mormon women. It also avoids discussion of the polygamy/suffrage link. It nonetheless presents an informative account of the work of the Territorial Suffrage Association and a useful overview of the original grant of the ballot to Utah women, its loss, and the successful effort to regain it. It also includes important voting statistics for the year 1900.

The second excerpt from the *History* is from volume six, written by Susa Young Gates. A second generation Utah suffragist, Gates carries the account through to passage of the National Amendment in 1920 giving suffrage to all American women. Some inaccuracies appear as she summarizes the earlier period though she presents a thorough overview of the period following Utah statehood. Her account gives credit to the many women, both Mormon and non-Mormon, who organized the Utah Council of Women, an organization to promote woman suffrage throughout the nation, and who entered Utah politics after gaining the vote and the right to hold office. These two reports provide an instructive summary of the fifty-year period between Utah women's first enfranchisement in 1870 and passage of the Constitutional Amendment in 1920.

While Eastern women had been agitating for broader legal and political rights for more than twenty years, Utah women became recipients of the elective franchise in 1870 with no public demonstrations or petitioning. But they were not all politically naive nor unaccustomed to some form of civic service, argues Lola Van Wagenen, in "In their Own Behalf: the Politicization of Mormon Women and the 1870 Franchise."[44] Mormon women, who dominated the female population in Utah, had a history of public activity, beginning with the organization of the Female Relief Society of Nauvoo, Illinois in 1842, a benevolent and moral reform society, and continuing through the public works assigned to the organization by Church President Brigham Young in Utah in 1867–68. The franchise, Van Wagenen argues, therefore did not appear as radical a change in the lives of early Mormon women as generally supposed. Moreover, she points out, a group of politically astute women in Salt Lake City in January 1870 actually resolved to demand the vote of the governor as part of their response to the proposed Cullom Bill, the most punitive to that point of anti-polygamy measures designed to enforce the anti-bigamy clause of the 1862 Morrill Act. Though the demand was not actually carried through, the women staged a rally at which they defended their religious rights and effectively demonstrated that they were articulate, intelligent arbiters of their own life choices.

What undoubtedly seemed to the women as a well-deserved response to their show of spirit, the Mormon legislative assembly passed a bill providing for woman suffrage which was reluctantly signed by the acting governor, non-Mormon Stephen Mann. Van Wagenen concludes that it was not an unusual demonstration of egalitarianism that prompted legislative action but rather the realization of the usefulness of enfranchised women in maintaining Mormon practices and policies against threatening federal legislation.

Among the elite female leadership in Salt Lake City none was more prominent than Eliza R. Snow, enjoying a position and prestige in the community held by no other LDS woman. One of the women who had attended the January 1870 meeting and one of two women selected in that meeting to go to Washington to plead for religious rights (a trip which did not materialize), Eliza R. Snow proposed and helped deliver a letter of appreciation to acting governor Mann for signing the woman suffrage bill.[45] She also suggested that women who traveled through the territory on Relief Society business might teach "woman's rights" if they wished.[46] But Eliza R. Snow viewed the woman question differently from the outspoken woman's rights advocates among her Mormon sisters, Jill Mulvay Derr points out in "Eliza R. Snow and the Woman Question."[47] While she was in favor of woman suffrage and saw its value to Mormon women and the Church, the elective franchise came to Mormon women, she believed, only when "God put it in the minds of the brethren to give us that right."[48] She was adamantly opposed to "strong minded women" agitating for their rights which could only lead to a "war between the sexes," for her an untenable thought. Cooperation with Church leaders, submission to religious authority, and compliance with Church principles and doctrines were for her the surer route to equality than public demonstrations for rights and privileges. Ironically, she was herself a prime example of a public spirited woman, enjoying unusual authority and facilitating the entry of Mormon women into public activity by organizing a variety of economic, social, and humanitarian programs. Few projects initiated by Mormon women during her lifetime were launched without her sanction, Derr notes. A woman's paper, a program of home industries, a call for medical doctors, a hospital, a woman's commission store, and the organization of a children's and young women's association all gave women opportunity for community service that helped "build Zion" while broadening women's experience and honing their administrative and organizational skills. Eliza R. Snow was instrumental in the implementing of all of these enterprises.

Despite the degree of autonomy and independence such public activity gave women, Snow maintained her belief that women could not gain equality without submission to Mormon doctrine and practices. She consistently preached the role of women as helpmeets to Church leadership. Empowerment, she insisted, came through spiritual channels, not secular, and was thus not subject to the secular indices of equality. She was herself a model of a strong, independent, and resourceful woman while fashioning her life and actions in harmony with her ecclesiastical superiors. Derr equates women's role, as perceived by Eliza R. Snow, with that of good stewards who magnify their responsibilities and receive commendation from their masters. Suffrage could thus be seen as giving women a wider field for civic involvement primarily to support the objectives of "kingdom building" which, during Snow's lifetime, encompassed the political and economic as well as religious life of Mormons.

In a brief overview of the relationship between Mormon women activists and the LDS Church in the latter part of the nineteenth century, Maureen Ursenbach Beecher, Carol Cornwall Madsen, and Jill Mulvay Derr have shown that those Utah women who spoke out on the woman question argued that both justice and the need for women's social contribution supported the expansion of rights for women. As the authors point out in "The Latter-day Saints and Women's Rights, 1870–1920: A Brief Survey,"[49] advocates of woman suffrage believed that justice demanded women have a voice in the laws that govern them and that the good of society demanded women's participation. The authors also indicate that not all of the rights urged by some activists in the nineteenth century, particularly "voluntary motherhood,"[50] found support among Mormons. But the expansion of educational, economic, legal, and political rights and opportunities was generally well received by both Latter-day Saint men and women and specifically supported by most Church leaders. The guiding hand of "propriety" was the key that governed women's choices, the authors note. They also caution that what seemed appropriate or inappropriate for women in the nineteenth century may not be so in the twentieth, and thus general conclusions or premises for current argument cannot always be drawn from the experiences of the past.

At the time of statehood, the authors note, woman suffrage was not universally accepted in Utah though it had been operative for seventeen years. It was a divisive issue among some LDS leaders, a division which became manifest in the constitutional convention in 1895 where the merits of woman suffrage in Utah were debated by three prominent Mormon leaders, Brigham H. Roberts, Orson F. Whitney, and Franklin S. Richards, all Democrats. The endorsement of Church leaders and the seventeen year experience of women with the ballot, however, helped convince many Mormons to support woman suffrage in the new state constitution.

The clause on woman suffrage in the constitution, the authors explain, clearly shows the progressive philosophy of the convention delegates, most of whom were LDS: "The right of the citizens of the State of Utah to vote and hold office shall not be denied or abridged on account of sex. Both male and female citizens of this state shall enjoy equally all civil, political, and religious rights and privileges." This statement closely resembles the proposed equal rights amendment of the 1970s, which, ironically, Utah soundly rejected.[51]

One of the first historians to explore the anomaly of woman suffrage in polygamous Utah is Thomas G. Alexander in "An Experiment in Progressive Legislation: The Granting of Woman Suffrage in Utah in 1870."[52] Noting the implementation of economic principles that privileged cooperation over competition, social policies that favored immigration and the utilization of women's skills in cooperative and reform movements, and familial ideals that rationalized plural marriage as a corrective to contemporary moral evils, Alexander describes Mormon society as a natural matrix for the radical idea of woman suffrage. He points out that some of the earliest public statements favoring woman suffrage were published in the *Utah Magazine*, written by editors E. L. T. Harrison and Edward Tullidge, who soon thereafter associated themselves with the Mormon schismatic group known as the New Movement.[53] Their comments were followed by equally enthusiastic articles in the *Deseret News* and *Ogden Junction* by LDS apostles George Q. Cannon and Franklin D. Richards. Shortly thereafter, the territorial legislature considered the measure, and Alexander follows the legislative process of the bill, noting the discussion, amendments, and final approval by the legislative assembly along with acting governor S. A. Mann's reluctant signing of the bill. When this progressive action on the part of the Utah legislative assembly did not provide the results anticipated by anti-polygamists, their enthusiasm for woman suffrage in Utah waned, Alexander found, and even provoked an anti-Utah woman suffrage movement.

Alexander deflates the Gentile view of the time that the Mormon hierarchy granted women the vote to shore up its political hold in the territory, explaining that Mormon numerical domination was never at risk. Rather, he concludes, the egalitarian views expressed by Church leaders should be taken at face value, suggesting that "Mormons were willing to move in where others feared to tread."

However, in "Woman Suffrage in Territorial Utah,"[54] Beverly Beeton asserts that giving the vote to Utah women in 1870 was not an egalitarian impulse of Mormon leaders but a tactical decision in furthering the goals of the Mormon hierarchy, more externally than internally influenced. It effectively dispelled the stereotype of the subjugated Mormon woman and connected enfranchised Mormon women with the national suffrage movement, she argues. National suffragists, Beeton points out, were unwilling to lose a suffrage enclave and thus served the interests of the Mormon leaders by countering legislation that advocated the repeal of woman suffrage as a punitive measure against polygamy. Beeton also argues that Mormon leaders hoped to win lobbying support from the suffragists for Utah statehood. Its association with Mormon polygamy, she concludes, damaged the image of the National Woman Suffrage Association and hindered the efforts of suffragists to gain support for their cause. The woman's movement, in focusing on suffrage as a panacea for women, Beeton also claims, lost an opportunity to make greater social changes in American society.

Because of the linkage between woman suffrage and polygamy and the connection between LDS and national suffragists, many historical accounts have ignored independent Utah suffragists and anti-polygamists. While Utah society has historically been bifurcated as Mormon and non-Mormon, a less noted group of nineteenth century dissident Mormon women was actively engaged in the anti-polygamy and national suffrage movement. Some of these disaffected Mormons teamed with non-Mormon women to form an anti-polygamy association in 1878 and worked arduously against woman suffrage in Utah.[55] Though some of them were supportive of enfranchising women elsewhere, the vote in the hands of LDS women, they claimed, simply entrenched Mormon political power and perpetuated the practice of plural marriage. Moreover, continued territorial status, they argued, protected non-Mormons from total Mormon domination, and they fought against every attempt at statehood. When statehood was imminent, five years after LDS President Wilford Woodruff issued his manifesto banning plural marriage, they were still suspicious of the political power of enfranchised Mormon women and joined the campaign to present the question of woman suffrage to the voters separately from the proposed constitution.[56]

Earlier in 1869 another dissident faction of Mormons had drawn away a number of discontented Mormons from the faithful fold. The New Movement, as noted earlier, adopted many of the tenets of spiritualism and advocated its philosophy of freedom from any form of authoritative constraint, particularly rebelling against Brigham Young's economic and political insularity. These ex-Mormons, also known as the Godbeites from one of their founders, William Godbe, though numbering only two or three hundred during their decade of prominence, nonetheless added another dimension to the polarization of Utah society and played a significant role in the woman suffrage story in Utah for a brief period during the 1870s.[57] Women of the New Movement organized a Ladies Improvement Society, headed by Fanny Stenhouse, a virulent opponent of plural marriage. Strongly supportive of giving the ballot to women, disclaiming any religious mandate for plural marriage, and eventually renouncing it altogether (requiring many of its leaders to separate from their plural wives), the New Movement provided national suffragists with a more "respectable" Utah connection than Mormons.[58] Overestimating the impact of the movement, national suffragists believed it to be the beginning of reform in Utah, thereby easing their embrace of suffragism in the territory.[59] The Ladies Improvement Society was instrumental in sending three of the four wives of William Godbe, Annie, Mary, and Charlotte, to represent Utah at the meetings of the National Woman Suffrage Association. These women were among the first Utah women to make contact with national suffrage leaders, the first to serve in various positions in the national association, and the first Utah women to contribute letters and essays to national woman suffrage publications.[60]

Charlotte Ives Cobb Godbe Kirby, Godbe's fourth wife, was the most constant of the three women in her campaign for woman suffrage. In her article, "A Feminist Among the Mormons: Charlotte Ives Cobb Godbe Kirby," Beverly Beeton has rescued her from anonymity and given her a voice through two letters in which Charlotte explains her suffrage activity to Church President Wilford Woodruff.[61]

A stepdaughter of Brigham Young, Charlotte Cobb married William S. Godbe only months before his excommunication from the LDS Church in 1869. Despite her husband's disaffection, Charlotte retained membership in the Church and soon separated from Godbe, as did his other plural wives when the New Movement rejected polygamy, finally divorcing him ten years after their marriage. Though Charlotte frequently defended Mormonism among her Eastern friends and worked tirelessly for woman suffrage, Mormon women did not accept her as their official representative in national suffrage circles, a stance no doubt influenced by her original association with the New Movement and particularly because of her later criticism of plural marriage. She came up against an equally zealous and ambitious suffragist in Emmeline B. Wells, who had the advantage of editing a newspaper and enjoying the support of LDS leaders. Charlotte's letters to LDS Church President Wilford Woodruff reveal not only the efforts she expended in behalf of woman suffrage in Utah but the personality of a determined, confident, and competitive worker in the cause.

While Beverly Beeton's survey of woman suffrage in Utah looks at many of the conflicting interests that surrounded this volatile issue during the 1870s and 1880s, Joan Smyth Iversen, in "The Mormon-Suffrage Relationship: Personal and Political Quandaries,"[62] examines in more detail the alliance of Mormon and national suffragists and the impact of polygamy on the national movement along with the personal relationships that evolved from that alliance. The ideological and methodological differences between the two national suffrage associations, she explains, intensified with the entrance of Mormon women into the movement and their affiliation with Anthony and Stanton's National Woman Suffrage Association. Because of the liberality of the National in befriending all supporters of woman suffrage,[63] the American Association distanced itself from the National and particularly from Mormon suffragists. A further problem for the National Association, Iversen points out, developed from the rise of the social purity movement with its strong anti-polygamy bias. The popularity of this reform crusade among women's groups delayed their joining the suffrage bandwagon and further isolated the National Association from mainstream American women.

Merger of the two national suffrage associations brought many social purists into the new organization, creating obstacles for continued Mormon affiliation. Iversen is less convinced of the negative impact of the Mormon connection on the movement or its leaders, however, than Beeton. While Anthony and other members of the National curtailed their involvement with Mormon women during the decade of congressional anti-polygamy legislation and continually disclaimed any sympathy toward plural marriage, they continued to protest the repeal of woman suffrage as part of that legislation, Iversen argues. They also successfully endorsed Mormon membership in the National and International Councils of Women, indicating not only respect for Mormon representation but regard for their personal relationships with Mormon women.

Iversen also explores marriage as a woman's rights issue, noting Stanton and Anthony's opposition to traditional forms of marriage. They argued that it robbed women of their legal identity and curtailed their sense of autonomy and self-identity. Both scorned plural marriage, although Stanton noted that polygamy might actually be less constraining to women than monogamy.[64] They were especially conscious of married women's legal disabilities under the common law, Iversen notes. Both women had lobbied earnestly for New York's first Married Women's Property Act, passed in 1848, and moved from that campaign into the woman's rights movement.

Iversen asserts that the triumph of Victorian domesticity, evident in the abandonment of Mormon polygamy, the popularity of the social purity movement, and the merger of the two suffrage associations, defused the earlier militancy of Mormon suffragists in defending their marriage practices. The challenge to traditional domestic values that the Mormon-suffrage alliance had represented dissipated in the success of the anti-polygamy movement and the more conservative stance of the suffrage movement reflected in the union of the two national associations, Iversen concludes.

When the woman's rights movement in the United States was inaugurated in 1848, it became apparent very early that its dependence on conventions and lecture tours for growth and the dissemination of its ideas was inadequate. The press became essential to its success. Since the mainstream press either castigated or ignored the movement, women initiated their own publications. *The Lily* (1849–56), originally a temperance paper, was one of the first woman's papers to address the issues raised at the Seneca Falls Convention. It was followed by the *Una* (1853–55), a short-lived but influential publication. The Civil War suspended concentrated focus on the movement, but when the suffrage alliance split after the war, the National Association was first to establish a publication, the *Revolution* (1868–70). It did not enjoy wide support because of its "radical" stance on women's issues, and it soon folded for want of funding. Close behind was the better funded, much more moderate, and longer lived Boston *Woman's Journal*, established in 1870 and published by the American Woman Suffrage Association under the editorship of Lucy Stone and her daughter Alice Stone Blackwell. Though these two are the best known of the woman suffrage newspapers, more than thirty-three were published between 1870 and 1890. These publications assisted the national movement by augmenting the audience, by creating a network of women with similar goals and values, and by identifying and creating the movement's leaders.[65]

Almost at the same time, enterprising women in the West published their own suffrage newspapers and enjoyed the same benefits. Sherilyn Cox Bennion explores the role of two of these publications operating in Oregon and Utah in *"The New Northwest* and *Woman's Exponent*: Early Voices for Suffrage."[66] In its initial issue, *The New Northwest* (1871–87), founded and edited by Abigail Scott Duniway, mother of the suffrage movement in Oregon, identified suffrage as its raison d'etre but carried other news, poetry, and fiction of interest to its female readers. The *Woman's Exponent* (1872–1914), founded a year later but lasting twenty-seven years longer, originally disclaimed any involvement in controversial women's issues, including suffrage (Utah women were already enfranchised). However, its editors (Louisa Greene Richards, 1872–77 and Emmeline B. Wells, 1877–1914) bowed to the times and their own inclinations and soon made woman's rights a staple of the paper, writing editorials and reprinting articles from other suffrage papers. The *Woman's Exponent* also carried other news items, poetry and fiction, and especially information relating to the LDS Church which it served as an unofficial organ of the woman's Relief Society.

Bennion notes that the two papers were engined mainly by the dogged determination of their editors who struggled with few subscribers and insufficient staff help. Both editors generated much of the copy and depended primarily on family help in the production of their papers. Although the papers were vehicles for their editors' political and feminist views, they were also outlets for their literary talents: both editors contributed much of the poetry and fiction for their publications.

While Duniway sold her paper after a run of just sixteen years and saw it sold again two years later, Emmeline B. Wells held on to her paper for thirty-seven years, despite its declining subscriptions, until it had outlived its usefulness. Both women have the distinction, Bennion points out, of being among the earliest westerners to advocate the right of women to vote through the medium of their newspapers.

While Congress wrestled with the polygamy issue in Utah, anti-polygamy sentiment arose on many sides. Tomes from the nation's pulpits, editorials from its presses, titillating novels from its publishers, resolutions from its women's associations, and cartoons from its popular artists all indicate the many fronts on which this unpopular practice was attacked. Cartoons were particularly effective in expressing public sentiment. When polygamy was coupled with woman suffrage, another favorite target of cartoonists, a single picture could lampoon both subjects with the same brush strokes. In their article, "Woman Suffrage, Popular Art, and Utah," Gary L. and Carol B. Bunker analyze attitudes toward woman suffrage in Utah as depicted in the popular mode of caricature. The prevailing theme throughout most of the nineteenth century by popular newspapers and magazines, the authors show, was defamation of Mormonism generally, derision of Mormon women particularly, and ridicule of woman suffragists.[67]

As early as 1869, a year before Utah women received the vote, a derisive cartoon speculating on how woman suffrage would enhance the voting power of Brigham Young because of his numerous wives appeared in a popular magazine.[68] It was an early pictorial comment on the prevailing stereotype of Mormon women, the authors note, as "gullible, docile, hoodwinked disciples" of Mormonism and Mormon men. However, when woman suffrage in Utah became linked with anti-polygamy legislation, cartoonists switched their characterization of LDS women to depict irate, militant women determined to hold on to their political rights. After Utah obtained statehood, with woman suffrage in its constitution, cartoonists found other targets for their humorous barbs. But when the final surge toward universal suffrage began and public opinion shifted, they joined the journalistic bandwagon and used their pens to support the escalating march to victory. The authors found that the "scorn and censure" common to the cartoons ridiculing Utah women's enfranchisement in 1870 gave way to "esteem and commendation" in the final stage of the national suffrage movement leading to the Nineteenth Amendment in 1920. Popular artists hailed Utah and the other suffrage states as vanguards in the movement and applauded their courage in overcoming prejudice.

When both Mormonism and woman suffrage were viewed as threats to prevailing social norms, cartoonists reflected public opinion in a humorous, entertaining, though often biting way, the authors explain. By the same token, they point out, when attitudes softened toward these two social challenges, cartoons changed as well. The Bunkers not only show the important role of popular art in depicting popular opinion, but also provide a thorough summary of some of the primary issues incident to the polygamy, suffrage, statehood political triad.

When the anti-polygamy Edmunds-Tucker Act of 1887 withdrew the right of Utah women to vote, suffragists set about almost immediately to organize a local movement to regain it. First organizing a territorial association, suffragists then created satellite associations in the various counties throughout Utah territory. Historians have generally focused on this grass-roots movement on the territorial level (see Thatcher, White, and Madsen in this volume), but Lisa Bryner Bohman has examined the records of two county associations and their methods of supporting the movement in "A Fresh Perspective: The Woman Suffrage Associations of Beaver and Farmington, Utah."[69] Bohman found that besides providing financial assistance to the territorial leaders, the county associations lobbied politicians, educated the populace in the value of woman suffrage, and persuaded skeptics.

Bohman's selection of Beaver in Southern Utah and Farmington in Northern Utah provides a comparative view of these two associations. Her study notes the varying social factors in each community that affected the type and extent of membership and the associations' impact on their communities. Bohman shows that despite a different population makeup in each community, the LDS Church was influential in both locations in terms of leadership and membership in the suffrage associations. She also points out that the local suffrage organizations attracted the "elite" of their communities: teachers, LDS auxiliary workers, and wives of prominent religious, political, and economic leaders, who were themselves often supporters of the movement.

Bohman concludes that Utah women's experience in county associations and in the movement itself prepared them for their reentry into politics and increased their awareness of contemporary women's issues and the national suffrage movement.

The success of the Territorial Suffrage Association was evident when the constitutional convention delegates met in Salt Lake City in March 1895 to draft a constitution for the impending state of Utah. With the Manifesto of LDS Church President Wilford Woodruff in 1890 pledging the Church's compliance with the law and promising no further plural marriages, statehood for Utah was finally on track toward reality. Congress passed the Enabling Act in 1894 providing for a constitutional convention the following year, and territorial party conventions were held to elect delegates. Both parties agreed to include woman suffrage as a plank in their platforms.

On the eve of statehood, Utah's woman suffragists felt confident that their hard work would bear fruit. But, as Jean Bickmore White explains in her seminal article, "Woman's Place Is in the Constitution: The Struggle for Equal Rights in Utah, 1895,"[70] there were surprises ahead, and supporters of woman suffrage were obliged to exert one more major effort to secure their political goal. White delineates the conditions leading up to the convention, the factors that put the issue of equal suffrage at risk, and the debate that consumed a disproportionate amount of the convention's allotted time. Three prominent Mormon Church leaders, all Democrats, lent their persuasive oratory to the debate on woman suffrage. Brigham H. Roberts, opposed to giving women the vote in general, argued that its presence in the constitution might jeopardize Congressional approval. His objection was logical and convincing. Orson F. Whitney and Franklin D. Richards argued just as persuasively for including women as voting citizens of the proposed state. Invoking democratic ideals of justice and equality, they made an emotional appeal for recognition of the value of women in the political process. The arguments of Whitney and Richards, with some help from fellow delegates, carried the day, and the Articles on Elections, which included woman suffrage, passed the convention on April 8, 1895. Because woman suffrage had been part of the political system in Utah for seventeen years and was not associated with radical crusaders, convention delegates felt comfortable in giving it serious consideration, White argues. Suffragists had developed a persuasive educational program, she explains, and had convinced a majority of delegates prior to the convention to support their cause. Wherever suffrage was won, White's article makes clear, success came only because hardworking, dedicated women were able to elicit the support of sympathetic male believers in whom rested the power to share this political right.

At the close of the constitutional convention, women celebrated their victory at the Rocky Mountain Regional Convention of the National Amer-

ican Woman Suffrage Association held in Salt Lake City. Susan B. Anthony
and the Reverend Anna Howard Shaw both attended, and the meetings were
packed with enthusiastic celebrants. It was a fitting conclusion to a six-year
campaign.

Soon after the convention, the question was raised as to whether or not
women would be permitted to vote at the election the following November
at which the constitution would be ratified and the new state officers
elected. While the question was being decided by the Territorial Supreme
Court, the two political parties turned their attention toward winning
women's loyalty. While the majority of LDS women followed their husbands
or their own inclinations into the Democratic Party, others preferred the
political philosophy of the Republican Party, despite its heavy non-Mormon
membership in Utah. Carol Cornwall Madsen explores the ramifications of
this political split, of the political focus on women during the summer of
1895, and the introduction of LDS women into party politics in "Schism in
the Sisterhood: Mormon Women and Partisan Politics, 1890–1900."[71]

With religion no longer a compulsory factor in politics, the heady
period following the constitutional convention prompted a spirited contest
between the two political parties to determine which one most valued
women in its ranks. Women were elected delegates to county and territorial
conventions as well as vice presidents and temporary chairpersons for the
meetings. Some were even nominated for office until the Territorial Supreme
Court ruled against their eligibility in late summer. The press made great fun
of the scramble for female voters and kept a close tab on women's activities
in their respective parties. The novelty of the situation made good copy.
Madsen identifies the period as singular in Utah women's political history and
found that after that initial flurry of attention, the traditional organizational
mode reasserted itself. Women no longer held special attention of party
leaders. Thus most politically minded women channeled their energies into
Republican and Democratic women's clubs. Utah women, like their national
counterparts after passage of the Nineteenth Amendment more than twenty
years later, discovered that their enfranchisement and office-holding right did
not necessarily translate into the political influence they had expected nor did
it draw women into the traditional channels of political power. Separatism,
or the process of working through their own female organizations, which had
worked so well in gaining the vote, Madsen found, still seemed a surer and
more familiar route to political influence for most women.

Behind the leaders whose names and faces commanded the spotlight
were the workers, whose efforts brought the vision of the more visible activists
to fruition. Ruth May Fox was a zealous supporter of woman suffrage. Her

single-minded devotion to the cause during the constitutional convention and the months immediately preceding and following it showed the intense effort many women made to become a vital part of the new political scene in Utah. Linda Thatcher allows Ruth May Fox to bring her experiences to light through her own words by editing a portion of her diary relating to the fight for woman suffrage and the political drama that preceded the ratification election.[72] Ruth May Fox, like many of the women in this volume, found public work of this kind a satisfying antidote to the domestic routine.[73]

Fox came under the political tutelage of Emmeline B. Wells, a major suffrage leader. She joined two writing clubs, the Reapers and the Utah Woman's Press Club, organized by Wells, and attended classes at the University of Utah in writing and grammar. She worked strenuously to ensure the passage of woman suffrage by the constitutional convention and then followed Wells into the Republican Party, an unpopular move since most LDS women favored the Democrats. Fox traversed the territory stumping for the Republican candidates, assisting to organize Republican women's clubs, and garnering female interest in party politics. It was a brief but significant foray into politics which interested her less than suffrage. The next year Ruth Fox gave birth to her last child, whom she named Emmeline Blanche after her friend and mentor, and then directed her prodigious talents and energies into LDS Church service, eventually becoming general president of the Young Women's Mutual Improvement Association. This brief insight into one woman's perspecive on a unique period of Utah women's history illuminates the factors that often led to such a whirl of public activity for some women, the methods and philosophy they generated in their advocacy of their causes, and the social power they felt from their female networks.

The final selection, a second article by Jean Bickmore White, closes the century and the volume. When the Utah Supreme Court ruled in August 1895 that women were not eligible to vote at the ratification election the following November nor to run for office, it was necessary for the Republicans, whose convention had been held prior to the ruling, to remove the names of three women from their slate of candidates. The absence of women candidates, however, was quickly remedied the following year when a number of women used their newly won political right to run for office. Dr. White has captured this initial experience for Utah women in her article, "Gentle Persuaders: Utah's First Women Legislators."[74] Three women won state offices in the election of 1896, and several others garnered county posts.

White focuses on the two female legislators, Eurithe K. LaBarthe, a four-year resident of Salt Lake City, and Sarah E. Anderson, a native Utahn from Ogden, who became members of the House, and on Martha

Hughes Cannon, the first female state senator in the United States. All were Democrats. All served only one term. Sarah Anderson died a year after her term expired. Eurithe LaBarthe moved to Denver following her term and died during a visit to Salt Lake City in 1910. These two representatives, White points out, did not necessarily distinguish themselves during their legislative service, but Martha Hughes Cannon became noteworthy for her legislation and her independent thinking in the Senate. As an Eastern-trained doctor, Martha Cannon was already a public figure in Utah. Married to Salt Lake LDS Stake President, Angus Cannon, she was joined to a prominent Utah family. Running for office on an open slate of ten candidates vying for five senate positions from the Third District, Martha found herself, one of five Democrats, running against her husband, one of five Republicans. All of the Democrats won, and Martha Hughes Cannon was subsequently featured in Ripley's *Believe it or Not* because of the unique circumstances surrounding her election. Cannon made substantive contributions during her term of office, originating a state board of public health, for which she served as its first chair. She also initiated a bill to provide protective measures for the health of female workers and another mandating compulsory education for deaf and blind children. She submitted additional bills in the second half of her term, all related to public sanitation and health. The birth of her third child soon after the expiration of her first term precluded her running for a second.

According to White, Utah's first female legislators did not immediately change the social landscape of Utah. Though Martha Hughes Cannon introduced significant new social legislation, it was implemented gradually, only as it generated public support. By and large, White argues, women did no better or worse than men as public servants. Their effectiveness, moreover, depended in large measure on the "courtesy" of their male colleagues, White concludes. Their lack of aggressiveness proved to be their best asset.

By the time the century turned, Utah had become a state with a unique political history. Its long effort toward statehood, the confrontations of the LDS Church with the federal government, the antagonism between Utah's Mormon and Gentile residents, and particularly its checkered history with woman suffrage contribute to a tale of conflict, compromise, capitulation, and finally cooperation. The enfranchisement of women brought neither the dramatic social improvements nor the direful consequences its advocates and detractors predicted. Nor did many women follow this new avenue into public service or professional work.

As suffragists continually noted, custom, habits, and attitudes long embedded in the social psyche, proved to be the largest impediment to change. Women, especially, seemed reluctant to define themselves in political terms or to take on civic responsibilities for which they had little experience or understanding. Those in the vanguard of social movements usually had to settle for less than they had hoped, and later generations have not always been generous to their failures. But changing attitudes proved to be more difficult than changing laws, and society did not quickly capitulate to the possibilities that legal and political rights offered women.

Woman suffrage was always a divisive issue because it was never free from a host of attendant social considerations. The national movement lost the support of male abolitionists over the Fifteenth Amendment. Even in Utah, with the pledged support of both parties, woman suffrage was almost derailed in the constitutional convention, not only by a lengthy debate on the merits of the question, but by a proposal to submit it separately from the constitution for voter approval. From the outset, enfranchising women proved to be a more complex issue than its supporters may have anticipated, especially in Utah where it was so entwined with polygamy and statehood.

But woman suffrage was most particularly and poignantly divisive among women. Women were among the strongest anti-suffragists in the long struggle, and there was always division among suffragists themselves, for whom their mutual goal could not always bridge philosophical and methodological differences. Their disagreements bitterly divided national suffragists for more than two decades before they were able to combine their prodigious energies and talents into a single national movement. The issue clearly divided the women in Utah. Ardent suffragist Emmeline B. Wells deeply regretted this divisiveness. "We never thought that woman could rise up against woman," she wrote in 1878 when her Gentile neighbors organized to defeat polygamy and support the repeal of woman suffrage in Utah. "It will be 'diamond cut diamond,' rest assured."[75] Her words rang with truth as women struggled over the right to define themselves and their relationship to each other, to men, and to the world in which they lived.

Prefiguring the battle for an equal rights amendment in the 1970s, the struggle for woman suffrage raised questions among women that are still reverberating. Long-held assumptions relating to women's role in the family and in society were at stake, and they did not easily yield even to the soul-stirring pleas for justice and equality. Another century and another woman's rights movement have not yet resolved the dilemmas left by the first. But gaining the vote, if nothing else, gave women an enduring symbol of the persistent determination of a few to win a constitutional right for all.

Notes

1. Until the middle of the nineteenth century, women had few political or legal rights and their lives were primarily circumscribed within the domestic sphere. For a comprehensive historical overview of women's experience see Susan Groag Bell and Karen M. Offen, *Women, the Family, and Freedom*, 2 vols. (Stanford: Stanford University Press, 1983).

2. Both the American and the French revolutions prompted a number of women to decry their marginality to the revolutionary claims and ideals.

3. See Elizabeth Clark, "Religion, Rights and Difference: The Origins of American Feminism, 1848–1860," in *Legal History Program, Working Papers, Series 2* (University of Wisconsin Law School: Institute for Legal Studies, 1987), 2.

4. Wollstonecraft's work was an early feminist manifesto enunciating women's claims to social justice and human rights. See reprint ed. (New York: W. W. Norton & Co., 1967). Nearly a century later British writer John Stuart Mill denounced the social inequality of men and women in *The Subjection of Women* (1869), a book widely distributed by suffragists during a divisive period in the American suffrage movement following the Civil War.

5. The phrase is from a letter dated 31 March 1776 which states, "I desire you would Remember the Ladies, and be more generous and favorable to them than your ancestors. Do not put such unlimited power into the hands of the Husbands. Remember all Men would be tyrants if they could. If particular care and attention is not paid to the Ladies we are determined to foment a Rebellion, and will not hold ourselves bound by any Laws in which we have no voice, or Representation." Alice Rossi includes several letters of Abigail Adams expressing her consciousness of women's social limitations in her compilation, *The Feminist Papers: From Adams to de Beauvoir* (New York: Columbia University Press, Bantam Edition, 1974),

6. Murray used the name "Constantia" in writing a series of articles on women's educational and religious status. See Rossi, 16–24, for a brief analysis of her feminism.

7. Rossi, 282–322.

8. An excellent discussion of the interaction of the convention planners and their connections with other social groups is Judith Wellman's, "The Seneca Falls Women's Rights Convention: A Study of Social Networks," *Journal of Women's History* 3 (Spring 1991), 9–37.

9. Elizabeth Cady Stanton, Susan B. Anthony, Matilda Joslyn Gage, and Ida Husted Harper, *The History of Woman Suffrage*, Vols. 1–4, (Rochester: Susan B. Anthony, 1881–1902), 1:68–73.

10. The common law of England, as codified by William Blackstone in the late eighteenth century, declared, in Blackstone's words, that "the very being or legal existence of the woman is suspended during marriage." This legal philosophy essentially removed all property rights from women upon marriage,

as well as legal control over their own persons and offspring. See Bell & Offen, 29–31; Marylyn Salmon, *Women and the Law of Property in Early America* (Chapel Hill: University of North Carolina Press, 1986); Norma Basch *In the Eyes of the Law: Women, Marriage, and Property in Nineteenth Century New York* (Ithaca: Cornell University Press, 1982).

11. Ellen Carol DuBois gives a detailed discussion of this alliance and its subsequent development in *Feminism and Suffrage: The Emergence of an Independent Woman's Movement in America, 1848–1869* (Ithaca: Cornell University Press, 1991) 21–104.

12. See DuBois on the differences between the two groups, 169–70.

13. DuBois, 170.

14. An account of the formation of the two associations is in DuBois, 190–202.

15. One of the earliest overviews of the suffrage movement is Eleanor Flexner's, *Century of Struggle* (New York: Atheneum, 1974).

16. This statement is in the introduction to a recent volume on the anti-suffrage movement by Jane Jerome Camhi, *Women Against Women: American Anti-Suffragism, 1880–1920* (Brooklyn: Carlson Publishing Inc, 1994), xvi.

17. Anne Firor Scott surveys the birth and development of women's volunteer societies in *Natural Allies: Women's Associations in American History* (Chicago, Urbana: University of Illinois Press, 1991).

18. Elizabeth Clark elaborates this idea in "Religion, Rights and Difference," 34.

19. Margaret Fuller, *Woman in the Nineteenth Century*, reprint ed. (Columbia, South Carolina: University of South Carolina Press, 1980), 27.

20. See Clark, 53. Die-hard suffragists such as Elizabeth Stanton, Matilda Joslyn Gage, and Susan B. Anthony, while recognizing the narrow focus of the suffrage quest and the limitations of political emancipation, nonetheless, channeled their efforts toward securing this political prize.

21. See DuBois, "The Radicalism of the Woman Suffrage Movement: Notes Toward the Reconstruction of Nineteenth Century Feminism," *Feminist Studies* 3 (1975), 63–71.

22. For example, by 1920 women were admitted to almost all universities, including graduate schools; most states had passed married women's property acts, giving women control of their property and earnings; and women were serving in federal and state positions and had gained entrance into traditional male professions such as law, medicine, and higher education.

23. They were not the first territories to consider enfranchising women. Washington Territory's legislative assembly in 1854 and Nebraska's in 1856 debated but did not pass bills to allow women the vote. The Civil War suspended further action in the states and territories. T. A. Larson notes these early attempts at woman suffrage in "Emancipating the West's Dolls, Vassals, and Hopeless Drudges: The Origins of Woman Suffrage in the West," in Roger Daniels, ed., *Essays in Western History* (Laramie: University of Wyoming Publications, 1971), 1–16.

24.   More correctly polygyny, though polygamy has become the preferred denotation.

25.   Until passage of the Poland Act in 1874, the probate courts of Utah, presided over by LDS bishops and other leaders, had enjoyed the power of original jurisdiction in both criminal and civil cases and provided a sympathetic alternative to the district courts governed by a federally appointed judiciary. The Poland Act restricted the probate courts to their traditional jurisdiction over wills and probate matters.

26.   Much of the proposed Congressional anti-polygamy legislation, as well as anti-Mormon sentiment, included the repeal of woman suffrage in Utah, beginning with the Cullom Bill. When eliminating Mormon political dominance in Utah was one of the major thrusts of the anti-Mormon crusade, it was logical to halve that political strength by removing the vote from women. The fact that this measure was included in the second of the only two bills that became law may in part be attributed to the lobbying power of national suffragists. A brief but detailed account of the anti-Mormon crusade can be found in Gustive O. Larson, "Government, Politics, and Conflict," and "The Crusade and the Manifesto," in Richard D. Poll et al., *Utah's History* (Provo, Utah: Brigham Young University Press, 1978), 243–74.

27.   It would be a mistake to equate "ex-Mormon" and "non-Mormon" with "anti-Mormon." There were those among these groups whose personal antipathy to Mormonism never erupted into overt opposition by way of the lecture circuit, the press, or the petition, and others who retained their support for woman suffrage in Utah despite its link with polygamy.

28.   This stance put them in strong opposition to moral crusaders who adopted the argument that woman suffrage in Utah supported the offending practice of plural marriage. Polygamy was a target of women's groups such as the Woman's Christian Temperance Union which embarked on a national purity crusade to rid society of unacceptable moral practices, including intemperance and prostitution. The concept of female moral authority during this period is discussed in Peggy Pascoe, *Relations of Rescue: The Search for Female Moral Authority in the American West, 1874–1939* (New York: Oxford University Press, 1990).

29.   The participation of these two women and the continuing suffrage activities of Emmeline B. Wells are discussed in Carol Cornwall Madsen, "Emmeline B. Wells: A Mormon Woman in Victorian America," Ph.D. dissertation, University of Utah, 1986, 195–229.

30.   See Larson, "The Crusade and the Manifesto," 266–73.

31.   Until statehood was actually granted in 1896, there were some non-Mormons who believed that any Mormon conciliation on the question of polygamy (expressed in the 1872, 1882, and 1887 attempts at statehood) was a stratagem to achieve home rule and a continuation of political and economic dominance. See, for instance, Larson, 269.

32. Their Anti-Polygamy Association, organized in 1878, and its organ, *The Anti-Polygamy Standard*, founded in 1880, had been instrumental in enlisting the sympathy and support of purity crusaders throughout the country, giving both breadth and strength to their campaign. Two prominent members of the organization, Jennie Froiseth, editor of the *Standard*, and Cornelia Paddock, wrote best-selling exposés of polygamy and worked tirelessly to eradicate it from Utah. It was not easy for them to reverse their position toward Mormons and polygamy after such strong and pervasive hostility expressed for more than a decade.

33. They included Margaret Blaine Salisbury, Corinne Allen, Emma J. McVicker, Isabella E. Bennett, and Lillie R. Pardee. Corinne Allen later became an ardent campaigner against post-manifesto plural marriages.

34. Several studies have explored the history of probate courts in Utah. See James B. Allen, "The Unusual Jurisdiction of County Probate Courts in the Territory of Utah," *Utah Historical Quarterly*, 36 (Spring 1968), 132–41; Jay E. Powell, "Fairness in the Salt Lake County Probate Courts," *Utah Historical Quarterly*, 38 (Summer 1970), 256–62; and Elizabeth D. Gee, "Justice for All or for the 'Elect'? Utah County Probate Court, 1855–1872," *Utah Historical Quarterly* 48 (Spring 1980), 129–47.

35. 14 January 1854, Section 1, 1853–54 Laws of Utah 16. Other Western states altered or adapted the common law to suit their own conditions when its precedents proved to be inapplicable. See Gordon M. Bakken, "The English Common Law in the Rocky Mountain West," *Arizona and the West* 11 (Summer 1969), 109–28, and Bakken, *The Development of Law on the Rocky Mountain Frontier* (Westport, Connecticut, 1983). A study on the common law in Utah is Shane Swindle, "The Struggle Over the Adoption of the Common Law in Utah," *The Thetean: A Student Journal of History* (May 1984, 76–97; and Michael W. Homer, "The Judiciary and the Common Law in Utah Territory, 1850–61," *Dialogue, A Journal of Mormon Thought* 21 (Spring 1986), 97–108.

36. An Act for the Regulation of Attorneys, Section 1, 18 February 1852, 1851–52 Laws of Utah 55.

37. There is no record that women availed themselves of this opportunity until 1872 when two women were formally admitted to the Utah bar: Phoebe Couzins, an attorney from Nebraska, and Georgiana Snow, daughter of Salt Lake attorney and Associate Justice of the Utah Supreme Court Zarubbabel Snow. See Carol Cornwall Madsen, "'Sisters at the Bar': Utah Women in Law," *Utah Historical Quarterly*, 61 (Summer 1993), 217–19.

38. The statute was in effect an early version of today's "no fault" divorce. It also included extremely lenient residency requirements. See "An Act in Relation to Bills of Divorce," Sections 2, 3, 1851–52 Laws of Utah. A detailed explanation of the principles of this divorce policy in Utah during this period is Carol Cornwall Madsen, "'At Their Peril': Utah Law and the Case of Plural Wives, 1850–1900," *Western Historical Quarterly* 21 (November 1990), 430–35.

39. The irony is that the non-Mormon, federally appointed officers in Utah, who viewed polygamy as a system of bondage for Mormon women, were those who strongly urged tightening the divorce laws in Utah. See Madsen, " 'At Their Peril,' " 433–34.

40. See Lisa M. Pearson, "The Legal Status of Women in Territorial Utah," copy in possession of author.

41. The full title is *The History of Woman Suffrage,* Vols. 1–4 (Rochester: Susan B. Anthony, 1881–1902); Vols 5–6 (New York: National American Woman Suffrage Association, 1922).

42. Anthony's scrapbooks reside in the Library of Congress.

43. Elisabeth Griffith details these events in *In Her Own Right: The Life of Elizabeth Cady Stanton* (New York: Oxford University Press, 1984), 176–78.

44. *Dialogue, A Journal of Mormon Thought* 24 (Winter 1991), 31–43.

45. Lola Van Wagenen, "Sister-Wives and Suffragists: Polygamy and the Politics of Woman Suffrage, 1870–1896," Ph.D. Dissertation, New York University, 1994, 36–37.

46. Van Wagenen, 39.

47. *Brigham Young University Studies* 16 (Winter 1976), 250–64.

48. Senior and Junior Cooperative Retrenchment Association Minutes, 8 August 1874, LDS Church Archives. This view was shared by Apostle Erastus Snow who noted in 1883, a year after polygamous wives and husbands lost the franchise by the Edmunds Act, that "it was the Lord who moved upon His servants and the Legislature of our Territory to be among the first to lead the van of human progress in the extension of the elective franchise to women as well as men, and to recognize the freedom and liberty which belongs to the fairer sex as well as the sterner; for the Gospel teaches that all things are to be done by common consent." See *Journal of Discourses*, 26 vols. (Liverpool, England, 1854–86), 14:69.

49. Task Papers in LDS History, No. 29 (Salt Lake City: Historical Department of the Church of Jesus Christ of Latter-day Saints, 1979).

50. This was the term used by birth control advocate Margaret Sanger in her campaign to limit the size of families and give women reproductive control.

51. Article 14, Section 1. Compare it with the proposed Equal Rights Amendment: "Equality of rights under the law shall not be denied or abridged by the United States or any State on account of sex" (Section 1).

52. *Utah Historical Quarterly* 38 (Winter 1970), 20–30.

53. See above for a more complete description of the group and its relationship to polygamy and woman suffrage.

54. *Utah Historical Quarterly* 46 (Spring 1978), 100–20. The information in this article is included in Beverly Beeton, *Women Vote in the West: The Woman Suffrage Movement, 1869–1896* (New York: Garland Publishing, 1986).

55. The anti-polygamists who supported repeal of woman suffrage in Utah were inadvertently helped by anti-suffragists who denounced "Mormonism, suffrag-

ism, socialism and Greenbackism" as un-American movements originating in the West. See Anne M. Benjamin, *A History of the Anti-Suffrage Movement in the United States From 1895 to 1920* (Lewiston, New York: The Edwin Mellen Press, 1991), 48. Two other excellent discussions of the anti-suffrage movement are Thomas J. Joblonsky, *The Home, Heaven, and Mother Party: Female Anti-Suffragists in the United States, 1868–1920* (Brooklyn: Carlson Publishing Inc, 1994) and Camhi, *Women Against Women*. An article which centers on anti-suffrage activities in the West is Billie Barnes Jensen, " 'In the Weird and Wooly West': Anti-Suffrage Women, Gender Issues, and Woman Suffrage in the West," *Journal of the West* 32 (July 1993), 41–51.

56. Jean Bickmore White describes this last-minute effort to stall the passage of woman suffrage in the new state constitution in "Woman's Place is in the Constitution: The Struggle for Equal Rights in Utah in 1895," page 221 of this volume.

57. Ronald Walker analyzes the rise and impact of the New Movement in "The Godbeite Protest in the Making of Modern Utah," Ph.D. dissertation, University of Utah, 1977.

58. Some national suffragists themselves were sympathetic to or deeply involved in spiritualism which may have contributed to their interest in the New Movement.

59. Lola Van Wagenen discusses the connection of national suffragists with the New Movement, including the visit in 1871 of Susan B. Anthony and Elizabeth Cady Stanton to Utah in "Sister-Wives and Suffragists: Polygamy and the Politics of Woman Suffrage."

60. Beeton, *Women Vote in the West*, 27–29.

61. *Utah Historical Quarterly* 59 (Winter 1991), 22–31. A second article on Charlotte Godbe by Beverly Beeton is "I Am an American Woman: Charlotte Ives Cobb Godbe Kirby," *Journal of the West* 27 (April 1988), 13–19.

62. *Frontiers: A Journal of Women's Studies* 11, no. 2 and 3 (1990), 8–16.

63. The most notorious member of the National Association, besides polygamists, was Victoria Woodhull, a New York stockbroker, spiritualist, and suffragist, whose personal life and advocacy of free love shocked the general public.

64. Elizabeth Stanton became self-supporting, and she and her seven children lived apart from her husband for most of her married life.

65. See Claire Jerry, "The Role of Newspapers in the Nineteenth Century Woman's Movement," in Martha M. Solomon, *A Voice of Their Own: The Woman Suffrage Press, 1840–1910* (Tuscaloosa and London: The University of Alabama Press, 1991), 17–29.

66. *Journalism Quarterly* 54 (Summer 1977), 286–92.

67. Cartooning was a popular form of debunking anti-suffrage sentiment as well. An informative study of pro-suffrage cartooning is Alice Sheppard's, *Cartooning for Suffrage* (Albuquerque: University of New Mexico Press, 1994).

68. *Frank Leslie's Illustrated Newspaper*, 2 October 1869, 56.

69.   *Utah Historical Quarterly* 59 (Winter 1991), 4–21.

70.   *Utah Historical Quarterly* 42 (Fall 1974), 344–69.

71.   In Davis Bitton and Maureen Ursenbach Beecher's, *New Views of Mormon History: A Collection of Essays in Honor of Leonard J. Arrington* (Salt Lake City: University of Utah Press, 1987), 212–41.

72.   " 'I Care Nothing for Politics': Ruth May Fox, Forgotten Suffragist," *Utah Historical Quarterly* 49 (Summer 1981), 239–53.

73.   It would appear that many women found public work to be an emotional catharsis when their husbands took additional wives. In some instances an additional wife in the family freed women to follow non-domestic interests.

74.   *Utah Historical Quarterly* 38 (Winter 1970), 31–49.

75.   *Woman's Exponent* 7 (1 December 1878), 102–3. The phrase is from a Thackeray novel.

I

The History of Woman Suffrage in Utah

1870–1900

EMMELINE B. WELLS

To write the history of woman suffrage in Utah one must turn backward to 1870, when the Legislature of the Territory passed a bill conferring the franchise upon women, to which acting-Governor S. A. Mann affixed his signature February 12. From that time women voted at all elections, while some of them took a practical interest in public matters and acted as delegates to political conventions and members of Territorial and county committees.[1]

The first attempt to elect a woman to any important office was made in Salt Lake City at the county convention of 1878, when Mrs. Emmeline B. Wells was nominated for treasurer. She received the vote of the entire delegation, but the statute including the word "male" was held to debar women from holding political offices. A bill was presented to the next Legislature with petitions numerously signed asking that this word be erased from the statutes, which was passed. Gov. George W. Emory, however, refused to sign it, and though other Legislatures passed similar bills by unanimous vote, none ever received his signature or that of any succeeding governor.

First published as "Utah," chapter 66 in Susan B. Anthony and Ida Husted Harper, eds., *The History of Woman Suffrage*, vol. 4 (Rochester: Susan B. Anthony, 1902): 936–56.

In June, 1871, Mrs. Elizabeth Cady Stanton and Miss Susan B. Anthony, the president and vice-president-at-large of the National Woman Suffrage Association, stopped at Salt Lake City on their way to the Pacific Coast and met many of the prominent men and women.

In 1872 the *Woman's Exponent* was established, and it is impossible to estimate the advantage this little paper gave to the women of this far western Territory. From its first issue it was the champion of the suffrage cause, and by exchanging with women's papers of the United States and England it brought news of women in all parts of the world to those of Utah. They also were thoroughly organized in the National Woman's Relief Society, a charitable and philanthropic body which stood for reform and progress in all directions. Through such an organization it was always comparatively easy to promote any specific object or work. The Hon. George Q. Cannon, Utah's delegate in the '70's, coming from a Territory where women had the ballot, interested himself in the suffrage question before Congress. He thus became acquainted with the prominent leaders of the movement, who went to Washington every winter and who manifested much interest in the women afar off in possession of the rights which they themselves had been so long and zealously advocating without apparent results. Among these were Mrs. Stanton, Miss Anthony, Mrs. Isabella Beecher Hooker and others of national reputation.

Women were appointed as representatives from Utah by the National Suffrage Association, and the correspondence between its officers and Mrs. Wells, who had been made a member of their Advisory Committee and vice-president for the Territory, as well as the fact that the women of Utah were so progressive on the suffrage question and had sent large petitions asking for the passage of a Sixteenth Amendment to the Federal Constitution to enfranchise all women, resulted in an invitation for her to attend its annual convention at Washington, in January, 1879. Mrs. Wells was accompanied by Mrs. Zina Young Williams and they were cordially welcomed by Mrs. Stanton and Miss Anthony. This was a valuable experience for these women, as, even though they had the right of suffrage, there was much to learn from the great leaders who had been laboring in the cause of woman's enfranchisement for more than thirty years. They were invited to address the convention, and selected with others to go before Congressional committees and the President of the United States, as well as to present important matters to the Lady of the White House. The kindness which they received from Mrs. Hayes and other noted women always will remain a pleasant memory of that first visit to the national capitol. On their return home they took up the subject of the ballot more energetically in its general sense than ever before through public speaking and writing.

Emmeline B. Wells. *Courtesy of Archives, Historical
Department, Church of Jesus Christ of Latter-day Saints.*

During the seventeen years, from 1870 to 1887, that the women of Utah enjoyed the privilege of the ballot several attempts were made to deprive them of it. In 1880 a case came before the Supreme Court of the Territory on a mandamus requiring the assessor and registrar to erase the names of Emmeline B. Wells, Maria M. Blythe and Cornelia Paddock from the registration list, also the names of all other women before a certain specified date, but the court decided in favor of the defendants.

In the spring of 1882 a convention was held to prepare a constitution and urge Congress to admit Utah as a State. Three women were elected— Ms. Sarah M. Kimball, Mrs. Elizabeth Howard and Mrs. Wells—and took part in framing this constitution, and their work was as satisfactory as that of the male members. Although this was a new departure, it caused no friction whatever and was good political discipline for the women, especially in parliamentary law and usage.

This year another case was brought, before the Third District Court, to test the validity of the statute conferring the elective franchise upon the women of the Territory. A registrar of Salt Lake City refused to place the names of women upon the list of voters, and Mrs. Florence L. Westcott asked for a writ compelling him to administer the oath, enter her name, etc. The case was called for argument Sept. 14, 1882, Chief Justice James A. Hunter on the bench, and able lawyers were employed on both sides of the question. The decision sustained the Legislative Act of 1870 under which women voted. Associate Justice Emerson agreed with Judge Hunter, and Associate Justice Twiss acknowledged the validity of the law, but insisted that women should be taxpayers to entitle them to the right. This test case decided all others and women continued to vote until the passage of the Edmunds-Tucker Law, in March, 1887. During this period women gained much political experience in practical matters, and their association with men acquainted with affairs of State, in council and on committees gave them a still wider knowledge of the manipulation of public affairs.

In September, 1882, the National W.S.A. held a conference in Omaha, Neb., and Mrs. Wells and Mrs. Zina D. H. Young attended. Miss Anthony, Mrs. May Wright Sewall, chairman of the Executive Committee, and many other distinguished women were in attendance. Mrs. Wells, as vice-president for Utah, presented an exhaustive report of the suffrage work in the Territory, which was received with a great deal of enthusiasm.

At the national convention in Washington the previous January the proposed disfranchisement of Utah women by the Edmunds Bill had been very fully discussed and a resolution adopted, that "the proposition to disfranchise the women of Utah for no cause whatever is a cruel display of the power which lies in might alone, and that this Congress has no more right to disfranchise the women of Utah than the men of Wyoming."[2] This sympathy was gratefully acknowledged by the women of the Territory.

The suffrage women throughout the various States made vigorous protests against the injustice of this pending measure. A committee appointed at the convention in Washington, in the winter of 1887, presented a memorial to the President of the United States requesting him not to sign the bills, but to veto any measure for the disfranchisement of the women of Utah.[3] Mrs. Belva A. Lockwood made an able speech before the convention on this question. There were at that time several bills before Congress to deprive Utah women of the elective franchise.

During the subsequent years of this agitation every issue of the *Woman's Exponent* contained burning articles, letters and editorials upon this uncalled-for and unwarranted interference with the affairs of the women of this Territory. The advocates of the rights of all women stood up boldly for those of Utah, notwithstanding the scoffs and obloquy cast upon them. It was a fierce battle of opinions and the weaker had to succumb. The strong power of Congress conquered at last, and the Edmunds-Tucker Act of 1887 wrested from all the women, Gentile and Mormon alike, the suffrage which they had exercised for seventeen years. Naturally they were very indignant at being arbitrarily deprived of a vested right, but were obliged to submit. They were determined, however, not to do so tamely but to teach their sons, brothers and all others the value of equal suffrage, and to use every effort in their power toward securing it whenever Statehood should be conferred.

Mrs. Arthur Brown and Mrs. Emily S. Richards were appointed to represent the Territory at the National Suffrage Convention in Washington in 1888, and were there authorized to form an association uniform with those in various States and Territories. Heretofore it had not been considered necessary to organize, as women were already in possession of the ballot.

Mrs. Elizabeth Lyle Saxon and Mrs. Clara Bewick Colby, who had been lecturing on suffrage in Oregon and Washington, visited Salt Lake in September, 1888. They spoke in the theater, and on the following day a reception was tendered them in the Gardo House, where they had the opportunity of meeting socially between five and six hundred people, both Gentiles and Mormons, men and women. The same evening another large audience in the theater greeted them, and on the day succeeding at 10 A.M. there was a meeting for women only in the Assembly Hall. These meetings were held under the auspices of the Woman's Relief Society, Mrs. Zina D. H. Young, president. Though they occurred at a time when the people were suffering from indignities heaped upon them because of unjust legislation, yet a strong impression was made on those (mostly Gentiles) who never previously had been converted to suffrage.

After careful deliberation and several preliminary meetings in the office of the *Woman's Exponent*, a public call was made through the daily papers, signed by the most influential women of Salt Lake City, for a meeting in the Assembly Hall, Jan. 10, 1889, to organize a Territorial Suffrage Association. Mrs. Richards occupied the chair and Mrs. Lydia D. Alder was elected secretary *pro tem*. Prayer was offered and the old-fashioned hymn, "Know this that every soul is free," was sung by the congregation.[4] One hundred names were enrolled and Mrs. Caine and Mrs. Richards were elected delegates to the National Convention. Mrs. Caine was already at the Capital with her husband, the Hon. John T. Caine, Utah's delegate in the House of Representatives. Mrs. Richards arrived in time to give a report of the new society, which was heard with much interest.

Within a few months fourteen counties had auxiliary societies. Possibly because of the former experience of the women there was very little necessity of urging these to keep up their enthusiasm. Towns and villages were soon organized auxiliary to the counties, and much good work was done in an educational way to arouse the new members to an appreciation of the ballot, and also to convince men of the benefits to be derived by all the people when women stood side by side with them and made common cause.

On April 11, three months after the Territorial Association was organized, a rousing meeting was held in the Assembly Hall, in Salt Lake City, Mrs. Alder, vice-president, in the chair. Eloquent addresses were made by Bishop O. F. Whitney, the Hon. C. W. Penrose, the Hon. George Q. Cannon, Dr. Martha P. Hughes (Cannon), Mrs. Zina D. H. Young, Mrs. Richards, Ida Snow Gibbs and Nellie R. Webber.

A largely attended meeting took place in the County Court House, Ogden City, in June, the local president, Elizabeth Stanford, in the chair. Besides brief addresses from members eloquent speeches were made by C. W. Penrose and the Hon. Lorin Farr, a veteran legislator. The women speakers of Salt Lake who had been thoroughly identified with the suffrage cause traveled through the Territory in 1889, making speeches and promoting local interests, and strong addresses were given also by distinguished men—the Hons. John T. Caine, John E. Booth, William H. King (delegate to Congress), bishops and legislators. The fact can not be controverted that the sentiment of the majority of the people of Utah always has been in favor of equal suffrage.

At the annual meeting, held in the Social Hall, Salt Lake City, in 1890, Mrs. Sarah M. Kimball, a woman of great executive ability, was elected president.[5]

In 1890 Mrs. Kimball and Maria Y. Dougall went as delegates to the National Convention and reached Washington in time to be present at the banquet given in honor of Miss Anthony's seventieth birthday. In Mrs. Kimball's report she stated that there were 300 paid-up members of the Territorial Association exclusive of the sixteen county organizations.

During 1890 the women worked unceasingly, obtaining new members and keeping up a vigorous campaign all the year round. Meetings were held in the most remote towns, and even the farmer's wife far away in some mountain nook did her part toward securing the suffrage.

On July 23, 1890, the day Wyoming celebrated her Statehood, the Suffrage Association of Utah assembled in Liberty Park, Salt Lake City, to rejoice in the good fortune of Wyoming women. The fine old trees were decorated with flags and bunting and martial music resounded through the park; speeches rich with independent thought were made by the foremost ladies, and a telegram of greeting was sent to Mrs. Amalia Post at Cheyenne.

Conventions were held yearly in Salt Lake City, with the best speakers among men and women, and the counties represented by delegates. Many classes in civil government also were formed throughout the Territory.

At the National Convention in Washington, in February, 1891, there were present from Utah ten representatives, and the number of paid-up members entitled the delegates to twenty votes, the largest number of any State except New York.

On Feb. 15, 1892, the association celebrated Susan B. Anthony's birthday in one of the largest halls in Salt Lake City, handsomely decorated and the Stars and Stripes waving over the pictures of Mrs. Stanton and Miss Anthony. Several members of the Legislature took part in the exercises, which were entirely of a suffrage character. A telegram was received from Miss Anthony which said, "Greetings, dear friends: that your citizens' right to vote may soon be secured is the prayer of your co-worker." A message of love and appreciation was returned.

On July 29, 1892, a grand rally in the interest of suffrage was held in American Fork, attended by the leaders from Salt Lake City and other parts of the Territory. Ladies wore the yellow ribbon and many gentlemen the sunflower; the visitors were met at the station with carriages and horses decorated in yellow, and bands of music were in attendance. Mrs. Hannah Lapish, the local president, had charge, a fine banquet was spread, and the entire day was a grand feast of suffrage sentiment. C.W. Penrose was the orator.

During 1892 Mrs. Wells traveled in California and Idaho, and wherever she went, in season and out of season, spoke a good word for the cause, often where women never had given the subject a thought, or had considered it brazen and unwomanly. The annual convention in October was an enthusiastic one, but the real work of the women during that year was for the Columbian Exposition, though a suffrage song book was published and much literature circulated, not only in Utah but broadcast throughout the West; and Mrs. Richards did some work in Southern Idaho.

In some striking respects 1893 was a woman's year, and much was done to advance the suffrage cause indirectly. The association gave a large garden party in Salt Lake, with addresses by Mrs. Minnie J. Snow, Mrs. Julia P. M. Farnsworth and the Hon. George Q. Cannon.

At the annual convention Mrs. Wells was elected president, Mrs. Richards vice-president, and they continued in office during the time of the struggle to obtain an equal suffrage clause in the State constitution. Mrs. Wells made personal visits throughout the Territory, urging the women to stand firm for the franchise and encourage the men who were likely to take part in the work toward Statehood to uphold the rights of the women who had helped to build up the country, as well as those who since then had been born in this goodly land, reminding them that their fathers had given women suffrage a quarter of a century before.

In February, 1894, Mrs. Wells called an assembly of citizens for the purpose of arousing a greater interest in a Statehood which should include equal rights for women as well as men. The audience was a large one of representative people. They sang Julia Ward Howe's "Battle Hymn of the Republic" and also "America," and brilliant addresses were made by the Hon. John E. Booth, the Hon. Samuel W. Richards, Dr. Richard A. Hasbrouck, a famous orator formerly of Ohio, Dr. Martha Hughes Cannon, Mrs. Zina D. H. Young and Mrs. Lucy A. Clark. As a result of this gathering parlor meetings were held in various parts of the city, arousing much serious thought upon the question, as the Territory was now on the verge of Statehood.

On July 16 President Grover Cleveland signed the enabling act and the *Woman's Exponent* chronicled the event with words of patriotic ardor, urging the women to stand by their guns and not allow the framers of the constitution to take any action whereby they might be defrauded of their sacred rights to equality. Miss Anthony's message was quoted, "Let it be the best basis for a State ever engrossed on parchment;" and never did the faith of its editor waver in the belief that this would be done.

From this time unremitting work was carried on by the women in all directions; every effort possible was made to secure a convention of men who would frame a constitution without sex distinction, and to provide that the woman suffrage article should be included in the document itself and not be submitted separately.

At the annual convention in October, 1894, a cordial resolution was unanimously adopted thanking the two political parties for having inserted in their platforms a plank approving suffrage for women.

The November election was most exciting. Women all over the Territory worked energetically to elect such delegates to the convention as would place equal suffrage in the constitution.

After the election, when the battle was in progress, women labored tactfully and industriously; they tried by every means to educate and convert the general public, circulated suffrage literature among neighbors and friends and in the most remote corners, for they knew well that even after the constitution was adopted by the convention it must be voted on by all the men of the Territory.

In January, 1895, the president, Mrs. Wells, went to Atlanta to the National Convention, accompanied by Mrs. Marilla M. Daniels and Mrs. Aurelia S. Rogers. In her report she stated that the women of Utah had not allied themselves with either party but labored assiduously with both Republicans and Democrats. In closing she said: "There are two good reasons why our women should have the ballot apart from the general reasons why all women should have it—first, because the franchise was given to them by the Territorial Legislature and they exercised it seventeen years, never abusing the privilege, and it was taken away from them by Congress without any cause assigned except that it was a political measure; second, there are undoubtedly more women in Utah who own their homes and pay taxes than in any other State with the same number of inhabitants, and Congress has, by its enactments in the past, virtually made many of these women heads of families."

A convention was held February 18 in the Probate Court room of the Salt Lake City and County building. Delegates came from far and near. Mrs. Wells presided, and vice-presidents were Mrs. Richards, Mrs. C. W. Bennett; secretary, Mrs. Nellie Little; assistant secretary, Mrs. Augusta W Grant; chaplain, Mrs. Zina D. H. Young. A committee was appointed by the Chair to prepare a memorial for the convention,[6] and stirring speeches were made by delegates from the various counties.

In the afternoon as many of the ladies as could gain admittance went into another hall in the same building, where the Constitutional Convention was in session, and where already some members had begun to oppose woman suffrage in the constitution proper and to suggest it as an amendment to be voted upon separately. The Hon. F. S. Richards, a prominent member, presented their memorial, which closed with the following paragraph: "We therefore ask you to provide in the constitution that the rights of citizens of the State of Utah to vote and hold office shall not be denied or abridged on account of sex, but that male and female citizens of the State shall equally enjoy all civil, political and religious rights and privileges." This was signed by Emmeline B. Wells, president, Woman Suffrage Association; Emily S. Richards, vice-president; Zina D. H. Young, president, National Woman's Relief Society; Jane S. Richards, vice-president, and all the county presidents.

The next morning a hearing was granted to the ladies before the Suffrage Committee. Carefully prepared papers were read by Mesdames Richards, Carlton, Cannon, Milton, Pardee and Pratt. Mrs. Wells spoke last, without notes, stating pertinent facts and appealing for justice.

There was much debate, pro and con, in the convention after this time, and open and fair discussions of the question in Committee of the Whole. The majority report was as follows:

Resolved, That the rights of citizens of the State of Utah to vote and hold office shall not be denied or abridged on account of sex. Both male and female citizens of this State shall equally enjoy all civil, political and religious rights and privileges.

The minority report submitted later was too weak and flimsy to be considered.

The women addressed a cordial letter of appreciation and thanks to the committee who had so nobly stood by their cause.[7] Having secured this favorable report the women had not supposed it would be necessary to continue their efforts, and it would not have been except for a faction led by Brigham H. Roberts who actively worked against the adoption of this article by the delegates.[8] Numerously signed petitions for woman suffrage from all parts of the Territory were at once sent to the convention.

On the morning of April 8 the section on equal suffrage which had passed its third reading was brought up for consideration, as had been previously decided. The hall was crowded to suffocation, but as the debate was limited to fifteen minutes it was soon disposed of without much argument from either side. The vote of the convention was 74 ayes, 6 noes, 12 absent. Every member afterwards signed the constitution.

On May 12, Miss Anthony and the Rev. Anna Howard Shaw, president and vice-president-at-large of the National Association, arrived, as promised, to hold a suffrage conference. They were accompanied by Mrs. Mary C. C. Bradford and Mrs. Ellis Meredith of Colorado. The conference met in the hall where the Constitutional Convention had adjourned a few days before. Mrs. Wells presided and Gov. Caleb W. West introduced Miss Anthony, assuring his audience it was a distinguished honor, and declaring that the new State constitution which included woman suffrage would be carried at the coming election by an overwhelming majority. Miss Anthony responded in a most acceptable manner. Governor West also introduced Miss Shaw who made an eloquent address. Mrs. Bradford and Mrs. Meredith were formally presented and welcome was extended by Mesdames Zina D. H. Young, W. Ferry, B. W. Smith, J. Milton, C. E. Allen, M. I. Horne, E. B. Ferguson and the Hon. J. R. Murdock, a pioneer suffragist and member of the late convention.

The same afternoon a reception was given in honor of the ladies at the handsome residence of the Hon. F. S. and Mrs. Richards, attended by over three hundred guests, including State officials, officers and ladies from the military post, and many people of distinction. The conference lasted two days, with large audiences, and the newspapers published glowing accounts of the proceedings and the enthusiasm. Many social courtesies were extended.

Miss Anthony and her party held meetings in Ogden and were honored in every possible way, the Hon. Franklin D. Richards and his wife and the Hon. D. H. Peery being among the entertainers there.

The question soon arose whether women should vote on the adoption of the constitution at the coming November election. The commission which had been appointed by the U.S. Government to superintend affairs in Utah, decided at their June meeting to submit the matter to the Attorney-General. There was considerable agitation by the public press; some newspapers favored the women's voting and others thought its legality would be questioned and thus the admission to Statehood would be hindered. The women generally were willing to abide by the highest judicial authority.

A test case was brought before the District Court in Ogden, August 10. The court room was crowded with attorneys and prominent citizens to hear the decision of Judge H. W. Smith, which was that women should register and vote. The case was then carried to the Supreme Court of the Territory and the decision given August 31. Chief Justice Samuel A. Merritt stated that Judge G. W. Bartch and himself had reached the conclusion that the Edmunds-Tucker Law had not been repealed and would remain effective till Statehood was achieved, and that he would file a written opinion reversing the judgment of the lower court. Judge William H. King, the other member, dissented and declared that "the disfranchisement of the women at this election he regarded as a wrong and an outrage."

The opinion of the Supreme Court could not be ignored and therefore the women citizens acquiesced with the best grace possible. Unremitting and effective work continued to be done by the suffrage association, although the foremost women soon affiliated with the respective parties and began regular duty in election matters. The leaders went through the Territory urging women everywhere to look after the interests of the election and see that men voted right on the constitution, which was not only of great importance to them and their posterity but to all women throughout the land.

Women attended conventions, were members of political committees and worked faithfully for the election of the men who had been nominated at the Territorial Convention. A few women also had been placed on the tickets—Mrs. Emma McVicker for Superintendent of Public Instruction, Mrs. Lillie Pardee for the Senate, and Mrs. E. B. Wells for the House of Representatives, on the Republican ticket, and it was held that although women were not allowed to vote, they might be voted for by men. But finally, so many fears were entertained lest the success of the ticket should be imperiled that the women were induced to withdraw. Mrs. Wells' name remained until the last, but the party continuing to insist, she very reluctantly yielded, informing the committee that she did it under protest. On Nov. 5, 1895, the Republican party carried the election by a large majority; the constitution was adopted by 28,618 ayes, 2,687 noes, and Full Suffrage was conferred on women.

President Cleveland signed the constitution of Utah, Jan. 4, 1896, and the inaugural ceremonies were held in the great tabernacle in Salt Lake City, January 6, "Utah completing the trinity of true Republics at the summit of the Rockies." Gov. Heber M. Wells took the oath administered by Chief Justice Charles S. Zane, and at a given signal the booming of artillery was heard from Capitol Hill. Secretary-of-State Hammond read the Governor's first proclamation convening the Legislature at 3 o'clock that day. Mrs. Pardee was elected clerk of the Senate and entered upon the duties of the office at the opening session, signing the credentials of the U.S. Senators—the first case of the kind on record. C. E. Allen had been elected representative to Congress, and the Legislature at once selected Frank J. Cannon and Arthur Brown as United States Senators.

At the National Suffrage Convention in Washington, the evening of January 27 was devoted to welcoming Utah. Representative Allen and wife were on the platform. The Rev. Miss Shaw tendered the welcome of the association. Senator Cannon, who had just arrived in the city, responded declaring that woman was the power needed to reform politics. Mrs. Allen and Mrs. S. A. Boyer spoke of the courage and persistence of the women, and Mrs. Richards gave a graphic account of the faithful work done by the Utah Suffrage Association.

In January, 1897, Mrs. Wells attended the National Convention in Des Moines, Iowa, and described the first year's accomplishments to an appreciative audience.

On Oct. 30, 1899, Mrs. Carrie Chapman Catt, chairman of the National organization committee, and Miss Mary G. Hay, secretary, came to Salt Lake City on the homeward way from Montana, and a meeting was held in the office of the *Woman's Exponent*, Mrs. Wells in the chair and about twenty-five ladies present, all ardent suffragists. After due deliberation a committee was appointed, Mrs. Richards, chairman, Mrs. J. Fewson Smith, secretary, to work for suffrage in other States, especially Arizona. Subsequently this committee organized properly, adopted the name Utah Council of Women, and did all in their power to raise means and carry on the proposed works, and dues were sent to the national treasury.

In February, 1900, Mrs. Richards, president, and Mrs. Lucy A. Clark, delegate, went to Washington and took part in the National Convention and the celebration of Miss Anthony's eightieth birthday. On this occasion the Utah Silk Commission presented to her a handsome black silk dress pattern, which possessed an especial value from the fact that the raising of the silk worms, the spinning of the thread and all the work connected with its manufacture except the weaving was done by women.

During this year the Council of Women worked assiduously, to make a creditable exhibit at the national suffrage bazaar, Mrs. Mary T. Gilmer having personal charge of it in New York City.

LAWS: Dower and curtesy are abolished. The law reserves for the widow one-third of all the real property possessed by the husband free from his debts, but the value of such portion of the homestead as is set apart for her shall be deducted from this share. If either husband or wife die without a will leaving only the one child or the lawful issue of one, the survivor takes one-half the real estate; if there are more than one or issue of one living, then one-third. If there is issue the survivor has one-half the personal estate. If none he or she is entitled to all the real and personal estate if not over $5,000 in value, exclusive of debts and expenses. Of all over that amount the survivor receives one-half and the parents of the deceased the other half in equal shares; if not living it goes to the brothers and sisters and their heirs.

Also the widow or widower is entitled to one-half the community property subject to community debts, and if there is no will, to the other half provided there are no children living.

A homestead not exceeding $2,000 in value and $250 additional for each minor child, together with all the personal property exempt from execution, shall be wholly exempt from the payment of the debts of decedent, and shall be the absolute property of the surviving husband or wife and minor children. This section shall not be construed to prevent the disposition by will of the homestead and exempt personal property.

A married woman has absolute control over her separate property and may mortgage or convey it or dispose of it by will without the husband's consent. The husband has the same right, but in conveying real estate which is community property, the wife's signature is necessary.

A married woman may engage in business in her own name and "her earnings, wages and savings become her separate estate without any express gift or contract of the husband, when she is permitted to receive and retain them and to loan and invest them in her own name and for her own benefit, and they are exempt from execution for her husband's debts." (1894.)

A married woman may make contracts, sue and be sued in her own name.

The father is the legal guardian of the children, and at his death the mother. The survivor may appoint a guardian.

Support for the wife may be granted by the court the same as alimony in divorce, if the husband have property in the State. If not there is no punishment for non-support. (1896.)

The "age of protection" for girls was raised from 10 to 13 years in 1888, and to 18 years in 1896. The penalty is imprisonment in the penitentiary not less than five years.

SUFFRAGE: The Territorial Legislature conferred the Full Suffrage on women in 1870, and they exercised it very generally until 1887 when they were deprived of it by Congress through what is known as the Edmunds-Tucker Act. Utah entered the Union in 1896 with Full Suffrage for women as an article of the State constitution.

That they exercise this privilege quite as extensively as men is shown by the following table prepared from the election statistics of 1900. It is not customary to make separate returns of the women's votes and these were obtained through the courtesy of Governor Wells, who, at the request of the Utah Council of Women, wrote personal letters to the county officials to secure them. Eleven of the more remote counties did not respond but those having the largest population did so, and, judging from previous statistics, the others would not change the proportion of the vote.

It will be seen that in five counties the registration and vote of women was larger than that of men, and in the State a considerably larger proportion of women than of men who registered voted. Women cast nearly 50 per cent. of the entire vote and yet the U.S. Census of this year showed that males comprised over 51 per cent. of the population.

All of the testimony which is given in the chapters on Wyoming, Colorado and Idaho might be duplicated for Utah. From Mormon and Gentile alike, from the press, from the highest officials, from all who represent

Counties	Registered			Voted		
	Men	**Women**	**Total**	**Men**	**Women**	**Total**
Salt Lake	14,083	13,328	**27,411**	13,102	12,802	**25,904**
Utah	5,921	5,922	**11,843**	5,649	5,650	**11,299**
Cache	3,112	3,210	**6,322**	2,946	3,085	**6,031**
Box Elder	1,759	1,548	**3,307**	1,677	1,466	**3,143**
Davis	1,175	1,327	**2,502**	1,133	1,277	**2,410**
Carbon	986	511	**1,497**	937	477	**1,414**
Uintah	851	683	**1,534**	796	622	**1,418**
Iron	743	672	**1,415**	708	646	**1,354**
Washington	690	752	**1,442**	690	752	**1,442**
Piute	409	264	**673**	399	246	**645**
Morgan	408	387	**795**	398	378	**775**
Rich	404	289	**693**	398	286	**684**
Wayne	342	302	**644**	318	309	**627**
Grand	285	135	**420**	263	129	**392**
Kane	280	341	**621**	219	285	**504**
San Juan	123	61	**184**	106	56	**162**

Total registration of men 31,571
Total vote of men 29,738
Registered but not voting 1,833

Total registration of women 29,732
Total vote of women 28,486
Registered but not voting 1,246

the best interests of the State, it is unanimously in favor of suffrage for women. The evidence proves beyond dispute that they use it judiciously and conscientiously, that it has tended to the benefit of themselves and their homes, and that political conditions have been distinctly improved.

OFFICE HOLDING: Governor Heber M. Wells at once carried into effect the spirit of the constitution, adopted in 1895, by appointing women on all State boards of public institutions where it was wise and possible. Two out of five places on the Board of the Deaf and Dumb Institute were given to women, Harriet F. Emerson and Dr. Martha Hughes Cannon.

The first Legislature, 1896, passed "An act for the establishment of sericulture" (raising of silk worms). Women had worked energetically to secure this measure, and it was appropriate that five of them, three Republican and two Democratic, should be appointed as a silk commission, Zina D. H. Young, Isabella E. Bennett, Margaret A. Caine, Ann C. Woodbury and

Mary A. Cazier. Each was required to give a thousand-dollar bond. A later Legislature appropriated $1,000 per annum to pay the secretary.

Two women were appointed on the Board of Regents of the State University, Mrs. Emma J. McVicker, Republican and Gentile; Mrs. Rebecca E. Little, Democrat and Mormon. Both are still serving. Two were appointed Regents of the Agricultural College, Mrs. Sarah B. Goodwin and Mrs. Emily S. Richards.

At the close of the Legislature the Republican State Central Committee was reorganized; Mrs. Emmeline B. Wells was made vice-chairman, Miss Julia Farnsworth, secretary. The Democratic party was quite as liberal toward women and the feeling prevailed that at the next election women would be placed in various State and county offices. There were many women delegates in the county and also in the State conventions of both parties in 1896, and a number of women were nominated.

It was a Democratic Victory and the women on that ticket were elected—Dr. Martha Hughes Cannon to the Senate, Eurithe La Barthe and Sarah E. Anderson to the House; Margaret A. Caine, auditor of Salt Lake County; Ellen Jakeman, treasurer Utah County; Delilah K. Olson, recorder Millard County; Fannie Graehl (Rep.), recorder Box Elder County, and possibly some others.

In the Legislature of 1897, Mrs. Le Barthe introduced a bill forbidding women to wear large hats in places of public entertainment, which was passed. Dr. Cannon championed the measure by which a State Board of Health was created, and was appointed by the Governor as one of its first members. She had part in the defeat of the strong lobby that sought to abolish the existing State Board of Public Examiners, which prevents incompetents from practicing medicine. She introduced a bill compelling the State to educate the deaf, mute and blind; another requiring seats for women employes; what was known as the Medical Bill, by which all the sanitary measures of the State are regulated and put in operation; and another providing for the erection of a hospital for the State School of the Deaf, Dumb and Blind, carrying with it the necessary appropriation. All the bills introduced or championed by Dr. Cannon became laws. She served on the Committees on Public Health, Apportionment, Fish and Game, Banks and Banking, Education, Labor, etc.

At the close of their second term the Senate presented her with a handsome silver-mounted album containing the autographs of all the Senators and employes. She had drawn what is known as the long term, and at its close she was chosen to present a handsome gavel to the president of the Senate in behalf of the members. Thus far she has been the only woman Senator.

In 1899 Mrs. Alice Merrill Horne (Dem.), the third woman elected to the House, was appointed chairman of the State University Land Site Committee, to which was referred the bill authorizing the State to take advantage of the congressional land grant offered for expending $301,000 in buildings and providing for the removal of the State University to the new site. At a jubilee in recognition of the gift, held by the faculty and students, at which the Governor and legislature were guests, Mrs. Horne was the only woman to make a speech and was introduced by President Joseph T. Kingsbury in most flattering terms for the work she had done in behalf of education. She championed the Free Scholarship Bill giving one hundred annual Normal School appointments, each for a term of four years; and one creating a State Institute of Art for the encouragement of the fine arts and for art in public school education and in manufactures, for an annual exhibition, a course of lectures and a State art collection, both of which passed. She was a member of committees on Art, Education, Rules and Insane Asylum; was the only member sent to visit the State Insane Asylum, going by direction of the Speaker of the House, as a committee of one, to surprise the superintendent and report actual conditions. Mrs. Horne was presented with a photographed group of the members of the House, herself the only woman in the picture.

The November election of 1900 was fraught with great interest to the women, as the State officials were to be elected as well as the Legislature, and they were anxious that there should be some women's names on the tickets for both the House and Senate, and that a woman should be nominated for State Superintendent of Public Instruction by both parties. For this office the Republican and the Democratic women presented candidates,—Mrs. Emma J. McVicker and Miss Ada Faust,—but both conventions gave the nomination to men. Meantime Dr. John R. Park, the superintendent, died suddenly and Gov. Wells appointed Mrs. McVicker as his successor for the unfinished term.

Mrs. J. Ellen Foster, of Washington, D.C., was sent to Utah by the Republican National Committee, and with Mrs. W. F. Boynton and others, made a spirited and successful campaign.

There never has been any scramble for office on the part of women, and here, as in the other States where they have the suffrage, there is but little disposition on the part of men to divide with them the "positions of emolument and trust." Only one woman was nominated for a State office in 1900, Mrs. Elizabeth Cohen for the Legislature, and she was defeated with the rest of the Democratic ticket. All of the women who have served in the Legislature have been elected by the Democrats.

Several women were elected to important city and county offices. In many of these offices more women than men are employed as deputies and clerks.

In 1900 Mrs. W. H. Jones was sent as delegate to the National Republican Convention in Philadelphia, and Mrs. Elizabeth Cohen to the Democratic in Kansas City, and both served throughout the sessions. This is the first instance of the kind on record, although women were sent as alternates from Wyoming to the National Republican Convention at Minneapolis in 1888.

Women are exempted from sitting on juries, the same as editors, lawyers and ministers, but they are not excluded if they wish to serve or the persons on trial desire them. None has thus far been summoned.

OCCUPATIONS: No profession or occupation is legally forbidden to women except that of working in mines.

EDUCATION: All of the higher institutions of learning are open to both sexes. In the public schools there are 527 men and 892 women teachers. The average monthly salary of men is $61.42; of the women, $41.19.

Women in Utah always have been conspicuous in organized work. The National Woman's Relief Society was established at Nauvoo, Ills., in 1842, and transferred to Salt Lake City in 1848. It is one of the oldest associations of women in the United States—the oldest perhaps of any considerable size. It has over 30,000 members and is one of the valuable institutions of the State. The National Young Ladies' Mutual Improvement Association has 21,700 members and in 1900 raised $3,000 partly for building purposes and partly to help the needy.[9] There are also a State Council of Women, Daughters of the Pioneers, Daughters of the Revolution, Council of Jewish Women, etc. Thirty-three clubs belong to the National Federation but this by no means includes all of them.

Notes

1. The History is indebted for this chapter to Mrs. Emmeline B. Wells of Salt Lake City, editor of the *Woman's Exponent*, and president of the Territorial Association during the campaign when Full Suffrage was secured. Valuable assistance has been rendered by Mrs. Emily S. Richards of that city, vice-president during the same period.
2. Committee: Lillie Devereux Blake of New York, Virginia L. Minor of St. Louis, Harriet R. Shattuck of Boston, May Wright Sewall of Indianapolis and Ellen H. Sheldon of Washington, D.C.

3. Committee: Lillie Devereux Blake, Matilda Joslyn Gage, Caroline Gilkey Rogers and Mary Seymour Howell, of New York; Clara B. Colby, Nebraska; Sarah T. Miller, Maryland; Elizabeth Boynton Harbert, Illinois; Harriet R. Shattuck, Massachusetts, and Louisa Southworth, Ohio.

4. The officers elected were: President, Margaret N. Caine; vice-presidents, Lydia D. Alder, Nellie R. Webber, Priscilla J. Riter; secretary, Cornelia N. Clayton; corresponding secretary, Charlotte I. Kirby; treasurer, Margie Dwyer; executive committee, Maria Y. Dougall, Nettie Y. Snell, Ann E. Groesbeck, Phoebe Y. Beatie and Jennie Rowe.

5. Vice-presidents, Mrs. Richards, Ann D. Groesbeck and Caroline E. Dye; recording secretary, Rachel Edwards; corresponding secretary, Julia C. Taylor; treasurer, Margie Dwyer; executive committee, Cornelia H. Clayton, Margaret Mitchell, Nellie Little, Theresa Hills and May Talmage.

6. Mesdames Richards, Young, Bennett, G. S. Carlton, J. S. Gilmer, Romania B. Pratt, Phebe Y. Beatie, Amelia F. Young, Martha H. Cannon, C. E. Allen, Emma McVicker, Ruth M. Fox, Priscilla Jennings, Lillie Pardee and Martha Parsons.

7. Hon. J. F. Chidester, chairman; A. S. Anderson, Joseph E. Robinson, Parley Christianson, Peter Lowe, James D. Murdock, Chester Call, Andreas Engberg, A. H. Raleigh, William Howard, F. A. Hammond, S. R. Thurman. In addition to this committee those who sustained the women and pleaded their cause were Messrs. Richards, Whitney, Evans, Cannon, Murdock, Rich, Hart, Ivins, Snow, Robinson, Allen, Miller, Farr, Preston, Maeser and Wells. There were others, but these were the foremost.

8. Mr. Roberts was elected to Congress on the Democratic ticket in 1900 [1898], although strenuously opposed by the women of Utah, irrespective of politics, but largely owing to the vigorous protests of the women of the whole United States, he was not permitted to take his seat. [Eds. of *History of Woman Suffrage*]

9. In 1889 Mrs. Susa Young Gates established the *Young Woman's Journal,* a monthly magazine, as the organ of this association, although it was for eight years financially a private enterprise. The president, Mrs. Elmina S. Taylor, was her constant help and inspiration. The first year Mrs. Lucy B. Young, mother of the editor, then past sixty, took her buggy and traveled over Utah explaining the venture and securing subscriptions. Two thousand numbers a year were published. Of late years the business managers have been women. In 1897 Mrs. Gates made over the magazine to the association without any consideration, but was retained as editor. There were at this time practically no debts and 7,000 subscribers, which later were increased to 10,000.

Susa Young Gates. *Courtesy of Archives, Historical Department, Church of Jesus Christ of Latter-day Saints.*

2

The History of Woman Suffrage in Utah

1900–1920

SUSA YOUNG GATES

The results of equal suffrage in Utah for fifty years—1870–1920—with an unavoidable interim of eight years, have demonstrated the sanity and poise of women in the exercise of their franchise. The Mormon women had had long training, for from the founding of their church by Joseph Smith in 1830 they had a vote in its affairs. Although the Territory of Wyoming was the first to give the suffrage to women—in November, 1869—the Legislature of Utah followed in January, 1870, and the bill was signed by [acting] Governor S. A. Mann February 12. Women voted at the regular election the next August and there was no election in Wyoming until September, so those of Utah had the distinction of being the pioneer women voters in the United States and there were over five times as many women in Utah as in Wyoming. The story of how their suffrage was taken away by an Act of Congress in 1887 and how it was restored in full by the men of Utah when they made their constitution for statehood in 1895 and adopted it by a vote of ten to one is related in detail in Volume IV of the History of Woman Suffrage. The women have voted since then in large numbers, filled many offices and been a recognized

First published as "Utah," chapter 43 in Ida Husted Harper, ed., *The History of Woman Suffrage*, vol. 6 (New York: National American Woman Suffrage Association, 1922): 644–50.

political influence for the benefit of the State.

The large and active Territorial Woman Suffrage Association held annual conventions until after it succeeded in gaining the franchise. In 1899, during a visit of Mrs. Carrie Chapman Catt to Salt Lake City, a meeting was called and steps taken to form a Utah Council of Women to assist the suffrage movement in other States and Mrs. Emily S. Richards was made president. This Council, composed of Mormons and non-Mormons, continued in existence for twenty years. For the first ten years there were monthly meetings and also special and committee meetings and prominent speakers addressed the annual gatherings, eulogizing and commemorating the lives and labors of the suffrage pioneers throughout the Union. Whenever the National American Suffrage Association called for financial aid it responded liberally. The suffrage having been gained it was hard to keep up the interest and after 1910 meetings were held only at the call of the president for the purpose of carrying out the wishes of the National Suffrage Association, at whose conventions the Council was always represented by delegates. In 1909–10, when the association was collecting its monster petition to Congress, the Council obtained 40,000 names as Utah's quota.

The official personnel remained practically the same from 1900. That noble exponent of the best there is in womanhood, Mrs. Emily S. Richards, preserved the spirit and genius of the Council, which recognized no party and whose members cast their votes for good men and measures without undue partisan bias. She was sustained by its capable and resourceful secretary, Mrs. Elizabeth M. Cohen, and both maintained a non-partisan attitude in the conduct of the Council. The officers were: Emmeline B. Wells, member national executive committee; Elizabeth A. Hayward, Mrs. Ira D. Wines, Dr. Jane Skolfield and Mrs. B. T. Pyper, vice-presidents; Anna T. Piercey, assistant secretary; Hannah S. Lapish, treasurer.

As Territory and State, every county, every town, every precinct has been served faithfully and well by women in various positions. It would be impossible to name all who have done yeoman service during the past years but the three women who have meant more than all others to the suffrage cause are Mrs. Sarah M. Kimball, who was appointed by Brigham Young and Eliza R. Snow as the standard bearer of that cause in the late '60's and who maintained her active hold upon politics until about 1885 [1893], when her able first lieutenant, Mrs. Emmeline B. Wells, took up the work dropped by the aged hands of Mrs. Kimball. She in turn carried the banner of equal civic freedom aloft, assisted by Mrs. Richards, until she relinquished it in 1896 and Mrs. Richards became the standard bearer. Many other splendid women have labored assiduously in this cause.

In legislative matters a committee from the Council has worked during every session since 1911 with associated committees from the other large organizations of women, the powerful Relief Society, the Young Ladies' Mutual Improvement Association and the Federated Clubs leading in all good movements. Results in the enactment of welfare laws for women and children have been very gratifying. The women's committees of the various organizations meet at the State Capitol during the legislative sessions and go over very carefully every bill in which they are interested. If after investigation a bill meets with their approval it is endorsed and every effort is made to secure its passage. From 1911 to 1917 the women's legislative committee secured copies of laws already in successful operation in other States and framed bills to meet their own needs. These were always submitted to two young lawyers, Dan B. Shields and Carl Badger, who corrected any flaws which might jeopardize their constitutionality. Among the women who comprise these committees are Mrs. Cohen, chairman, Miss Sarah McLelland of the Relief Society; Mrs. Adella W. Eardley and Mrs. Julia Brixen of the Y.L.M.I.A.; Mrs. Richards and Mrs. Hayward of the Suffrage Council; Mrs. C. M. McMahon, president, Mrs. Peter A. Simpkin, Mrs. A. V. Taylor and Mrs. Seldon I. Clawson, members of the Federation of Women's Clubs.

In many Legislatures since statehood there have been women members and their work has been along expected lines. In 1896, the year Utah was admitted to the Union, Dr. Martha Hughes Cannon was elected to the State Senate, the first woman in the United States to receive that honor. Several women were elected to the Lower House then and others in the years following. Needed reform measures were secured by Mrs. Mary G. Coulter, who sat in the Lower House and was made chairman of the Judiciary Committee in 1903. There was a long interim when no women were sent to the Legislature but in 1913 four were elected, Mrs. Annie Wells Cannon, Dr. Skolfield, Mrs. Elizabeth Ellerbeck Reid and Mrs. Annie H. King. They were instrumental in securing the Mothers' Pension Law and the Minimum Wage Law and through Mrs. Cannon the bureau of emigration labor was provided with a woman deputy to look after the women and children workers. Utah already had an equal guardianship law but largely through the efforts of Mrs. Cannon it was improved and is now regarded as a model and has been copied by other States. She is a representative daughter of Mrs. Wells.

In 1915 Mrs. Elizabeth A. Hayward and Mrs. Lily C. Wolstenholme were elected and to the former the improved child labor law must be credited. In 1917 she was re-elected and Dr. Grace Stratton Airy and Mrs. Daisy C. Allen became members of the Lower House. During 1915–1917 laws raising the age of protection for girls to 18 and requiring equal pay for equal work were enacted. Mrs. Hayward, at the request of the women's Legislative Council, introduced the resolution calling on Congress to submit the Federal Amendment. In 1918 she was elected State Senator. In 1919 Dr. Airy was re-elected and Mrs. Anna G. Piercy and Mrs. Delora Blakely were elected to the Lower House. Altogether there have been thirteen women members of the Legislature. No State has better laws relating to women and children than Utah.

It has been difficult to persuade the women to stand for important offices. The modern furious pace set by campaigners and the severance of home ties for long periods are not alluring to wives and mothers but they find many public activities through which to exercise their executive abilities. They sit on the boards of many State and local institutions and serve on committees for civic and educational work. A considerable number have filled and are now filling city and county offices. Mrs. L. M. Crawford has a responsible position in the office of the State Land Board. Mrs. McVicker was State Superintendent of Schools. In 1917 a new department was added to the office of the Adjutant General to secure pensions for those veterans who had served in the Indian wars of Utah. Mrs. Elizabeth M. Cohen was given early custody of the old Indian War Records and was named Commissioner of Pensions. In order to prove the claims of these men and women she cooperated with the Pension Bureau at Washington, D.C. Up to date out of a possible 1,500 whose claims have merit nearly 700 pensions have been granted, bringing into the State the sum of $400,000.

When Brigham Young established those monuments to his name, the Brigham Young University of Provo and the Brigham Young College of Logan in 1874 he placed women on their boards. Mrs. Martha J. Coray of Provo served ten years for the former and Professor Ida M. Cook for the latter. Mrs. Gates was made a trustee of the university in 1891, which position she still occupies, while her sister, Mrs. Zina Young Card, has been a trustee since 1914. Mrs. Gates was on the board of the State Agricultural College 1905–1913. Mrs. A. W. McCune was on this board ten years, seven of them its vice-president. Mrs. Rebecca M. Little, Mrs. Antoinette B. Kinney and Dr. Belle A. Gummel have been regents of the university. Professor Maude May Babcock has been dean of physical education and expression since 1892 and a trustee since 1897. Her culture and personality have left an indelible impress on the history of this State.

From the beginning women have allied themselves with the different political parties, ocasionally [sic] uniting on a great issue like that of Prohibition. From the time they were enfranchised by the State constitution they have received the recognition of the parties. In 1900 women were sent as delegates and alternates to both national presidential conventions and Mrs. Cohen seconded the nomination of William Jennings Bryan. A number were sent in following years. In 1908 Mrs. Margaret Zane Cherdron was a delegate and a presidential elector, carrying the vote to Washington. She was one of the two received by President Taft and was royally entertained while in the capital. Among other women who have acted as delegates and alternates since 1900 are Mrs. William H. Jones, Mrs. Hayward, Mrs. Sarah Ventrees, Mrs. Gates, Mrs. Lucy A. Clark, Mrs. B. T. Pyper, Mrs. L. M. Crawford, Mrs. Alice E. Paddison.

Women have their representation on all political committees—Mrs. Hayward is a member of the Democratic National Committee—and their participation in politics is accepted without question. There are about 10,000 more women voters than men voters. As a rule about 90 per cent of the women vote and about 85 per cent of the men, as some of the latter are in the mines or out of the State for various reasons. Among the Republican leaders are Mrs. Wells, Mrs. Gates, Mrs. Cherdron, Mrs. Jannette A. Hyde, Mrs. Cannon, Mrs. Wolstenholm, Mrs. Loufborough, Mrs. William Spry, Mrs. Reed Smoot; Mrs Martha B. Keeler of Provo and Mrs. Georgina G. Marriott of Ogden. The Democratic party has had among its leading women Mrs. Richards, Mrs. Alice Merrill Horne, Mrs. Cohen, Mrs. Hayward, Gwen Lewis Little, Mrs. Piercy, Mrs. S. S. Smith, Mrs. Annice Dee, Mrs. Inez Knight Allen and Miss Alice Reynolds.

No State exceeded Utah in the proportion of the work done by women during the World War. Mrs. Clarissa Smith Williams was the unanimous choice for chairman of the State branch of the Woman's Council of National Defense. She was eminently fitted for this position through her long experience as first counsellor to Mrs. Emmeline B. Wells, head of the Relief Society, and every demand of the Government was fully met.

RATIFICATION. At the request of the Suffrage Council and without urging, Governor Simon Bamberger called a special session of the Legislature for Sept. 30, 1919, to ratify the Federal Suffrage Amendment submitted the preceding June. The resolution was presented by Senator Elizabeth A. Hayward and was ratified unanimously by both Houses within thirty minutes. The Governor signed it without delay. The women and the Legislature had helped in every possible way to secure the Amendment and the entire Utah delegation in Congress had voted for it.

A striking event in the train of possible fruitful activities left behind was the visit of the great leader, Mrs. Carrie Chapman Catt, president of the

National American Suffrage Association, with her able young assistants, who came to Utah for Nov. 16–18, 1919. She was accompanied by Dr. Valerie Parker and Mrs. Jean Nelson Penfield, chairmen in the National League of Women Voters, and Miss Marjorie Shuler, director of publicity for the National Association. The convention, held in the Assembly Hall, was in charge of the Suffrage Council, its president, Mrs. Richards, assisted by Mrs. Cohen and Mrs. E. E. Corfman. A long and valuable program was carried out. Mrs. Catt spoke in the Tabernacle on Sunday afternoon, introduced by President Charles W. Penrose with a glowing tribute to her power as a leader, to the sincerity and womanliness of her character and to the catholicity of her vision and sympathy. There were banquets, teas and receptions.

At the close of the convention the Suffrage Council, which had rendered such splendid service for the past twenty years, was merged into the State League of Women Voters and Mrs. Richards willingly resigned her leadership to its chairman, Mrs. Clesson S. Kinney.

On Feb. 12, 1920, a jubilee celebration was held in honor of the fiftieth anniversary of the signing of the woman suffrage bill by the Territorial [Acting] Governor S. A. Mann. There was also celebrated the granting of the complete franchise by the immense majority of the voters in 1895.

Utah celebrated in Salt Lake City August 30, with a great demonstration, the triumph of woman suffrage in the United States through the ratification of the Federal Amendment, which had been proclaimed August 26. It was introduced with an impressive parade led by bands of music and the program of ceremonies was carried out on the steps of the State Capitol. Governor Bamberger, former Governor Heber M. Wells, Congressman E. O. Leatherwood and Mayor C. Clarence Neslen joined the women in congratulatory addresses. Mrs. Richards, Mrs. Hannah Lapish and Mrs. Lydia Alder, veteran suffragists, told of the early struggles and Mrs. Beulah Storrs Lewis appealed to women to keep high the standard in order to lead men out of the darkness of war into the light of brotherly love and make ready for world peace. Mrs. Annie Wells Cannon and Mrs. Susa Young Gates were appointed to send a telegram of congratulation to Mrs. Catt. The celebration was under the auspices of the League of Women Voters, whose chairman, Mrs. Kinney, presided. The most impressive figure on the platform was President Emmeline B. Wells, 92 years old, who had voted since 1870 and who had labored all these years for this glorious achievement. What those dim eyes had seen of history in the making, what those old ears had heard and what that clear brain had conceived and carried out only her close associates knew. She was the incarnate figure of tender, delicate, eternally determined womanhood, arrived and triumphant.

Notes

1. *The History* is indebted for this chapter to Mrs. Susa Young Gates, member of the General Board of the Woman's Relief Society and editor of the Relief Society's Magazine since it was established in 1913 and historian of the activities of Utah women.

3

In Their Own Behalf

The Politicization of Mormon Women and the 1870 Franchise

Lola Van Wagenen

Immediately upon the passage of territorial legislation enfranchising Utah's women in 1870, almost fifty years before the Nineteenth Amendment extended the vote to American women, arguments erupted between the Mormon and non-Mormon community over the reasons behind this legislation. Since that time, historians have continued to disagree about the motives of the Mormon-dominated legislature. Some dismiss this early woman suffrage in Utah as a fluke; others believe Mormon women were passive recipients of the vote or pawns of the male leadership. Still others are convinced the act was progressive, the result of a generally egalitarian ideology.[1]

Amidst this array of opinions, it is somewhat surprising to find that what has been overlooked is the possibility that Mormon women themselves had a role in securing their suffrage. This oversight is no doubt due in part to the fact that Mormon women did not publicly draft petitions, nor did they hold public demonstrations to seek enfranchisement. As a result, many historians have concluded that they were not politically active until after suffrage, and then only in response to attempts to disfranchise them.[2] Had

First published in *Dialogue: A Journal of Mormon Thought* 24 (Winter 1991): 31–43. Reprinted by permission.

these scholars studied the actions of Mormon women within their church, a different view might have emerged.

There is ample evidence that Mormon women were not disinterested recipients of the vote. Their reaction to enfranchisement readily demonstrates their involvement. Moreover, they had *not* been politicized overnight: many were well prepared in 1870 to assume an active political role in their communities (Scott 1986–87). Both their religious and community activities politicized Mormons and helped lead to the 1870 franchise. Although Mormon women did not openly seek suffrage, I believe they were activists in their own behalf, and their actions contributed to their enfranchisement. The record also shows that Mormon women were not totally isolated in far-away Utah. They engaged many of the same problems and sought similar solutions as did women's advocates in the States.

For Mormon women, 1870 signaled the end of a politicization that had begun in the 1840s and the beginning of a visible and aggressive political activism. This process occurred in three stages. The first began in Nauvoo, where some Mormon women were taught that all the doctrines of the restored gospel, including polygamy, signaled a new era for women. Promised equality and privileges greater than they had ever known, women participated in Church governance through the "religious franchise," the Church's method of voting (Cannon 1869; Gates n.d.; Gates and Widtsoe 1928, 7–9).

Clear evidence of a new era was most expressly manifest by the founding of the Female Relief Society of Nauvoo in 1842. Sarah Kimball is credited with the original idea for the society, although the Prophet Joseph Smith blessed and sanctified the organization (Derr 1987; Crocheron 1884, 27; Derr 1976; Jenson 1901, 4:373). The Relief Society helped the sisters develop many of the same skills other American women were learning in similar benevolent associations (see Berg 1978). But in addition, Mormon women took their first united political action when they drafted—and delivered— a petition to the governor of Illinois seeking protection for the community of Nauvoo.[3] Sarah Kimball later claimed that when the Relief Society was established, "the sure foundations of the suffrage cause were deeply and permanently laid" (1892). In the upheaval following the death of Joseph Smith, the Relief Society was temporarily disbanded by Brigham Young. The Mormon sisters, however, resented giving up their organization and were firm in their conviction that they had specific powers in relationship to it. Angered by these assertions, Brigham Young lashed out saying, "When I want Sisters or the Wives of the members of the church to get up Relief Society I will summon them to my aid but until that time let them stay at home & if you see Females huddling together veto the concern and if they say

Joseph started it tell them it is a damned lie for I know he never encouraged it" (in Derr 1987, 163).

The women, however, were steadfast in their belief that the Society was rightfully their own organization. They frequently asserted their convictions by quoting Joseph Smith's promise: "I now turn the key to you in the name of God and this Society shall rejoice and knowledge and intelligence shall flow down from this time" (Minutes, Nauvoo, 28 April 1842). The activism that Mormon women initiated in Nauvoo established a pattern of participation that defined the first critical stage of their process of politicization. By the time the Saints were forced to leave Nauvoo, an inchoate sisterhood had emerged, one that quickened on the Great Plains. Survival on the westward trek dictated cooperation among Mormon women, and many learned through that ordeal and what followed both leadership and independence.

The second stage of politicization dates from the Saints' 1847 arrival in the Great Basin to the end of the Civil War. It was time of severe stress for Mormon women. Plural marriage, combined with the frequent calling of males on Church missions, left many women alone to provide materially and emotionally for the welfare of their families. In addition, Leonard Arrington has described this era as marked by "harsh hyperbole, offensive rhetoric and militant posturing" on the part of Brigham Young and federal officials. The passage of the 1862 Antibigamy Act reinforced the national attitudes toward Mormons and polygamy (1985, 300). When that rhetoric was directed toward Mormon women, it appears, at best, insensitive and at worst anti-female (Evans 1980, 13). These were difficult years for Sarah Kimball, who taught school for several years under "very trying circumstances," and, according to an early biography, became "even more than ever convinced" of the need to change working conditions for women who were in competition with men. She saw "no other method that could be so effectual as the elective franchise" (Jenson 1901, 4:190). It is not clear, however, how broadly her sentiments were shared.

In spite of these difficulties and constraints, Mormon women continued their organizational efforts. They established a Female Council of Health in 1851 to discuss personal health matters and were active participants in the Polysophical Society, a western version of the lyceum which sponsored lectures by visiting scholars or dignitaries. Finally, on women's initiative, between 1847 and 1856, various forms of the Relief Society made brief reappearances in a decentralized and ad hoc form (Jensen 1983; Naisbitt 1899; Beecher 1975,1). Throughout this second stage, 1847–65, women participated in various public efforts to help their own poor as well as Native Americans in the territory and promoted the health and well-being of other women. In these efforts, they learned to move forward carefully enough to avoid problems, but forcefully enough to break new ground.

The third stage of politicization ran from 1865 to the end of the decade. Though benign, the Utah War had been expensive for the Saints, and anti-Mormon sentiment was on the rise. Realizing that he had to find a less combative way to deal with the national government, Brigham Young began reassessing past economic policies and renewed an emphasis on cooperative efforts, including home manufacturing. In this climate, Mormon women worked for the permanent reestablishment of the Relief Society. Eliza R. Snow, President Young's most trusted female counsel, was not officially set apart as president of the "sisterhood" until 1880 but was authorized to reorganize the Relief Society in 1867 (Derr 1987, 172). "The time had come," she stated, "for sisters to act in a wider sphere" (Minutes 1867).

While each ward Relief Society was officially under the "guidance" of the bishop, programs and priorities reflected the counsel of Eliza R. Snow and the vision of individual ward presidents. In the Salt Lake City Fifteenth Ward, Sarah Kimball was determined to prove that women could contribute economically to the community. She tenaciously promoted home manufacturing, which included a variety of homecrafts such as straw hats and handmade gloves as well as food items, and the construction of a storehouse financed, owned, and operated by women (Minutes 4 Jan., 15 Feb., 18 June, 16 July, 14 Aug. 1868). Her statement when the Salt Lake City Fifteenth Ward chapel's cornerstone was laid indicates her support for women's economic independence: "A woman's allotted sphere of labor is not sufficiently extensive and varied to enable her to exercise all [her] God-given powers . . . nor are her labors made sufficiently remunerative to afford her that independence compatible with true womanly dignity" (Minutes 12 Nov. 1868).

Whether Kimball, Snow, and others saw economic independence as a step toward political activity is unclear. However, Kimball thought it right for women to be independent, but she was careful not to appear too autonomous. Programs were always approved by local male authorities. Eliza Snow also promoted programs of self-improvement and instructed the sisters that the time would come "when we will have to be in large places and act in responsible situations" (Minutes 25 April 1868). At the same time, she consistently reminded women of their duty as wives and mothers and of the importance of obedience. Nevertheless, the practical experience in domestic commercial enterprises, the commitment to self-improvement, and the constant affirmation of their spiritual powers had produced a vibrant sense of sisterhood. The Relief Society provided a sanctioned setting in which to discuss women's rights and responsibilities.

Fifteenth Ward Relief Society Hall.

By 1869, the success of various Relief Society efforts was gaining public attention in Zion—many men who had been skeptical began praising the women's accomplishments. Among the women, pride and growing self-esteem were palpable. Change was aloft in the community of Mormon women. As an example, in the past when they were portrayed in anti-polygamy attacks as degraded victims, Mormon women had chosen not to respond; now increasingly they came to their own defense.

Ironically, finding a way to end polygamy was the motivation behind the earliest proposal to enfranchise Utah's women. The underlying assumption among non-Mormons was that Mormon women would vote to end polygamy. This tactic was suggested by the *New York Times* in 1867 (reprint, *Deseret News*, 15 Jan. 1867; Beeton 1986, x)[4] and was subsequently introduced as a bill in the United States Congress. To the surprise of the bill's sponsors, both Utah's territorial representative and the press in Utah received the proposal favorably; as a result it was subsequently abandoned. But from this time forward, the issue of woman suffrage was increasingly discussed in the territory—by women as well as men.

January 1870 signaled a turning point in the politicization of Mormon women. They had strengthened the position of their most valuable activist organization, the Relief Society. Widening their sphere of activity, they had thoroughly debated women's roles. Their gender consciousness appears clear. They had moved into a highly visible public arena that they energetically sustained for the rest of the century.

Two events mark 1870 as a watershed in the history of Mormon women and political activism. First, in early January three thousand women gathered in a "great indignation meeting" to protest anti-polygamy legislation introduced in the national Congress. Then in February, acting Governor S. A. Mann, a non-Mormon, signed the woman suffrage bill passed by the territorial legislature. The circumstances surrounding these events show Mormon women as outspoken public activists in their own behalf.

The arrival in the territory in December 1869 of a new anti-polygamy bill, the Cullom Act, propelled Mormon women into political activism. Among other things, the Cullom Bill stipulated that anyone believing in polygamy would be denied the right to vote or serve on a jury. Though the Saints no doubt knew the bill had been introduced in Congress, seeing it in print must have been a shock—both the substance and language were outrageous and insulting. In fact, a number of non-Mormons found the bill offensive and spoke against its passage (*Deseret News*, 9 March 1870).

Mormon women were especially outraged, which was nothing new, but now their response was boldly public. They called for a meeting 6 January to plan a women's public protest; in probability it was approved by Church leaders.[5] Sarah Kimball opened the discussion stating, "Mormon women would be unworthy of the names we bear or of the blood in our veins, should we longer remain silent." Eliza Snow added that it was "high time" for Mormon women to "rise up in the dignity of our calling and speak for ourselves." The group voted unanimously to hold a protest, and a committee drafted resolutions. After the resolutions were read and approved, the meeting took an even more aggressive turn. Bathsheba Smith stated that she was pleased with the actions thus far, then moved "that we demand of the Gov. the right of franchise." The women voted, and the "vote carried." Then Lucy W. Kimball, stating that "we had borne in silence as long as it was our duty to bear," moved that the women "be represented in Washington." Eliza Snow and Sarah Kimball were "elected as representatives" (Minutes, 19 Feb. 1870).

In response to such bold action, one might have expected newspaper headlines the next day to have read "Women to Seek Franchise from Utah Governor," or "Snow and Kimball Elected to Represent Mormon Women in Washington." Instead *five* days later, the *Deseret News* headline read, "Minutes of a Ladies Mass Meeting." The article, which included the comments by Sarah Kimball and Eliza Snow as well as a full copy of the protest resolution, blandly concluded: "Miss E. R. Snow, Mrs. L. W. Kimball and Mrs. B. Smith made a few very appropriate remarks expressing their hearty concurrence in the movement and in the measures adopted by the meeting." The article was signed by Sarah Kimball.[6] It fails to mention both the motion to seek the franchise and Eliza Snow's and Sarah Kimball's election as representatives to Washington.

This represents a fascinating editorial decision. While the organizing meeting minutes show solid evidence of the quickening political behavior of Mormon women, excluding both motions from the public record obscured their efforts from immediate public (and eventual historical) scrutiny. There are several possible reasons for the omission. The sisters themselves may have worried about appearing too aggressive or about using the Relief Society for their own agenda—accusations that had been leveled at Emma Smith in Nauvoo—thereby endangering the position of the Relief Society; or the women may have wanted to discuss their resolutions with the Brethren before announcing them publicly. The discrepancy may also show one reason why Mormon women's political activities are so difficult to trace: the women were more interested in being effective than visual. A low profile may have been critical to their success, and they knew it. Clearly, however, Mormon women had been talking privately about suffrage, and prior to their enfranchisement they were trying to do something about it.

Another possible reason for not publicizing their 6 January action on woman suffrage was the immediately upcoming mass protest meeting, which needed planning. This "Great Indignation Meeting" held 13 January 1870, brought three thousand women to the Salt Lake Tabernacle to hear the "leading sisters" of the Church speak from its pulpit for the first time. Though the meeting's stated agenda was to protest the Cullom anti-polygamy bill, proceedings indicate that some Mormon women had come to see polygamy as a women's rights issue. Although nine of the fourteen recorded speakers spoke directly to the defense of polygamy without raising the issue of women's rights or suffrage, five did broach the topic. In a surprising opening remark, Sarah Kimball stated, "We are not here to advocate woman's rights but man's rights" (*Deseret News*, 16 Feb. 1870). Those anxious about the danger of "strong-minded" women would undoubtedly be reassured by Kimball's comment. Most likely, that was her intent. She did not, however, overlook women's interests. She ended her speech, noting that not only would the legislation "deprive our fathers, husbands and brothers" of their constitutional privileges, but "would also deprive us, as women, of the privilege of selecting our husbands, and against *this* we most unqualifiedly protest" (*Deseret News*, 14 Jan. 1870, emphasis added).

Ultimately the protest served a number of purposes. Mormon women at last had a chance to show the outside world that they were articulate and willing to defend their beliefs. The newspaper coverage was perhaps the most positive account ever given of Mormon women, and that reflected well on the whole community. The *Ogden Junction* on 23 March commented, "If the Cragin and Cullom legislative burlesques have no other good effect, they have drawn out the ladies of Utah from silence and obscurity, exhibited them before the world as women of thought, force and ability, who are able to make strong resolutions and defend them with boldness and eloquence."

The anti-polygamy campaign had unintended consequences for Mormon women as well. The protest meeting proved to Mormon men that the women could organize a successful public demonstration and could be, in a "wider sphere" of action, a valuable asset "to the cause of Zion." Mormon men could only applaud the women's public defense of polygamy. The women would not be accused of acting outside their appropriate sphere; defending polygamy became a sanctioned mechanism by which women increased their public participation.

Only four months before the meeting, Brigham Young had commented that he wished more women would assume their rights: "the right to stop all folly in [their] conversation" and "the right to ask their husbands to fix up the front yard" (*JD* 14:105; Evans 1980, 13). Obviously he was not grappling seriously with woman's rights or suffrage. However, almost immediately following the protest meeting, attitudes changed; male Church leaders moved in support of woman suffrage. Historian Leonard Arrington asserts that in the "aftermath" of the meeting, "Brigham and other Mormon leaders—both men and women—decided it would be helpful if the Utah legislature should pass an act granting woman suffrage" (1985, 364). By 12 February the territorial legislature had passed the woman suffrage legislation. Women actively lobbied acting governor S. A. Mann, and, a week later he signed the bill into law (Arrington 1985, 365).

At a subsequent meeting on 19 February at the Salt Lake City Fifteenth Ward, Eliza Snow suggested a committee draft an "expression of gratitude" to the acting governor (Minutes 19 Feb. 1870).[7] The task completed, the meeting became a "feast of woman's anticipations" (Tullidge 1877, 502). If this group shared a single political perception, it was that they had entered a new phase in the "era of women." Several speakers expressed their pleasure in gaining the vote, which they referred to as the "reform." Prescenda Kimball said she was "glad to see our daughters elevated with man," while Bathsheba Smith "believed that woman was coming up in the world." Other women expressed words of caution. Margaret Smoot said that she "never had any desire for more rights," that she had considered "politics aside from the sphere of woman." But Willmirth East disagreed. "I cannot agree with Sister Smoot in regard to woman's rights," she declared, adding that she had always wanted "a voice in the politics of the nation, as well as to rear a family." Phebe Woodruff said she had "looked for this day for years. . . . [The] yoke on woman is partly removed," she noted, adding "Let us lay by, and wait till the time comes to use it, and not run headlong and abuse the privilege" (Minutes 19 Feb. 1870).

For Sarah Kimball, however, suffrage was a turning point. She told the women that she had "waited patiently a long time, and now that we were granted the right of suffrage, she would openly declare herself a woman's rights woman." She then "called upon those who would do so to back her up, whereupon many manifested their approval" (Minutes 19 Feb. 1870). These are not the words of a woman who had been recently politicized. Moreover, the rights she was referring to were not religious rights, but the secular rights of women: political, economic, and social. It is hardly surprising that some women at the meeting were unready to "manifest their approval" and "back up" Sarah Kimball on woman's rights. Declaring oneself a "woman's rights woman" was no doubt a bold move for any woman. The implication is that Kimball now allied herself with the more militant American suffragists. The statement was so daring, in fact, that Sarah Kimball waited until after suffrage was granted to declare herself publicly.

Woman suffrage refocused the political activity of Mormon women. No sooner were they enfranchised than the outside world moved to disfranchise them. For the rest of the century, they were defenders of their own suffrage and were joined in that defense by many woman suffrage activists from the States. In turn, Mormon women were activists for the passage of woman's rights. The degree of help that Mormon women received in return was uneven. Anti-polygamy activists tried to dissuade national suffrage advocates from defending woman suffrage in Utah, claiming that it only reinforced the power of the Mormon church and the strength of polygamy. As a result, support for Mormon women waxed and waned at various times for twenty-five years, and it differed between woman suffrage organizations and among individual suffragists.

Despite the efforts of many national and local advocates of woman suffrage, in 1887 all women in Utah were disfranchised by a federal law designed to destroy polygamy and to reduce the political and economic power of the Church. Three years later the Mormons officially discontinued plural marriage and began a vigorous campaign to secularize political life and to secure statehood. In 1895 woman suffrage was vigorously debated during the constitutional convention, and despite fears that its inclusion might damage the bid for statehood, its advocates prevailed.

A month later national suffrage leaders, including a vigorous but aging Susan B. Anthony, were on hand to celebrate the victory with their sister-suffragists in Utah. In a tribute to Anthony, Sarah Kimball discussed the difficulty of the early years of the woman suffrage movement in Utah. She said that when she first read Anthony's publication, the *Revolution* (1869), she would not have "dared to say the bold, grand things that Miss Anthony said. . . . That," she states, would have made her "so unpopular," she would have hardly "dared to shoulder it." She continued, "As time rolled on we were very careful" ("Conference" 1895).

If a single word could describe the operative mode for Mormon women, it would be "careful." They consistently guarded their words and actions to make sure the hierarchy never felt threatened or interpreted the women's goals as inconsistent with the goals of the church. But the women tenaciously defended their right to participate in the political process. They knew that success was essential, but it was equally critical to succeed in the right way. A year after they were enfranchised, the leading sisters wrote a circular stating that "God through His servants had conferred on us the right of franchise for a wise purpose. This privilege has been granted without our solicitation, and in this as well as in many other respects, we realize that women in Utah possess advantages greatly superior to women elsewhere" (Gates n.d.). The document is a good example of the careful way Mormon women operated. They bypass credit, express their gratitude, and yet secure their continuing activity, in this instance by claiming divine purpose for their enfranchisement. By deflecting credit for their achievements, however, Mormon women themselves contributed to the illusion that they were not agents in their own behalf. Hiding their agency was not uncommon for other nineteenth-century women, and it is not uncommon today. But is it one reason their political activism prior to 1870 has been overlooked.

Mormon women helped gain suffrage by being activists in their own behalf. Suffrage was not granted women in 1870 because of an overwhelming egalitarian impulse on the part of the Brethren; rather the usual pragmatic decision-making process was at work. Four months before women were enfranchised, the male leadership was still undecided about the wisdom of woman suffrage.[8] The women of Utah appear to have been enfranchised only after they had proved their potential for political usefulness. And, in fact, Mormon women did much to buffer growing criticism of the Church and of polygamy by securing the support of many non-Mormon suffragists and by presenting to the American public an alternative vision of Mormon womanhood. Between 1870 and 1890, Mormon women defended plural marriage as a First Amendment right and woman's rights issue, but they also continued to agitate for woman suffrage after polygamy was no longer a central issue. In 1895 when woman suffrage was restored, support for woman's political equality in Utah, while not unanimous, clearly was broadly based. Thus the advocacy of woman suffrage was more than just expedient.

By the time women in Utah were reenfranchised, Mormon suffragists had earned the respect and friendship of many of their sister-suffragists, even though they steadfastly maintained the divinity of their church and continued to sustain and obey its male leaders. But apart from religious issues, when it came to political, economic, and social rights of women, Mormon women were, as Sarah Kimball would have said, "heart and hand" with the female activists of the world.

Notes

1. Eleanor Flexner notes a difference between Mormon and non-Mormon interpretations of this event. Mormon historians, she states, see the enfranchisement as the "logical extension of an egalitarian attitude toward women basic to the Mormon creed." But to Flexner, a non-Mormon, woman suffrage was an in-

terplay of other forces, the most significant being the need of the hierarchy to "enlist the help of women" against the passage of anti-polygamy legislation (1959, 165). In contrast, non-Mormon historians Mari Jo Buhle and Paul Buhle see woman suffrage in Utah as the act of a "progressive Mormon hierarchy" (1978, Introduction); likewise Mormon historian Thomas Alexander states that woman suffrage was a reflection of "progressive sentiment in advance of the rest of the nation" (1970, 38), while another Mormon historian, Richard Van Wagoner, sees the activities of Mormon women as "orchestrated by the Mormon hierarchy" (1986, 109). Beverly Beeton concludes that Mormon women were "pawns" (1986, 37), and Anne F. Scott sees woman suffrage as "to some extent a gift from the male hierarchy" (1986–87, 10). Today, as in other aspects of Mormon history, the old line between Mormon and non-Mormon interpretations is becoming increasingly blurred.

2. Several sources suggest but do not develop the idea of women's activism. See Arrington in *Brigham Young* (New York: Alfred A. Knopf, 1985, 364–5). Maureen Ursenbach Beecher, Carol Cornwall Madsen, and Jill Mulvay Derr, "The Latter-day Saints and Women's Rights, 1870–1920: A Brief Survey," *Task Papers in LDS History,* No. 29 (Salt Lake City: Historical Department of the Church of Jesus Christ of Latter-day Saints, 1979). Edward Tullidge, *Woman of Mormondom* (1877; Salt Lake City, 1975) states that women worked for passage but does not document the statement.

3. Several hundred Mormon women signed the petition, which Emma Smith and other women then took to the governor. Joseph Smith attended a Relief Society meeting in August of 1842 and thanked the women for having taken "the most active part" in his defense ("Minutes," Nauvoo, Aug. 1842; Crocheron 1884, 3; Newell and Avery 1984, 127).

4. Gary Bunker and Carol Bunker note that the first suggestion that woman suffrage could be an "antidote" to polygamy came from William Ray in 1856 (1991, 33).

5. The *Deseret News* 9 March 1870. Sixteen years later, in 1886, Mormon women requested permission from President John Taylor to hold a similar meeting (Kimball, Pratt, and Horne 1886).

6. Two different essays by historians report on this part of the meeting, but neither refers to a vote on the suffrage motion or to Lucy W. Kimball's motion. Beverly Beeton states: "A 'Sister Smith' even demanded of the governor that women be allowed to vote. At the close of the meeting Eliza Snow . . ." (1986, 31). Reported in this way, what happened becomes only one insignificant woman demanding the vote, rather than a motion made and passed by the whole Society. Maureen Ursenbach Beecher, Carol Cornwall Madsen, and Jill Mulvay Derr state: "Later in the meeting one Sister Smith rose to move that 'we demand of the governor the right of franchise.' Whether the motion was carried or not, and whether or not the demand reached the legislature is not known" (1979, 10).

7. The 23 February *Deseret News* reported that after the meeting, a committee took the letter of thanks to the governor, who told the women "that the subject has been much agitated . . . [and] will be watched with profound interest." He hoped, he added, that "the women would act so as to prove the wisdom of the legislation." According to George A. Smith, "the ladies said they thought the Governor was about as much embarrassed as they were" (1870).

8. For comments showing a lack of resolve on woman suffrage from both George Q. Cannon and Brigham Young, see *Deseret News*, 6 August 1869, and the *JD* 14:105.

Bibliography

Alexander, Thomas. "An Experiment in Progressive Legislation: The Granting of Woman Suffrage in 1870." *Utah Historical Quarterly* 38, no. 1 (1970): 20–30.

Arrington, Leonard. *Brigham Young: American Moses*. Alfred A. Knopf, 1985.

Beecher, Maureen Ursenbach. "Three Women and the Life of the Mind." *Utah Historical Quarterly* 43, no. 1 (1975): 26–40.

———, Carol Cornwall Madsen, and Jill Mulvay Derr. "The Latter-day Saints and Women's Rights, 1870–1920: A Brief History." *Task Papers in LDS History*, no. 29. Salt Lake City: Historical Department of the Church of Jesus Christ of Latter-day Saints, 1975.

Beeton, Beverly. *Women Vote in the West: The Woman Suffrage Movement, 1869–1896*. New York and London: Garland Publishing Outstanding Dissertation Series, 1986.

Berg, Barbara J. *The Remembered Gate: Origins of American Feminism*. New York: Oxford University Press, 1978.

Buhle, Mari Jo, and Paul Buhle. *The Concise History of Woman Suffrage*. Urbana: University of Illinois Press, 1978.

Bunker, Gary L., and Carol B. Bunker. "Woman Suffrage, Popular Art, and Utah." *Utah Historical Quarterly* 59 (Winter 1991): 32–51.

Cannon, George Q. Untitled article. *Deseret News*, 6 August 1869.

"Conference N.A.W.S.A. . . . May 13 and 14, 1895." *Woman's Exponent*, 15 August 1895.

Crocheron, Augusta Joyce. *Representative Women of Deseret*. Salt Lake City: J.C. Graham and Co., 1884.

Derr, Jill Mulvay. " 'Strength in Our Union': The Making of Mormon Sisterhood." In *Sisters in Spirit*, edited by Maureen Ursenbach Beecher and Lavina Fielding Anderson, 153–207. Chicago: University of Illinois Press, 1987.

———. "The Liberal Shall Be Blessed: Sarah M. Kimball." *Utah Historical Quarterly* 44 (Summer 1976): 205–21.

Evans, Vella. "Woman's Role and Pioneer Mormon Rhetoric." Unpublished paper presented at the University of Utah, 1980. Copy in possession of author.

Flexner, Eleanor. *A Century of Struggle.* Cambridge, Mass.: Harvard University Press, 1959.

Gates, Susa Young. Susa Young Gates Collection, Box 17, Manuscript Collection, Utah State Historical Society, Salt Lake City, Utah.

————, and Leah D. Widtsoe. *Women of the "Mormon" Church.* Independence, Mo.: Press of Zions Printing and Publishing Co., 1928.

JD. *Journal of Discourses.* 26 vols. Liverpool and London: LDS Booksellers, 1855–86.

Jensen, Richard L. "Forgotten Relief Societies, 1844–67." *Dialogue* 16 (Spring 1983): 105–25.

Jenson, Andrew. *Latter-day Saint Biographical Encyclopedia.* 4 vols. Salt Lake City: The Andrew Jensen History Company, 1901.

Kimball, Sarah M. *Woman Suffrage Leaflet.* Salt Lake City: n.p., 1892. LDS Church Archives.

————, R. B. Pratt, and Mrs. Horne. Letter to President John Taylor, 20 February 1886. John Taylor Letterbooks, Special Collections, Marriott Library, University of Utah, Salt Lake City, Utah.

Minutes, Female Relief Society of Nauvoo. Photocopy in my possession, courtesy of Maureen Beecher. Original in LDS Church Archives.

Minutes, Salt Lake City Eighth Ward Female Relief Society. 16 December 1867. LDS Church Archives.

Minutes, Salt Lake City Thirteenth Ward Female Relief Society. 25 April 1868. LDS Church Archives.

Naisbitt, Henry W. " 'Polysophical' and 'Mutual.' " *Improvement Era* 2 (1899): 745.

Newell, Linda King, and Valeen Tippets Avery. *Mormon Enigma: Emma Hale Smith.* Chicago: University of Chicago Press, 1984.

Scott, Anne F. "Mormon Women, Other Women." *The Journal of Mormon History* 13 (1986–87): 3–19.

Smith, George A. Letter to Wm. Hooper, 19 February 1870. Copybooks. LDS Church Archives.

Tullidge, Edward. *The Women of Mormondom.* Salt Lake City: Tullidge and Crandall, 1877.

Van Wagoner, Richard. *Mormon Polygamy: A History.* Salt Lake City: Signature Books, 1986.

Eliza R. Snow. *Courtesy of Archives, Historical Department, Church of Jesus Christ of Latter-day Saints.*

4

Eliza R. Snow and the Woman Question

JILL MULVAY DERR

And what is Woman's calling? What her place?
Is she destined to honor, or disgrace?
                                        —*Eliza R. Snow, "Woman"*

In the 1830s, contemporary with the beginning of Mormonism, a new woman's movement was stirring in America. A small but vocal group of American women involved in the abolitionist cause had come to a frightening awareness of their own lack of legal and property rights. Increasingly women recognized their ability to organize and speak out for their own cause, and in 1848, with the early woman's rights convention at Seneca Falls, New York, an organized woman's movement was underway. With that movement came the questions that Americans would actively ask until 1920 when the suffrage amendment was finally ratified: What is woman's position? What are her rights? What is her sphere? Feminists concluded that woman's rights had been usurped and her sphere confined. They were eager to break down the established order that had so long kept woman under what Elizabeth Cady Stanton termed the "absolute tyranny" of man.

Women converted to The Church of Jesus Christ of Latter-day Saints in the years following its 1830 organization, however, were not concerned with breaking down an existing order, but rather with establishing a new order—the Kingdom of God. As that kingdom grew, the sphere of Mormon

First published in *BYU Studies* 16 (Winter 1976): 250–64, under the author's birth name, Jill C. Mulvay. Reprinted by permission.

women was enlarged. Sisters were early encouraged to exercise spiritual gifts such as speaking in tongues; later, they participated in baptisms for the dead and temple ordinances; and they administered to the sick by the laying on of hands. Early in the 1830s Latter-day Saint women began voting in general Church assemblies.[1] In 1842 the Prophet Joseph Smith responded to the women's desire to be organized, and established the Female Relief Society of Nauvoo "to look to the wants of the poor," "to teach the female part of the community," and "to save souls."[2]

All of this was part of the growing Kingdom, a kingdom directed by the priesthood-bearing hierarchy of the Church. The rights, sphere, and position of Mormon women were determined by the pronouncements of its male prophets, seers, and revelators. But Mormon women themselves distinguished subjugation to man's "absolute tyranny" from submission to the priesthood. They insisted upon defending their role, not defining it. Beginning in the early 1870s, in response to anti-polygamy legislation and a nationwide characterization of Mormon women as "poor and degraded," Latter-day Saint sisters became increasingly vocal about their position as women within the Church.

"Do you know of any place on the face of the earth, where woman has more liberty, and where she enjoys such high and glorious privileges as she does here, as a Latter-day Saint?"[3] Eliza R. Snow asked some five or six thousand women gathered in the Salt Lake Tabernacle in January 1870 to protest against anti-polygamy legislation. Zion's poetess and Female Relief Society president would never complain of usurped rights or a confined sphere of activity, and she promised her sisters that no woman in Zion would need to mourn because her sphere was too narrow. Eliza Snow's assertions were not mere rhetoric. During the 1870s the sphere of the nineteenth century Mormon woman was expanding. By the 1880s Mormon women had significant duties and responsibilities inside and outside their homes. At the first meeting of the International Council of Women at Washington, D.C. in 1888, Utah's delegate reported that 400 Relief Societies in Utah held property valued at $95,000, many societies owning the halls in which they met.[4] Mormon women published their own biweekly newspaper titled the *Woman's Exponent*. The Relief Society managed a hospital with a woman as resident surgeon. And the women of Zion had contributed significantly to the territory's economy through their participation in silk production and their mercantile cooperatives promoting home manufacture.[5] By the turn of the century Mormon women had made political, economic and social gains within their own culture comparable to gains made by their more vocal national colleagues in the larger American culture.

This host of Utah women was for more than twenty years captained by Eliza Roxcy Snow, "presidentess" of all Latter-day Saint organizations for women. Designated by her sisters an "elect lady," she was said to have precedence "in almost everything pertaining to woman's advancement among her people."[6] Not only was she an able administrator, she was an eloquent enunciator who proclaimed Church doctrine to her sisters in poetry, prose, and oratory that would fill volumes. Add to these distinctions the eminence of being a wife, consecutively, of both Joseph Smith and Brigham Young, and the aura of spiritual gifts such as speaking in tongues and healing, and it is not difficult to understand why this poetess-presidentess-priestess-prophetess was probably the most widely heard and widely heeded woman in nineteenth century Mormondom.[7] What is woman's position? What are her rights? What is her sphere? Eliza R. Snow certainly influenced (if not sometimes dictated) both practical and theoretical responses of Mormon women to the woman question.

The focal point of late nineteenth century women's issues was suffrage. In that matter Mormon women were for some years ahead of women involved in the national suffrage movement, women in Utah receiving in 1870 the franchise for which their Eastern sisters would battle for the next five decades. They had staged no demonstrations and apparently circulated no petitions. The signature of Eliza R. Snow headed fourteen signatures on a memorandum to acting territorial governor Stephen Mann praising his "liberality and gentlemanly kindness" in signing the bill granting suffrage. But Eliza never would have led her sisters in an effort to take the right of suffrage by storm. She distrusted "that class known as 'strong minded' who are strenuously and unflinchingly advocating 'woman's rights,' and some of them at least, claiming 'woman's sovereignty' vainly flattering themselves with the idea that with ingress to the ballot box and access to financial offices, they shall accomplish the elevation of woman-kind." She explained, "Not that we are opposed to woman suffrage. . . . But to think of a war of sexes which the woman's rights movement would inevitably inaugurate, . . . creates an involuntary shudder!"[8]

In 1872, while Susan B. Anthony was being arrested in Rochester, New York for her attempt to register and vote, Eliza R. Snow encouraged Mormon women to cast their more easily secured ballots. She possessed enough political acumen to see the advantages of female suffrage, especially in Utah. "Your vote counts as much, weighs as heavily, as President Young's, Brother G. A. Smith's or Brother D. H. Well's, hence you should consider yourselves important on election day," she counseled her sisters. She told Ogden Relief Societies, "[God] has given us the right of franchise," and it is "as necessary to vote as to pray." With Illinois and Missouri persecutions vivid enough in her memory, she advised, "Unless we maintain our rights we will be driven from place to place."[9]

As a political force the women of Utah were destined to create controversy. When their votes strengthened the Church-dominated People's Party, the anti-Mormon Liberal Party complained that "the female dupes of the priesthood" were "arrayed at the polls against them."[10] Consequently, liberal forces lined up against female suffrage, while generally conservative Church authorities and women rose in its defense. In the struggle Eliza R. Snow, who had earlier polemicized against "female conventionists," called Mormon women together in suffrage meetings to garner support for the proposed "Anthony Amendment" which guaranteed that the right to vote in federal or state elections would not be denied on the basis of sex.

The alliance with the national suffrage movement was tenuous at best, and under the leadership of Sister Snow Mormon women did not become closely involved with national suffrage leaders. By 1882 Mormon women had attended only two of the annual woman's suffrage conventions, indicating as one sister put it, that they had been "so busily engaged in cleaning up the House of Zion . . . that seemingly the fact has not been considered that there might be safety in having a few sentinels stationed on the towers afar off."[11] In Utah the major battle for suffrage took place after the disfranchisement resulting from passage of the anti-Mormon Edmunds-Tucker Bill in 1887, and Eliza died before that year was out.

Perhaps Eliza R. Snow unintentionally prepared the field for the suffrage struggle in other ways, especially in organizing the Relief Societies which became the focal point for the activities of Mormon women. She had served as secretary of the Female Relief Society of Nauvoo, and with prophetic hindsight she later recalled: "When Joseph organized the sisters in Nauvoo I saw different positions for women to occupy besides tending to their household duties as wives and mothers."[12] Having dutifully kept minutes for the Nauvoo meetings—minutes Joseph Smith said would be the constitution and law of the society—Eliza brought them across the Plains to Salt Lake City. Such a constitution became useful when Brigham Young commissioned Eliza to assist bishops in organizing ward Relief Societies, and eventually called her to preside over all Relief Societies.

In 1868 the Relief Society was erecting its first hall in the Fifteenth Ward and at the same time Brigham Young was suggesting classes through the University of Deseret "giving ladies a thorough business education, qualifying them for bookkeepers, accountants, clerks, cashiers, tellers, payers, telegraphic operators, reporters, and other branches of employment suitable to their sex."[13] Eliza backed him up with the words of her first and best-loved Prophet: "Joseph Smith counseled the sisters to do business."[14]

More than once Eliza Snow helped Brigham Young in his requests for women to meet specific community needs. In 1873 when the President asked women to help with printing, Eliza made up her mind "to go from house to house if required to procure young ladies, to learn."[15] President Young suggested that young ladies volunteer to study obstetrics and nursing, and to become physicians. "We want sister physicians that can officiate in any capacity that gentlemen are called upon to officiate. . . . Women can occupy precisely the same footing that men occupy as physicians and surgeons," declared Eliza.[16] Small groups of women began their own classes in physiology and anatomy, and several women went East to study medicine, some with financial aid from their sisters. By 1879, plans for a hospital were underway, and in 1882, under the direction of Eliza R. Snow, president of its founding association, the Deseret Hospital opened its doors and an LDS woman was installed as resident surgeon.

The first issue of the *Woman's Exponent*, a paper, "owned by, controlled by and edited by Utah ladies," appeared in 1872. In several early issues the editor described the purpose and terms of the paper, including this note: "Miss Eliza R. Snow, President of the entire Female Relief Societies, cordially approves of the journal, and will be a contributor to it as she has leisure from her numerous duties."[17] Eliza's official sanction was crucial to any Mormon woman's enterprise. In the hundreds of issues of the *Exponent* printed before her death, Eliza R. Snow's name was connected with every major movement among Mormon women from retrenchment to publication of Edward Tullidge's *Women of Mormondom*.[18] Few, if any, of the movements originated with her, but many benefited from her phenomenal executive skill, and all—home industry, silk production, ladies' commission stores, physiology classes, grain storage, MIAs and Primaries—received her personal endorsement as she traveled by train and wagon to every settlement in the territory.

With the coming of the railroad which brought foreign goods within easy reach, and Retrenchment Associations whose purpose was to curb the appetite for Eastern finery, came Brigham Young's push for home industry. Support home industries, Eliza emphasized, "in accordance with the requirements of the Priesthood."[19] Sustain home straw manufacture and "if we can get sufficient encouragement, we shall make hats for men and boys, women and girls."[20] Eliza considered "each successful Branch of Home Manufactures, an additional stone in laying the foundation for the upbuilding of Zion," and she considered a woman who stepped forward and assisted efficiently in home industries (including silk culture, straw weaving, tailoring, and home canning) to be "doing just as much as an Elder who went forth to preach the Gospel."[21] Sister Snow did not preach idly. She and her sisters in the Fourteenth Ward commenced a Cooperative Tailoring Establishment to "fill orders for men and boys' clothing, on short notice and at low prices."[22]

In 1876, President Young asked the women to "form an association to start business in the capacity of disposing homemade articles, such as are manufactured among ourselves."[23] Eliza Snow was elected president of the Relief Society Woman's Mercantile Association and the women opened their store in the Old Constitution Building on Main Street in Salt Lake City. Because they had no capital to commence their enterprise, they sold on commission and the project came to be known as the Woman's Commission Store. The first year of operation Eliza superintended the store from eight in the morning until six at night, carefully looking after the minute details— evidently quite capably. Once, refusing to let one of Brigham Young's clerks dictate the terms of commission on Young's goods, Eliza haughtily wrote the President: "Although we are novices in the mercantile business, we are not green enough for that kind of management."[24]

"Presidentess" Snow told the Brigham City Relief Society, "Sometimes I think we can do more than the brethren."[25] For years the men had tried unsuccessfully to store grain, but Brigham Young finally assigned grain storage to the Relief Society. Individual ward Relief Societies built their own granaries and by 1880 their holdings were strong enough that John Taylor was advising the women that their sisters had voted at general conference to lend their respective bishops "so much wheat as they may consider requisite to meet the necessities of the deserving poor," and at the same time admonishing the bishops to pay back their loans in full.[26]

As Retrenchment Associations grew up among the young ladies, many recognized the need for similar associations for the young men. Eliza told her sisters, "I have suggested that the boys be organized but of course we ladies cannot dictate."[27] Dictate she did not, but campaign she did. In 1875 she traveled to Lehi and held a meeting for the young ladies and instructed them to bring their beaux. She later reported:

> I asked the young men to vote and told them I wanted them to
> sustain the young ladies in their positions; and also if they did not
> leave off their drinking and tobacco where were the young girls to
> get husbands? The young men did not wish the young girls to be in

advance of them. I heard the next morning that the young men had been after the Bishop to organize them before night.[28]

The same year, President Young called Junius Wells to head the Young Men's Mutual Improvement Association. "We ladies cannot dictate," Eliza admitted, but the Prophet Joseph Smith had told the women at that first meeting of the Relief Society in Nauvoo that they might "provoke the brethren to good works."[29]

By the mid-1880s Mormon women had achieved with distinction. Relief Societies, Mutual Improvement Associations, and Primary Associations had been established throughout the territory, largely through the efforts of women under the direction of Eliza R. Snow.[30] Women's efforts in these organizations, in home industry and grain storage, and their willingness to be trained in skills meeting specific needs of the growing Kingdom made theirs a contribution in no way inferior to that of their brethren.

Certainly by the standard of gentile crusaders for women, the "poor, degraded women of Utah," were making significant contributions. Topics discussed at the first meeting of the International Council of Women held in Washington, D. C. in 1888 indicate that Mormon women were engaged in many of the same activities as their gentile counterparts: "Women in Journalism," "Women as Educators," "Women in the Trades," "Women in Medicine," "Hospitals Managed by and for Women," "How to Reach the Children," "Woman as Missionary," "Constitutional Rights of Women of the United States," "The Moral Power of the Ballot."[31] Apparently nineteenth century feminists and Mormon women expanded their responsibilities and influence in similar directions.

But however similar their directions, their points of departure were diametrically opposite. Feminists attacked a male-dominated society; Eliza R. Snow defended it. Miss Anthony decried "Woman's utter dependence on man"; Eliza Snow deemed it essential to woman's salvation. Mrs. Stanton attacked established religion for placing women in an inferior position; "Presidentess Snow," the most influential woman in a sect yet unbound by centuries of tradition, acknowledged man's superiority and never ceased to defend it doctrinally. Eliza R. Snow seemed to advocate every tenet radical feminists were working to uproot.[32]

Eliza did not ignore the woman question, but rather attempted to synthesize an assortment of Mormon doctrines into a neat package that would provide for the eternal expansion of woman's role. For Eliza, woman's earthly position had been unalterably determined. Aware of feminist campaigns for equality, she asserted, "We have no occasion to clamor about equality, or to battle for supremacy. We understand our true position—God has defined the sphere of woman wherever His Priesthood is acknowledged."[33] Woman

> . . . led in the transgression, and was plac'd
> By Eloheim's unchangeable decree,
> In a subservient and dependent sphere:—[34]

"Order is heaven's first law," Eliza instructed, "and it is utterly impossible for order to exist without . . . gradation."[35] In that gradation, men and women did not occupy the same position. Apostle Orson Hyde, in 1857, addressed his audience "Brethren and sisters," rather than "Ladies and gentlemen," because, he said, "the order of heaven places man in the front rank; hence he is first to be addressed. Woman follows under the protection of his counsels, and the superior strength of his arm. Her desire should be unto her husband, and he should rule over her."[36] Countless times in her travels, Sister Snow enlarged upon that doctrine for her sisters. In the beginning, she explained, male and female were addressed as one, but the Fall brought about a change, and thus the "curse of Eve" rested upon all womankind. Regarding that curse, Brigham Young stated, "I do not know what the Lord could have put upon women worse than he did upon Mother Eve, where he told her: 'Thy desire shall be to thy husband.' . . . I would be glad if it were otherwise."[37]

Elizabeth Stanton's 1848 Declaration of Sentiments included her outrage that "the history of mankind is a history of repeated injuries and usurpations on the part of men toward woman, having in direct object the establishment of absolute tyranny over her."[38] However, Latter-day Saints felt that man's unrighteous dominion over woman was not only a result of his wickedness, but a result of the curse that woman's desire should be to her husband. George Q. Canon explained:

> Why, women, in their yearning after the other sex and in their desire for maternity, will do anything to gratify that instinct of their nature and yield to anything and be dishonored even rather than not to gratify it.[39]

Woman's degradation was a fact. For gentile women the only recourse was to burst the bonds of slavery, but for Eliza and her sisters there was a different path. They proclaimed: "We stand in a different position from the ladies of the world; we have made a covenant with God, we understand his order, and know that that order requires submission on the part of women."[40] Mormon women did stand in a different position from the women of the world. They could submit to the rule of their righteous husbands and brethren, with the knowledge that they were honoring God through honoring his priesthood. Eliza boasted:

> Let those fair champions of "female rights,"
> Female conventionists come here.
>   Yes, in
> These mountain vales . . .
>   . . . are noble men,
> Whom woman may be proud t'acknowledge for
> Her own superior.[41]

Latter-day Saint women did not admit that just any man could guide and direct woman. It was not the mere fact of masculinity; it was the righteous exercise of priesthood which gave a man wisdom and power that was from God and thus qualified him as woman's leader and protector. Eliza lamented the futile efforts of the feminists:

> With all their efforts to remove the curse,
> Matters are daily growing worse and worse;
> They can as well unlock without a key
> As change the tide of man's degeneracy,
> Without the Holy Priesthood: 'tis at most
> Like reck'ning bills in absence of the host.[42]

When Eliza saw her gentile sisters working to eliminate prostitution and desertion, she disparaged their efforts, and taught instead that "man's wisdom is not sufficient—God alone can prescribe the remedy." The remedy was plural marriage. Sister Snow continued,

> Here in Utah, through his servants and handmaidens [God] is establishing a nucleus of domestic and social purity, confidence and happiness, which will, so far as its influence extends, eradicate and prevent, in future, all those blighting evils. . . . God loves purity, and he has introduced the principle of plurality of wives to restore and preserve the chastity of woman. . . . It is truly woman's cause— a cause which deeply involves, not only her present but her eternal interests.[43]

For the LDS ladies of Utah, the concept of woman's rights and woman's cause became inextricably tied to the principle of plural marriage. Consequently, when they held mass meetings, their orations were without exception dominated by testimonies supporting polygamy. Proud of their superior understanding of woman, Mormon ladies affirmed that they were in favor of woman's rights, interpreting the term to fit their own values. Eliza suggested:

> If those who're advocating "Woman's Rights,"
> Will plead the right of wedlock for the sex,
>
> . . . .
>   they'll win a meed
> Of everlasting gratitude and praise.[44]

The right to "holy, honorable wedlock" was the right of all women, not just a few. By this means alone could women be redeemed and since plural marriage was the only system in which all women could have the opportunity to marry righteous men, "those who stepped forward as volunteers" were laboring "in the cause of woman's redemption."[45]

Rather than ignore or deny the biblical curse upon womankind, as did some contemporary feminists, Mormon women concerned themselves with woman's redemption. Eliza asked her sisters if the curse upon woman would never be removed and she "stand in her primeval condition." Then she answered her own question:

> The Lord has placed the means in our hands, in the Gospel, where by we can regain our lost position. But how? Can it be done by rising, as women are doing in the world, to clamor for our rights? No. It was through disobedience that woman came into her present position, and it is only by obedience, honoring God in all the institutions he has revealed to us, that we can come out from under that curse, regain the position originally occupied by Eve, and attain to a fulness of exaltation in the presence of God.[46]

Consistent with that philosophy, Eliza Snow stressed that women would benefit if they would obey the priesthood in whatever they tried to accomplish. She was advocating not passivity, but righteous submission. "As sure as the sisters arise and take hold of the work," she exclaimed, "the brethren will wake up, because they must be at the head."[47] Relief Society president Willmirth East wrote Eliza from Arizona concerning her bishop's objection to frequent Relief Society visits from sisters to members. Sister Snow replied that the bishops might not be "properly informed relative to the Teacher's visits," and that it might be well for the sisters "to explain to him, but not oppose his wishes." She concluded her response with her consistent instructions to all Relief Society sisters: "We will do as we are directed by the Priesthood."[48]

Sarah Grimké and other leaders in the nation's woman's movement had asserted that whatever was right for a man to do was likewise right for a woman to do. Perhaps this sentiment was present among some Mormon sisters. Evidently as women became increasingly active in Church positions of leadership and responsibility they became confused regarding their status and authority. Church President John Taylor in 1880 explained that sisters "ordained" to Relief Society positions were not ordained to the priesthood. Subsequently, to avoid confusion women were "set apart" for these positions, rather than "ordained." As enthusiastic sisters organized MIAs and Primary Associations, some question arose regarding woman's authority to organize and reorganize Relief Societies. Eliza R. Snow, with twenty years of experience, was called upon to clarify woman's role. At a Sevier Stake conference she

> spoke on the subject of organization; said there were some societies which women had a right to organize, such as the Y[oung] L[adies'] and Primary Associations, but they had no right to organize a Relief Society; but they could *assist* the priesthood in doing so . . . Sister Eliza explained that she had been given a mission to *assist* the priesthood in organizing Relief Societies; hence, some had conceived the idea that she organized.[49]

Lest Relief Society sisters think that the strength of their accomplishments entitled them to strike out on their own, against the wishes of bishops and stake presidents, John Taylor admonished them: "While we appreciate the labors of our sisters, it must not be forgotten that the man holds the Priesthood, and is the head of the woman, as Christ is the head of the Church."[50]

Women should be helpmeets to the priesthood, and they should assist their brothers, in Eliza's imagery, "like the devout and steadfast Miriam in upholding the hands of Moses."[51] Unlike her national contemporaries, Eliza was not even anxious to give woman the last word. Happy to see the brethren at Relief Society meetings and conferences, she invited them to speak last. Relief Society president Margaret T. Smoot from Provo explained, "Sister

Snow says it is proper for us to speak first, and let the stronger follow the weak, that if we say anything that needs correcting it can be corrected."[52]

The accomplishments of Eliza R. Snow and Mormon women in general are not reduced in light of this absolute submission to the priesthood. They did not consider themselves slaves; they were stewards. The many who were faithful in their assignments epitomized the wise stewards who in the parable of the talents doubled the talents for which they were held responsible and were given more. Stewards relieve their masters of certain tasks and in that process make decisions of consequence. Just so, the purpose of the Relief Society was to relieve the bishops and Eliza advised, "Do not run to him with every trifle."[53] "If possible we should relieve the Bishops instead of adding to their multitudinous labors."[54] Stewardship is not passivity and the steward who fearfully hid his talent in the earth was condemned. "Many of the women of Zion [have gone] astray with the idea that they [have] no time to attend meetings, or to give to the culture of their minds, but that their whole being and time must be given to the drudgery of life."[55] But, "Do we realize our responsibilities? And that we have as much to do with the salvation of our souls as the brethren? They can not save us, we must save ourselves."[56] She counseled, "It is a choosing time and we should do the choosing ourselves."[57]

Eliza Snow was speaking to thousands of Mormon mothers with children. What would she, a childless "mother in Israel," have them choose? "Let your first business be to perform your duties at home."[58] "The sisters in Zion are required to form the characters of the sons who are to be rulers and bishops in the kingdom of God."[59] This "is a mother's first duty, but it is not *all* her duty."[60]

> Inasmuch as you are wise stewards, you will find time for social duties, because these are incumbent upon us as daughters and mothers in Zion. By seeking to perform every duty you will find that your capacity will increase, and you will be astonished at what you can accomplish.[61]

The wise stewards did find time for other duties, and there were not only presidents and counselors for Relief Societies, MIAs and Primaries, but also storekeepers, printers, telegraphers, silk growers, surgeons and hospital directors.

Feminists taught women that through asserting themselves they could achieve social, political, and economic equality with men. Eliza R. Snow consistently held that only through obedience, and faithfulness in her stewardship, would woman change her sphere:

Inasmuch as we continue faithful, we shall be those that will be crowned in the presence of God and the lamb. You, my sisters, if you are faithful, will become Queens of Queens, and Priestesses unto the Most High God. These are your callings. We have only to discharge our duties.[62]

In the parable of the talents, a promise was given the stewards who discharged their duties: "Thou hast been faithful over a few things, I will make thee ruler over many things" (Matthew 25:23). Or, in the words of Zion's Poetess who penned these lines so carefully for her sisters:

> What we experience here, is but a school
> Wherein the ruled will be prepared to rule.
> . . . .
> And thro' obedience, Woman will obtain
> The *power of reigning, and the right to reign.*[63]

Notes

1. For a detailed discussion of woman's position in the pre-Utah Church, see Ileen Ann Waspe, "The Status of Woman in the Philosophy of Mormonism from 1830 to 1845" (Master's thesis, Brigham Young University, 1942), especially 81–136.

2. Relief Society General Board Minutes 1842–1914, 17 March 1842, microfilm of holograph, Library-Archives, Church Historical Department. Hereafter cited as Church Library-Archives. In these unpublished minutes and those cited hereafter, spelling and punctuation have been standardized.

3. Eliza R. Snow address, "Great Indignation Meeting," *Deseret News Weekly*, 19 January 1870.

4. "The Women of Utah Represented at the International Council of Woman, Washington, D.C.," *Woman's Exponent*, 1 April 1888.

5. See Leonard J. Arrington, "The Economic Role of Pioneer Mormon Women," *Western Humanities Review* 9 (Spring 1955): 145–64.

6. Annie W. Cannon, "Women of Utah," *Woman's Exponent*, 15 July 1888.

7. See Maureen Ursenbach, "The Eliza Enigma: The Life and Legend of Eliza R. Snow," lecture delivered for the Charles Redd Center for Western Studies, Brigham Young University, Provo, Utah, 24 October 1974, manuscript on file in the office of the Church Historian, Church Historical Department.

8. Eliza R. Snow address, "Celebration of the Twenty-fourth at Ogden," *Deseret News Weekly,* 26 July 1871.

9. Salt Lake Stake, [General or Cooperative] Retrenchment Association Minutes 1871–1875, 19 July 1873, Church Library-Archives; Weber Stake, Ogden City Wards Joint Session [Relief Society] Minutes 1879–1888, 6 February 1879, Church Library-Archives.

10. "The Woman Suffrage Law," *Salt Lake Daily Tribune*, 23 December 1877.

11. Romania B. Pratt, "Woman Suffrage Convention," *Woman's Exponent*, 1 March 1882.

12. Park Stake, First Ward Relief Society Minutes 1870–1893, 26 November 1874, Church Library-Archives.

13. General Epistle, January-February 1868, Brigham Young Circular Letters, Church Library-Archives,25.

14. Box Elder Stake Relief Society Minutes 1878–1890, 10 September 1878, Church Library-Archives.

15. Salt Lake Stake, [General or Cooperative] Retrenchment Association Minutes 1871–1875, 19 July 1873.

16. Ibid., 13 September 1873.

17. "Woman's Exponent, A Utah Ladies' Journal," *Woman's Exponent*, 1 June 1872.

18. Edward W. Tullidge's *The Women of Mormondom* (New York: n.p., 1877) was financed through shares purchased by ward Relief Societies. Eliza R. Snow collected sketches of Mormon women for the volume and read and revised the manuscript. See Emmeline B. Wells, "Pen Sketch of an Illustrious Woman," *Woman's Exponent*, 15 August 1881.

19. "Notice to the Officers and Members of each Branch of the Relief Society . . . ," *Woman's Exponent*, 1 April 1875.

20. Ibid.

21. E. R. Snow to Mrs. L. G. Richards, *Woman's Exponent*, 15 April 1875; First Ward Relief Society Minutes, 7 June 1877, in *Woman's Exponent*, 15 November 1877. Daniel H. Wells, second counselor to Brigham Young, told the Relief Society: "Any man or woman engaged in any of these callings [building, manufacturing, agriculture] with pure motives, is just as much on a mission as if teaching the gospel." "Dedication of the Kaysville Relief Society," *Woman's Exponent*, 1 March 1877.

22. "Tailoring Establishment," *Woman's Exponent*, 1 May 1875.

23. President Young to the President and Members of the Relief Societies, 4 October 1876, in *Woman's Exponent*, 15 October 1876.

24. Eliza R. Snow to Brigham Young, 10 February 1877, Brigham Young Collection, Church-Library-Archives.

25. Box Elder Stake [old] Relief Society Minutes 1875–1884, 6 November 1877, Church Library-Archives.

26. John Taylor, "Circular," *Woman's Exponent*, 1 May 1880.

27. Park Stake, First Ward Relief Society Minutes 1870–1893, 5 September 1872, Church Library-Archives.

28. Salt Lake Stake, [General or Cooperative] Retrenchment Association Minutes 1871–1875, 1 May 1875.

29. Relief Society General Board Minutes 1842–1914, 17 March 1842.

30. The concept of a Primary Association, an organization to train young children in the teachings of the Church, originated with Aurelia S. Rogers, who with the support of Eliza R. Snow and under the direction of her bishop, organized the first Primary Association in Farmington, Utah, in 1878. Sister Snow and other women immediately took up the task of organizing Primaries throughout the territory. See Aurelia Spencer Rogers, *Life Sketches of Orson Spencer and Others, and History of Primary Work* (Salt Lake City: George Q. Cannon & Sons, 1898), 210–23.

31. "International Council of Women," *Woman's Exponent*, 15 March 1888.

32. As early as 1869 the national suffrage movement was split along radical-conservative lines into the National Woman Suffrage Association and the American Woman Suffrage Association. Elizabeth Cady Stanton and Susan B. Anthony were leaders of NWSA, the more radical of the groups. Though the NWSA alienated many religious American women, the AWSA made an effort not to lose the influence of the churches, and though Mrs. Stanton and Miss Anthony would have disagreed violently with the doctrine Miss Snow propounded, some of that doctrine was traditionally Christian and would have been accepted by many of the American women working for woman suffrage. See Eleanor Flexner, *Century of Struggle: The Woman's Rights Movement in the United States* (New York: Atheneum, 1973), 151–55.

33. Snow address, "Celebration of the Twenty-fourth at Ogden."

34. Eliza R. Snow, "The New Year, 1852," *Deseret News*, 10 January 1852.

35. Snow, "Celebration of the Twenty-fourth at Ogden."

36. Orson Hyde, Sermon, *Deseret News*, 18 March 1857.

37. Brigham Young in *Journal of Discourses*, 26 vols. (London: Latter-day Saints Book Depot, 1855–1886), 16:167.

38. Elizabeth Cady Stanton, quoted in Flexner, *Century of Struggle*, 75.

39. George Q. Cannon in *Journal of Discourses*, 13:207.

40. "Miss E. R. Snow's Address to the Female Relief Societies of Weber County," *Latter-day Saints' Millennial Star* 33 (12 September 1871): 578.

41. Snow, "The New Year, 1852."

42. Eliza R. Snow, "Woman," *Poems, Religious, Historical and Political*, 2 vols. (Salt Lake City: LDS Printing and Publishing Establishment, 1877), 2:174.

43. Eliza R. Snow, "Degradation of Woman in Utah," *Deseret News Weekly*, 27 April 1870.

44. Eliza R. Snow, "How '70 Leaves Us and How '71 Finds Us," *Deseret News Weekly*, 11 January 1871.

45. "E. R. Snow's Address to the Relief Societies of Weber," 579.
46. Ibid., 578.
47. Salt Lake Stake, [General or Cooperative] Retrenchment Association Minutes 1871–1875, 30 August 1873.
48. Eliza R. Snow to Willmirth East, 23 April 1883, photocopy of holograph, Eliza R. Snow Papers, Church Library-Archives.
49. Sevier Stake Relief Society Minutes, 24 and 25 October 1880, in *Woman's Exponent*, 15 November 1880.
50. Juab Stake Relief Society Minutes, 20 April 1879, in *Woman's Exponent*, 1 June 1879.
51. Snow address, "Great Indignation Meeting."
52. Provo Stake Relief Society Minutes, 27 May 1881, in *Woman's Exponent*, 1 July 1881.
53. Sugar House Ward Relief Society Minutes, 20 July 1868, in *Woman's Exponent*, 1 May 1891.
54. E. R. Snow Smith to the branches of the Relief Society, *Woman's Exponent*, 15 September 1884.
55. Provo City Relief Society Minutes, 17 June 1875, in *Woman's Exponent*, 15 July 1875.
56. Ephraim Relief Society Minutes, 25 June 1875, in *Woman's Exponent*, 15 August 1875.
57. Nineteenth Ward Relief Society Minutes, 18 August 1875, in *Woman's Exponent*, 1 October 1875.
58. "An Address by Miss Eliza R. Snow . . . August 14, 1873," *Latter-day Saints' Millennial Star* 36 (13 January 1874): 21.
59. Ephraim Relief Society Minutes, 25 June 1875.
60. Weber Stake Relief Society Minutes, 9 June 1882, in *Woman's Exponent*, 1 July 1882.
61. "An Address by Miss Eliza R. Snow . . . August 14, 1873," 21.
62. Ibid.
63. Snow, "Woman," 178.

5

The Latter-day Saints and Women's Rights, 1870–1920

A Brief Survey

MAUREEN URSENBACH BEECHER
CAROL CORNWALL MADSEN
JILL MULVAY DERR

Wrote Apostle Orson F. Whitney in 1906: "Among the outward evidences of the divine origin of 'Mormonism,' there is nothing that testifies more clearly or eloquently to the truth of the Latter-day work, than the provision made therein for the uplifting and advancement of woman; for the salvation and exaltation, in this world and in the world to come, of woman as well as man."[1] It is evident from a perusal of recorded sermons, diaries, and news accounts of the late nineteenth and early twentieth centuries that Elder Whitney articulated the feelings of the leaders of The Church of Jesus Christ of Latter-day Saints, as they related not only to doctrine, but also to the public life of the Territory or later State of Utah.

How these sentiments expressed themselves on the various issues then considered under the rubric "woman's rights," or the more general, if slightly derogatory term "the woman question," provides material more suited to a dissertation than simply a brief report. But in skimming the surface, the following might suggest some themes of significance to women.

Two fundamental approaches to the position of women vis-a-vis men

---

First published as Task Papers in LDS History No. 29 (Salt Lake City: History Division, Historical Department, Church of Jesus Christ of Latter-day Saints, September 1979). Reprinted by permission.

and the society as a whole thread their way through the rhetoric of Mormon consideration of the various issues as they arise, and change very little from year to year, from issue to issue. One, that earliest articulated by British Mary Wollstonecraft in 1792 in her *Vindication of the Rights of Women*, declared women and men to be partakers of a common humanity, both endowed by a supreme creator with the capacity for rational thought, and the implied shared responsibility for their own and society's perfectibility. In the ideal society, there was no place for externally imposed designations of "inferior," or "superior," nor could restraints on individual growth for either sex be condoned. In Wollstonecraft's view, education was the key to woman's full participation in the social process, in the attempt "to render the social compact truly equitable." Human justice demanded sexual equality.

Also woven through the statements of Church leaders can be found a later logic, one which valued the same goals of woman's emancipation less for their approach to ideal justice than for their ultimate benefit to the social order. "Sexual propriety," more than equality, in the early nineteenth century determined woman's proper place. Her distinctiveness, not her similarity to man, suggested a unique woman's sphere in which she performed specifically designated female duties, different from male responsibilities, but equally valued. While not disallowing the uniqueness of woman's sphere or nature, mid-nineteenth century polemics advocated the widening of woman's field of influence and the utilizing of her distinctive attributes for the benefit of both society and the domestic circle. These themes of gender equality and sexual propriety thus become interwoven in the statements of Mormon leaders who addressed the subject during the period under question.

Of the issues which today, lumped together or taken individually, reflect the women's movement, only some were considered significant in the Mormon milieu a hundred years ago. Four will be considered here as reflecting the attitudes of Church leaders as they found expression in in-house as well as public forums.

The question of a woman's right to control her fertility, an issue which in the decades after "the pill" focuses almost solely on abortion, in the earlier century included not only the then difficult procedures of contraception, but also abortion itself (foeticide) and the practice of infanticide. All were equally condemned in public statements of General Authorities, though there is little evidence that the latter was ever common among either Mormon or non-Mormon populations in America. Reflecting a national concern which peaked in the 1870s, Utah, then a territory, enacted its first anti-abortion law. Although there had been sporadic references to abortion in the discourses of Mormon leaders from 1840 on, in 1878 the subject became a common theme, arising, it appears, not so much from an observed problem in Utah as from a wish to join forces on the side of family values in the public eye. Abortion was unequivocally termed "murder" by Church leaders, who lumped together the practices of foeticide and infanticide. In the words of George Q. Cannon, those who participated in the practice, male or female, "will be damned with the deepest damnation; because it is the damnation of shedding innocent blood, for which there is no forgiveness."[2] Birth control procedures also came under attack, though with less fervor, in a statement by Erastus Snow who applauded those who resisted the worldly incursions. The Saints, he said, "do not patronize the vendor of noxious, poisonous, destructive medicines to procure abortion, infanticide, and other wicked devices whereby to check the manipulation of their species, in order to facilitate the gratification of fleshly lusts. . . ."[3]

Elder Snow joined Elder Cannon in the condemnation of the practices of the great cities of Babylon, where many were "taking steps to destroy their own offspring, committing infanticide and foeticide, all of whom, and their aiders and abettors, are but ripening for the damnation of hell."[4]

The eventual separation of the three practices, each thereafter to be considered a separate act, can be traced through statements from General Authorities in subsequent years, directed more to the Saints themselves and less to the world outside, expressing their disapproval of worldly practices. The attitude toward abortion altered but little, but some justification for planning families was seen in official statements such as that of President Joseph F. Smith printed in the *Improvement Era* in 1908. While normally healthy men and women would bring "a host of social evils" into the community and the nation by preventing conception, "there are weak and sickly people who in wisdom, discretion and common sense should be counted as exceptions. . . ."[5]

A decade later, as the efforts of reformer Margaret Sanger moved out of the domain of the radicals and became the practice of "fashionable women," the *Relief Society Magazine* under editor Susa Young Gates published responses of six apostles and the Presiding Bishop. The articles were in essential agreement, condemning the practice of family limitation, and pointing out the effects of the practice on the mental and physical health of those who indulged. The series precipitated "animated and sometimes heated discussion" of the topic. At one point the First Presidency wrote, "We give our unqualified endorsement to these articles, . . . and commend the sentiments to members and non-members . . . everywhere."[6] Abortion then was not the issue, the assumption being that its seriousness set it above debate.

The position on birth control has consistently moderated, to the point represented in Heber J. Grant's 1939 addendum to the strong 1917 statement of Joseph F. Smith's often cited. President Smith said, in part: ". . . I believe that where people undertake to curtail or prevent the birth of their children that they are going to reap disappointment by and by. I have no hesitancy in saying that I believe this is one of the greatest crimes in the world today, this evil practice. . . ."[7] President Grant added: "Married couples who . . . have themselves been blessed with mental and physical vigor are recreant in their duty if they refuse to meet the natural and rightful responsibility of parenthood. Of course, in every ideal home the health of the mother, as well as the intelligence and health of the children should receive careful consideration."

In the late nineteenth century the basic issue of education for women— that they were entitled to it—had been resolved, at least in theory, for most Americans. In Utah, in practice, the sense of "sexual propriety" maintained; both at the University of Deseret, which admitted eighty-eight women and ninety-nine men in its first year, and at the colleges founded by Brigham Young, beginning with his Academy in Provo, education for women focused on the traditional "womanly" occupations: child care, homemaking, teaching, and/or replacing men in shops and offices to free them for the more arduous labors of the community. Brigham Young's famous "let them study law, or physic . . ." quote[9] seems in actual practice more bright dreams of the future than reasonable expectations of the 1870s; even so, the achievements of Utah colleges reflect well a commitment to higher education for women and for men. The introduction by Susa Young Gates at Brigham Young University of a department of Domestic Science, for example, predates by about ten years the sweep of that study across the nation, but follows the stated goals of the Academy, which prescribed: "Both men and women shall be taught how to live in the home . . . some branch of mechanics suitable to taste and capacity. Men should receive instructions in industrial areas and women in domestic work."[10]

By 1894, the *Young Woman's Journal*, edited by Susa Young Gates, was admonishing the girls of the Church to consider, as they set their educational goals, the possibility that they might be required to support themselves and their families. "The young woman who aims to perfect herself in any kind of professional work must know definitely the end in view and toward this the course of her training must be directed. She must decide what her natural aptitudes and inclinations are, and so far as lies in her power let these determine her choice of work."[11]

In the areas of employment itself there have been statements, though not so frequently from General Authorities as from women themselves, pleading for fair and equitable practices for women in what was basically men's sphere. Under her pseudonym Blanch Beechwood, later editor Emmeline B. Wells wrote for the *Woman's Exponent* in 1876 a plea for those "working girls" forced to submit to sweatshop ethics of the times. "Give them equality in all respects [she pleaded], and let each work with the same chance of success according to the labor performed, without the consideration of sex, and there would soon be a vast change which would be of material benefit to the existing state of society." And added, "Let [women] have the same opportunities for an education, observation and experience in public and private for a succession of years, and then see if she is not equally endowed with man and prepared to bear her part on all general questions socially, politically, industrially and educationally as well as spiritually."[12]

An early statement of the propriety of the concept of equal pay for equal work was summarized in that same journal as articulated by Joseph F. Smith, then president of the Quorum of the Twelve: "The woman who performed the same kind and quality of work that a man did, should receive therefore the same wages of pay. If a woman as school teacher, clerk, accountant or cook excelled a man in those same occupations, she should receive superior pay, and it is a poor rule that did not work both ways."[13] And representative of the opening of the professional schools to women is the 1872 statement, most likely of Emmeline B. Wells (she signs the piece simply "E"), that woman "should have access to every avenue of employment for which she has physical and mental capacity." The piece goes on: "Custom has, that women must only earn a living by a few circumscribed modes of employment; and although there is a reaction against this worse than absurd idea, the custom still obtains too largely, and the needle and midnight candle are yet considered, by too many, the proper appliances of woman's sphere."[14]

During the decade in which Sister Wells wrote, Utah women were to find their way into the professions: the 1870s produced Utah's first native-born women doctors, lawyers, journalists, participants in higher education, as well as a continuation of women in commerce, and the many-faceted work of women's organizations, notably the Relief Society and its auxiliary organizations, the YLMIA and the Primary. It is significant that that decade began auspiciously with the participation of Utah women in the election of public officers.

It must be understood in reading the *Woman's Exponent* that statements on women in the work force must be matched with labor conditions of the time; hence many of them are inappropriate to the present situation, in much the same way that, as a Utah woman legislator once said, (paraphrase) "those measures of 'protective legislation' which I worked so hard to promote, so that women would not have to work such long hours, now prevent women from rising in their jobs from the menial to the administrative levels, because a foreman has to be ready to work overtime. What helped in the 1930s hinders in the 1970s!"[15]

By the same token, care must be exercised in applying the rhetoric of suffrage to the general approach to women's rights currently. The wail is heard among Mormon feminists, "The Brethren supported the women's movements in the last century; why don't they now!?" The strong support given to women in the great suffrage struggle of the nineteenth century, a struggle won in Utah a half century before it was concluded in the nation at large, is evident in the accounts which follow. But that support was for one issue of the movement, the cause of woman suffrage; as this paper has attempted to demonstrate, it did not apply equally to the assortment of women's issues which might be included as "women's rights." When, for example, Elizabeth Cady Stanton, accompanying Susan B. Anthony to Utah on a suffrage tour, chose to preach birth control to the women assembled in the Old Tabernacle, she found herself very quickly *persona non grata* among the Saints. But Anthony, whose message was consistently the franchise for women, continued to be warmly received among Mormon women, and reciprocated in kind when their representatives visited conferences in the East.

Briefly summarizing what should—and does—take a dissertation to recount, the history of woman suffrage in Utah focuses around three dates: 1870, when the legislature of Utah Territory first awarded women the vote, after the example of Wyoming Territory, and with the approval of the federal government; 1887, when, as a result of the Edmunds-Tucker act aimed against the practice of plural marriage the franchise was withdrawn; and 1895, when Utahns in constitutional convention chose to include woman suffrage as a condition of their statehood.

Contemporary with the initial granting of the franchise to women in 1870 there is little recorded in newspapers and journals. Two studies on the subject ascribe conflicting motivations to the principals in the piece, the one focusing on the act essentially as a fluke committed by the federal government in its attempt to dispose of polygamy,[16] the other looking more at Utah sources and so seeing it as a natural continuation of Mormon feeling for the essential justice of universal suffrage.[17] Each, of course, acknowledges the interworking of many factors culminating in the Utah legislature's enactment of the bill.

There is no question that there was ready support in Utah for the franchise for women. Elder George Q. Cannon had editorialized in favor of women's involvement in the public sphere in the *Deseret News*:

With women to aid in the great cause of reform, what wonderful changes can be effected! Without her aid how slow the progress! Give her responsibility, and she will prove that she is capable of great things; but deprive her of opportunities, make a doll of her, leave her nothing to occupy her mind but the reading of novels, gossip, the fashions and all the frivolity of this frivolous age, and her influence is lost, and instead of being a help-meet to man, as originally intended, she becomes a drag and an encumbrance. Such women may answer in other places and among other people; but they would be out of place here.[18]

The history of Mormon women bears out Elder Cannon's high opinion of their contributions, and proves him prophetic, perhaps, in this next special case. It seems apparent that many of the moves involving women have originated among the women themselves and were, in very large measure, "grass-roots" motions which found favor with priesthood or political leadership. It may well be that the following is another instance of that phenomenon.

It is evident to any historian that the great mass meeting through which the women registered their contempt of the Cullom anti-polygamy bill pending in Washington, wielded an influence on the territorial legislature to raise and debate the issue of suffrage. The mass meeting was January 13, 1870; duplications followed in most of the settlements the month following; and on February 12 the suffrage bill, having cleared legislature and council, was signed into law by Acting Governor Stephen A. Mann. The minutes of the Salt Lake Stake Fifteenth Ward Relief Society reveal, however, a prelude to that indignation meeting, a prime mover, perhaps, of the whole series of events. None other than Sarah M. Kimball, that same strong sister in whose Nauvoo home the original pre-organization meeting of the Relief Society was held, called her women together in their Relief Society Hall to express, voluntarily, their indignation at the pending Cullom bill. Eliza R. Snow, general president of the Relief Society, was there, and approved the action, adding, "The ladies of Utah [have] too long remained silent while they [are] being so falsely represented to the world. . . . It is high time that we should rise up in the dignity of our calling and speak for ourselves."

Later in the meeting Sister Bathsheba Smith rose to move that "we demand of the governor the right of franchise."[19] Whether the motion carried or not, and whether or not the demand reached the legislature is not known. But it is evident that the desire for suffrage, a desire fed by the writings of suffragists in the East which reached into the not-so-isolated Rocky Mountain territory, was alive and growing among the women of Utah.

Following the signing of the act granting them the electoral franchise, the women of the Fifteenth Ward met again, this time in celebration. Their first business was to compose a letter of appreciation to Mann for his part in the business; then they turned to expressing to each other their feelings in a testimony-bearing format. Sister Kimball, recorded the secretary, "had waited patiently a long time, and now that we were granted the right of suffrage, she would openly declare herself a woman's rights woman." Many concurred, but not all. Margaret Smoot felt that she had "never had any desire for more rights" than she had. "I have always sought to vote at conference, and I then felt I had done all I desire to do," she said, adding of political matters that "I have always considered these things beneath the sphere of women." Not one to drag her feet, however, she agreed that "as things progress I feel it is right that we should vote." "My sisters," concluded Willmirth East, "this is a bright day, but we need more wisdom and humility than ever before." Then, implying that there had earlier been active support of the now accomplished fact, she added, "I am glad to be associated with you, those who have borne the heat and burden of the day, and I ask God to pour blessings on [your] heads continually."[20]

The detail recorded here bespeaks a careful secretary; it seems probable that such sentiments were more widespread than simply in the Fifteenth Ward. The extent of the contribution of the women themselves to the granting of suffrage in 1870 must yet be explored in depth.

That their brethren rejoiced with the women in their political rights is evident in this quotation from an April conference of Erastus Snow, given in 1883, ironically, four years before the franchise would be withdrawn from them:

> It is a source of satisfaction to me that the Lord has moved upon His servants and the Legislature of our Territory to be among the first to lead the van of human progress in the extension of the elective franchise to women as well as men, and to recognize the freedom and liberty which belongs to the fairer sex as well as the sterner; for the Gospel teaches that all things are done among us by common consent, and the Prophet Joseph commanded and introduced in our midst the custom which we are following today. . . .[21]

It was the constitutional convention of 1895, however, which brought out the grand rhetoric in support of the inclusion of a suffrage plank in the organic law of the soon-to-be state. Considering that both political parties in Utah supported the concept, it is strange that so much of the time of the convention was taken up in debate, but there were those of the delegates who felt, not that suffrage was not right and proper, but that the constitution might lose some public support if the clause were included.

The interchange between Brigham H. Roberts, "the delegate from Davis County," and Orson F. Whitney is one of the most rhetorically dramatic in the proceedings of the convention. Whitney seems to have echoed the majority view of Church leaders in his support of universal suffrage—President Woodruff is quoted as having advised Roberts not to oppose it—but in both cases the arguments were the standard ones, couched in flaming rhetoric and interpreted into Utah's peculiar circumstances (the non-Mormon women, whose natural bent would have favored the liberal position, found themselves opposing the measure, arguing that it would solidify power in Mormon hands). Elder Roberts was persuasive in his opposition; his fear was not only that women would spoil politics, or that politics would ruin women, but that the inclusion of a universal suffrage clause would endanger the long-sought statehood so necessary to the growth of the territory, the people, and the Church.[22]

At this time the women were not absent from the action. As the pressure mounted, they mobilized their Woman Suffrage Association of Utah and obtained signatures on petitions demonstrating mass support for suffrage, countering the opposition's 15,366 names favoring a separate submission to the electorate clause with their own 24,801 names preferring its inclusion in the constitution package.[23]

Personal statements of leaders of the Church at this time, as well as those of women and men generally, demonstrated such overwhelming support of the cause that it is easy in retrospect to anticipate the resounding support the constitution would have. Then Apostle Heber J. Grant recorded publicly that he was "decidedly in favor of equal suffrage for the sexes,"[24] and privately in a letter to Anthon H. Lund that "I am as ardent a woman's suffrage man as can be found."[25] President Joseph F. Smith was summarized in his comments to a large group of women as saying, referring to the 1887 disfranchisement of women, that "The women of Utah once enjoyed the elective franchise, and they used it wisely, and it was an outrage that it was stricken from them, and he hoped the day would soon come when it should be restored to them. . . ."[26]

Further to his convention address, Bishop Whitney told an audience in the Tabernacle that he regarded the suffrage movement "as one of the levers by which the Almighty is lifting up this fallen world." He went on, "It is a measure of progress, a step in the march of human liberty, and will sweep from its path all opposition that lifts its puny arm and voice against it. I feel this in every fibre of my being."[27]

One aspect of the Utah State Constitution, however, which has been less ardently investigated is the general statement of philosophy with which it begins, a philosophy which would of itself require equal suffrage. It declares that "both male and female citizens of this state shall enjoy equally all civil, political, and religious rights and privileges,"[28] a clause which in the light of twentieth century movements was, like the granting of suffrage, years ahead of its time.

That the political climate of Utah should have been so favorable to women's rights and responsibilities is obvious in the light of the doctrines of the Church. In an impassioned address to women of the Relief Society gathered in general conference, President Joseph F. Smith supported doctrinally his ardor in favor of women's rights:

> Man and woman are begotten of the same father, are born of the same mother, possess the same life, breathe the same air, feel the same cold or heat, hunger or thirst, pleasure or pain; eat the same food, wear the same fabric wrought only in different forms and fashions; exist by the same means; both bear the divine image and possess the same divine nature. They are born, live and die and live again for the one great and glorious purpose. They are indispensable to each other, each is the complement of the other, both for this world and the world to come, for time and for all eternity. Then why shall one enjoy civil rights and the other be denied them?[29]

Then, in specific terms, speaking to the problems of women in the late nineteenth century, he continues:

> Why shall one be admitted to all the avenues of mental and physical progress and prosperity and the other be prohibited, and prescribed within certain narrow limits, to her material abridgement and detriment? . . . Shall men be favored as bread-winners, and women be handicapped in their effort to win bread? Shall a man be paid higher wages than is paid to a woman for doing no better than she does the very same work? Shall the avenues for employment be multiplied to men and diminished to women by the mere dictum or selfishness of men? If a man can perform labor for which woman is physically disqualified, let him enjoy the monopoly of it; let the same be said of woman. By what process of reasoning can it be shown that a woman

standing at the head of a family, with all the responsibility resting upon her to provide for them, should be deprived of the avenues and ways or means that a man in like circumstances may enjoy to provide for them? Yet many of these unwholesome conditions do exist, and that too vastly to the detriment of women. . . .

Then, turning to the converse of his point, President Smith goes on:

> . . . notwithstanding which, strange to say, women may be found who seem to glory in their enthralled condition, and who caress and fondle the very chains and manacles which fetter and enslave them! Let those who love this helpless dependent condition and prefer to remain in it; but for conscience and for mercy's sake let them not stand in the way of those of their sisters who would be, and of right ought to be *free* [italics his throughout]. Let them who will not enter into the door of equal rights and impartial suffrage step aside, and leave the passage clear to those who desire to enter.

Recognizing the responsibilities which irrefutably adhere to the possession of rights, President Smith acknowledges that "if the women have equal rights they must bear equal burdens with the men." Speaking of the women of the Church, he maintains that "they do this already, except that their burdens are made unequal in that they are deprived of the enjoyment of equal rights."

> Yes but, says the objector, they must sit on juries, they must serve as marshals, soldiers, &c. Well, let them do so if they want to, and can *get* such office. But what nonsense this is; it is all right for them to be qualified for any and all positions, and to possess the right or privilege to fill them, but that they *must* do so does not follow. There are many men in every community who never sat on a jury, never having been called to do so, nor to be a soldier, or to do any duty, nor to be sheriff, policemen, marshals, nor even governors or judges, and yet they have possessed all the qualifications to fill any of these positions. Therefore why shall the women be *compelled* to do things because she has the franchise that men are not compelled to do!

The speech, or at least the newspaper account of the speech, ends with the berating of propagandists who attempt to "frighten" women from seeking their rights, and the hope that "no woman be deterred for a moment from her whole duty, by such contemptible twaddle."

Contemporary with President Smith's address is another statement of Bishop Whitney's, included here as much for its prose style as for its content:

> It is woman's destiny to have a voice in the affairs of government. She was designed for it. She has a right to it. This great social upheaval, this woman's movement that is making itself heard and felt, means something more than that certain women are ambitious to vote and hold office. I regard it as one of the great levelers by which the Almighty is lifting up this fallen world, lifting it nearer to the throne of its creator.[30]

And, remembering the dichotomy of "sexual equality," or the inherent justice argument, and "sexual propriety," the argument of value to the social order, let us conclude with one more statement, that of James E. Talmage, from a Woman's Suffrage Association meeting in 1889, which interweaves both approaches in a way characteristically Mormon, yet universally applicable: "The conclusions at which I have arrived in the consideration of the subject are based upon no comparison of legal political advantages or disadvantages likely to result from conferring the rights of suffrage upon women; but upon the justice of her claims to these rights as witnessed by the word of the Almighty."[31] Then the "value" argument:

> Man, in his studied wisdom, has learned this great lesson of Nature— that the Creator has fitted every object of His care to the purpose of its being. Is it then to be thought that woman is less completely endowed with the capacities of her calling than is man for his? It has been often said that woman, in the sphere allotted to her existence, is as perfect as man. I would say in place of this, that in her sphere woman is as much the superior of man as does man excel in his proper powers. Nature has been as liberal in endowing woman—Jehovah's daughter—as in blessing man—His son.

Notes

1. Orson F. Whitney, "Woman's Work and 'Mormonism,'" *Young Woman's Journal* 27 (July 1906): 293.
2. The basic study of this subject is that of Lester E. Bush, Jr., "Birth Control Among the Mormons: Introduction to an Insistent Question," *Dialogue: A*

Journal of Mormon Thought 10 (Autumn 1976): 12–44. The quotation here is from George Q. Cannon, *Journal of Discourses* 26 (1884): 14–15.

3. Erastus Snow, *Journal of Discourses* 25 (1884): 111–12.
4. Ibid., 24 (1883): 69.
5. Joseph F. Smith, *Improvement Era* 11 (October 1908): 959–61.
6. *Relief Society Magazine* 4 (1917): 68.
7. Ibid., 317–18.
8. Lester Bush, "Birth Control," 25, cites a letter of Heber J. Grant to Arnold Haymore, 1 May 1939, copy in his possession.
9. Brigham Young, *Journal of Discourses* 13 (18 July 1869): 61. The quotation reads as follows:

> As I have often told my sisters in the Female Relief societies, we have sisters here who, if they had the privilege of studying, would make just as good mathematicians or accounts as any man; and we think they ought to have the privilege to study these branches of knowledge that they may develop the powers with which they are endowed. We believe that women are useful, not only to sweep houses, wash dishes, make beds, and raise babies, but that they should stand behind the counter, study law or physic, or become good book-keepers and be able to do the business in any counting house, and all this to enlarge their sphere of usefulness for the benefit of society at large. In following these things they but answer the design of their creation.

10. Articles of Incorporation, 1875: 13, Brigham Young University Archives, as quoted in Virginia B. Poulson, History of College of Family Living (Provo, Utah: College of Family Living, [1975]).
11. "Advice to Girls," *Young Woman's Journal* 6 (December 1894): 137. To which Louisa Lula Greene, founding editor of the *Woman's Exponent* added a statement of personal responsibility which seems very much in keeping with what LDS women are hearing from their women leaders today:

> Let women shine by the intelligence of their own minds and not by that reflected from man. Let women be qualified to stand alone, if necessary, and then if she become a wife or mother, she can act with wisdom and judgement; and if her path be in smooth and quiet places, she is none the less womanly because of her innate powers. But should her lot be cast in rough and thorny paths, how great her need of strength from within and without to endure. Remember there are many lonely walks in life, and it is necessary to be well armed with courage and fortitude. *Woman's Exponent* 5 (1 July 1876): 20.

12. Blanch Beechwood [Emmeline B. Wells], "Action or Indifference," *Woman's Exponent* 5 (1 September 1876): 54. The thought of Emmeline B. Wells is

summarized in Carol Cornwall Madsen, " 'Remember the Women of Zion': A Study of the Editorial Content of the *Women's Exponent*, a Mormon Woman's Journal," Master's thesis, University of Utah, 1977.

13.   Joseph F. Smith, ibid., 20 [15 March 1892]: 133.

14.   [Wells], "Woman's Rights and Wrongs," ibid., 1 (1 June 1872): n.p.

15.   Reva Beck Bosone, as noted in the remarks at Brigham Young University, February 1977.

16.   Beverly Beeton, "Woman Suffrage in the American West, 1869–1896," Ph.D. dissertation, University of Utah, 1976.

17.   Thomas G. Alexander, "An Experiment in Progressive Legislation: The Granting of Woman Suffrage in Utah in 1870," *Utah Historical Quarterly* 38 (Winter 1970): 20–30.

18.   *Deseret News Weekly*, 26 May 1869.

19.   Salt Lake Stake Fifteenth Ward Relief Society, Minutes 1868–1873, 6 January 1870, Church Archives, Historical Department, The Church of Jesus Christ of Latter-day Saints.

20.   Ibid., 19 February 1870. A typescript of the minutes was made by Jill Mulvay Derr and published in *Exponent II* 1 (December 1974): 14.

21.   Erastus Snow, *Journal of Discourses* 24 (6 April 1883): 69.

22.   The exchange is provided in full in Utah, Constitutional Convention, 1895, *Official Report of the Proceedings and Debates*, 2 vols. (Salt Lake City, 1898). Historical background is interwoven into the text in Jean Bickmore White, "Woman's Place is in the Constitution," *Utah Historical Quarterly* 42 (Fall 1974): 344–69.

23.   White, "Woman's Place," 363.

24.   "Equal Suffrage Department," *Young Woman's Journal* 6 (February 1895): 225.

25.   Heber J. Grant to Anthon H. Lund, 20 September 1895, Heber J. Grant Letter Press Copy Book 21, 175–77, Church Archives.

26.   "Speech of Pres. Jos. F. Smith," *Woman's Exponent* 20 (15 March 1892): 133.

27.   *Woman's Exponent* 24 (15 June 1895): 10.

28.   As quoted in Maureen Ursenbach Beecher and Kathryn L. MacKay, "Women in Twentieth-century Utah," *Utah's History*, ed. Richard D. Poll et al. (Provo: BYU Press, 1978), 573.

29.   "Relief Society Conference," *Woman's Exponent* 24 (15 August 1895): 44–46. All quoted sections here are from this source. We have corrected typographical errors in a few instances.

30.   Orson F. Whitney, "Speech in Support of Woman Suffrage," *Men and Women* 1 (14 May 1895): 11. The publication reprinted the text of Whitney's speech from the constitutional convention of Utah, 30 March 1895.

31.   "Woman's Suffrage Meeting," *Woman's Exponent* 17 (15 February 1889): 138. Both sections are from this source. For additional quotations similar to those in this paper, taken primarily from Latter-day Saint women's journals, see Carol Lynn Pearson, *The Flight and the Nest* (Salt Lake City: Bookcraft, 1975).

6

An Experiment in Progressive Legislation

The Granting of Woman Suffrage in Utah in 1870

THOMAS G. ALEXANDER

In 1869 and 1870, as the nation agonized over the adoption of the Fifteenth Amendment and universal manhood suffrage, the people of Utah considered a suffrage question which was so far ahead of its time that the nation did not adopt it until 1920. At that time these mountain westerners debated universal adult suffrage, female suffrage as it was then called, or woman suffrage as it is generally called today.[1]

Utah was not the first state or territory to adopt this measure.[2] New Jersey had allowed women to vote from 1790 to 1807 and various other states had in the meantime allowed the suffrage to women for various reasons, often because they happened to be property owners. Also, in the State of Deseret prior to the organization of Utah Territory, women voted in civil elections just as they had always voted on ecclesiastical matters in the Church of Jesus Christ of Latter-day Saints or Mormon church.

The first modern territory to adopt universal adult suffrage was Wyoming Territory whose governor, John A. Campbell, signed a law providing for woman suffrage on December 10, 1869. The adoption of suffrage in Wyoming Territory where men outnumbered women by a ratio of six to

First published in *Utah Historical Quarterly* 38 (Winter 1970): 20–30. Reprinted by permission.

one could not have had the impact it did in Utah where the numbers were approximately equal.

Nineteenth century Utah appeared to non-Mormons or Gentiles, as they were called in the Mormon territory, to be a retrograde and barbarian place only slightly more advanced than the Moslem lands of the Near East, with which it was often compared.[3] The people of Utah, however, considered themselves to be socially enlightened, and by the standards which obtained in the United States when universal suffrage was adopted they appear so today.

Surrounded by a roaring frontier country which emphasized the acquisitive, individualistic, and violent, Mormons in 1869 and 1870 talked about cooperation, self-sacrifice, and a sense of community. In April 1869, Brigham Young announced a cooperative movement which, for the good of the people, would "shut off," many businessmen so the community could be benefited by central purchasing, manufacturing, and marketing.[4]

In the same vein George Q. Cannon, editor of the *Deseret News* and a counselor to President Young, emphasized the need to consider the good of the community and not simply individual advantage in other matters. In an editorial he lamented the plight of the American workingman and the problems caused by the rapid centralization of wealth,

> in the hands of the very few in this country [which] is unparalleled, and the unprincipled use of the power thus acquired, as witnessed during the recent Wall Street gambling operations [which] cannot but cause wide spread distress.
>
> [This shows that] here as elsewhere, when power and wealth are acquired and exercised by the few who are not guided by principle, they are not used *pro bono publico*, but are made to answer private interests and to subserve selfish ends.[5]

Like the later Progressives, Cannon was convinced that man was basically good and that the evil he did grew from environmental influences.

> Man's inclination to do evil, is, in most instances, the result of habits which grow out of defective and improper education and training. When men are rightly trained, they will be unable to perceive a single advantage which they can gain by doing wrong. If society were properly organized, there would be nothing that men could legitimately desire which they could not obtain by doing right, and, of course, under such circumstances, there would be no temptation to do wrong.

Unlike many in his own time, Cannon, an immigrant himself, opposed the movement for immigration restriction, even the restriction upon the immigration of orientals.[6]

In another editorial, he lauded the efforts to bring women into the promotion of the cooperative and reform movements.

> With women to aid in the great cause of reform, what wonderful changes can be effected! Without her aid how slow the progress! Give her responsibility, and she will prove that she is capable of great things; but deprive her of opportunities, make a doll of her, leave her nothing to occupy her mind but the reading of novels, gossip, the fashions and all the frivolity of this frivolous age, and her influence is lost, and instead of being a help meet to man, as originally intended, she becomes a drag and an encumbrance. Such women may answer in other places and among other people; but they would be out of place here.[7]

Even polygamy, or plural marriage as Mormons preferred to call it, which was viewed as retrograde and uncivilized by Gentiles, was seen as a method of reforming society and eradicating social evils by contemporary Mormons. Church leaders saw this reform as a way of freeing women from slavery to the lusts of men and making them honored wives and mothers with homes of their own and social position. By entering polygamy women achieved a place in a society where the family formed the basic social unit. There is some evidence that Mormon women shared this view because so many of those who were active in the campaign for woman's rights were plural wives of prominent Utah citizens. Rather than simply tacitly accepting polygamy as their burden, these women used their social position to promote a better life for others in society.[8]

It is hardly surprising, then, that the predominant sentiment of the community favored woman suffrage as soon as it was proposed. Representative George W. Julian of Indiana introduced a bill entitled, "A Bill to Discourage Polygamy in Utah," which simply granted women the right to vote. Professor J. K. H. Willcox of the Universal Franchise Association in argument before the House Committee on Territories said that if the experiment succeeded in Utah it could be extended elsewhere. By this means, he was certain, "polygamy would be destroyed." Delegate William H. Hooper said that he favored the bill and opined that the leading citizens of Utah would also. The bill never came to a vote.[9]

As the time for the legislative session of 1870 neared, the press of

Utah demonstrated considerable interest in the proposal. The *Utah Magazine* through its editor E. L. T. Harrison and his associate Edward W. Tullidge published several articles supporting the idea. Harrison said that suffrage ought to be granted to women because it was inevitable in the progression of things. Tullidge argued that:

> The nation which does not assign to women a very high part to play not only in the home circle but also in all the vital concerns of humanity, is barbaric in its notions and estate. True civilization had not yet reached that nation.[10]

A woman correspondent of the magazine took the position that women have the talent to occupy any professional position which men could hold and justified the right to vote by the Mormon doctrine of free agency. She was of the opinion that women's votes would not change things much because, just as in congregational voting, women would vote pretty much the same as men. She said, however, that they had the right to express themselves just the same. Harrison was sympathetic with the view.[11]

Not until the legislature had already passed the act providing for woman suffrage did church authorities comment editorially on the provision, but their approval seems to have been unanimous. President Cannon wrote in the *Deseret News* that the right of suffrage ought to be granted to all who can exercise it intelligently. He took the view that neither men nor women could exercise their full rights while "the other labors under disability, however limited." He was convinced that women would do more to promote "legislation of such a character as would tend more to diminish prostitution and the various social evils which overwhelm society than anything hitherto devised under universal male suffrage."[12]

Franklin D. Richards in his newly established *Ogden Junction* took a similar tack and emphasized Mormon unity on social and political questions. "Mormonism," he said, "seeks to provide for, educate and make useful to the State the whole feminine portion of the race." He was quick to point out, however, that women ought not be raised "above the level of man to be his governor, guide or lawgiver," or invested "with powers for which nature has not fitted her."[13]

It is not at all surprising, given the sentiment in favor of the move, that the legislature considered the proposal early in 1870.[14] On January 27, 1870, Representative Abram Hatch of Wasatch County moved that the Committee on Elections be instructed to inquire into the propriety of passing a bill granting the suffrage to women. That afternoon, under the chairmanship of

Representative John C. Wright of Box Elder County, the Committee of the Whole took up Hatch's motion and asked the Committee on Elections to consider the matter further.

On February 2, Wright reported that the Committee on Elections recommended passage of the measure. The report pointed out that the Organic Act granted suffrage to every free white male inhabitant over twenty-one years of age and limited the right to hold office to citizens of the United States. The legislature appeared to have the right to extend the suffrage to any other group it wished. It recommended, also, that the suffrage be extended to women who were wives or daughters of citizens, because, the report said, a federal act of April 14, 1802, had granted citizenship to widows and children of aliens who had received their first papers. "According to this," the committee reasoned, "we should naturally infer that if the widow and children of an alien who had not perfected his citizenship, became citizens, that the wife of a citizen became a citizen by being united in marriage to her husband." By exercising the franchise, the committee report continued, women would be placed "in a position to protect their own rights by an appeal to the ballot box which we think they are quite as competent to use as uneducated foreigners, the negro or chinese." The committee also recommended that women be ineligible to hold high judicial, legislative, or executive offices, though they might be allowed to hold minor positions.

On the basis of this recommendation, Peter Maughan of Cache County, chairman of the House Committee on Elections reported back a bill on February 5, 1870. The Maughan bill passed all three readings on that day, was approved unanimously, and sent to the Council. It provided simply that any woman twenty-one or older, a resident of the territory for six months, who was born or naturalized in the United States or who was the wife, widow, or daughter of a citizen was entitled to vote in any election.

On February 9, the Council passed the bill with some amendments which the House refused to accept. A conference committee agreed to accept the House bill and on February 10, both the House and Council passed the amended version. Orson Pratt, speaker of the House, sent the bill to Territorial Secretary and Acting Governor S. A. Mann. Though Mann said he had "very grave and serious doubts of the wisdom and soundness of that political economy which makes the act a law of this Territory," he signed it on February 12, 1870, because both the House and Council had passed it unanimously. Governor J. Wilson Shafer, who was still in Washington at the time, told Delegate Hooper that he intended to wire Mann to veto the bill, but he failed to do so.[15]

In true Utah fashion the Ghost Government of the Ghost State of

Sarah Melissa Granger Kimball. *Courtesy of Archives, Historical Department, Church of Jesus Christ of Latter-day Saints.*

Deseret considered the proposal. On February 21, 1870, the territorial legislature reconvened itself as the Senate and House of the State of Deseret, heard the message of Governor Brigham Young, and adopted the laws of the Territory of Utah for the State of Deseret. In addition the legislature passed and Young approved a joint resolution to submit an amendment to the constitution of the State of Deseret to the people which would allow the vote to all women over the age of twenty-one.[16]

Though the women of Utah had had little to do with the actual passage of the bill, they were gratified at its enactment. At a meeting of the Female Relief Society in Salt Lake City on February 19, seven days after the passage of the act, Eliza R. Snow, a plural wife of both Joseph Smith and Brigham Young, proposed an expression of gratitude to Acting Governor Mann for signing the bill. The proposal was adopted and a committee made up of wives of some of the most prominent men in the territory drafted the resolution and presented it to the acting governor.[17]

Already, on February 14, 1870, two days after the passage of the bill, women had voted in a municipal election in Salt Lake City. Though it probably would have been difficult to prove, contemporaries say that the first woman voter was Miss Saraph Young, daughter of Brigham H. Young and grand niece of Brigham Young. Even though the women of Wyoming got the suffrage first, women in Utah voted before their neighbors to the east, owing to the timing of the municipal election.[18]

After the suffrage was granted, the women of Utah did not simply rest with their newly won freedom. Mrs. Sarah M. Kimball, a leader in the Relief Society and later a nationally known woman's rights advocate, began a program of civic education for the women of the territory. She helped form clubs, organized classes in history and political science, and directed the work generally. Mrs. Kimball and others saw that the Relief Society was put to good use in the promotion of activities and classes. Relief Society meetings became classes in government, mock trials, and symposia on parliamentary law [19]

Women began to take an active part in public affairs. On one occasion, Brigham Young was asked if he wanted women in such offices as sheriff. He replied that if one of his wives, Harriet Cook Young, who had signed the memorial to Governor Mann and who happened to be six feet tall, "went out after a man she would get him every time." In keeping with Young's ideas, women began to participate in civic activities. Miss Georgia Snow, a niece of Judge Zerubbabel Snow, among others, was admitted to the bar. Women were placed on school boards in various districts, and as early as September 1874, two women served on a coroner's jury at Little Cottonwood.[20]

The majority of the people in Utah appear to have been pleased with this experiment in democracy. Louise L. Greene, editor of the *Woman's Exponent*, the organ of the Female Relief Society, expressed this feeling in June 1872 in an early number of the periodical when she said that she was proud that the women of Utah did not have to bear the burden of disfranchisement which the women of most of the United States did. Women ought to have the right "to say who shall disburse those taxes [which many of them pay], how that government shall be conducted, or who shall decide on a question of peace or war which may involve the lives of their sons, brothers, fathers, and husbands."[21] In April 1883, Apostle Erastus Snow said that it was the Lord who

> moved upon His servants and the Legislature of our Territory to be among the first to lead the van of human progress in the extension of the elective franchise to women as well as men, and to recognize the freedom and liberty, which belongs to the fairer sex as well as the sterner; for the Gospel teaches that all things are to be done by common consent. . . .[22]

Though comment outside Utah initially saw woman suffrage as an enlightened move, that view gradually disappeared. The principal reason for its dissipation appears to have been that women of Utah neither forced an end to polygamy, nor did they elect Gentiles to undermine the power of the Mormon church in Utah. Even the passage of the Edmunds Act (in 1882) did not change the situation, in spite of the disfranchisement of all polygamous men and women. Charges were thrown around about the illegal voting of alien women and under-aged girls, some of which were probably true—though the act did allow some women, who would normally have been considered aliens, to vote. As Congress considered the Edmunds-Tucker Act in 1886 and 1887, this sentiment in Utah reached a peak, and a provision of the act disfranchised all women in Utah Territory.[23]

Thus ended a seventeen-year experiment in political equality between the sexes. It had burst on the rock of national anti-Mormon and anti-polygamy sentiment because the enterprise had not had the effect which national leaders expected it to have. It had not brought an end to polygamy and church domination in Utah.

One question remains unanswered. Did the Mormon hierarchy promote woman suffrage in an attempt to strengthen its hold on Utah politics as some Gentiles believed? This seems hardly to have been the case. Never, throughout the history of Utah up to the time of granting the suffrage to women, was there any real possibility that Gentile men might outnumber

Mormon men. Though the possibility existed that the coming of the railroad in 1869 might have changed this, there is little evidence that the church leaders expected it to happen.

It appears, rather, that the reasons given in public for granting woman suffrage in 1870 are the real ones because they are congruent with the progressive sentiment among the Mormons at the time. Cannon's editorials in the *Deseret News*, the church organ, are progressive and optimistic in tone. They speak of the perfectability of man, the need for equality in the community, and the high place of women in Mormon society. Though women did not hold ecclesiastical offices, they had always voted on matters brought before the congregation and Eliza R. Snow and her companions led the Relief Society and the "Young Ladies' Department of the Co-operative Retrenchment Association" which evolved into the Young Women's Mutual Improvement Association. Women were encouraged by church leaders to participate in public affairs, and such leaders as Sarah M. Kimball had a high place in the public esteem.

It was only natural that church leaders and the majority of the people of Utah, given the community sentiment, should favor legal participation for women in public life. It is not at all surprising that when the people of Utah were again given the opportunity to express their feelings on woman suffrage in the 1895 Constitution, they favored it overwhelmingly. It is also not surprising, that principal opposition came from non-Mormons in the mining districts of Utah.[24] It seems probable, then, that in 1870, progressive sentiment was simply in advance of the rest of the nation and because of their experience and beliefs, the Mormons were willing to move in where others feared to tread.

Notes

1. General treatments of woman suffrage will be found in Carrie Chapman Catt and Nettie Rogers Shuler, *Woman Suffrage and Politics: The Inner Story of the Suffrage Movement* (New York, 1926); The National American Woman Suffrage Association, *Victory: How Women Won It; A Centennial Symposium, 1840–1940* (New York, 1940); and Kate B. Carter, comp., *Woman Suffrage in the West* ([Salt Lake City], 1943).

2. Susa Young Gates, "History, Chapter, Woman Suffrage in Utah" (typescript, Susan Young Gates Miscellaneous File in the Widtsoe Collection, Utah State Historical Society). (Hereafter this file will be cited as Gates File, USHS.) Ralph Lorenzo Jack, "Woman Suffrage in Utah as an Issue in the Mormon and Non-

Mormon Press of the Territory, 1870–1887" (master's thesis, Brigham Young University, 1954), 22; B. H. Roberts, *A Comprehensive History of the Church of Jesus Christ of Latter-day Saints, Century I* (6 vols., Salt Lake City, 1930), V, 325; T. A. Larson, *History of Wyoming* (Lincoln, Nebraska, 1965), 78–84. Roberts states wrongly that Campbell vetoed the bill.

3.   Leonard J. Arrington and Jon Haupt, "Intolerable Zion: The Image of Mormonism in Nineteenth-Century American Literature," *Western Humanities Review*, XXII (Summer, 1968), 243–60. Stanley S. Ivins, "Notes on Mormon Polygamy," *Utah Historical Quarterly*, 34 (Fall, 1967), 309–21.

4.   Leonard J. Arrington, *Great Basin Kingdom: An Economic History of the Latter-day Saints, 1830–1900* (Cambridge, 1958), 305.

5.   *Deseret News Weekly* (Salt Lake City), February 10, 1869 (hereafter cited as *DNW* with the date).

6.   Ibid., June 2 and 30, 1869.

7.   Ibid., May 26, 1869.

8.   Ibid., February 16, 1870. Speech of George Q. Cannon, July 7, 1878, in *Journal of Discourses* (26 vols., Liverpool, England, 1854–1886), XX, 36–37; Susa Young Gates and Leah D. Widtsoe, *Women of the "Mormon" Church* (Jackson County, Missouri, 1928); and Edward W. Tullidge, *The Women of Mormondom* (New York, 1877). In a conversation with the author, Leonard J. Arrington pointed out that so many polygamous wives could be freed for community service because of their position and other wives who could assist them by caring for children and taking other household duties. See also Ivins, "Notes on Mormon Polygamy," *U.H.Q.*, 34, 309–21.

9.   *DNW*, March 24, 1869; Jack, "Woman Suffrage in Utah," 15–18; Roberts, *Comprehensive History*, V, 324; Edward W. Tullidge, *History of Salt Lake City* (Salt Lake City, 1886), 435.

10.   "Women's Sphere in Utah," *The Utah Magazine*, II (February 13, 1869), 252; E. W. Tullidge, "Woman and Her Sphere," ibid., III (June 26, 1869), 119.

11.   "A Utah Woman's Thoughts on Womanly Employments, Marriage, etc." *The Utah Magazine*, III (July 31, 1869), 199; see also "Talk About Woman's Wages," ibid., 203.

12.   *DNW*, January 22, 1870. See also *Mormon Tribune* (Salt Lake City), January 22, 1870, for similar comments by a non-Mormon.

13.   *Ogden Junction*, February 9, 1870.

14.   The consideration in the legislature is based upon Utah Territory, Legislature, Minutes of the Utah Territorial Legislature, MS, Manuscript Section, File Box on Utah Territory, Legislature (Church of Jesus Christ of Latter-day Saints Historian's Library, Salt Lake City); *DNW*, February 16, 1870.

15.   Jack, "Woman Suffrage in Utah," 19.

16.   See note 14 and *DNW*, February 23, 1870.

17.   Many of the women were also plural wives. *DNW*, March 2, 1870; Tullidge, *Salt Lake City*, 435; Jack, "Woman Suffrage in Utah," 32.

18. Tullidge, *Salt Lake City*, 437; Jack, "Woman Suffrage in Utah," 21; *Deseret Evening News* (Salt Lake City), May 9, 1947.

19. Susa Young Gates, "The Suffrage Movement," MS and "History, Chapter, Woman Suffrage in Utah," 16, Gates File, USHS.

20. Gates, "History, Chapter, Woman Suffrage in Utah," 17 and "Copy," MS, Gates File, USHS.

21. *Woman's Exponent*, I (June 1, 1872), 5.

22. Speech of Erastus Snow, April 6, 1883, in *Journal of Discourses*, XIV, 69.

23. Tullidge, *Salt Lake City*, 433 and 435; Jack, "Woman Suffrage in Utah," 26, 27, and 32; Statement of Mrs. Angie F. Newman, June 8, 1886, in U.S., Congress, Senate, *Miscellaneous Document 122*, 49th Cong., 1st Sess., 1885–86, Serial 2346.

24. Stanley S. Ivins, "A Constitution for Utah," *U.H.Q.*, XXV (April, 1957), 102–6 and 115–16.

7

Woman Suffrage in Territorial Utah

BEVERLY BEETON

> *Utah is the land of marvels. She gives us, first, polygamy, which seems to be an outrage against "woman's right," and then offers to the nation a "Female Suffrage Bill."* . . . *Was there ever a greater anomaly known in the history of society?*
>
> —The Phrenological Journal, *November 1871*

The political franchise was extended to women in the United States in 1920 with the ratification of the Nineteenth Amendment, but in some areas of the American West women had been voting for a half-century. Although organized efforts to achieve woman suffrage in the late nineteenth century were concentrated in New England and New York, women were first allowed to vote in the Rocky Mountain West.[1]

Desiring to publicize the newly created Wyoming Territory and attract investors and settlers, the Territorial Assembly of Wyoming passed legislation giving women the right to vote in December 1869.[2] Two months later the women of Utah Territory were enfranchised. But the experiment with woman suffrage in Utah received much more attention because Utah had nearly forty times as many females in its population as Wyoming; moreover, most of those Utah women followed a religious faith that practiced plural marriage.

Reformers as well as critics intently watched the development of the female franchise among the Mormons. The principal preoccupation was: how could what appeared to be the most liberal view of women's rights—

First published in *Utah Historical Quarterly* 46 (Spring 1978): 100–120. Reprinted by permission.

suffrage—and the most enslaving marital arrangement—polygamy—develop and coexist in the same environment.

Assuming that woman suffrage and polygamy were inherently antithetical, earlier reformers had suggested that woman suffrage be employed to destroy polygamy. For at least three years prior to the legislation vesting the women of Utah with the political franchise, this idea had been discussed in the East. The United States Congress had gone so far as to consider enfranchising Utah women on the assumption that the women would immediately vote down polygamy. When discussed by easterners, the right of Utah women to vote was almost always seen as a means to eliminate polygamy. The assumption, as illustrated by Reconstruction legislation, was that the ballot would be used to free those in slavery from their oppressors. The argument held that plural marriage existed only where women were degraded; therefore, it would disappear if women were elevated. And political power was seen as the means of elevation. In their zeal to eradicate "the second twin relic of barbarism," many Reconstruction reformers seized the idea of having Mormon women vote.

In 1867–68 when New York suffragist Hamilton Willcox proposed experimenting with woman suffrage in the territories, he gave particular emphasis to the value of testing the idea in Utah. Not only could the system be observed in a territory where there was a large female population; but, as a fringe benefit, the Mormon system of plural wives would be eliminated.[3] The *New York Times* popularized this proposal, suggesting that perhaps the enfranchisement of Utah women would result in the casting out of polygamy as well as Mormonism. At the very least, Utah would be a good place to experiment with woman suffrage.

In the spring of 1869, when his legislation designed to enfranchise the women of the western territories stalled in Congress, Indiana Republican George Washington Julian followed Willcox's lead and limited his woman suffrage bill to Utah with the justification that women there would use the ballot to stop the practice of taking multiple wives. The Utah delegate to Congress, William Henry Hooper, spoke in favor of the bill, but it never came to a vote.

Generally, this national concern with women in Utah amused the Mormons. Assuring his readers that Utah women could be enfranchised "without running wild or becoming unsexed," George Q. Cannon, editor of the Mormon *Deseret News*, voiced approval of woman suffrage, calling it an opportunity for the Mormons to be an example to the world. The newspaper also noted that both Mormon men and women voted in the semiannual church conferences on all matters brought before the membership.

In 1869, when the subject of the women of Utah was before the national Congress, many easterners traveled to Salt Lake City on the newly completed transcontinental railroad and returned home with tales of the Mormon mecca. As one Christian worker summarized the situation for the *Chicago Advance*: Nearly all the Mormons believed in polygamy but less than one-fourth practiced it. Moreover, if the women were left to themselves nine-tenths of them "would vote it so thoroughly out of existence that it would never be heard of again."[4]

The headliners of the period who made political names for themselves, and considerable sums of money, touring the country lecturing on the Mormons were Anna Dickenson, Kate Field, and Vice-president Schuyler Colfax. Colfax, who in 1872 was himself the subject of an expose when the *New York Sun* charged him with accepting stock of the Credit Mobilier in return for political influence, delivered his lecture "Across the Continent" to numerous audiences, including members of Congress. Famous for his public piety, the Indiana politician enhanced his nickname, "the Christian Statesman," by his revelations about Mormonism.

Anna Dickenson, an advocate of woman suffrage, toured the East after her visit to Salt Lake City in 1869 in the company of the United States House of Representatives Ways and Means Committee. Her specialty at those appearances was a message of the "Whited Sepulchres" in which she depicted the condition of Mormon women as deplorable. She told of their haggard countenances, their dejected looks, and their slavish obedience. A Mormon missionary in Connecticut reported that Anna Dickenson was paid $150 for an hour and a half lecture in which she called for the nation to put down polygamy as it had Black slavery. In the years after the Civil War, Dickenson had been one of the most popular lecturers on the lyceum circuit, averaging 150 lectures a season and earning as much as $20,000 annually. Although it was just one of her regular lectures, the "Sepulchres" speech popularized the image of the degraded Utah women. Reporting the lecture success of the "incorrigible spinster," as Mormon elder John Jacques referred to Dickenson, the *Millennial Star* writer visualized a confrontation between the suffragist lecturer and her "fellow-labourer in the cause of human progress," George Francis Train. Jacques decided they "would make a magnificent team, especially when pulling in opposite directions."[5]

And opposing Anna Dickenson was exactly what George Francis Train did. Avid Democrat and friend of unconventional people and radical movements, Train had been a friend of the suffragist leaders Susan B. Anthony and Elizabeth Cady Stanton during the 1867 Kansas Suffrage campaign; later he sponsored the suffrage newspaper *Revolution*. In numerous speeches and newspaper articles he countered the critics of the Mormon marriage system. After his visit to Salt Lake City in 1869, while campaigning for the United States presidency, "Citizen Train," as he liked to be called, lectured before two thousand people in New York's Tammany Hall. As an obvious challenge to Anna Dickenson, his oration was entitled "Old Fogies of the Bible and Blackened Sepulchres." That "conglomeration of oddities and eccentricities," as the Mormon press affectionately referred to Train, was a lifelong supporter of Mormon virtues and Utah's right to statehood. In fact, he was such an avid defender of the Saints that he was once asked if he was a Mormon. He answered by declaring he had only one wife and was not a Mormon, but he was not sure that he would not become one. In 1870, while lecturing in the Salt Lake Theatre as Brigham Young's guest, Train jokingly conceded that he never committed adultery and was therefore almost a Mormon, adding, "No wonder they call me a crazy man."[6]

Train's continuing praise of Brigham Young, whom he called the "Napoleon of colonists," won Train a place in the hearts of the Mormons. Brigham Young returned Train's compliment by describing the eccentric entrepreneur as a gentleman and scholar who had brains and decency even though he would occasionally play the buffoon when it appeared profitable. When Brigham Young died in 1877, Train published a long poem in the Buffalo, New York, *Agitator* commemorating his friend and reaffirming his affection for the Mormons, ending with the following play on words:

And though too *Young* to miss the *Train*
We *never shall shake hands again!*
Tell my Utah friends to Hold the Fort
And I will guarantee support.

Through the years the Mormons were reluctant to be too closely identified with Train because of his wild campaigns in support of Woodhull and Claflin, Fenians, Paris Communards, Anarchists, and Young America, and because of his public displays such as protest fasting and his eighty-day whirl around the world that inspired Jules Verne's famous story. Nevertheless, Train continually lauded the Utah experiment with woman suffrage, campaigned for Utah statehood, and generally defended the Mormons against their defamers. But, because of Train's reputation, his defense of the Mormons did not always do them service. As an observer in the *Salt Lake Tribune* saw it, Train was inclined "to rush in with his mad force . . . and make Deseret his hobby."[7]

In this period the Mormons attracted supporters who were considered at least radical if not the lunatic fringe of eastern society. Even P. T. Barnum, master promoter of oddities, freaks, and fakes, wrote a letter to the editor of the *New York Tribune* after his trip to Salt Lake Valley in the spring of 1870, defending the Mormons against Anna Dickenson's accusations about their treatment of their women.

While "the Mormon Question," as the polygamy problem was referred to, was being aired in the press and on the lecture circuit, the idea of experimenting with woman suffrage in Utah became more popular. However the stock argument that the vote would cause women to migrate to the territory was not used in the case of Utah, both because the Mormons promoted their marital system as a means to deal with surplus women[8] and because easterners did not want to encourage more women to move to Utah because they feared they might become plural wives. On the contrary, the principal ends easterners hoped to serve by enfranchising women in the Mormon region were, first, to eliminate polygamy and, second, to experiment with the idea of woman suffrage. Even the National Woman Suffrage Association at its 1870 convention resolved that the enfranchisement of Utah women was the one safe, sure, and swift means to abolish polygamy in that territory.

Responding to the proposed experiment with the female franchise, the Mormon press cynically noted, "It is only the 'Mormons' who will suffer; they will have all the trouble, and the people of the East can look calmly on until the question is settled."[9]

Because the proposal to enfranchise Utah women was tied to the desire of many people to eliminate polygamy, the fortunes of the female franchise in Utah would rise and fall for the next twenty years with the battle over plural marriage. Additionally, women's right to vote would be argued on the local and national scene each time the question of statehood for Utah was considered.

This concern of people outside the territory for women's right to vote in Utah was the most influential force in bringing about the enfranchisement of Utah women. Nonetheless, there were women suffrage advocates in the territory. The first talk of woman suffrage within Utah was heard from a group of liberal Mormon intellectuals who published their ideas in the *Utah Magazine*, which developed into the *Mormon Tribune* that in turn became the *Salt Lake Tribune*. These Mormon reformers—the principals being William S. Godbe, Edward W. Tullidge, E. L. T. Harrison, Amasa M. Lyman, Henry W. Lawrence, William H. Shearman, and Eli B. Kelsey—created a scheme to end the economic and social insularity of the Mormon community in the Great Basin. At the time of the completion of the transcontinental railroad, these liberals suggested that the Mormons should cooperate with Gentiles[10] to develop manufacturing and mining. Mormon church officials, however, defended their policy of remaining an agricultural, self-sufficient kingdom. In addition to being estranged from Brigham Young's concept of Zion, the reformers wanted to infuse spiritualism into Mormonism. Conflict ensued, the end result of which was that Godbe and most of his followers were excommunicated or voluntarily left the church.[11]

One of the issues championed by the Godbeites was the equality of women.[12] In the next twenty-five years, the *Deseret News* often credited them with initiating the push for the enfranchisement of women. Why were these liberal Mormon men advocates of woman suffrage? All the principal leaders—except Godbe and Lawrence who were first and foremost merchants—had served as missionaries in England during the liberal era. Since most of them were directly involved in the editing of the *Millennial Star*, the Mormon newspaper there, they must have heard the arguments in favor of equality from reformers of the day such as John Stuart Mill. Godbe, on the other hand, frequently traveled to the East Coast to purchase goods for his mercantile enterprises and thus was exposed to the frequently discussed ideas of the day.

Early women's rights activities in Utah centered around the Godbe family. William S. Godbe and three of his four polygamous wives—Annie Thompson Godbe, Mary Hampton Godbe, and Charlotte Ives Cobb Godbe—were active in the women's rights movement. They made the initial contacts with eastern suffrage leaders and convened the first meeting in Utah Territory dealing with woman suffrage. Of all the people identified with the Godbeite movement, Charlotte Godbe was the most important figure in woman suffrage.

After William Godbe's excommunication all his wives left the Mormon Church except Charlotte, who did not abandon the religion because of her mother. Charlotte's mother was Augusta Adams Cobb Young, Brigham Young's fifth wife. Charlotte had been raised as one of Young's daughters, even living for a time in the Lion House. Thirty years earlier, Charlotte's mother, a member of the prominent Adams family, had fled Boston to become one of Brigham Young's wives and in so doing abandoned her husband and five of her children, taking with her six-year-old Charlotte and an infant who later died.[13]

Many years later Charlotte wrote to Wilford Woodruff, who was then president of the Mormon church, explaining that when her mother had lived in Boston she had been an acquaintance of suffragist Lucy Stone and had maintained contact with her over the years. Charlotte attributed the commencement of woman suffrage activities in Utah to her mother and reported that it had been her mother's deathbed wish that Charlotte continue the work she had begun.[14] Charlotte did make woman suffrage her life's work.

In April 1869, seven months before he excommunicated William Godbe, Brigham Young had sealed Charlotte to Godbe as his fourth wife. This marriage, which Charlotte later referred to as her "painful domestic experience in polygamy," ended ten years later with a divorce after a number of years of separation. Though she did not leave the church, Charlotte was never listed among the Mormon women speaking out for woman suffrage or protesting anti-polygamy legislation. The Mormons' refusal to accept her as one of their own may have been as much a result of her spiritualistic activities as the fact that she was married to Godbe. Nevertheless, for many years Charlotte continued her women's rights work independently, through letters to the editor and feminist speeches. In those early years she also had considerable contact with eastern suffragists.

Nearly twenty years later Charlotte recounted how she had "assumed a prominence among" the women of the national suffrage movement and been elected by them "to speak before the House Committee on this subject, and claim for all women the right [to vote]."[15] In 1871 in Boston's Fremont Temple she did speak before a large audience on woman suffrage and on "the fine and noble women" of Utah. In doing so, she became the first American woman with voting rights to address eastern suffragists. Although the ten minutes of her discourse devoted to a defense of Mormon women earned her the praise of Boston newspapers, they called down the damnation of Emmeline B. Wells, prominent leader of the polygamous women of Salt Lake City and editor of the *Woman's Exponent*, a Utah journal established in 1872 as the explicit vehicle whereby Mormon women could explain themselves to the world and report the labors of their Relief Society. In an article in the *Exponent*, Emmeline discussed Charlotte's unsuccessful polygamous marriage to Godbe and concluded that Charlotte "was not now an advocate for this principle of the Church, hence could not be a representative for the women here [in Utah]." As Charlotte later reported, "the *motive* for this I saw a year after when E.B.W. *tried* to be—what I was—a representative woman in *political* circles."[16]

The contest between Charlotte and Emmeline would continue through their long careers. Charlotte was a feminist, while Emmeline stood as the symbol of the polygamous wife. Both remained members of the Mormon church, and both worked for woman suffrage from their own point of view. Charlotte persisted because, as she often said, it was morally right for women to participate in their government. Emmeline worked for woman suffrage as a means to promote Mormon women, their Relief Society, and the church's goals such as statehood for Utah. The conflict between these two proud, effective women was constantly being renewed; when Charlotte made a feminist statement or observation about Mormon women in the national or suffrage press, Emmeline usually countered in the *Exponent*.

Like Charlotte, Annie Thompson Godbe was an active suffragist in touch with national movement leaders. She was probably the "Mrs. Godby [*sic*], wife of the leading reform advocates of Utah," who with Margaret Lucas, sister of English woman suffrage advocate Jacob Bright, was among the distinguished guests at the twentieth anniversary celebration of the inauguration of the women's rights movement held in New York City in 1870. The organizer of the meeting, Pauline W. Davis, concluded, "In Utah it [woman suffrage] is of less account [than the Wyoming example] because the women are more under a hierarchy than elsewhere, and as yet vote only as directed."[17]

Within the ranks of the Mormon faithful there were people who favored woman suffrage at this early date. In 1868 the editor of the *Deseret News* noted some justice in women's claim to the right to vote; referring to the recent enfranchisement of Black men, he noted women's intelligence and said he saw no reason why they should not be admitted to the polls also. In addition, the editor speculated, "before long, probably in Massachusetts at any rate, they will have the privilege granted to them."[18] Over the years the *Deseret News* was supportive of woman suffrage. Editors George Q. Cannon and Charles W. Penrose not only used the paper to promote woman suffrage but often pursued the cause on the lecture platform. Likewise, Franklin D. Richards, who edited the *Ogden Junction* in Utah's second city, supported woman suffrage in both arenas.

Franklin D. Richards, his wife Jane S. Richards, their son Franklin S. Richards, and the latter's wife Emily S. Tanner Richards were among the most forceful voices in favor of women's rights within the Mormon church. The Richards family frequently hosted eastern suffragists during their stopovers in Utah; and since Frankin S. was often in the national capital in his role as attorney for the church, he and Emily had occasion to make the acquaintance of prominent suffragists. As a worker for women's rights, Emily would serve on the Board of Lady Managers of the 1892 World's Fair in Chicago and as a delegate to the International Council of Women. Ultimately she would be the initiator of the organization of the first woman suffrage association in Utah in 1888.

When the question of extending the vote to women was considered by the Utah Territorial Legislature in 1870 national attention was focused on the Mormons. Vice-president Colfax was carrying out a vigorous anti-

Mormon newspaper and lecture campaign. At the same time, Congress was inundated with legislation relating to the Mormons. As George A. Smith noted in a letter to his cousin Hannah P. Butler, "I understand about a dozen bills have been presented to the Congress in relation to Utah." These bills varied from schemes to partition Utah, giving segments to the surrounding territories and states, to proposals disfranchising the Mormons, disqualifying them from holding public office and sitting on juries, depriving them of the right to homestead or preempt public lands, or disinheriting their children.[19]

But the legislation that sparked the greatest response in Mormondom was that introduced by the chairman of the House Committee on Territories, Shelby M. Cullom. He sponsored a bill designed to enforce the anti-polygamy law of 1862. In a letter to William H. Hooper, Utah's delegate to congress, Brigham Young assessed reaction to the Cullom bill, saying: "Our sisters here are in high dudgeon over it."[20] During the first week of January 1870 the women of the Fifteenth Ward in Salt Lake City met to express their opposition to Cullom's legislation. With Sarah M. Kimball presiding, the women unanimously protested the bill and resolved to bring their moral influence to bear against it. A Sister Smith even demanded of the governor that women be allowed to vote. At the close of the meeting Eliza R. Snow, who had successively been married to Joseph Smith, Jr., and Brigham Young and was recognized as the voice of the Mormon leadership on subjects relating to women, suggested that the example of the women of the Fifteenth Ward be followed by the sisterhood throughout the territory.[21]

On January 13 "a great indignation meeting" was held at the Old Tabernacle on Temple Square. Despite the inclement weather over 5,000 women of all ages rallied to hear their sisters decry Cullom's "mean, foul legislation." For the next six weeks women throughout the territory responded to the call to voice their objection to Congressman Cullom's proposal. From Providence in the north to Manti in the south, mass meetings of women were convened to sustain resolutions protesting the proposed legislation. These gatherings demonstrated how effectively the church organizational structure could be utilized to gather and to display support for a cause. In subsequent years this tactic would be used frequently.

Referring to "the great indignation meeting" as one of the grandest female assemblages in all history, the *New York Herald* editorialized:

> It will not be denied that the Mormon women have both brains and tongues. Some of the speeches give evidence that in general knowledge, in logic, and in rhetoric the so-called degraded ladies of Mormondom are quite equal to the women's rights women of the East.[22]

Most eastern newspapers of the day had some positive comments to make about Mormon women as a result of these mass meetings. The New York *Journal of Commerce* confessed that the arguments presented by the women in Utah were fully up to the mark of the best efforts of Mrs. Mott, Mrs. Stanton, Miss Anthony, or any of the female suffrage women who were trying to stir up public sentiment east of the Rocky Mountains.[23]

Against this background, the Utah Legislative Assembly considered the advisability of extending the ballot to women. Though the council aired some reservations, after two weeks of discussion members of both houses, by unanimous vote, passed a bill enfranchising women.[24] The motives behind the approval of this bill were explained to Congress by Delegate William H. Hooper:

> To convince the country how utterly without foundation the popular assertions were concerning the women of the Territory, some members of the Legislative Assembly were in favor of passing the law; . . . others favored it, convinced of its propriety by the arguments of the friends of the great political reform.[25]

On February 12, 1870, Territorial Secretary S. A. Mann, serving as acting governor, signed into law the act conferring the elective franchise upon women twenty-one years of age or older who had resided in the territory six months, were born or naturalized in the United States, or were the wives, widows, or daughters of native-born or naturalized citizens. Though he expressed his personal doubts as to the wisdom of this legislation, Mann justified his signing of the bill by the unanimous legislative vote.

Mann was not a Mormon, yet he was popular with the Saints.[26] His prompt signing of this legislation endeared him to the women, who quickly convened a meeting and drew up a resolution expressing their appreciation. The resolution was delivered to Mann by a delegation of women headed by poet Eliza R. Snow. In response he penned a letter philosophizing about the intelligent use of the ballot, cautioning that the application of woman suffrage in Utah would "be watched with profound interest, for upon its consistent and harmonious working depends in a great measure its universal adoption in the Republic."[27]

Mormon faithful William Clayton was less philosophical when he noted, "the poor, enslaved downtrodden!!! women of Utah can now act for themselves and take revenge on the men of Israel." But as Clayton gleefully observed, those who expected the Mormon women to use the vote against polygamy would "gnash their teeth with rage" and "foam worse than ever," for "there are not many women here but will sustain all the measures of the authorities better than some of the men do."[28]

Once the news was out, messages came in commending the Mormons for their action. "Congratulations. Woman Suffrage, Greenbacks, Protection, Morality, Temperance, Statesmanship, Presidential Platform." So read the telegram sent by that perennial friend of the Mormons, George Francis Train, upon the passage of the bill. Brigham Young's reply to Train was a cautious, "Family and friends all well. Return congratulations. Truth, liberty, happiness, and mountain air are lovely and desirable."

The British press reacted differently. The *London Daily Telegraph* rhetorically addressed its comments to philosopher John Stuart Mill and asked how the women of Utah could vote yet sustain plural marriage, as "the great indignation meeting" appeared to do.

Two days after the act was signed into law, municipal elections were held in Salt Lake City, and, according to Brigham Young, twenty-five women exercised their newly gained right to vote. Reportedly, Seraph Young, Brigham's niece, was the first woman to cast her ballot.[30] The *New York Globe* summarized the historic occasion:

A morning dispatch informs us that the women of Utah vote to-day, since female suffrage has become a law in that territory. We expect they will go to the polls in a quiet orderly, lady-like manner, and deposit their votes without any jeers or opposition from the gentlemen. If this thing can be done in the "wicked and immoral" city of Salt Lake, where women are supposed to be held in less estimation than they are in the high-toned and healthy cities of New York and Boston, why may it not be accomplished in every town and hamlet in the Union? That the women of Utah will to-day vote to abolish polygamy, we do not expect. They are as much in favor of that system as the men. It is wrong to expect this of women of Utah, and it will be unfair to call female suffrage a failure if they do refuse to abolish polygamy. The question, however, is not up for decision.[31]

Woman suffrage was a reality in Utah Territory. Mormon women had registered their dismay with the Cullom bill and in so doing had, to a degree, sustained the patriarchal family system of multiple wives practiced by the Saints. Now the Mormons were able to say to the world that women were not held in bondage but were free, thinking beings willingly participating in plural marriage. Nevertheless, Senator Cullom continued to push for legislation to abolish polygamy. When the House approved his bill, many newspapers talked of imminent war if it became law. Back in Zion, Mormon military regiments drilled while committees throughout the territory held mass meetings of men and women to draw up remonstrances protesting the pending legislation as tyrannical.[32]

These mass meetings were well planned and aimed for long-range results. Acting under Brigham Young's direction, Daniel H. Wells corresponded with Delegate Hooper, advising him that John T. Caine would be arriving in Washington, D. C., to deliver proceedings of the mass meetings and to assist Hooper with some "efficient aid, by forming public opinion through the press and otherwise, not only paving the way towards the defeat of the Cullom bill in the Senate, but also in the matter of our admission as a State into the Union."[33]

As agitation against the "second twin relic of barbarism" reached a high pitch in the national capital, even the Godbeites, who had been excommunicated from the Mormon church or had left voluntarily, met with non-Mormon friends at the Masonic Hall in Salt Lake City to draft a memorial to the Senate asking for a modification of the most obnoxious portions of the Cullom bill as passed by the House. Most attending the meeting voiced their objection to polygamy but noted that the proposed legislation against it appeared unjust and overly severe

The House of Representatives had approved the bill after amending it to remove the sections empowering the president to send troops to Utah. And although Utah women had been enfranchised less than three months, a clause had been added to Cullom's bill withdrawing that privilege. This section of the legislation would have deprived the women of suffrage and the right to serve on juries. Senator Cullom was pushing hard; he had tried to make it the official mission of the Republican party to eradicate polygamy along with slavery. However, the Senate adjourned for the summer without acting on the matter.

During the summer of 1870, national concern about the Mormons was amplified by the agitation of Rev. J. P. Newman, Methodist preacher and chaplain of the United States Senate. In reaction to the Cullom bill debates and Delegate Hooper's defense of polygamy, Newman delivered numerous speeches in Washington, D. C., against polygamy. That summer he appeared in Salt Lake City to challenge Brigham Young to debate the question of whether or not the Bible sanctions polygamy. Young refused Newman's challenge, but Orson Pratt did present the Mormon view in a debate staged in the Salt Lake Tabernacle. Upon returning to the national capital, Newman's wife organized a Woman's Christian Association for the benefit of Utah women with a Mrs. Hollister, Vice-president Colfax's sister, in charge of the activities of the association in Salt Lake City.[34]

Six months after the passage of the act permitting Utah women to vote, and amid talk of having the legislation pronounced unconstitutional by the territorial supreme court, the women of Utah went to the polls to cast their ballots in territorial elections. Despite a considerable amount of what men referred to as "good humored chaffing," a large number of women entered the polling places through the separate women's entrances and cast their votes. A few individualists took their feminism seriously and voted for women for public office. "One lady voted for a lady to be a Commissioner to locate University Lands, also for one to be a Representative in the Territorial Legislature, and for one to be County Treasurer."[35] A visiting observer was not impressed. As he saw it, "the Mormon women cared but little for the privilege of voting and cast their ballots just as their Bishops directed."[36]

No doubt many Mormon women were ambivalent about their newly gained political role; some were even openly opposed to women taking part in political affairs. The minutes of women's meetings in the Salt Lake City Fifteenth Ward reflect the full spectrum of views on voting. Some women clearly declared themselves for women's rights; some said they had little interest in politics but would vote "for good men in office not enemies." Others admitted they had always considered politics beneath women and were thus not interested in voting.[37]

Brigham Young's analysis of Utah women's first experience at the polls was that the ladies of Mormondom had gone "forth in force and voted for the only man who raised his voice in the Halls of Congress in defense of a pluralities of wives"[38]—William H. Hooper. In short, the women had used their political power to affirm the institution of polygamy by reelecting Hooper. It is doubtful that this was a conscious affirmation on the part of women. Hooper was, after all, an aggressive advocate of woman suffrage during his days as delegate to Congress.

Reportedly, it was Hooper, possibly inspired by Charlotte Godbe, who had proposed the idea of granting Utah women the franchise in 1869 when Congress was considering imposing female suffrage on Utah. Hooper was also credited with engineering the signing of the bill by Acting Governor Mann. Hooper, who was in Washington when the territorial legislature passed the enfranchising bill, allegedly persuaded Thomas Fitch, congressman from Nevada, to telegraph Mann to sign the bill. Gov. J. Wilson Shaffer, who was also in Washington, was about to instruct Mann to veto the bill when Hooper and Fitch convinced him that the whole woman suffrage thing was a hoax.[39]

While the Mormons pointed to the reality of women voting in Utah as a refutation of Anna Dickenson's "Whited Sepulchres" and "Woman's Cry from Utah" speeches, Hamilton Willcox, in a *Revolution* article, insisted that women's enfranchisement had sealed polygamy's doom. Utah women held their future in their own hands, he said; therefore, Congress should let Utah alone. At the same time, the *Revolution* articles objected to the Cullom bill since it had been altered to take the right of suffrage from Utah women.

At this juncture the Mormons repeatedly reminded Congress that the idea of enfranchising women in Utah had been first pursued by Congress and that the territorial legislature had passed its female franchise act at the very time that similar measures were being considered in Washington. "Bah!" was the *Salt Lake Herald's* response to the frequently heard accusation that the Mormon-dominated legislature had given the women the vote as a means of strengthening their potential power against non-Mormons in Utah.

Still, most analysts see the reason for the enfranchisement of Utah women solely in terms of the dynamics within the territory, and most accept the theory that it resulted from an effort on the part of the Mormons to increase their political power in hopes of keeping political control out of the hands of non-Mormons. As Alan P. Grimes argues in his *Puritan Ethic and Woman Suffrage*, "Women voters were not so much pawns in this struggle as reserve troops to be called upon when needed."[40]

One contemporary version credits Brigham Young—supposedly afraid of the influx of miners into the territory—with devising the scheme of granting the right to vote to women:

> Capitalists and prospectors multiplied. The wily deceiver then evolved from his narrow soul the magnanimous scheme of *enfranchising the women*. The Mormon legislature passed the bill. The Gentile miners were mostly unmarried men, or had left their families in the East. Every Mormon citizen thus had his civil power extended in correspondence with his numerous alliances.[41]

Certainly, some Mormons may have feared that the territory would be overrun by outsiders once the railroad provided easy access. Nevertheless, at the time the woman suffrage legislation was passed in 1870, the territory's population was 87,000—less than 4,500 of whom were non-Mormons.[42] Although the *Deseret News* admitted that such an influx was possible, it did "not anticipate such a result." Even when the non-Mormon population did increase, the Mormons securely maintained their political superiority. During the final twenty-five territorial years, the Mormon men alone outnumbered the non-Mormon men four to one. If there were already more than four Mormon voters for every non-Mormon voter, it obviously was not necessary to double the Mormon electorate by giving women the vote. "Reserve troops" would never be needed, not even if the men who practiced polygamy (probably around one-fourth of the total Mormon men) were disfranchised. Speculation based solely on events within the territory might, instead, lead to the conclusion that the Mormon leaders, shaken by the liberal schism, were not afraid of growing non-Mormon political power but were questioning their own ability to maintain Mormon political solidarity.

Though motives for enfranchising the women of Utah can be found within the territory and within the Mormon structure, the most compelling reasons were external: the need to counter the image of downtrodden Mormon women, thus stemming the tide of anti-polygamy legislation, and the desire to find lobbying power and congressional support in the move to achieve statehood. Some astute Mormon politicians saw that the enfranchisement of women in Utah territory would rally the eastern-based woman suffrage organizations and congressmen favorable to women voting and that these lobbyists would counter attempts by some members of Congress to pass legislation designed to eradicate polygamy. The Mormon leaders also saw the possibility that this same women suffrage lobby could be recruited to assist with statehood. As George Q. Cannon, the Utah delegate to Congress following Hooper, summarized it, "The extension of suffrage to our women was a most excellent measure. It brought to our aid the friends of women suffrage."[43]

If motives derived from the Mormons' relationship with the larger American society and the federal government are accepted, then Mormon women and eastern suffragists were pawns, not reserve voting troops. The woman suffrage movement gave the Mormons a national stage upon which they could demonstrate that polygamous wives were intelligent beings capable of thinking for themselves and therefore willing participants in plural marriage, not the downtrodden slaves painted by lecture-bureau circuit riders.

National suffrage leaders carefully watched the Utah experiment. Susan B. Anthony and Elizabeth Cady Stanton of the National Woman Suffrage Association were particularly concerned. The "maidenly Susan B." and the "motherly Stanton," as the *Deseret News* referred to them, visited Utah in the 1870s to see firsthand what impact the ballot in the hands of women was having. Stanton held a five-hour meeting with a large gathering of Mormon women in the Old Tabernacle. Having discussed various possible marital arrangements, Stanton concluded that none was ideal from the female point of view. She talked openly of what would be termed "family planning" today. She advised Mormon women that "quality rather quantity" should be sought in their offspring and that they should not become mothers oftener than once in five years. Subsequently, Stanton was barred from Mormon podiums.

From 1870, when women were enfranchised in Utah, until 1887 when Congress took the vote from Utah women with the Edmunds-Tucker Act, the National Woman Suffrage Association lobbied Congress in defense of Utah women's rights. Belva Lockwood, the first woman lawyer to be permitted to practice before the Supreme Court, led the suffragists' defense of Mormon women in Washington. As Lockwood saw it, the fight against the numerous bills designed to "elevate" women of Utah and "relieve" them from their "bondage" by repealing the territorial act giving them the franchise was "not only a fight for 'Mormon' female votes—it is a contest for women's equal rights on principle."[44] While national suffrage leaders such as Anthony and Lockwood were defending Mormon women's rights, anti-polygamy associations that were closely tied to the early Women's Christian Temperance Union were campaigning against women voting in Utah. The issue came to full boil in 1887 when Congress disfranchised Utah women.

In 1895 during the Utah Constitutional Convention the hottest subject of debate was the woman suffrage question. Should the Utah State Constitution define the electorate to include women? Most Mormons said yes and most non-Mormons said no. One articulate Mormon, the delegate from Davis County, Brigham Henry Roberts (also known for his work as a historian), aggressively opposed women voting. First, he said, it would endanger statehood; but, when pushed, he admitted that he did not believe women should be involved in politics. Roberts's "manly stand" made him a hero in some circles. In recognition of his efforts against woman suffrage, he received bouquets of roses from anonymous admirers and members' privileges for thirty days at the all-male Alta Club in Salt Lake City.

In response, the Utah Woman Suffrage Association rallied its supporters. Franklin S. Richards and Orson F. Whitney, another historian, debated against Roberts. The final decision was in favor of including woman suffrage in the constitution which became effective when Utah became a state in 1896.[45] With statehood, women in Utah gained full voting privileges. Women in the surrounding states of Wyoming, Colorado, and Idaho also were permitted to vote in 1896, but it would be another twenty-four years before the Nineteenth Amendment would be ratified making it illegal to deny access to the polling place on the basis of one's sex in all states of the Union.

The national suffragists' experience with the question of woman suffrage in Utah helped to move them closer to what is referred to as the Victorian Compromise and preoccupation with the franchise. The National Woman Suffrage Association—which had been most critical of the monogamous marital system—had been pressured, as William L. O'Neill has said, not to allow the organization to be used by Victoria Woodhull to promote free love. Likewise, moderate suffragists objected to Belva Lockwood defending Mormon women in words often interpreted as a defense of plural marriage. For two decades the National Woman Suffrage Association championed Utah women's right to vote and in so doing damaged its image. That wing of the suffrage movement was discredited because of its identification with the nontraditional family structure and its critiques of monogamous marriage. Faced with attacks from all sides if they attempted to analyze the traditional family structure, women's rights advocates began at the turn of the century to confine themselves more and more to one subject—the vote. Suffrage became the panacea. Thus, a feminist ideology of woman's role in society, which might have resulted in a much greater change in society than woman suffrage produced, was not forthcoming.

Notes

1. The single most comprehensive, basic source of original material on the woman suffrage movement in the United States is the six-volume *History of Woman Suffrage* edited by Elizabeth Cady Stanton, Susan B. Anthony, Matilda J. Gage, and Ida H. Harper and originally published during 1881–1922 (reprint ed., New York: Arno, 1969). Chapter 66 of volume 4 is devoted to activities in Utah, based on information provided by Emmeline B. Wells and Emily S. Richards. An analysis entitled *Woman Suffrage and Politics: The Inner Story of the Suffrage Movement* by Carrie Chapman Catt and Nettie Rogers Shuler was published in 1923; recently it was reprinted with an introduction by T. A. Larson (Seattle: University of Washington, 1969). Pauline W. Davis's small volume, *A History of the National Woman's Rights Movement* (New York, 1871), reprinted by Source Book Press in 1970, is a good source of details on woman suffrage for the years 1870–71. William L. O'Neill, *Everyone Was Brave: The Rise and Fall of Feminism in America* (Chicago: Quadrangle, 1969), presents an interesting analysis of suffrage. The two best interpretive studies of woman suffrage are Eleanor Flexner's *Century of Struggle: The Woman's Rights Movement in the United States* (Cambridge, Mass.: Harvard University, 1958) which is an institutional study and Aileen Kraditor's ideological study, *The Ideas of the Woman's Suffrage Movement, 1890–1920* (New York: Columbia University, 1965).

    Susa Young Gates brought together most of the information on woman suffrage in Utah that found its way into official histories of the suffrage movement in the United States. Additional information can be found in the Susa Young Gates Collection at the Utah State Historical Society, Salt Lake City. Kate B. Carter compiled selections from newspapers, histories, and summary accounts, especially those of Gates, on woman suffrage in the West for volume 5 of *Heart Throbs of the West* (Salt Lake City: Daughters of Utah Pioneers, 1944). Ralph Lorenzo Jack's "Woman Suffrage in Utah as an Issue in the Mormon and Non-Mormon Press of the Territory, 1870–1887" (M.S. thesis, Brigham Young University, 1954) does not attempt to analyze the woman suffrage activities in detail, but it does demonstrate how the two sides used the idea of woman suffrage to promote their cause. In her February 14, 1974, Charles Redd Lecture at Brigham Young University, Jean B. White detailed the events surrounding the inclusion of woman suffrage in the Utah constitution. See "Woman's Place Is in the Constitution: The Struggle for Equal Rights in Utah in 1895," *Utah Historical Quarterly* 42 (1974): 344–69. In *The Puritan Ethic and Woman Suffrage* (New York: Oxford, 1967), which deals primarily with woman suffrage in the West, Alan P. Grimes, employing status anxiety techniques similar to those developed by Richard Hofstader, argues that "the constituency granting woman suffrage was composed of those who also supported prohibition and immigration restriction and felt woman suffrage would further their enactment." In his article, "An Experiment in Progressive Legislation: The Granting of Woman Suffrage in Utah in 1870," *Utah Historical Quarterly* 38 (1970): 20–30, Thomas Alexander argues that the Mormons were progressive, ahead of their time in supporting woman suffrage.

2. T. A. Larson has made the most detailed study of suffrage in Wyoming. The most thoroughly documented version of his analysis is "Emancipating the West's Dolls, Vassals, Hapless Drudges: The Origins of Woman Suffrage in the West," in Roger Daniels, ed., *Essays in Western History in Honor of T. A. Larson* (Laramie: University of Wyoming, 1971), 1–16.

3. In an 1871 article in *Revolution* (New York), Willcox gave the Universal Franchise Association, of which he was a leading member, credit for woman suffrage in Utah. Three years later in an address before the House Committee on Territories he publicly took credit for originating the idea of enfranchising Utah women; George Q. Cannon admitted that Willcox's statement was substantially correct. See *Sacramento Union*, January 14, 1874; *Woman's Journal* (Boston), January 24, 1874.

4. "Journal History of the Church," July 5, 1869, Archives Division, Historical Department, Church of Jesus Christ of Latter-day Saints, Salt Lake City.

5. *Millennial Star* (Liverpool, England), October 1869, 683.

6. *Deseret News*, July 23, 1870.

7. *Salt Lake Tribune*, November 23, 1871.

8. In both England and the United States in the second half of the nineteenth century considerable discussion centered on what was called the "surplus women problem." While society was resisting efforts by some to allow women greater independence and fuller participation, it was also concerned about the

excess number of females over males. In a culture that prescribed that woman's role was to serve as mother and wife in a monogamous family, the fact that there were more women of marriageable age than men was a real problem. Immigration to the United States was seen by some as one alternative.

In their proselyting efforts in England, the Mormons capitalized on this problem by actively seeking female converts and advertising the opportunities for prosperity and social mobility in America. However, they never officially proposed polygamous marriage as a solution to the "surplus women problem." Instead, they consistently defended plural marriage in terms of religious conscience. The *Deseret News*, nevertheless, printed countless articles on the subject of surplus women and reprinted stories from all over the world on the problem.

9.   *Deseret News*, March 18, 1869.

10.   "Gentile" was used by Mormons to describe anyone outside their faith.

11.   Leonard J. Arrington, *Great Basin Kingdom: An Economic History of the Latter-day Saints, 1830–1900* (Cambridge, Mass.: Harvard University Press, 1958), 243–44. The July 1871 *Phrenological Journal* ran a detailed biographical article on the "Leaders of the Mormon Reform Movement—with Portraits." A more recent analysis of the Godbeites is Ronald W. Walker, "The Commencement of the Godbeite Protest: Another View," *Utah Historical Quarterly* 42 (1974): 216–44.

12.   "Manifesto from W. S. Godbe and E. L. T. Harrison," *Utah Magazine*, November 27, 1869, 470–73. The 1869 issues of the magazine carried a number of articles in support of women's rights.

13.   Mary Cable, "She Who Shall Be Nameless," *American Heritage*, February 1965, 50–55.

14.   Kirby to Woodruff, February 16, 1869, Incoming Letters, Wilford Woodruff Papers, LDS Archives.

15.   Kirby to Woodruff, February 5, 1889.

16.   Ibid.

17.   Davis, *A History of the National Woman's Rights Movement*, 25; see also 4–5.

18.   *Deseret News*, December 2, 1868.

19.   Smith to Butler, February 1, 1870, in "Journal History."

20.   Young to Hooper, January 11, 1870, Young Letterbooks, Brigham Young Papers, LDS Archives.

21.   Riverside Stake, Fifteenth Ward Relief Society Minutes, January 6, 1870, LDS Archives. This ward was in the Salt Lake Stake until 1940. See also *Deseret News*, January 11, 1870.

22.   *New York Herald*, January 23, 1870.

23.   *New York Evening Express*, January 26, 1870.

24.   For details of the legislature's considerations and the actions of Deseret's "ghost government," see Alexander, "An Experiment in Progressive Legislation," 25–26.

25. Hooper's speech before the House on January 29, 1873, was reported in the *Deseret News*, February 14, 1873.

26. George A. Smith to J. S. Harris, May 27, 1870, in "Journal History."

27. Mann to Eliza R. Snow, Bathsheba W. Smith, Marinda M. Hyde, Phoebe W. Woodruff, Amelia H. Young et al., February 19, 1870, Mann Papers, LDS Archives.

28. Clayton to Brother Jesse and Clayton to Brother East, February 13, 1870, Clayton Letterbooks, microfilm, LDS Archives.

29. "Journal History," May 14, 1870.

30. *Deseret News*, February 15, 1870.

31. *New York Globe*, February 14, 1870.

32. "Journal History," March 26, 29, 1870.

33. Wells to Hooper, April 2, 1870, Young Letterbooks.

34. *Deseret News*, May 17, 1871; "Journal History," August 8, 12 and October 20, 1870.

35. *Deseret News*, August 3, 1870.

36. Wilford H. Munro, "Among the Mormons in the Days of Brigham Young," *Proceedings of the American Antiquarian Society*, new series 36, October 1926, 229.

37. Fifteenth Ward Relief Society Minutes, July 20, 1871; see also January 6 and February 19, 1870.

38. *Millennial Star*, August 30, 1870, 550.

39. "William H. Hooper, the Utah Delegate and Female Advocate," *Phrenological Journal*, November 1870, 330–31; see also Kirby to Woodruff, February 5, 1889.

40. Grimes, *The Puritan Ethic and Woman Suffrage*, 41.

41. U. S., Congress, Senate, 49th Cong., 1st sess., 1886, *Miscellaneous Documents*, 122:3.

42. The 1880 census data show that there were 120,000 Mormons in Utah and 24,000 other residents.

43. Cannon made similar comments on a number of occasions, but his most revealing statement is in his letter of February 7, 1880, to John Taylor, Mormon church president, in George Q. Cannon Papers, LDS Archives.

44. See Belva A. Lockwood's speech before the National Woman Suffrage Association, January 24, 1883, as printed in the *Ogden Daily Herald* of June 9, 1883.

45. For an analysis of the constitutional convention debate see White, "Woman's Place Is in the Constitution," 344–69.

In the beauty of the lilies, Christ was born across the sea,
With a glory in His bosom that transfigures you and me;
As He died to make men holy let us die to make men free;
    While God is marching on.

Julia Ward Howe.

EQUAL RIGHTS.

TUNE:—"Hail Columbia."

RISE, Columbia's daughters, rise;
Heaven has surely heard your cries,
Yet to the world we must appeal.
Arise, ye mothers of the race,
Enjoy your heaven-appointed place,
Demand the rights the world accords
Freely to "creation's lords,"
Now let woman's watchword be—
"Equal Rights and Liberty."

CHORUS:

    Sisters, brave of heart and true,
    Now for simple justice sue;
    Claim the birthright of the free—
    "Equal Rights and Liberty."

Shall we longer count as naught,
Rights for which our fathers fought?
The rights which all their sons enjoy?
Can impartial justice sleep?
Servile silence shall we keep?
Need we bear for evermore
All our wrongs so deep and sore?
Why should women still be banned
Virtual slaves, in freedom's land?

CHORUS:

"Equal Rights," for small and great;
"Equal Rights," whate'er our state—
No more, no less than this we claim.
Let others think 'tis woman's fate
Always submissively to wait ;
For equity we'll still contend,
And work to gain the wish'd for end.
Take courage, friends, and don't forget—
That "Equal Rights" await us yet.

CHORUS:

Emily H. Woodmansee.

WOMAN, ARISE.

TUNE:—"Hope of Israel."

FREEDOM'S daughter, rouse from slumber;
    See, the curtains are withdrawn
Which so long thy mind hath shrouded ;
    Lo ! thy day begins to dawn.

CHORUS:

    Woman, 'rise, thy penance o'er,
    Sit thou in the dust no more;
    Seize the scepter, hold the van,
    Equal with thy brother, man.

Truth and virtue be thy motto,
    Temp'rance, liberty and peace,
Light shall shine and darkness vanish,
    Love shall reign, oppression cease.

CHORUS: Woman, 'rise, etc.

Cover and sample pages from *Utah Woman Suffrage Song Book. Courtesy of Archives, Historical Department, Church of Jesus Christ of Latter-day Saints.*

8

A Feminist among the Mormons

Charlotte Ives Cobb Godbe Kirby

BEVERLY BEETON

Charlotte Ives Cobb Godbe Kirby, who held that the question of one's sex did not prevent the full and free expression of intelligence, was a feminist of the nineteenth century.[1] A woman who fought for the rights of all women, Charlotte urged women to stand by each other and work unitedly for the whole of womanhood. This message of union she delivered to a suffrage meeting at Boston's Fremont Temple and to a congregation of the Church of Jesus Christ of Latter-day Saints in the Mormon Tabernacle in Logan, Utah. Charlotte was a feminist, a suffragist, a plural wife, a Mormon.

She was one of the first in Utah Territory to speak in favor of the enfranchisement of women; as early as 1869 she was arguing for equal political rights for women. While forcefully articulating the case for women's rights, Charlotte remained a member of the Mormon church. As the letters[2] addressed to the president of the Church of Jesus Christ of Latter-day Saints, Wilford Woodruff, demonstrate, her religion was important to her.

Both her piety and her close attachment to her mother caused Charlotte to remain close to the church. Her mother, Augusta Adams Cobb Young, was Mormon leader Brigham Young's fifth wife. In the 1840s Augusta, a

First published in *Utah Historical Quarterly* 59 (Winter 1991): 22–31. Reprinted by permission.

Charlotte Cobb Godbe Kirby. *Utah State Historical
Society. All rights reserved. Used by permission.*

member of the prominent Adams family, had fled Boston to become one of Young's wives. At that time she abandoned her husband and five of their children, taking with her six-year-old Charlotte and an infant who later died. Charlotte was raised as one of Young's daughters and lived for a time in Brigham Young's Lion House with his polygamous wives and their children.

In April 1869 Charlotte was married and according to Mormon practice "sealed for time and all eternity" to William S. Godbe. She was one of Godbe's four wives. This marriage, which Charlotte later described as her "painful domestic experience in polygamy," ended in divorce ten years later after several years of separation. Though she did not leave the church when Godbe was excommunicated, shortly after their marriage, Charlotte was never listed by the Mormons as one of their women promoting woman suffrage or protesting anti-polygamy legislation even though she did both. The Mormons' refusal to accept her as one of their own may have been as much a result of her involvement in spiritualism as the fact that she was married to Godbe.

In 1884, a few years after her divorce from Godbe, Charlotte married a wealthy non-Mormon mine owner by the name of John Kirby who was twenty years younger than she was. Living the remainder of her life in Salt Lake City, until her death in 1908, Charlotte continued her campaign for women's rights, especially woman suffrage. She made speeches, wrote letters to editors, and lobbied politicians on the local and national scene to unite women and gain support for women's political rights.

Charlotte was actively working for woman suffrage in Utah and on the national scene in 1870 when women in Utah Territory were first granted the right to vote as a result of legislation passed by the territorial legislature, in 1887 when the United States Congress in an effort to eliminate polygamy took the vote from women in Utah, and in 1896 when Utah joined the Union with a constitution that once again enfranchised women. In 1889, at a time when Utah women were trying to regain the right to vote, Charlotte sought to have her leadership in the movement recognized by Utah women and LDS church officials. Over the years she had vied for the leadership role on suffrage issues with Emmeline B. Wells, and in 1889 she thought she was a better leader because she was not a polygamous wife as Wells was. The following letters are Charlotte's own account of her suffrage work from 1869 to 1889.

Salt Lake City Feb 5/89

Pres. [Wilford] Woodruff,

I hope you will pardon me, for troubling you with a matter that may be of no interest to you. Since it is a matter of history & of importance to me,

& I do not know, whom to communicate with unless it be the President of the Church, in which I was reared, & of which I am still a member.

A number of years ago as long as when Capt[ain] Hooper[3] was our Delegate to Congress, I being East at the time, took an active interest in Woman's Suffrage, & th'ro[ugh] a personal influence used among my relatives & friends in Washington, New York, & Boston, also letters I wrote to leading papers, & words I spoke at conventions of W.[oman] S.[uffrage] Meetings, assisted *indirectly* perhaps in helping the bill to pass which gave to the women of Utah the right to *Vote.* Capt[ain] Hooper wrote to me a note, while sitting in the Gallery of the House, (he being on the floor) "Persevere in the spirit you now are & you will not only bless yourself—but the Community among whom you were reared." I persevered & became a member of the W.[oman] S.[uffrage] A.[ssociation]. The bill passed which made *me* a literal representative of the question that my sister women in the U.[nited] S.[tates] were only theorizing about, hence I at once assumed a prominence among them, was elected at the next convention to speak before the House Committee on this subject, & claim for all women the right I have had bestowed upon me. (Some years later when it was known here). Postmaster General Howe[4] & his good wife were my friends, he was chairman of the Committee on Territories. I *know* my words to him influenced him favorably in his decision on Utah affairs, at this time.

I spoke at a W.[oman] S.[uffrage] Convention in Boston, before thousands of people in Fremont Temple. The evening being given to Wendall Phillips,[5] & Mary A. Livermore,[6] they insisted that I take half an hour, & speak of Suffrage for *all* women, I told them I would speak twenty minutes for W.[oman] S.[uffrage] if they would let me speak ten minutes for the pure & noble women I knew in Utah, they consented, & I never spoke better in my life, for *both* causes,—

The Boston papers next morning said, in criticism "The Mormon women are fortunate in having so brave a champion as M*rs* Charlotte Ives Godbe and they would do well to send her to the coming Congress for Women as a Delegate." This was read in Utah by a *little* woman Ed.[itor] of a little paper[7] pub.[lished] in Salt Lake City, she immediately took her pen in hand to show *why* I was not eligible to such an office, & *cruelly* gave to the *world* thro'[ugh] the same paper—that had kindly criticized me,—my painful domestic experience in polygamy, adding that I was not now an advocate for this principle of the church, hence could not be a representative for the women here. This did much *harm* to the course I was advocating, Woman Suffrage in Utah, & M*rs* Livermore said to me "is this one of your *grand* women, you spoke so eloquently of at the meeting in Fremont Temple?" The *motive* for

this I saw a year after when she E.[mmeline] B.[lanche] W.[ells] *tried* to be—
what I was—a representative woman in *political circles*, it was not, that I was
not doing a good work in this way for Utah. Prejudice melted before me, &
I made many influential friends beat down the b[ar]riers & made it possible
for those women who followed me, to speak at these conventions. For *ten*
years she has *systematically mis*represented me, & *never* has my name appeared
in her *little* paper with credit. Altho[ugh] she would Eulogize, the women I
had made friends to Utah's question.

Belva Lockwood[8] was *very* much prejudiced, when I first met her,
gradually this worked away, & the next year after my return to Utah, she wrote
me a letter saying "Get a petition signed by some of your most influential
women protesting against the Suffrage being taken from you, & I will see
that it is *not thrown under the table.*" I took it to a meeting in the 15th Ward,
& asked the privilege of reading it. Sister [Isabella M.] Horne & a few of
the sisters presiding looked at it, & then invited Zina Young, Aunt Zina's[9]
daughter to read it—it was a *Lawyer's* penmanship, & with great difficulty
she made out to get at the *point* of the letter; it was then handed back to me,
no comments. But there was *one* who saw the *points*, she, E[m]meline Wells,
immediately set about raising money to *buy* my friend; & our poor sisters
were called upon to donate to this fund five hundred dollars, to pay Belva,
for doing that which she had offered me to do for nothing.

It is just such things as these that has made me more confident in the
decernment of many Mormon women,—I always seem to know by instinct,
whom it *will do* to trust, & people who are true to *themselves*, will usually
be true to everybody else. I wish women could loose *themselves*, for a time in
great questions, as men do, & work for the *question* at issue, & not *all* want to
be *Generals!* But up hold the hands of *any* woman who is doing good work
for their side. I have been reading of late with interest, The leaves from your
Journal, published. & the *unity* that existed between the founders of this
Faith, must have been one cause of its establishment then.

A movement is now made for a W.[oman] S.[uffrage] A.[ssociation] of
Utah,[10] I have been invited to join, & while *I do not wish* to be a General,
I would like some respect shown me, as the first woman, who spoke for
W.[oman] S.[uffrage] for Utah, and as an earnest worker in the cause for
several years, & the *dis*ability—Mrs E.[mmeline] B.[lanche] W.[ells] tried to
show ten years ago, *now* forms my *ability* in working for this cause. Had I
have been *permitted* to go on in my good work—it seems *to me* as if W.[oman]
S.[uffrage] in Utah would have been ten years ahead. "Mais But L'homme
Ropose [*sic*] et Dieu Dispose."

President Woodruff, if I *know* my own heart, I must be true, to myself

& to my fellows, I come of that stock. After my painful experience in plural marriage, it would be strange if I could *feel* other than I do. But upon this subject, I have never had *anything* to say publicly & never wish too [*sic*] have. Politics & religion won't mix.—& we are now trying, to form a political association for women entirely free from religious ties, into which the Methodist & Catholic woman can come & work, while holding her own consciencious [*sic*] views. The women of other religions are not willing to admit or work with women as officers who are in any way connected with polygamy. Hence some of the best workers will have to be left out publicly, but if they will uphold the hands of those who *can* work.[11] One year, will show God's providence in this, as in all His Works. With kind wishes, I am your's truly

Charlotte Ives Cobb Kirby

February 11, 1889

Mrs. Charlotte I. C. Kirby,

Your favor of Feb. 5th, relating to your labors in the cause of Woman's Suffrage for many years past, has been received and perused with much interest.

It would seem, from your statement of labors performed, that they should have been appreciated by the ladies of this Territory, and no doubt they were by a great many, but of whom we do not hear from. I have not been personally conversant with these matters in the past, so I am not able to say much upon that subject. I have noticed the recent organization of the Woman's Suffrage Association in the territory that you have been selected as Corresponding Secretary,[12] in which position I trust you will be able to find scope for your talents, not only in writing, but in speaking upon a subject which has been so familiar to you, and thus be able to assist in bringing the women of this fair Territory to that place they should occupy, and be acknowledged by the women of our great nation as worthy of their association and support.

I trust that amicable and friendly feelings may be cultivated, so that a harmonious working together may be had and the best of feeling engendered.

Wilford Woodruff

Salt Lake City Feb 16th/89

Pres. [Wilford] Woodruff,

Your kind answer to my personal recital, is rec—[eive]d, thanks. I have always found that "Man's extremity was God's opportunity," & in all my trials of that character, I have been driven more closely to the Arm of God, &

have so learned to lean upon Him, that it would seem to me almost *sacrilege* to now lean on man or look to him for guidance[.] Christ says "give me thine heart."—I feel in my inmost soul that my heart is given to Christ; & to the furtherance of His great work upon this Planet, which dawns upon me more fully day by day. I believe that you will be able to understand me! I see thro'[ugh] all your writings an implicit reliance on faith on *God*, & love for the beautiful in literature & art, & the strong evidences you have had of God's goodness are only confermations [*sic*] to me, that *you are* the right man in the right place. If we could only *always* know this, & when a man or woman comes to the front, the very fact of their having the courage of conviction, shows that they are called of God.

I know that the present work now opening before me is my work, my life works[;] five years ago I said to Aunt Zina.—(in answer to her wish that I would work *with* the women, & throw a useful life in with their's[).]

"Aunt Zina—when *you* are at the head of the women here I shall feel very differently, & when the women of Utah touch Suffrage, I shall come to the front for that is my work." This must have been prophetic, for both conditions are now here. Altho'[ugh] Aunt Zina said, at this time, *she* did not believe she would take that place. I want the confidence of my sisters & in time shall *win it*. My heart & interest are both in this cause & I *know how* to further the work. I wrote an open letter to the women of America as a *greeting*, on the formation, of our New Society, it was read at our last meeting, & the vote carried that it should be published in Eastern papers.—After the meeting Dr. R.[omania B.] Pratt[13] came up to the stand, & said she thought it presumptious [*sic*] in us to send such a letter, & she would not like to have our organization appear ridiculous. I said you should have *voted* a contrary mind, *then*.—it is too late now.

This little circumstance was of great value to me—& showed me a *wisdom*, in my being placed where I was, I could write such a letter, & have it warmly rec—[eive]d by the women to whom it was addressed for my *personal* acquaintance with them, made it possible, & a social standing I held in Washington, made Belva Lockwood say, "The lady from Utah has a strong friend at Court in her brother-in[-]law, John W. Candler."[14] Mr Candler was a personal friend of Gen. Garfield went into office with him,—he is a warm friend of Woman Suffrage, & told me if I needed a friend to call upon him.

Lucy Stone,[15] the leader of the movement in Mass.[achusetts] knew my blessed mother. I have just written her a long *personal* letter in which I gave her an account of dear mother's last hours, so *full* of heavenly beauty & sweet peace. I told her how I asked dear mother, if in these long years of privation & suffering, she had *never* regretted the step she took in leaving a home of luxury & a lovely family. & her reply, "*Never*, my Redeemer called & I obeyed, & I *know* where I am going."

Lucy Stone asked me the last time I visited Boston if mother was still a firm adherant to the Mormon faith. Said she attended that first Mormon meeting in Marlboro Chapel Boston & saw mother there.

It was dear mother['s] last wish that I continue the work she had commenced. This is now my own desire. & while I may not always persue [*sic*] the Modus Opperandi [*sic*] that another woman differently constituted may, still, the *result* may show a fore-sight on my part, & so that my heart is committed to this work of Woman Suffrage. I may err in judgement some times, but my zeal will pardon that when the object for which we work is *attained!* I had a long talk with br.[other] Angus Can[n]on. A satisfactory one to me.—& I believe I shall be able to satisfy the brethren, as to my public work—past, & present, & my sisters much try to *trust* me, until they can understand the whys, & wherefores. I honor & admire a beautiful religious life, like my Mother's,—I am myself a prayful woman. Yet unlike my Mother, I enjoy, a fine spirited argument, the life of a political campaign, the trushing up of old ideas, the introduction of new ones.—

With kindest feelings.—

Yours truly

C. I. Kirby.

Notes

1. Throughout my research on woman suffrage in the nineteenth-century American West, I kept encountering radical statements attributed to Charlotte Ives Cobb Godbe, Mrs. C. Godby, E. I. C. G., C. G., and Mrs. Kirby. Realizing there was a similarity in this rhetoric, I asked myself, "Could this be one person?" After considerable piecing together of citations found in local and national archives, I documented that it was one person—Charlotte Ives Cobb Godbe Kirby.

2. These three letters, located in the Wilford Woodruff Papers, LDS Church Library-Archives, Salt Lake City, are published by permission of the LDS Church Historical Department. The author is indebted to Hampton Godbe of Salt Lake City for his notes on the Godbe family history which verified archival findings.

3. William Henry Hooper, a Mormon, was the delegate to Congress from Utah Territory, 1859–1861, then again from 1865 to 1873. A successful merchant and banker, he served the Mormon community in various political offices.

Prior to his election as the Utah delegate, Hooper was the secretary of Utah Territory and later served in the territorial senate. Hooper, a supporter of woman suffrage, spoke in favor of enfranchising the women in Utah in 1869 when Congress was considering the proposal sponsored by Indiana Republican Congressman George Washington Julian. Hooper had urged Brigham Young to have the territorial legislature pass a bill enfranchising the women of Utah "to convince the country how utterly without foundation the popular assertions were concerning the women of the Territory." Later, Hooper, working through his colleagues in Washington D.C., was instrumental in persuading the non-Mormon acting governor, S. A. Mann, to sign the enfranchising bill. See *Desert News*, February 14, 1873; "William H. Hooper, the Utah Delegate and Female Advocate," *Phrenological Journal* (November 1870): 330–31; James L. Harrison, *Biographical Directory of American Congress, 1774–1949* (Washington: Government Printing Office, 1950), 1328.

4.   Timothy Otis Howe served as postmaster general in President Chester A. Authur's cabinet from 1881 until his death in 1883. In the two prior decades Howe had served as a Republican senator from Wisconsin; it was in this capacity that he chaired the Senate Committee on Territories. Harrison, *Biographical Directory*, 1338.

5.   The reformer Wendall Phillips was a friend and supporter of woman suffrage.

6.   At the 1869 organizing meeting of the American Woman Suffrage Association, Mary A. Livermore was elected vice-president of the new group, and before long she was invited to be editor of the organization's Boston-based weekly newspaper, the *Woman's Journal*. In addition to woman suffrage, Livermore was a supporter of temperance and a devotee of spiritualism. When Charlotte visited Boston in the early 1870s she stayed at Mary Livermore's home where the two women undoubtedly indulged in late-hour discussions on their mutual interests of woman suffrage, temperance, and spiritualism. Many years later Charlotte would acknowledge that Livermore had first interested her in temperance.

During the final three decades of the nineteenth century, tall, matronly, auburn-haired Livermore was one of the most popular speakers on the Redpath lecture circuit, delivering over 150 lectures annually. In the spring of 1889, when Livermore planned to visit Salt Lake City on a lecture tour, she contacted Charlotte Kirby to arrange a hall and prepare the publicity. Charlotte wrote numerous articles for the local newspapers on the upcoming visit of the "Queen of the Lecture Bureau." Edward T. James and Janet Wilson James, *Notable American Women, 1607–1950: A Biographical Dictionary* (Cambridge, Mass.: Belnap, 1971), 2:411–13; Salt Lake City newspaper articles spring of 1889; and Kirby to Wilford Woodruff, March 10, 1889, Woodruff Papers.

7.   The *"little"* woman referred to was Emmeline Blanche Woodward Wells, who edited the *Woman's Exponent*. A native of Worcester County, Massachusetts, Emmeline Wells and her family were early converts to the Church of Jesus

Christ of Latter-day Saints. Emmeline moved to Nauvoo and later to Utah. In 1852, after two marriages, one of which ended with her being deserted by her husband, the other with the death of her husband, Emmeline became the seventh wife of Daniel Hanmer Wells, a leading official of the church and general of its military arm, the Nauvoo Legion.

Educated as a teacher, Emmeline was an effective administrator and writer. For over forty years she edited the *Woman's Exponent*, a newspaper initiated to report the works of the Women's Relief Society, the ladies auxiliary of the LDS church. Emmeline, also a devoted worker for woman suffrage, did not hesitate to use the Relief Society organization or its journal to promote the suffrage cause.

The difference between Charlotte and Emmeline was that Charlotte advocated woman suffrage from an ideological, feminist base; while Emmeline employed woman suffrage as a means to improve the image of Mormon women and promote the goals of the church, such as statehood. From Emmeline's point of view, she was first a polygamous wife and mother, then an advocate of woman suffrage.

In 1879 when Emmeline and Zina Williams, daughter of Zina D. H. Young and Brigham Young, left Salt Lake City by train to go to the national capital to attend the National Woman Suffrage Association convention and present a petition to Mrs. Rutherford B. Hayes asking that the anti-polygamy law of 1862 not be enforced, the *Deseret News* acclaimed the two Mormon women "as representatives of plural marriage as well as other woman's rights." *Deseret News*, January 11, 1879; James and James, *Notable American Women*, 3:561–63; Andrew Jenson, *Latter-day Saint Biographical Encyclopedia*, 4 vols. (Salt Lake City, 1901), 1:731–34, 4:199–200.

8. Finding herself a young widow with a child to support, Belva McNall left her upstate New York home and moved to Washington, D.C., on the eve of the Civil War, where she opened one of the earliest private coeducational schools in the city. In 1868 she married a former Baptist minister and dentist, Ezekiel Lockwood, who took over the daily management of the school, thus freeing Belva to study law at the National University Law School. Though she completed her law courses, she found it necessary to write to President Ulysses S. Grant, who served as the school's ex-officio president, demanding her diploma before she could receive her law degree. She was admitted to the bar of the District of Columbia, the rule prohibiting women to practice law in the district having been changed two years earlier; however, it took a special act of Congress, promoted by two prosuffrage senators, Aaron A. Sargent of California and George F. Hoar of Massachusetts, for her to be permitted to argue cases before the Supreme Court and the Federal Court of Claims. The bulk of her work as an attorney consisted of pension claims against the government; later in her career, at the age of seventy-five, she argued before the Supreme Court on behalf of the Eastern Cherokee Indians which resulted in the award

of five million dollars to the Indians for purchase of land taken at the time of their 1835 removal.

From her early days in Washington, D.C., Belva was an advocate of women's rights; she was one of the founders of that city's Universal Franchise Association. In addition to lobbying for woman suffrage, she campaigned for Victoria Woodhull in 1872 in her unsuccessful candidacy for the presidency of the United States. Belva believed in an independent woman's political party. In 1884 she herself was nominated by the Equal Rights party as its candidate for the presidency. She ran on a platform that promised equality and justice regardless of color, sex, or nationality; voting and property rights for women; uniform marriage and divorce laws; prohibition of the liquor trade; citizenship for Indians; pensions for soldiers; and universal peace. In spite of Lockwood's strong feminist platform, woman suffragists such as Susan B. Anthony and Elizabeth Cady Stanton supported the candidacy of the Republican James G. Blaine. When the votes were counted, Lockwood came in a slow fifth in the race; yet she vowed she would campaign again in 1888.

As the *Salt Lake Daily Herald* of July 5, 1885, phrased it, Belva Lockwood had "ever been a warm and consistent friend of the people of Utah." The summer after her unsuccessful bid for the presidency, Lockwood was in Salt Lake City for a week at the request of Emily S. and Franklin S. Richards delivering lectures on women and politics.

Shortly after her stay in Utah, Lockwood wrote a long letter to President Grover Cleveland defending the Mormons and advising him that there was no need to send troops to Utah to put down a conflict between the Mormons and non-Mormons for no such outbreak was imminent.

The following year she would again write to the Utah delegate to Congress, John T. Caine, advising him to make a determined move to have Utah admitted as a state. She warned, "Evidently the *polygamy part must be relinquished*, and it is better that, that portion should be conceded, before your people, men and women, are disfranchised, and the Church dispoiled."

She also worked closely with Brigham Young's son, John W. Young, in an effort to find examples of prominent men in Washington D.C. who had more than one wife so that the Edmunds-Tucker Act could be enforced in the nation's capital. The goal was to create a reaction against the law, but Lockwood was not able to bring charges against prominent men, only "common bigamists and adulterers."

Nonetheless, she continued her lecture campaign in support of the Mormons. One of her best-known speeches was "The Mormon Question: The Other Side," in which she assured audiences that she did not advocate polygamy and was not herself a Mormon and then attempted to persuade them that Mormons were sincere in submitting a constitution for admission as a state which forbade polygamy. She did criticize the Mormons for failing to include women in the electorate of the proposed state by saying, "if there is any substantial reason why the Fiftieth Congress should not admit Utah as a state, it is the fact that they tamely submitted to the disfranchisement of their women, and have entirely left them out of their new State Constitution." Lockwood to Caine, February 14, 1886; broadside in LDS Church Library-Archives; James and James, *Notable American Woman*, 2: 413–16.

9. Zina Diantha Huntington Young, one of Joseph Smith's wives, married Brigham Young in 1846 after Smith's death. By Young she had a child named Zina. This daughter, Zina Young Williams, was a leader in the Women's Relief Society, and in 1878 she presented a major address before the mass meeting of women assembled to protest pending legislation in the United States Congress designed to eliminate polygamy. Jenson, *LDS Biographical Encyclopedia*, 1: 697–99.

10. Emily S. Richards, wife of the Mormon church lawyer, Franklin S. Richards, obtained special permission to organize a woman suffrage association for Utah Territory as an auxiliary of the National Woman Suffrage Association. Special permission was necessary because Jennie Froiseth, a principal leader of the anti-polygamy league, was against allowing women in Utah to vote.

   On January 2, 1889, the apostles of the church met with representatives of the Relief Society at the church historian's office to lay out a plan for the creation of a territorial woman suffrage association. In attendance at the meeting were Wilford Woodruff, Franklin D. Richards, Brigham Young, Jr., John Henry Smith, Bathsheba W. Smith, Sarah M. Kimball, Emmeline B. Wells, and Emily S. Richards. Once the gathering decided that the women should proceed to organize a territorial suffrage association and possibly send one or more delegates to the annual National Woman Suffrage Association conference, President Woodruff suggested that Emily S. Richards be the delegate, if anyone went. She was the best choice, he said, because she was "posted in these matters and had previously reported the Labors of the Ladies of this Territory at Washington." L. John Nuttal Draft Journal and Journal, January 2, 1889; also November 14 and December 31, 1888; Franklin D. Richards Journal, January 2, 10, 14, 1889; and Woodruff to "Jason Mack" [Joseph Fielding Smith], January 8, 1889, Wilford Woodruff Letterbooks, LDS Church Library-Archives.

11. Polygamous wives were conspicuously absent from the roster of the officers of the new suffrage association. One week after the meeting of church officials, a gathering of predominately Mormon women at the Assembly Hall in Salt Lake City formed the Woman Suffrage Association for Utah Territory and unanimously elected as their president Margaret N. Caine, wife of Utah's delegate to Congress, John T. Caine. Charlotte Kirby was elected corresponding secretary.

12. On March 13, 1889, the *Salt Lake Herald* published a letter to the editor from "a friend," announcing that with Charlotte I. Kirby as the corresponding secretary of the Utah Territorial Woman Suffrage Association "the subject is

not likely to go to sleep." Charlotte probably wrote this letter of self-praise, because it recited the same version of the story of her earlier lecture in Boston that she had written to Wilford Woodruff. In this public letter, however, she did not attack Emmeline B. Wells.

13. Romania B. Pratt was a physician in Salt Lake City specializing in obstetrics. Like a number of other Mormon "lady doctors," she was a strong advocate of woman suffrage.

14. Congressman John Wilson Candler, a Republican from Massachusetts in the Forty-seventh and the Fifty-first Congresses, was defeated in his reelection bid in 1890. Candler was first elected to Congress in the 1880 election when James A. Garfield was elected president. In 1881 the president of the LDS church, John Taylor, commissioned Charlotte to go to Washington, D. C., to present a woman suffrage petition and speech to Congress. Harrison, *Biographical Directory*, 944.

15. Educated at Oberlin College, Lucy Stone was an early advocate and speaker for the abolition of slavery and for women's rights. After Elizabeth Cady Stanton and Susan B. Anthony had formed the National Woman Suffrage Association in 1869, Lucy Stone and her husband, Henry B. Blackwell, along with others, such as Julia Ward Howe, formed the American Woman Suffrage Association and launched the *Woman's Journal*. This Boston-based faction of the woman's movement was more conservative than the Stanton-Anthony group. For example, Lucy Stone and her followers held a states' rights view on the subject of woman suffrage, preferring to petition state legislators rather than lobby Congress, as Stanton and Anthony did, for an amendment to the federal Constitution to prohibit denying access to the ballot on the basis of sex.

This schism within the woman's movement persisted until 1890 when the two groups merged into the National American Woman Suffrage Association which came to be dominated by the methods and philosophy of Lucy Stone and to be led by a new generation of suffragists such as Carrie Chapman Catt who, in keeping with the Progressive Era philosophy, stressed what women would do with the vote to improve the world rather than the liberal tradition arguments of women's inherent natural right to the ballot. James and James, *Notable American Women*, 3:387–90.

9

The Mormon-Suffrage Relationship

Personal and Political Quandries

JOAN IVERSEN

The nineteenth-century history of the women's suffrage movement, the schism between the National (Anthony-Stanton) and the American (Stone-Blackwell) suffrage associations, and the rise of the mass of women energized by the temperance crusade has a rarely told subplot, the story of the Mormon-suffrage relationship—an alliance fraught with political, ideological, and personal difficulties. This relationship exacerbated the tensions between the rival suffrage groups, and when the middle-class evangelical women of the social purity movement turned to an anti-polygamy crusade in the 1880s, the individuals within the alliance confronted both personal and political dilemmas. Along the uneasy path of the Mormon-suffrage relationship, leading suffragists took positions that sometimes were dictated by political expediency and at other times evolved from strongly held views of marriage, morality, and/or civil liberties. This paper examines the political and personal quandaries created for some of the leaders of the movement as the Mormon-suffrage relationship developed.

First published in *Frontiers: A Journal of Women Studies* 11, no. 2&3 (1990): 8–16. Reprinted by permission.

The Anomaly of Polygamous Suffragists

The women of Utah presented the National Woman Suffrage Association with a perplexing political anomaly: polygamous suffragists. The Church of Jesus Christ of Latter-day Saints (LDS) had announced plural marriage as a religious tenet in 1852, shortly after the Mormon migration to Utah. Even before the Civil War, polygamy had been linked by reform Republicans with slavery as the "twin relic[s] of barbarism." After the war, opposition to the practice grew increasingly intense, manifesting itself in punitive federal laws and opposition to Utah statehood. Woman suffrage, originally proposed in the East as a means to rid the territory of the scourge of polygamy, was unexpectedly adopted in 1870 by the Mormon-dominated territorial legislature, which anticipated—correctly—that Mormon women would demonstrate their loyalty to their religion by upholding the principle of plural marriage.[1]

While the franchise was not used to end polygamy, it did develop political activism among leading Mormon women, who founded their own woman's paper, the *Woman's Exponent*, held mass protest meetings, and undertook a militant defense of their religious marital practices. Faced with this undesired outcome, anti-Mormon and antisuffrage forces in Congress launched repeated attempts to disfranchise Utah's women. The leaders of the National Woman Suffrage Association protested these attempts, and in 1879 invited two Mormon women to attend their Washington convention.[2] From this point on, Utah's Mormon women were affiliated with the National Woman Suffrage Association. This connection brought the National the benefits of a strong western link, but also associated it with the despised practice of polygamy and with the patriarchal LDS church.

The Mormon alliance immediately exacerbated the rift between the National and its rival organization, the American Woman Suffrage Association, and would become even more controversial in the coming decade as the social purity agenda expanded to include an anti-polygamy crusade that also became enmeshed with the suffrage movement. For the Mormons, there were clear advantages in recruiting women's rights advocates to their side of the battle; for example, the Mormon women attending the 1879 convention had the opportunity to deliver a memorial from the women of their church to Congress and the president.[3] But as the anti-Mormon crusade accelerated, Mormon women endured hurtful snubs, and the defense of polygamy became increasingly untenable. For both suffrage and Mormon women leaders, the relationship engendered enduring friendships as well as opportunities for growth, but it was not to be tranquil.

Most of the early suffrage leaders expected, in 1870, that having received political freedom, the Mormon women would overthrow a system that was widely perceived as degrading to women—indeed, as an equivalent of the Turkish harem.[4] Mormon women, however, considered plural marriage to be of divine origin and an important part of their religion, even though many of them were personally ambivalent about it and often unhappy with the system. They viewed their marital practices as a form of utopian experiment that contributed to the development of woman's strength and character; and in actual practice, polygamy did require that Mormon women develop emotional independence and often some financial independence. Polygamy's profound—though unexpressed—assault upon nineteenth-century concepts of romantic love contributed to their feminist identification. Romantic love as the monogamous, exclusive sexual relationship of a man and a woman obviously could not be incorporated into plural marriage, and in fact, plural wives spoke of the necessity for emotional distancing and the need for self-reliance.[5] So while the majority of Americans saw them as living in bondage to patriarchy, Mormon suffragists refused to find polygamy and feminism incongruous. At the same time, ironically, Mormon women's moral values did not differ greatly from those of other nineteenth-century women: they argued defensively that polygamy was superior to monogamy in taming male sexuality and that it resulted in a society free from adultery and prostitution.[6]

Elizabeth Cady Stanton, alone of the major suffragists, actually discussed their marital system with a large audience of Mormon women. She and Susan B. Anthony had been invited to Salt Lake City in 1870 by the leaders of a recent group of Mormon apostates (Godbeites) who had broken with the LDS Church over economic and religious questions but were nonetheless committed to woman suffrage. Before Stanton and Anthony arrived in Salt Lake City, however, Brigham Young, leader of the Mormon people, invited the two women to speak at the Mormon Tabernacle.

Stanton enthusiastically seized this opportunity to speak candidly about her own views on the early matriarchate, the history of marriage, and the origins of monogamy. She wrote, "As Susan and I felt that they [we] would never be allowed back again, we decided to say all we had to say at the first session." The meeting, with about three hundred women, lasted for five hours, into which Stanton "crowded an immense amount of science and philosophy, [and] history." She reported that "we had a full and free discussion of every phase of the question" and that the Mormon women "stoutly defend[ed] their own religion." The Mormon women obviously scored a few points as well; Stanton was impressed that their marital system deferred to the "sacredness of motherhood" with strictures against sexual intercourse during pregnancy and lactation. Characteristically, Stanton was satisfied that she and her audience had found some common ground: "We all agreed that we were still far from having reached the ideal position for women in marriage, however satisfied man might be with his various experiments . . . and the Mormon women, like all others, . . . are no more satisfied than any other sect."[7]

Stanton's own views had been expressed in "The Man Marriage" (1868), in which she explained that marriage in its present state was a one-sided, distorted institution, based upon the subjugation of woman. Ideal marriage—essentially a companionate marriage of equals—could be realized only under conditions of "moral health," that is, the achievement of "equality, self-respect [and] independence" for women. "Until men and women view each other as equals," she argued, ". . . marriage will be in most cases a long hard struggle to make the best of a bad bargain."[8] In the meantime most marriages were unsatisfactory and even polygamous. "How can we have a monogamic relation with only one party true to its requirements?" In her essay on "Home Life" Stanton went so far as to label as polygamy the "well known" form of marriage of a man with "many mistresses."[9]

Nevertheless, Stanton was not horrified or outraged by the "immorality" of polygamy as were many members of the nineteenth-century women's movement. Where social purity advocates argued against polygamy in favor of the conventional purity of the religious home, Stanton understood that polygamy was supported in the Bible; in fact, she believed that monogamy had come to civilization through pagan Rome. Her opposition to polygamy was tempered by this historical perspective and matched by her criticism of the conventional monogamy advocated by traditional religion. Indeed, her view of religion itself was vastly different from the prevailing conservative acceptance of "divine truth." The Mormon women's adherence to polygamy, she thought, resulted from religious delusion, but the Mormons were no more deluded than any woman who accepted the biblical concept of woman's inferiority and patriarchal marriage. "When women understand that governments and religions are human inventions; that Bibles, prayer books, catechisms, and encyclical letters are all emanations from the brain of man, they will no longer be oppressed." Only when women were lifted from all religious superstition and when the social revolution had achieved changes that would "go deep down to the very foundations of society" could ideal, monogamic marriage be realized.[10]

Stanton's equanimity in the face of polygamy was not duplicated by Susan B. Anthony. Anthony found polygamy repugnant; she blamed it for the fact that she saw "scarcely a sunny, joyous countenance" in the Tabernacle, and, during her 1871 visit with the Godbeites, she openly challenged its practice.[11] Yet it was Anthony who was to become personally closer to the Mormon women over the next thirty years—not only because of Stanton's absence in England but also because of her own single-minded and pragmatic commitment to organization building. But, as we shall see, Anthony's views were more elusive and understated, shaped by political constraints as well as by her personal rejection of marriage.

Origin of the Alliance

Mormon women could hardly embrace Stanton's anti-Christianity and her view of them as "deluded." Nor would they reach out to the National Woman Suffrage Association for eight more years—that is, until leaders of the National protested in Washington against escalating attacks on Utah woman suffrage and the Mormons were faced at home with the newly organized Anti-Polygamy Society. Mormon women, appreciative of the suffragists' defense, sent "sincere and heartfelt thanks" to the National leaders from a mass protest meeting held in November 1878.[12] Subsequent private correspondence led to an invitation to Emmeline B. Wells, editor of the *Woman's Exponent*, to attend the NWSA convention. Perceiving the advantages of such an opportunity, the Mormon leadership sent both Emmeline Wells and Zina Young Williams, daughter of Brigham Young, to Washington, where, accompanied by several of the suffragists, they defended the practice of plural marriage both to the House Judiciary Committee and to President Rutherford B. Hayes. Although the NWSA women were careful not to endorse polygamy, one member of the delegation later published an account of the event praising the "two Mormon ladies." Mrs. Sara Spencer, strongest in support, also accompanied the Mormon women to the House Judiciary Committee, urging the congressmen to recognize them as a people who had made the desert "blossom as the rose."[13]

Criticism of this new alliance came immediately from within the suffrage movement. Only a month after the Washington meeting, the *Woman's Journal*, official publication of the American Woman Suffrage Association, published an incensed letter under the heading, "Polygamy Degrades Womanhood." The author, Amanda Dickinson, expressed regret that the NWSA had permitted "any appearance of affiliation" with women who defended a system that plunged woman "into her lowest depths of degradation."[14] Elizabeth Cady Stanton bristled at this attack. Angry that Lucy Stone had printed this letter without defending the National women, Stanton wrote to Matilda J. Gage, editor of the *National Citizen and Ballot Box*:

> If George Q. Cannon can sit in the Congress of the United States
> without compromising that body . . . I should think Mormon
> women might sit on our platform without making us responsible
> for their religious faith. . . . When the women of a whole territory
> are threatened with disfranchisement where should they go . . . but
> to the platform of the National Suffrage Association.[15]

Gage published Stanton's letter and attacked the rival suffrage leadership
as male-identified women who claimed equality for their sex but so catered
to public opinion as to curry favor with men, thus wearing "the brand
of the slave." Continuing with unusual vehemence, Gage launched an "ad
hominem" attack on the *Woman's Journal* editors, Lucy Stone and Henry
Blackwell: "Lucy Stone's own married life . . . is a protest against the laws
of marriage as recognized by the Christian Church . . . it ill becomes those
living in the Glass House, the *Woman's Journal*, to throw stones at Mormon
women."[16]

Gage had already used the polygamy issue as a vehicle to attack
hypocrisy within the reform ranks. The previous year, she had assailed the
"sham morality" evident in those who decried plural marriages but said
nothing about eastern male sinners. In a thinly disguised reference to the
Beecher scandal, Gage urged that the anti-polygamy forces "Let Utah alone
and begin with the male sinners of the Empire State."[17]

This controversy over the Mormon question highlights some of the
ideological differences between the rival suffrage groups at midcentury. For
both Stanton and Gage the crux of woman's subordination was male authority
in religion—in a patriarchal society, all religion. Gage noted that "Mormon
elders" were not alone in keeping women in "spiritual bondage." This
perspective, combined with the NWSA's stated goal to welcome "women
of every class, condition, rank," supported the organization's affiliation with
the Mormon women.[18] Ultimately, justifications offered for the alliance were
firmly rooted in the Stanton group's commitment to a broad vision of human
liberation that encompassed all women.

By contrast, Henry Blackwell of the American Woman Suffrage Association saw polygamy only in terms shaped by the pre-Civil War reform
era, which linked it with slavery as barbarism. "Polygamy is the slavery of
sex," he cried; it had put women into "chains, morally and materially." Its
abolition, however, he believed must be gradual in order to protect Mormon
plural wives and ensure the legitimacy of the children of plural homes.[19] Sim-
ilarly, Lucy Stone was scandalized by the Stanton-Anthony association with
the Mormon women.[20]

Not surprisingly, the *Woman's Journal* was an early supporter of the rising anti-polygamy movement, reprinting the horror stories sent by Utah's activists. The most prominent women of the American Woman Suffrage Association, Harriet Beecher Stowe and Julia Ward Howe, offered their names to anti-polygamy publications. Although Lucy Stone, her husband, and her daughter consistently protested all attempts to disfranchise the Utah women, their paper and organization were uncompromising about polygamy even when the anti-polygamy crusade had barely begun.

The Anti-Polygamy Crusade, 1880–1887

The anti-polygamy crusade originated in Utah but rapidly achieved momentum as it became an integral part of the broader nineteenth-century evangelical women's culture. Anti-polygamy activism followed the growing influence of the temperance and social purity campaigns into the national suffrage movement. In November 1878 Gentile and apostate Mormon women in Salt Lake City formed the Anti-Polygamy Society, and within two years they began publishing a paper, the *Anti-Polygamy Standard*, which carried an opening appeal from Harriet Beecher Stowe. Both suffrage journals printed subscription appeals for this paper. To arouse the non-Mormon world, the anti-polygamy women also published lurid, sensationalized fictional tracts that in effect appealed to the prurient instincts as well as the domestic ideology and nativist fears of the respectable nineteenth-century woman reader.

The crusade had wide appeal, because polygamy threatened the very heart of the midcentury consensus about motherhood and domesticity: the ideology of the "Empire of Mother," which wove the precepts of domesticity into the very foundation of the republic.[21] Opposition to polygamy rapidly became a national woman's cause, spawning a national organization with chapters in Brooklyn and Chicago by 1880. The founders of the Utah Anti-Polygamy Society also sent an appeal to First Lady Lucy Rutherford Hayes. Her help was not long in coming; she became president of the Woman's Home Missionary Society of the Methodist Episcopal Church, formed in 1880 with a stated objective of aiding the "suffering sisters in Utah."[22]

Soon the crusade could point to major triumphs. It had replaced Utah's polygamist representative to Congress, George Cannon, with a monogamist Mormon, John T. Caine, and soon achieved legislative success with the passage of the 1882 Edmunds Act, which criminalized polygamy and established the Utah Commission to enforce federal rulings in the territory. The law was written to enable prosecution for cohabitation; federal marshals were given broad authority to force children and wives to testify and to hunt down polygamists. Mormon religious leaders served penitentiary sentences, and plural wives lived "on the run" to hide pregnancies that might reveal cohabitation. These violations of privacy and civil rights served only to increase the resistance of the polygamous Saints.

Meanwhile, prominent Mormon women suffragists continued to maintain a dignified and stoic public stance. Emmeline Wells expressed an almost resigned attitude toward the attacks. "It seems to have been . . . the fate of Mormons to be slandered," she observed.[23] But Mormon women in general could hardly remain unresentful. They were often described in propaganda literature as coarse, ignorant, and unrefined. On a trip east, Brigham Young's wife Zina was approached after a public meeting by a woman who exclaimed in surprise that Mrs. Young did not "look very degraded." Even given their determination to rise above their critics, the Mormon women who traveled out of Utah found the hostility and ignorance difficult to endure.[24] The anti-polygamy cant that most rankled Mormon women was the accusation that children of plural marriages were slow-witted and inferior, an assertion based upon a popular nineteenth-century notion that moral depravity led to inherited physical degeneracy. Alice Stone Blackwell, daughter of Lucy Stone, was apparently influenced by this thinking, reporting on her visit to Salt Lake City that many of the men appeared "low-browed and brutish" and that the mass of Mormons fell into two classes, "the dull and the wild."[25]

This bigotry by itself would have made contacts with the suffrage association difficult, but problems were compounded by Susan B. Anthony's efforts to broaden the base of suffrage support by welcoming into the NWSA temperance leaders who advocated the ballot for "Home Protection." The suffrage movement was aligning itself with the very forces that backed the anti-polygamy crusade. Additional difficulties came with increased attacks on Utah's woman suffrage. Claiming to be believers in woman suffrage everywhere *but* Utah, the leaders of the Utah anti-polygamy movement published an "Open Letter to Suffragists" in the *Anti-Polygamy Standard* (1882) calling on them to oppose the woman's vote in Utah. Suffrage leaders were finding the Mormon issue more difficult; they could not support disfranchisement of any women, yet, since they argued for the vote on the grounds that it would reform and purify American society, Utah woman suffrage and polygamy were embarrassments. Suffragists, understandably, grew increasingly defensive about being associated with polygamy. The always anomalous Mormon-suffrage relationship was stretched thin by the separate agendas of its components.[26]

The Mormon women tried to gain support from reform friends in the East to combat the anti-polygamy forces. In the fall of 1881 Dr. Ellen Ferguson, LDS convert, accompanied by Brigham Young's wife Zina Huntington Young, visited Hartford, Connecticut, and spoke at the liberal Unity Church there. Ferguson made a favorable impression and even earned an invitation from Harriet Beecher Stowe to speak at the coming Woman's Congress in Buffalo. However, when the Mormon women arrived at the congress in October they were denied the right to speak because of their association with polygamy and had to listen to a platform speaker urge support for the anti-polygamy forces.[27]

A few months after the Buffalo rejection, the same two Mormon women, now joined by Dr. Romania Pratt, attempted to present their case at the New York State Woman Suffrage Convention, where they were again not allowed to speak. In a private conversation with them Susan B. Anthony justified this action on the grounds that the suffrage organization had to be careful not to appear to be endorsing polygamy. She even had the temerity to ask Pratt for the name of someone in Utah who could write the anti-Mormon side of the suffrage question for the forthcoming *History of Woman Suffrage*. Pratt replied angrily that Mormon women would not face so much misrepresentation if Anthony were as "eager to hear our side . . . as you are the anti-side." Evidently, Anthony was redefining her support for Utah's woman suffrage so as to separate it clearly from the larger Mormon cause. The Mormon women who had planned to attend the National Woman Suffrage convention in Washington did not go.[28]

The absence of support from suffrage friends was a disappointment to Mormon suffragists. As the anti-polygamy crusade accelerated in Utah, Emmeline Wells expressed frustration. "We do not expect the world to believe in celestial marriage," she noted. "Mormon women are not asking for pity from any source, they simply want justice, nothing more."[29] Should not Mormons receive what was accorded by the Constitution to all citizens—religious freedom? The issue raised by the aggressive federal enforcement of anti-polygamy legislation *was* one of civil rights, yet only one woman leader of the suffrage organization spoke out in defense of the Mormons—Belva Lockwood, prominent Washington, D.C., attorney and member of the NWSA. Lockwood's unique advocacy of the Mormons earned her the accusation of being on retainer from them. She alone of the suffragists at this time publicly criticized the 1882 Edmunds Act's invasion of family life and privacy, observing that the law operated retroactively to criminalize polygamy and prosecute marriages made previously on the basis of religious belief.[30]

When Lockwood, at the NWSA convention in 1884, attempted to

gain support for the Mormons' struggle against the anti-polygamy crusade, Susan B. Anthony interrupted her speech and hastened, at its conclusion, to dissociate herself from Lockwood's views. Anthony declared, to loud applause, that the organization could defend woman suffrage in Utah but should not criticize the "general laws" of Congress.[31] We can only speculate about her motives. Was she catering to the popularity of the anti-polygamy movement within suffrage ranks, or was she simply adhering to her often-noted pragmatic, single-issue approach to the suffrage cause?

It is easy to understand why the Mormon women singled out Belva Lockwood to thank for "moral courage" in defense of their constitutional rights. For her own part, Lockwood repeatedly had to insist that she herself was a "thorough monogamist." "I do not believe in polygamy and am not a convert to the Mormon faith; but I do believe in Humanity and justice, . . . in the inviolability of personal and property rights, [and] in . . . freedom of religious convictions." Lockwood's defense of the Mormons was not without cost, and one historian believes that it both weakened the suffrage struggle and alienated her from the suffrage movement.[32] Years later, Elizabeth Cady Stanton would refer to the anti-polygamy persecutions of the 1880s and echo Lockwood's position that federal enforcement had violated Mormon civil liberties as well as the separation of church and state. But since she was in England during this period and there is no record of her speaking out at the time, we cannot know whether she would have urged a different position upon Anthony and the suffrage organization.

The Nadir Years, 1887–1890

No efforts could forestall further congressional anti-Mormon legislation. Having disfranchised all polygamists with the 1882 Edmunds Act yet failed to end polygamy, Congress now moved to more punitive legislation, the Edmunds-Tucker Act of 1887, which removed the vote from *all* the women of Utah. All the suffrage leaders of both organizations protested this act, and twenty women from the NWSA, including Lillie Devereaux Blake, president of the New York Suffrage Association, formed a delegation to present a Mormon women's petition to President Grover Cleveland asking him to veto the bill. Susan B. Anthony, however, would not join this delegation.[33]

The three years following the Edmunds-Tucker Act were most difficult for Mormon women in the suffrage ranks; federal prosecution of polygamists continued at home while political maneuvering within the suffrage movement, as the two rival organizations took steps toward a merger, threatened to exclude Mormon women. The American had proposed merger to the National in 1887, and a committee comprising representatives from each association was formed to plan for the consolidation.

Anti-polygamy women were now well represented in both organizations. Mrs. Jennie Froiseth, editor of the *Anti-Polygamy Standard*, had been listed for several years as one of NWSA's vice presidents for Utah. Intending to fight for representation in the national women's movement, the Mormons sent delegates to the April 1888 meeting of the International Council of Women called to found the National Council of Women, a coalition of the important national women's organizations that had proliferated throughout the nineteenth century. The idea of the meeting, which would commemorate the fortieth anniversary of Seneca Falls, was Anthony's. The Mormon women had made significant contributions to convening the National Council, and one of their delegates, Mrs. Emily Richards, was to present a report from the influential Mormon Women's Relief Society. The presiding officer forgot to introduce her and was about to adjourn when Anthony intervened and led Richards to the rostrum. This incident, reported in the *Woman's Exponent*, was not as trivial as it may seem.[34] Clearly there was a struggle going on behind the scenes that would become clearer at the National Suffrage Convention, held immediately following the International Council.

To this convention the Mormons had sent two monogamist women, Richards and Mrs. Arthur Brown, with authorization to form a state suffrage association uniform to the others within the National.[35] Since until 1887 Utah's women had had the franchise there had been no need, until now, for such an association. But Froiseth and other anti-polygamy women from Utah opposed both Mormon membership in the National and Utah woman suffrage. The resulting controversy was resolved when Mrs. Harriet Robinson, Massachusetts suffragist and former Lowell worker, offered a compromise resolution that restated the National's commitment to retaining in its membership "women of all classes, all races and all religions." The two monogamist Mormon women were appointed vice presidents for Utah. Emmeline Wells, remaining in Salt Lake City and relegated to a less visible position by an LDS leadership now relying upon monogamist representatives, was ambivalent in reporting the convention proceedings. While she expressed appreciation of Robinson's efforts to effect a compromise, she wondered why "any resolution should be necessary to admit Utah women," who had voted for seventeen years. Despite irate Gentile opposition in Salt Lake City, the actions at both meetings indicated that Anthony would not abandon the Mormon affiliation in the process of seeking merger.[36]

The rest of the summer of 1888 was tense in Salt Lake City as anti-polygamy Utah women still hoped to exclude Mormon women from the coming merged organization. Froiseth campaigned strenuously to win prominent suffrage leaders to an anti-Mormon position. When Julia Ward Howe visited Salt Lake City that summer she was met and entertained by Froiseth but apparently refused the Mormon women's invitation to present a lecture.[37] Emmeline Wells sent several messages, persistent in her wish to meet with Howe. She came to that meeting bringing flowers and later wrote a glowing tribute in her paper about the eastern suffragist, ironically adding that it was surprising that a woman of Howe's "breadth of thought" would visit Salt Lake City and not meet with the Mormons.[38]

As a direct result of this incident, Clara Colby, editor of the *Woman's Tribune* and a member of the committee planning the National-American merger, offered to come to Salt Lake City in September with Mrs. Elizabeth Saxon, suffragist and social purity lecturer. The expedition was an unqualified success. The women toured a day nursery run jointly by Gentile and Mormon women. Clara Colby carefully recorded the visit in her paper, noting the dignity and courtesy demonstrated by the Mormon women during very difficult times. "You don't have to ask the Mormons to learn of these hardships [federal prosecutions of polygamists]," she observed, "you need only to read the Gentile papers to see the painful experiences these people endure for relationships formed *before* they were illegal."[39] Annoyed, Froiseth asked the Woman's Relief Corps to raise money to send her to the Detroit Woman's Congress to answer Colby, who was expected to give a favorable report there about the Mormons. At the congress, presided over by Julia Ward Howe, Froiseth gave her anti-Mormon speech on the same platform with Frances Willard. She also seized the opportunity to invite other leading women at this congress, all members of the American Woman Suffrage Association, including Antoinette Blackwell, Mary Livermore, and Harriet Boutwell, to visit Salt Lake City. When they arrived the following year, Emmeline Wells despaired in her diary, "I suppose Mrs. Froiseth will fill them full of Mormon slanders."[40]

One positive outcome of the Colby-Saxon visit was that it provided the impetus for the formation of the Utah Woman Suffrage Association in January 1889. The new organization had the participation of a few Gentile women as well as LDS endorsement. The Mormon women chosen for prominent roles in the organization were, however, monogamist. Emmeline Wells was called upon to help with the organizing and writing but not given a prominent position in the new organization.[41] The Edmunds-Tucker Act had confiscated church property, and it was becoming clear, especially to monogamist Mormons, that it was necessary to retreat from the principle of plural marriage in order to save the church and achieve statehood.[42] While the Mormons had

Emily Sophia Tanner Richards. *Courtesy of Archives, Historical Department, Church of Jesus Christ of Latter-day Saints.*

decided to downplay polygamy, they were not totally abandoning woman suffrage. To have retreated on this issue would have vindicated opponents who claimed that Utah woman suffrage had been merely a sham to retain Mormon dominance. Furthermore, suffragists might still be important allies in obtaining Utah statehood.

As Mormon and anti-polygamy women battled in Utah, the time moved closer to the merger of the American and National suffrage associations. Some of Anthony's earlier associates were appalled at the coming alliance with the more religious, conservative women of the American Woman Suffrage Association, whose growing importance could be traced through the pages of the *Woman's Journal*. Anthony, who would not retreat from the merger, was convinced of the benefits to be gained from the addition of the Christian reform women to the ranks of suffrage. It is clear that she was seduced by the advantage of numbers. Unfortunately, there is no record of her reaction to the struggle to exclude the Mormon women from the coming merged organization, nor any evidence of her relationship with Emmeline Wells in this period.

Meanwhile, Anthony's former ally Matilda Gage, appalled at the religious and conservative sentiments expressed at the 1888 International Council meeting, began a campaign to oppose the alliance with the conservative, religious faction. Writing to Elizabeth Cady Stanton in a letter published by Colby's *Woman's Tribune*, Gage recorded her dismay at the coming merger, referring to Frances Willard as a "dangerous woman," and calling for Stanton to join her in an explicitly anticlerical position. Anthony viewed Gage's statements as a "secession" movement.[43]

Although Stanton shared Gage's distrust of the religious reformers, she did not oppose Anthony's steps toward merger. Stanton had been isolated from the suffrage movement in the 1880s, living abroad, as the anti-polygamy crusade grew into a national movement. It now appeared that Stanton would nevertheless retain her role in the new organization. In spite of the opposition of such leaders of the American as Stone, Blackwell, and Howe, Stanton was elected president with about 60 percent of the vote. Julia Ward Howe bitterly noted in her diary that Stanton had the votes of all the Mormon delegates.[44]

In her acceptance speech before the newly merged National American Woman Suffrage Association (NAWSA), Stanton directed remarks to the purity reformers who had attempted to exclude the Mormon women.

> Wherever and whatever any class of women suffer whether in the home, the Church, the Courts . . . a voice in their behalf should be heard in our conventions. . . . We must manifest a broad Catholic

spirit for all. . . . *Colored women, Indian women, Mormon women* . . . have been heard in these Washington Conventions & I trust they always will be. (Emphasis mine)[45]

Stanton's later remarks seem to be directed to Anthony herself. While Anthony had never abandoned affiliation with the Mormon women, her actions during the height of the anti-polygamy crusade were very cautious. Now Stanton criticized this kind of timidity, declaring, "There is such a thing as being too anxious lest some one 'hurt the cause' by what she may say or do."[46]

But Stanton's position was clearly in the minority, and she was not to hold the presidency of the NAWSA much longer. By 1896 the organization had rejected her *Woman's Bible*, a rationalist explication of scriptural male bias—ironically, at the same convention that honored Utah's entrance as a new woman suffrage state. By then the LDS church had issued its 1890 Woodruff Manifesto retreating from plural marriage. It is interesting that many of the women who defended Stanton's book at that convention, where the battle divided between the more liberal, free-thinking suffragists and the "Christian Party," which now made up the majority, were those who had always been supportive of the Mormon alliance. Stanton was bitter about the bigotry of the "religious women zealots."[47]

The Respectable Years, 1890–1899

After the Woodruff Manifesto the Mormon women found greater acceptance in the national women's movement; indeed, the three years following the manifesto were a high point in cooperation, as the Mormon and Gentile women prepared for the Columbian Exposition. These years of relative political calm brought gratifying occasions of recognition. As members of the National Council of Women, Mormon women participated in the 1895 birthday celebration of Elizabeth Cady Stanton, sending her a miniature ballot box made of Utah onyx and silver. Later that year Wells attended the Intermountain Woman Suffrage Convention, where she was deeply touched when Susan Anthony embraced her at the conclusion of her speech. She wrote in her diary, "It was a tribute of personal affection as well as a flattering compliment to the Territory."[48] The culminating triumph of these years came with the reenfranchisement that accompanied statehood in Utah. Susan B. Anthony and Dr. Anna Shaw arrived in Salt Lake City in time to celebrate the victory.

But this period of acceptance was soon ended as the nation and women's groups were aroused anew to the issue of polygamy. Methodist and Presbyterian ministers in Utah, incensed by the continued practice of polygamy, declared the Woodruff Manifesto a farce and claimed that over 2,000 plural marriages had taken place there since statehood. As statehood now placed Utah's marital practices beyond the authority of Congress, the ministers called for a constitutional amendment to ban polygamy. This campaign escalated to a national level when an admitted polygamist, B. H. Roberts, was elected to the House of Representatives in November 1898 and the Ministerial Alliance of Salt Lake City appealed for national support to prevent Roberts from assuming his seat. By January the movement against Roberts had been joined by the Women's Board of Home Missions of the Presbyterian, Methodist, and Baptist groups, and the National Congress of Mothers had passed a resolution against Roberts's admission to Congress. Ultimately, seven million signatures protesting Roberts's election were received by Congress.[49]

The groundswell of opposition to Roberts from women's groups was carried to the triennial meeting of the National Council of Women in February 1899. Once again, Mormon women active in national organizations were forced into a defensive position by polygamy. Ironically, Roberts had been an opponent of Utah woman suffrage and had also antagonized the church leadership. But though the six Mormon women delegates had no reason to support him personally, the condemnation of Roberts implied the repudiation of their church, and they knew that if the National Council passed such a resolution they would be forced to abandon membership in an organization they greatly valued.[50] It must have been difficult for the Mormon delegates to resist the pressures to which they were subjected before the meeting began. President May Sewall urged the women to condemn Roberts in order to demonstrate their sincerity as anti-polygamists. Emmeline Wells proposed a substitute resolution that diffused the criticism of Roberts, and by implication the LDS church, by calling for all congressional representatives to be "law abiding." The floor debate was highly emotional. At one point, Susa Young Gates, journalist and daughter of Brigham Young, broke into tears as she attempted to explain how important the membership in the National Council was to Mormon women. "I wanted to bring you arguments, but I see I can only bring you emotion and sentiment," she managed to say before leaving the platform in tears. Susan Anthony left the platform to sit beside Gates and embrace her as she wept.[51]

Many of the former allies and friends of the Mormon women again rallied to their side. Sara Spencer, Belva Lockwood, and Clara Colby argued for their position. But the tide was turned by Anthony, who observed that Congress was undoubtedly full of men who had violated monogamic marriage and gone unpunished. "Why should we go away out to Utah to seek a man to punish?" she asked.[52] The outcome was a political victory for the Mormon women leaders and, as even the hostile *Salt Lake Tribune* acknowledged, a personal tribute to them. Emmeline Wells's years of work in the suffrage movement had earned her the respect of the delegates.

For Anthony, however, support of the Mormon women had placed her in opposition to her dear friend Dr. Anna Shaw and other social purity leaders. The issue of Roberts plagued Anthony throughout the year. At the Rochester convention of the New York State Federation of Women's Clubs, she opposed another resolution calling for Roberts's expulsion. Although she had not intended to speak, when the president called on her for her position, Anthony stated her views. Given the double standard of morality in most of America, men in Congress could hardly condemn Roberts for immorality. Echoing the debate of twenty years earlier, Anthony noted that "people who live in glass houses should not throw stones." Public reaction was so negative that Anthony had to clarify her position later in the New York *World*, reiterating that she abhorred polygamy.[53]

In defending Roberts, Anthony revealed that her position on polygamy had not changed from her first visit to Salt Lake City in 1871, when she had declared, "No person could abhor polygamy more than myself. . . . The system of the subjection of women here [Salt Lake City] finds its limit, and she touches the lowest depths of her degradation."[54] Nevertheless, Anthony did not join the anti-polygamy forces; indeed, she explicitly forbade the Anti-Polygamy League for Amending the Constitution to use her name on its national committee. Nor would she ever abandon her personal and political affiliation with the Mormon women. But when Susa Young Gates wrote to ask permission to identify Anthony in a book as a courageous supporter of Mormons, Anthony refused.

You, like others, do not seem to note the difference between endorsing a movement itself and upholding the affiliation with the National Council of organizations. . . . I do not consider that I endorsed Mormonism. . . . You fail to comprehend that I am among those who hate polygamy and all the subjection of women in the Mormon faith.[55]

Like Stanton's, Anthony's views on polygamy are closely intertwined with her position on marriage. Anthony, too, held that marriage should be an association of complete equality, possible only when women had full political rights. But for Anthony, equality in marriage was almost always expressed solely in the puzzling terms of economic independence. "What women most need is . . . a self-respect which shall scorn to eat the bread of dependence. Whoever consents to live by the sweat of the brow of another human being inevitably humiliates and degrades herself," she declared. When she first confronted polygamy in Utah in 1871 it was this economic dependence that she condemned. "Their life of dependence on men is even more dreadful than that of monogamy, for here it is two, six, a dozen women . . . all dependent on the one man."[56]

When Anthony refused to allow Gates to use her name she added a revealing comment: "When you justify polygamy as a requirement of religious faith you make it entirely too respectable. I recognize no excuse for it."[57] The operative word here is "respectable," and it differentiates her position from Stanton's. While both Stanton and Anthony defended Mormon polygamy by pointing to the inadequacies of contemporary marriage and the hypocrisy of Gentile adultery, Anthony's disapproval of polygamy appears more visceral. Susa Young Gates herself noted this repugnance, explaining that "Miss Anthony had the natural Puritanic horror of what she deemed promiscuous marriage. She did not or would not comprehend the spiritual principle which differentiated a religious sacrament from a loose marital custom."[58] While one cannot totally accept Gates's assessment, it is apparent that Anthony's repugnance to polygamy went beyond her insistence upon woman's need for economic independence.

A possible explanation of that repugnance is suggested by Kathleen Barry, recent biographer of Anthony, who notes that at the base of Anthony's "critique of marriage was an analysis and awareness of sex as domination"— a critique held tacitly.[59] Underlying Anthony's expressed horror of woman's economic dependence in marriage, her fear that "woman's subsistence enslaves her will, degrades her pride and vitiates her whole moral nature," was her unexpressed rejection of the sexual domination inherent in the Victorian marriage. For Anthony, marriage without equality for woman meant she was "fit only to minister to man's animal instincts."[60] Anthony's anti-polygamy views were, in the last analysis, closely related to her own rejection of marriage and to her lifelong commitment to work first for the full political and economic empowerment of woman. She never wavered in her acceptance of the Mormon suffragists as allies in this struggle, compartmentalizing her disapproval of plural marriage. Yet she was too politically astute to allow the suffrage association to become too identified with the Mormon struggle. In spite of her personal distaste for polygamy and her careful political disavowal of Mormon sympathies, it was Anthony who was the suffrage leader most revered by the Mormon women active in the suffrage movement. Reflecting years later on her suffrage allies, Susa Gates praised them for advancing the development and acceptance of Mormon women, noting that these leaders were "more liberal, nay more just, than woman is by nature."[61]

There was to be another major attack on Mormons in the first part of the twentieth century, but for the most part Mormon women's groups retained their respectability, continuing as members of the National Council of Women. Gradually, however, Mormon women became less identified with the women's rights struggle—a change that Mormon scholars have both documented and sought to account for. By the time the postsuffrage period brought greater legal and social emancipation to many American women, the Mormon women were "no longer setting their own agenda . . . drawn under the umbrella of church policy."[62] The story recorded here suggests a partial explanation.

In the early years of the nineteenth-century woman's movement, leaders like Stanton attempted a challenge to the conservative ideology of Victorian domesticity—arguing for the full equality and development of women, calling for the restructuring of home and family away from patriarchal authority, aiming for a coalition of all women around these common concerns. Instead, the rising of the middle-class "woman" movement of the last decades of the century coalesced around a "politics of domesticity"—a female evangelicism that manifested itself in the temperance, social purity, and anti-polygamy movements, insisting upon the elevation of woman's status within the ideal Victorian home, without challenging patriarchal authority. Ironically, the Mormon women had more in common ideologically with this female evangelicism than with Stanton's vision of the restructured home. While they were forced, in defending plural marriage, to argue for their practice as a utopian solution, they did so without challenging patriarchal authority within the home; and, most important, they did so in support of their church and culture. Once that culture had abandoned polygamy, Mormon women had no rationale or need for continued militance. The potential challenge to Victorian domesticity within the early Mormon-suffrage alliance was lost in the triumph of the anti-polygamy movement and the merger of the rival suffrage organizations.

Notes

1. Utah woman suffrage is explained in Beverly Beeton, *Women Vote in the West: The Woman Suffrage Movement 1869–1896* (New York: Garland Publishing, 1986); Beverly Beeton, "Woman Suffrage in the American West, 1865–96" (Ph.D. diss., University of Utah, 1976); Beverly Beeton, "Woman Suffrage in Territorial Utah," *Utah Historical Quarterly* 46 (Spring 1978): 101–21. A different interpretation is given by Thomas G. Alexander, "An Experiment in Progressive Legislation: The Granting of Woman Suffrage in Utah in 1870," *Utah Historical Quarterly* 38 (Winter 1970): 20–30.

2. Beeton, *Women Vote in the West*, chap. 3, *passim*.

3. John Taylor to George Q. Cannon, 17 January 1879. John Taylor Letter Book, Taylor Family Papers, University of Utah.

4. James K. Hamilton Wilcox, "Utah's Woman Suffrage," *Woman's Journal* 12 (January 1882): 421; *Woman's Journal* 1 (12 November 1870): 355.

5. Joan Iversen, "Feminist Implications of Mormon Polygyny," *Feminist Studies* 10 (Fall 1984): 515–16.

6. Julie Dunfey, " 'Living the Principle' of Plural Marriage: Mormon Women, Utopia, and Female Sexuality in the Nineteenth Century," *Feminist Studies* 10 (Fall 1984): 523–37; Kathleen Marquis, "Diamond Cut Diamond: Mormon Women and the Cult of Domesticity in the Nineteenth Century," *University of Michigan Papers in Women's Studies* 2 (1976): 105–24.

7. Theodore Stanton and Harriot Stanton Blatch. *Elizabeth Cady Stanton, As Revealed in Her Letters, Diary and Reminiscences* (1922; reprint, New York: Arno Press, 1969), 2:132–33; Elizabeth Cady Stanton, *Eighty Years and More: Reminiscences 1815–1897* (1898; reprint, New York: Arno Press, 1969), 283.

8. Elizabeth Cady Stanton, "The Man Marriage," *The Revolution* (8 April 1869): 217–18.

9. Elizabeth Cady Stanton, "Home Life," August 1878. Elizabeth Cady Stanton Papers, Library of Congress (microfilm, Seneca Falls National Park).

10. Stanton, *Eighty Years and More*, 284–85; "The Man Marriage," 217–18.

11. Ida Husted Harper, *The Life and Work of Susan B. Anthony* (1908; reprint, New York: Arno Press. 1969), 1:390.

12. " 'Mormon' Women on Plural Marriage." Pamphlet reporting Mass Meeting. 16 November 1878, Salt Lake City, Utah.

13. "Letter from Miss Grundy," *National Citizen and Ballot Box* 3 (January 1879): 7, describes the meeting with President Hayes at which she was present; Mrs. Spencer is quoted in an article reprinted from the *Washington Star* in *National Citizen and Ballot Box* 5 (February 1979): 7.

14. Amanda E. Dickinson, "Polygamy Degrades Womanhood," *Woman's Journal* 10 (29 March 1879): 97.

15. "The Brand of the Slave," *National Citizen and Ballot Box* 4 (May 1879): 2.

16. "The Brand of the Slave," 2.

17. Matilda Joslyn Gage, "The Utah Question Once More," *National Citizen and Ballot Box* 3 (December 1878): 2.

18. "Note from Editor," *National Citizen and Ballot Box* 5 (August 1880): 3.

19. Henry Blackwell, "Anti-Polygamy," *Woman's Journal* 12 (13 August 1881): 260; "Polygamy in Utah," *Woman's Journal* 1 (19 February 1870): 49.

20. Lucy Stone to Harriet Robinson, 4 March 1879, Robinson-Shattuck Papers, Schlesinger Library (microfilm available through interlibrary loan).

21. Mary Ryan, *Empire of the Mother: American Writing about Domesticity, 1830–1860* (New York: The Institute for Research in History and Haworth Press, 1982), 140ff.

22. Barbara Haywood, "Utah's Anti-polygamy Society, 1878–1884" (M.A. thesis, Brigham Young University, 1980), 48; "Memorial of the Woman's Home Missionary Society to the General Conference of the Methodist Episcopal Church" (Philadelphia, Pa., 1 May 1884).

23. "Woman against Woman," *Woman's Exponent* 7 (1 May 1879): 180.

24. "Letter from Romania Pratt," *Woman's Exponent* 10 (1 March 1881): 146; Jane Snyder Richards, "Reminiscences" (Bancroft Library, University of California, 1880), 51.

25. Lester E. Bush, Jr., "Mormon 'Physiology,' 1850–1875," *Bulletin of the History of Medicine* 56 (Spring 1982): 218–39; Alice Stone Blackwell, "In Salt Lake City," *Woman's Journal* 14 (7 July 1883): 212–13.

26. Beeton, *Women Vote in the West*, 67.

27. Ann Gardner Stone, "Ellen B. Ferguson," *Sister Saints*, ed. Vicky Burgess-Olson (Provo, Utah: Brigham Young University Press, 1978), 330–32; "Dr. Ferguson's Letter," *Woman's Exponent* 10 (15 November 1881): 90.

28. Romania Pratt, "Woman Suffrage Convention," *Woman's Exponent* 10 (1 March 1882): 143, 146.

29. Emmeline B. Wells, "What They Say," *Woman's Exponent* 12 (15 November 1883): 92.

30. Belva A. Lockwood, "The Disfranchisement of the Women of Utah," *Ogden Daily Herald* (Ogden City, Utah), 9 June 1883, 4.

31. Emmeline B. Wells, "Washington Convention," *Woman's Exponent* 13 (15 March 1884): 156.

32. " 'Mormon' Women's Protest, An Appeal for Freedom, Justice and Equal Rights," Pamphlet reporting Mass Meeting, 6 March 1886 (Salt Lake City, Utah), 19; *Journal History of the LDS Church*, 21 February 1888 (Scrapbook history located at LDS Archives); Beeton, *Women Vote in the West*, 79.

33. Katherine Devereaux Blake and Margaret Louise Wallace, *Champion of Women: The Life of Lillie Devereaux Blake* (New York: Fleming H. Revell Company, 1943), 167.

34. *Woman's Exponent* 16 (15 April 1888): 169–70.

35. Emmeline Wells, "Utah." *The History of Woman Suffrage*. vol. 4, ed. Susan

B. Anthony and Ida Husted Harper (Indianapolis: Hollenbeck Press, 1902; reprint, New York: Arno Press, 1969), 4:940.

36. "Editorial Thoughts," *Woman's Exponent* 16 (1 May 1888): 180; "They Captured the Convention," *Salt Lake Daily Tribune*, 15 April 1888, 2.

37. Julia Ward Howe, Diary, 24 June 1888, Houghton Library, Harvard University; Augusta Joyce Corocheran, "Appreciation of Mrs. Howe," *Woman's Exponent* 17 (1 August 1888): 35.

38. Emmeline B. Wells, Diary 23–26 June 1888, Typescript, Brigham Young University, Provo, Utah; "Julia Ward Howe," *Woman's Exponent* 17 (1 July 1888): 17–18.

39. "Holiday Notes," *Woman's Tribune* 6 (20 October 1888), in "Woman's Tribune Clippings Book," Huntington Library, San Marino, California, 191–93.

40. "In the Line of Duty," *Salt Lake Daily Tribune*, 11 October 1888, 2; "Utah Seen by the East," *Salt Lake Daily Tribune*, 23 November 1888, 4; Wells Diary, 17 October 1889.

41. Wells, "Utah," *History of Woman Suffrage*, 4:940; Carol Cornwall Madsen, "A Mormon Woman in Victorian America" (Ph.D. diss., University of Utah, 1985), 248–49.

42. Richards Interviews, Samuel W. Richards Collection, Historial Department, LDS Church, Salt Lake City, Utah. Folders 1, 2.

43. Susan B. Anthony to Eliza Wright Osborne, 5 February 1890, Anthony Family Correspondence, AF 80, Huntington Library, San Marino, California.

44. Julia Ward Howe, Diary, 17 February 1890, Houghton Library, Harvard University, 44M-314.

45. Elizabeth Cady Stanton, "Change Is the Law of Progress," 12 February 1890, Stanton Papers. Stanton added the words "Christian" and "Infidel" in the margin of her handwritten draft, but it is clear that at first writing she had the Mormon women primarily in mind.

46. Stanton, "Change Is the Law of Progress."

47. Stanton, letter fragment, n.d., Stanton papers, reel 5.

48. Emmeline Wells to Samuel Richards, 7 October 1895 and 4 November 1895, Samuel W. Richards Collection; Wells, Diary, 2 February 1895.

49. Hon. Marcus E. Jones, "The Present Situation in Utah as a Result of Statehood," *The Kinsman* 1 (5 February 1898): 2; William White, Jr., "The Feminist Campaign for the Exclusion of Brigham Henry Roberts from the Fifty-Sixth Congress," *Journal of the West* 17 (January 1978): 45–52; *Journal History of the LDS Church*, 17 February 1899.

50. Utah Woman's Press Club, Minute Book 1894–1898, Utah Historical Society; Beeton, *Women Vote in the West*, 90.

51. *Salt Lake Tribune*, 17–19 February 1899; Susa Y. Gates, "The Recent Triennial in Washington," *Young Woman's Journal* 10 (May 1899): 207–8.

52. *Salt Lake Tribune*, 19 February 1899.

53. "Miss Anthony on Roberts," *Woman's Exponent* 28 (15 November and 1 December 1899): 80; Harper, *The Life and Work of Susan B. Anthony*, 3:1151ff.

54. Harper, *The Life and Work of Susan B. Anthony*, 3:1151; 1:390.

55. Harper, *The Life and Work of Susan B. Anthony*, 3:1153.

56. Quoted in Lee Virginia Chambers-Schiller, *Liberty, a Better Husband. Single Women in America: The Generations of 1740–1840* (New Haven: Yale University Press, 1984), 68; Harper, *The Life of Susan B. Anthony*, 1:390.

57. Harper, *The Life and Work of Susan B. Anthony*, 3:1153.

58. Susa Young Gates, *Woman in History*, Typescript, Utah Historical Society, Salt Lake City, Utah (microfilm, Archives of the LDS Church), chapter "Statehood and Woman's Interests," 4.

59. Kathleen Barry, *Susan B. Anthony: A Biography of a Singular Feminist* (New York: New York University Press, 1988), 124.

60. Barry, *Susan B. Anthony*, 123–24; Chambers-Schiller, *Liberty, a Better Husband*, 68.

61. Susa Young Gates, *Woman in History*, MIC 1152–1169, Typescript, Utah Historical Society, chapter, "National and International Relations of Mormon Women," 45.

62. Anne Firor Scott, "Mormon Women, Other Women: Paradoxes and Challenges," *Journal of Mormon History* 13 (1986–87): 14. One of the most comprehensive books referring to this transformation in Mormon women's lives is *Sisters in Spirit: Mormon Women in Historical and Cultural Perspective*, ed. Maureen Ursenbach Beecher and Lavina Fielding Anderson (Urbana: University of Illinois Press, 1987).

10

The New Northwest *and* Woman's Exponent

Early Voices for Suffrage

SHERILYN COX BENNION

Although San Francisco was the home of what was probably the West's first woman suffrage paper,[1] two more long-lived suffrage publications took root in Portland, Ore., and in Salt Lake City, Utah. The Oregon paper was *The New Northwest*, a weekly founded in 1871 by Abigail Scott Duniway and edited and published by her until its death in 1887. In Utah the *Woman's Exponent* was issued twice a month from 1872 until 1914. Founded by and for Mormon women, it was edited during its first five years by Louisa Green Richards, with Emmeline B. Wells serving as editor for the remainder of its life.

The two papers were founded for different reasons and aimed at different audiences, but both were ardent voices in favor of women obtaining the right to vote. In spite of their differences, a comparison of the editors and their publications reveals some striking similarities and demonstrates that women's concerns found published expression in the West, as well as in the East, very early in the struggle for suffrage.

Along with calling attention to the contributions of Western women journalists in the campaign for suffrage, this paper attempts to look at

First published in *Journalism Quarterly* 54 (Summer 1977): 286–92. Reprinted by permission.

two of these women as editors. What sort of persons were they? Were their philosophies reflected in their papers? How did they feel about their newspaper careers? What were their papers like? One master's thesis has been written about Duniway's career as editor of *The New Northwest*, but no detailed examination of Wells, Richards or the *Exponent* exists, and no prior effort has been made to compare the two papers.[2]

The Editors

All three editors participated in the pioneer movements to the West, but Richards was only three years old when her family made the trek to the Mormon Zion in Utah. Wells was born in 1828 in Massachusetts, Duniway in 1834 in Illinois, and Richards in 1849 in Iowa. Since Wells saw the *Exponent* through 37 of its 42 years, this analysis will concentrate on her and Duniway.

Wells' father died when she was only four years old, and nine years later, still in Massachusetts, her mother joined the Mormon Church. Emmeline was baptized the next year. At 15, she began teaching school and also married James Harvey Harris, whose father was a leader in the Orange, Mass., Mormon congregation. The Harrises moved to Mormon headquarters at Nauvoo, Ill., in 1844, just a few weeks before the martyrdom of the Mormon prophet, Joseph Smith. Emmeline was deeply and favorably impressed by Smith, but her husband's parents apparently did not have similar feelings, for they soon left both Nauvoo and the Church. After a baby boy was born to Emmeline and died a month later, James, too, left Nauvoo. Emmeline never saw him again.

In 1845 she became the polygamous second wife of Mormon Presiding Bishop Newel K. Whitney. Emmeline had taught school at both Nauvoo and Winter Quarters, the jumping-off place for Mormon migrants, and after Whitney died in 1850 she taught in Salt Lake City. By that time, she had two daughters. Three more daughters were born after she married Daniel H. Wells, a prominent figure in religious and political affairs of the new territory. The youngest was 15 by the time Emmeline, at 49, became editor of the *Exponent*. Emmeline died in 1921, at the age of 93.

The basic facts of Duniway's life are similar, polygamous marriages excepted. Her mother and a younger brother died during the Scott family's move west from Illinois in 1852, but her father pushed on, and Abigail obtained a teaching position in a small town near Salem after the family arrived in Oregon, although she had less than a sixth-grade education. In 1853, after only one season of teaching, she married Benjamin Duniway, another recent emigrant from Illinois. In 1862, with four children, the Duniways lost their farm, which Ben had offered as security for a loan, and support of the family was left to Abigail a short time later when Ben was incapacitated by a back injury.

She first tried running boarding schools, then opened a millinery shop in Albany. This was sufficiently successful to finance a move to Portland, where Ben was able to get a job at the Customs House through the influence of Abigail's brother, Harvey, editor of the Portland *Oregonian* and a lifelong opponent of woman suffrage. Abigail was 36 and had six children—five sons and one daughter—when she started *The New Northwest*. She died in 1915, just before her 81st birthday. According to one account, her death was brought on by an infected toe that she had tried to cure herself; blood poisoning developed.[3]

Both editors had early aspirations toward careers as writers. Duniway was the keeper of the diary for the Scotts' journey to Oregon, and she published a novel based on the journey in 1859. Called *Captain Gray's Company, or Crossing the Plains and Living in Oregon*, it collected bad reviews and lost money. A year of contributing to the San Francisco suffrage paper, the *Pioneer*, prepared Duniway to found her own. Wells reported that she wrote her first verse at age four and that years later when her husband asked her what her dearest ambition was she replied immediately, "I would like to be the editor of a magazine."[4] She began contributing to the *Exponent* almost as soon as it was started.

Once they became editors, the women had ready forums for fiction and poetry, as well as articles and editorials. They regularly produced poems and serial novels for their papers, and some of these also were published separately. Duniway had a volume of poetry, *Musings*, published in 1875 and a book-length poem, *David and Anna Matson*, in 1876. She revised *Captain Gray's Company* for republication in 1905 and completed her autobiography, *Path-Breaking*, in 1914. Wells' book of poetry, which came out in 1896, was called *Musings and Memories*.

The editors came to support suffrage from quite different orientations. Duniway saw her mother as a victim of the backbreaking labor to which pioneer women were subjected. In her millinery shop she met women from whom she heard stories of husbands who left them to repay debts the wives had known nothing about or appropriated money the wives had earned selling butter and eggs. When, during a family conversation, Ben suggested that women could remedy such situations if they had the vote, Abigail saw the light. Of course! If women could vote, they could not only insure their own independence, they could clean up politics and perhaps even usher in an era of world peace.[5]

Wells' feelings about suffrage were tied up with her religious convictions. Even though women were excluded from the Mormon priesthood, they had always held voting rights in church congregations, and Utah women were given the vote in 1870, only three months after Wyoming women were the first in the nation to receive it. Wells was one of the first Utah women to cast a ballot, and was nominated for county treasurer, in 1878, but women did not yet have the right to hold office. She was anxious for all women to share in the blessings of the vote, as well as in what she saw as other advantages of Mormonism.

Between 1882, when wives of polygamous men were denied the vote by the Edmunds Bill (the Edmunds-Tucker Bill disenfranchised all women in Utah territory in 1887) and 1896, when statehood restored it, Mormon women were fighting to regain their privileged status. Suffrage was a religious, as well as a political, cause for Wells.

In spite of their support for the radical cause of woman suffrage, both Duniway and Wells were basically conservative in their views on woman's place. Women should, indeed, have the right to practice any suitable trade, but their first responsibility remained the home and family, as both editors frequently pointed out in their papers. One of the advantages of activities outside the home was that they made women more interesting wives and mothers. Giving them the vote would not make them masculine, Duniway promised, agreeing that there was "nothing more detestable to be seen or endured upon the earth than a feminine man, unless it be a masculine woman."[6]

The philosophies of both editors grew from their own experiences, and they saw their papers as vehicles to other women. This practical outlook also was manifest in their use of family help in the production of their papers. Duniway's sons and Wells' daughters set type and did editorial work. Duniway's sister, Catherine Coburn, and Wells' daughter, Annie Wells Cannon, had major responsibility for the papers while their editors organized and supervised out-of-town meetings.

Meetings occupied a major portion of both Wells' and Duniway's time. In Duniway's case, most of the meetings were to promote suffrage. She reported that she spoke an average of four times a week during the period of her editorship.[7] Temperance organizations received her support, and she served as president of the Oregon State Federation of Woman's Clubs after working for some time with the Portland Woman's Club. She ran for mayor of Portland in 1873.[8]

Wells was a long-time officer of the Mormon organization for women, the Relief Society, acting as general president from 1910 until her death. Related to her Relief Society positions were her leadership in such Church projects as a wheat storage campaign and the operation of a hospital and a mercantile association. Like Duniway, she organized and led suffrage groups and women's clubs, including the Utah Woman's Press Club, the Utah Woman's Republican League and the Utah Society of Daughters of the Revolution.

Obviously, both editors possessed tremendous stamina and drive. They had ideas and knew how to carry them through. This led to some impatience with those who did not share their visions or lend support in their struggles. For instance, neither woman could understand why readers needed to be reminded to renew and pay for subscriptions. At the end of 1886, Duniway wrote that she had produced more than 400 original columns of printed matter for *The New Northwest* and other papers during that year and had canvassed every town she had visited for subscriptions and renewals, adding,

> . . . we do feel abused, and insist that we have a right to say so, when suffragists, many of whom, as in Washington Territory, have received their liberties mainly through these efforts, and many others, as in Oregon, who owe their property rights and whatever of fame they have gained to the influence of this journal, withhold from it their support.[9]

Wells offered a similar scolding in 1893:

> It seems remarkably strange that the very women whose influence should be used to uphold and maintain the paper, should realize its importance so little as to think because times are hard and there is a depression in the money market and the value of silver is low, that they cannot afford to take a paper at a dollar a year, which would not average the amount of one third of a cent a day the year round. . . . To make flimsy excuses such as are often sent in letters to this office is childish.[10]

It was probably inevitable that two such peripatetic journalists with so much in common would meet. They began their acquaintance by exchanging papers, a practice common at that time, and occasionally printing excerpts from each other's publications. Duniway's comments about the women of Utah were friendly, and she insisted that they should not be denied the vote, but she never became reconciled to their practice of polygamy. Apparently she did not discuss that sensitive topic on her first lecture tour in Utah in 1872, because an early *Exponent* reported only that she gave an excellent discourse on the founding of her paper and her life's work in women's rights.[11] However, when she came in 1876 to give two lectures, she advised against polygamy, leading the *Exponent* to print a reply from "A Farmer's Daughter." This writer quoted Duniway as urging girls to marry when they were old and strong enough but asking them not to "imagine that I would have you take fractional husbands, as many of the women of Utah seem perfectly willing to do," then went on to defend polygamy.[12] Duniway reprinted the entire *Exponent* article in *The New Northwest*.

The Papers

While *The New Northwest* was founded expressly as a suffrage paper, the *Woman's Exponent* had broader purposes. The first number announced that it would discuss all subjects interesting and valuable to women, report Mormon Relief Society meetings and other matters connected with the workings of that organization, encourage both new and established writers and provide an outlet for their work, and furnish to the world an accurate view of the grossly misrepresented women of Utah. Its primary purpose was not to be an advocate of women's privileges, but it would support the struggle for just treatment.[13]

Duniway's inaugural editorial focused on women's rights:

> We see, under the existing customs of society, one half of the women over-taxed and underpaid; hopeless, yet struggling toilers in the world's drudgery; while the other half are frivolous, idle and expensive. Both of these conditions of society are wrong. Both have resulted from woman's lack of political and consequent pecuniary and moral responsibility. To prove this, and to elevate woman, that thereby herself and son and brother man may be benefitted and the world made better, purer, and happier, is the aim of this publication.[14]

Both editors were astute enough to realize that they would need more than high-minded purposes and impassioned editorial pleas to attract and hold readers. Their papers were lively collections of news, advice, humor, poetry and fiction.

The news usually appeared in the form of brief notes under headings like "Record of Recent Events" or "Local News" in *The New Northwest* and "Home Affairs" or "Local Notes" in the *Exponent*. Reports of meetings provided another sort of news; both papers carried lengthy summaries of meetings of the various organizations with which the editors were involved. A third type of news appeared in the columns of miscellaneous notes that both papers published. These might place a paragraph from a speech supporting suffrage next to an announcement that a new periodical for ladies had appeared in London and follow that with a brief polemic against Paris fashions, as one *Exponent* "News and Views" column did.[15]

Advice appeared in articles, editorials and helpful hints. The dress reform question was a preoccupation of both papers. The first page of the first number of *The New Northwest* carried articles about "Fashions for Gentlemen" and "Fashions for Ladies," stressing the necessity of tempering fashion consciousness with good sense, and a satire on "The Unwritten Heroism of Fashion-Ridden Women," an outgrowth, perhaps, of Duniway's experiences in her millinery shops. The *Exponent* warned that fads in fashion must be examined closely. Puffs and rats in hair were "unwholesome for the brain . . . and likely to produce disease, if not death."[16]

The helpful hints covered a wide area. The *Exponent* offered a "cure for Asthma" and suggested how "To Remove an Offensive Breath" and how "To Cleanse the Hair."[17] In answering a reader's question about bedbugs, Duniway wrote:

> The only effectual remedy for bed-bugs is to burn your house down and run away by the light of it. There is no other species of vermin so pestiferous, abominable, unendurable and un-get-rid-of-able as an Oregon bed-bug. We once bought a house that was infested with these odoriferous monsters, and after five years of drudgery in the attempt at extermination, we were glad to beat an ignominious retreat.[18]

Other advice was more directly related to the editorial convictions of the papers. They agreed that women needed to be educated, so that they could be both better wives and mothers and better citizens of their communities. They advised their readers to go beyond house-keeping and cookery and take an active part in community life but insisted that this would not result in any sacrifice of femininity. They urged support for temperance, although Duniway resisted tying this cause to suffrage, and opposed prohibition.

As pointed out, Duniway also opposed the Mormon practice of polygamy, which the *Exponent* vigorously defended, and she took a generally critical view of organized religion, as well, so this was another difference in the two papers. *The New Northwest* carried objections to religious hypocrisy and outdated dogma, while urging conformity to Christian ideals, but the

Woman's Exponent.

VOL. I.   SALT LAKE CITY, UTAH, JUNE 1, 1872.   No. 1.

NEWS AND VIEWS.

Women are now admitted to fifty American colleges.

Rev. De Witt Talmage is pronounced a success as a sensation preacher.

Theodore Tilton says the best brains in northern New York are wearing white hats. They might wear chapeaux of a more objectionable color.

Daniel W. Voorhees in one day destroyed the political record of a life-time, and that was when he became henchman to a judge with an eclesiastical mission.

An Alabama editor writes "United State," and refuses to write "United States"—a straw to show how Southern sentiment runs. What a state he must be in?

The season of scattering intellectual filth has set in over the country. It occurs quadrennially in the United States, commencing a few months before the Presidential election.

Dr. Newman failed to become a Bishop at the Methodist General Conference, and Dr. Newman mourns this second great defeat. He has remembrances of Salt Lake in connection with the previous one.

Great outcry is raised against the much marrying of the Latter-day Saints. The tendency of the age is to disregard marriage altogether, but there seems no indication of a desire to have the race die out.

The "Alabama" muddle like "confusion worse confounded" becomes worse mixed the more it is stirred. It stretches itself over the path of time, and "like a wounded snake drags its slow length along." The country has become heartily sick of it.

Some Eastern journals head their Utah news with "Deseret." With keen appreciation of the coming and inevitable, they accept the mellifluous name chosen for the region wrested by that industry which "the honey bee" represents, from the barren wilds of nature.

George Francis Train sends us a bundle of Train Ligues. The compliment is appreciated, but the act is like sweetness wasted. We can vote, but not for "the next President of America." Utah has not become Deseret yet, nor can it participate in Presidentmaking.

The last week of May, 1872, will be memorable in American annals as the first time since the first ordinance of secession was passed in the South, that both houses of Congress had their full list of members. Statesmanship can retain a complete Federal Legislature, but the article has grown somewhat scarce.

To pardon the worst class of criminals on condition that they emigrate to the United States, is growing in favor with European mouarchies. Germany and Greece so far have done the largest business in this line, the latest batch of villains thus disposed of being the Marathon murderers from Greece. Orders have been forwarded by President Grant to New Orleans, to which port it is understood they have been sent, to prevent their landing. They should be captured, ironed, returned to Athens with Uncle Samuel's compliments, and a bill for direct and "consequential" damages presented.

News comes from France that trailing dresses for street wear are going out of fashion. So many absurd and ridiculous fashions come from Paris that the wonder is thinking American women do not, with honest republican spirit, reject them entirely. This latter one, however, is so sensible that its immediate adoption will be an evidence of good sense wisely directed.

The anti-Mormon bill of Judge Bingham seems to have fared no better in the judiciary committee of the House of Representatives than the one to which Mr. Voorhees stood sponsor. It is gratifying to think that a majority of that committee yet respect the antiquated and once revered instrument still occasionally referred to as the Constitution.

Rev. James Freeman Clark claims "that if it is an advantage to vote, women ought to have it; if a disadvantage men ought not to be obliged to bear it alone." Speaking from experience we feel safe in affirming that the Rev. gentleman is right, and we hope for a time when this immunity may be universally enjoyed by our pure-minded and light-loving sisters. We don't presume that those belonging to the opposite class care anything about it.

Mrs. Carrie F. Young, editor of the "Pacific Journal of Health," has been lecturing in Idaho on Temperance and Woman Suffrage. The editor of the "Idaho World" was not present, but did not regret his absence. He says, "We feel a most decided repugnance to the exhibition of a woman upon the rostrum, advocating such degrading theories as 'woman suffrage' and other cognate subjects." He omits to state whether "Temperance" is one of the "degrading theories" to which he refers.

Force is ever the argument of a bad cause. The principles which cannot be overcome except by the exercise of physical power, present a front that arrests the attention of thinking minds. Where argument fails and force is employed to overcome an opponent, the power of the principles to which opposition is made is admitted. Will those who urge repressive legislation against the people of Utah think of it? Witness the Voorhees bill as an illustration.

A notable event, as a result of the late terrible Franco-German war, is the opening of the German University in Strasbourg, which takes place June 1st—to-day. That famous city on the Rhine, after a siege memorable in the annals of warfare, passed into the hands of the Germans, and now they take the surest means to permanently consolidate their power, by establishing there one of those seats of learning for which Germany has become enviably famous.

Miss Susan B. Anthony, it is said, declared before the Cincinnati Convention met, that if it gave her cause "the cold shoulder," she would go to Philadelphia and pledge the ballots of the women of America to U. S. Grant. As the women of America are yet without ballots, and as it is very questionable, if they had them, whether they would authorize any single individual to pledge them for any caudidate, the supposition is fair that Miss Anthony possesses too much good sense to have made any such declaration.

Rev. Mr. Peirce, a Methodist clergyman who has made Salt Lake his headquarters for some time, in lecturing east proposed the extinction of polygamy by the introduction here of vast quantities of expensive millinery goods, and by inducing "Gentile" women to dress in gorgeous style that "Mormon" women might imitate them and run up such heavy dry goods bills that it would be impossible for a man to support more than one wife, if even one. Mr. Peirce, no doubt, preaches modesty and humility occasionally, by way of variety; now he recommends the encouragement of pride, vanity and extravagance to accomplish his "Christian" designs. The course he advises has been largely followed in many places, has tenanted brothels, aided to fill prisons, broken up families, hurled women of reputation and position down to degradation and infamy, and has met heavy denunciations from inspired men whom Mr. Peirce professes to revere. He would steal the livery of evil to serve religion in. There is not much of this reverend gentleman, and what little there is must be either very silly or very wicked.

The editor of "The Present Age" has been to a church and heard an orthodox sermon, in which the preacher took occasion to say that all religious "isms," including Mohammedanism, Mormonism and Spiritualism, rested their claims for being true "upon miracles." The "Age" is a Spiritualist and denies that his "ism" basis its claims to be true upon miracles. Latter-day Saints deny that Mormonism basis any claim for credence in it on miracles; the reverse is the truth. The "Age" defines a miracle to be "the setting aside for the time being of a natural law to meet an unexpected emergency." Had he said a miracle was the bringing into operation of certain natural laws not generally understood or comprehended, he would have been nearer correct. When somebody can tell how a natural law may be or can be set aside, except by the operation of some other natural law, his definition, which is the generally received one, may be entitled to more consideration. We imagine the working of the overland telegraph is as great a miracle to the Cheyenne Indians as any recorded miracle that the "Age" or the orthodox minister can quote.

Mrs. Laura De Force Gordon attended the Cincinnati Convention and claimed a seat as a delegate from California. Her claim was treated with hisses and laughter. She took a position in front of the stand and endeavored to speak, but her voice was drowned by a tumultuous discord. Her persistence in seeking to address an assemblage that treated her claim in such a manner was undignified; while the action of the Convention in receiving her with hisses and uproarious laughter, was disgraceful. The Liberal Republicans assembled in Cincinnati for a general work of purification and reform, evidently stood greatly in need of general reform themselves, in the matter of manners as well as in politics. Mrs. Gordon was as much entitled to a seat in that Convention as Carl Schurz himself, for we have yet to learn that the call for it specified that "male" Republicans only were admissable.

A new periodical in London is called "The Ladies."

First issue of the *Woman's Exponent* (1872–1914). *Courtesy of Archives, Historical Department, Church of Jesus Christ of Latter-day Saints.*

major portion of its religious wrath was reserved for those who used the Bible to sanction the subordination of women.

Replies to critics of her paper and her views gave Duniway another opportunity to exercise her indignation. She regularly printed comments, both favorable and unfavorable, from letters to the editor and from other publications. Her replies to these were one more means of conveying her own opinions. The *Woman's Exponent* used far fewer comments from outside sources about its editorial views.

Another difference was the amount of space devoted to biography. *The New Northwest* printed occasional sketches of such notables as Margaret Fuller and Alice Cary, but biographies and autobiographies—and obituaries—were mainstays of the *Exponent*, perhaps because, as that paper reported, Mormon Church President Brigham Young had directed that "the lives of prominent women in the Church, those who had associated in the early days in active measures for the benefit and establishment of Mormonism, . . . should be written up."[19]

Fiction in the *Exponent* was sometimes difficult to distinguish from biography. Wells wrote a substantial amount of both, and when she was trying to get subscriptions for a volume of her short stories in 1902, she claimed that all were based on fact, which may account for some of the confusion.[20] Her fictional works, usually published in the *Exponent* as serials, had a common formula: A strong, noble heroine, either born a Mormon or converted during the course of the story, triumphed eventually over tremendous odds and temptations, found her true love and produced a crop of children whose adventures both complicated and lengthened the chronicle.

The formula of Duniway's serials was somewhat different, but they were equally didactic. Her strong, noble heroines were oppressed by bigoted husbands or frontier hardships but defied convention to pursue careers and eventually find marriages based on true love and respect. Her stories usually were written, Duniway admitted, week by week to meet the demands of the paper's deadlines. An exception was noted in an 1880 ad for her upcoming effort, a "good portion" of which was already finished and showed "a care in its construction unknown in her previous successful efforts."[21]

Both editors also wrote poetry for their papers and used a considerable amount by other authors, in addition. That in *The New Northwest* was often by nationally-known poets, while the *Exponent* relied almost entirely on its own readers for poetry. In fact, the amount of material from reader-contributors was another major difference between the two papers. The *Exponent* had as one of its expressed purposes the cultivation of literary talent among its readers. This was not a goal of *The New Northwest*.

The subjects of the poetry used by the papers were similar: Nature, joys (or sometimes trials, in the case of *The New Northwest*) of womanhood, friendship, desirable character traits, important events, tributes. Like the serial novels, the poems were sentimental and moralistic.

Another type of content used by both *The New Northwest* and the *Exponent* was advertising, although both relied primarily on subscriptions for revenue. The *Exponent* carried more ads during the 1870s than at any other time, perhaps because advertising was sought more assiduously then. As Wells took on more and more responsibilities in the multitudinous organizations to which she belonged, she may have neglected the business affairs of the paper. Advertisers ranged from furniture stores to patent medicines. Advertising in *The New Northwest* was similar—and more plentiful. Both papers offered advertisers support in their editorial columns by telling readers when shipments of goods arrived or special values were offered and by urging patronage of advertisers.

The editors also sought new subscribers through advertisements. Another method used by the *Exponent* to recruit readers was the organization of subscription clubs, which were offered one free subscription for each 10 paid-up ones they sent in. Both papers had agents in various communities who received a commission for subscriptions they turned in, and both offered premiums for those who were especially successful. *The New Northwest* started its 1871 premium list with a shuttle sewing machine and moved up to an organ. At that time, every subscriber also received three months of *Woodhull and Claflin's Weekly* free. Duniway later expressed disapproval of Victoria Woodhull's private career and substituted other publications as bonuses.[22] The *Exponent* in 1886 gave each new subscriber a portrait suitable for framing of Lucy Mack Smith, mother of the prophet Joseph Smith.

These inducements never seemed to be as effective as the editors expected. Finally, both reduced prices, *The New Northwest* from $3.00 to $2.50 for a year's subscription at the beginning of 1886, the *Woman's Exponent* from $2.00 to $1.00 in 1889. Still, as evidenced by the editors' frequent pleas and scoldings, circulation did not jump. Exact figures are difficult to find. *The New Northwest* probably peaked at 3,000 subscribers in 1884.[23] Ayer's *American Newspaper Annual* estimated the *Exponent's* circulation at only 700 in 1902,[24] but it had been higher in earlier years. A Relief Society membership report in 1881 listed 754 subscribers among the groups reporting but gave no indication of how many units did not report.[25]

Duniway wearied of the battle for readers considerably sooner than did Wells. She had other problems, as well, during 1886. Her only daughter died, and, during the summer, two sons left to go into ranching in Idaho.

Then her husband became seriously ill. In January 1887, at the age of 53, she sold the paper to a Portland businessman and his daughter, announcing in *The New Northwest* of Jan. 6:

> Over and over again during the past few years I have warned the readers of this journal that I would sever my business relations with it unless they would more promptly remit their maturing subscriptions and relieve me of the compulsory labor of regularly visiting their many different localities in order to collect its dues. Advancing years and increasing calls in the lecture field have made the financial load heavy that I once carried with comparative ease.[26]

Duniway promised that she would continue to write for the paper, but the Feb. 24 number contained an announcement that she had ceased to be connected with it.[27] The new owners kept *The New Northwest* for two years, then sold it.

Wells never actually threatened to abandon the *Woman's Exponent*. In fact, after 25 years as editor, she wrote that "altogether it has been a labor of love, no matter how arduous the work or how numerous the fault finders, never once has the writer been tempted to withdraw."[28] By that time the paper was appearing with numbers combined, occasionally missing numbers altogether.

In 1912, Wells decided that she would give the *Exponent* to the Mormon Relief Society, the organization for which it had been unofficial voice since its founding. However, she requested that she be retained as editor and her daughter as assistant editor. Apparently, the organization was not willing to accept the paper on its 84-year-old president's terms, and two years later it was discontinued, to be replaced in 1915 with *The Relief Society Magazine*.

Wells lived long enough to see the 19th amendment ratified in 1920, after the vote had been restored to Utah women in 1896, and Duniway was the heroine of the day when woman's suffrage was approved by Oregon in 1912, so both editors lived to see their fight for woman suffrage at least partially won. They must have felt satisfaction in the fact that their papers had been among the earliest—East or West—to advocate the right of women to vote.

Notes

1.   The *San Francisco Pioneer*, published from 1869 to 1873 and edited by Emily Pitt Stevens.

2. The master's thesis is Gayle R. Bandow's " 'In Pursuit of a Purpose:' Abigail Scott Duniway and the New Northwest" (University of Oregon M.A. Thesis 1973). Duniway writes little of her editorship in her autobiography, *Path-Breaking* (Portland, Ore.: James, Kerns and Abbott Co., 1914), and her newspaper career is not covered at length in the biography by Helen Krebs Smith, *The Presumptuous Dreamers* (Lake Oswego, Ore.: Smith, Smith and Smith Publishing Company, 1974), although Smith does include a useful bibliography. Periodical articles about her, such as the recent one by Elinor Richey, "The Unsinkable Abigail," *American Heritage*, XXVI (February 1975), usually mention her editorship only in passing.

No book-length works have been written about Richards or Wells. Biographical information for them may be culled from articles in Mormon periodicals, such as *The Relief Society Magazine*, the *Improvement Era*, and *The Instructor*, and from manuscripts in the collection of The Historical Department of The Church of Jesus Christ of Latter-day Saints, Salt Lake City, which also holds a typescript history of the *Exponent* by Susa A. Young Gates.

The papers themselves are the best sources of information about the women as editors. Both are on microfilm. For this article, copies at the Mormon Historical Department and the University of Oregon were used.

3. Elinor Richey, op. cit., 89.

4. "Emmeline B. Wells," *The Relief Society Magazine*, VII, 136 (March 1920).

5. Helen Krebs Smith, op. cit., 112.

6. "Feminine Men and Masculine Women," *The New Northwest*, May 15, 1871: 2.

7. Gayle R. Bandow, op. cit., 11.

8. "The Sex," *Woman's Exponent*, July 15, 1873: 31.

9. "Record of a Year's Work," *The New Northwest*, Dec. 16, 1886: 1.

10. "The Woman's Exponent," *Woman's Exponent*, July 1 and 15, 1893: 184.

11. "Editorial Notes," *Woman's Exponent*, July 15, 1873: 29.

12. "A Farmer's Daughter," *Woman's Exponent*, Sept. 1, 1876: 49.

13. "Woman's Exponent," "Our Position," "Woman's Rights and Wrongs," *Woman's Exponent*, June 1, 1872: 8, 4, 5.

14. "About Ourself," *The New Northwest*, May 5, 1871: 2.

15. "News and Views," *Woman's Exponent*, June 1, 1872: 1.

16. "Extremes in Dress," *Woman's Exponent*, October 1910: 28.

17. "Household Hints," *Woman's Exponent*, June 1, 1872: 3.

18. "Correspondence," *The New Northwest*, Oct. 6, 1871: 1.

19. "A Word to the Relief Society," *Woman's Exponent*, June 1904: 4.

20. "A Book for the Holidays," *Woman's Exponent*, Oct. 1 and 15, 1902: 36.

21. "New Serial Story" and "A New Story," *The New Northwest*, Nov. 6, 1879: 2, 3.

22. "Erratic Women," *The New Northwest*, July 21, 1871: 1.

23. Gayle R. Bandow, op. cit., 44.

24. N. W. Ayer and Son, *American Newspaper Annual* (Philadelphia: N. W. Ayer and Son, 1902), 850.

25. "Relief Society Report," *Woman's Exponent*, Nov. 1., 1887: 4.
26. "Personal Announcement," *The New Northwest*, Jan. 6, 1887: 4.
27. "Announcement," *The New Northwest*, Feb. 24, 1887: 1.
28. "Editorial Work," *Woman's Exponent*, July 1 and 15, 1902: 12.

I I

Woman Suffrage, Popular Art, and Utah

GARY L. BUNKER
CAROL B. BUNKER

From the earliest stirrings of the woman suffrage movement in Utah, popular artists represented or misrepresented the partisans of women's rights up to the adoption of the Nineteenth Amendment to the Constitution.[1] Neither Utah nor woman suffrage was a stranger to social caricature, since artists had long feasted at a banquet of controversy that both Mormonism and suffrage advocates served.[2] But the half-century tie between Utah and woman suffrage gave illustrators the luxury of maligning or praising Utahns and the proponents of suffrage with strokes from the same brush in a single, usually humorous, print.

The illustrations were unevenly distributed over a fifty-year span, which may be subdivided into four logical stages: (1) enfranchisement, (2) disfranchisement, (3) statehood and reenfranchisement, and (4) the quest for national suffrage. Although cartoonists depicted all four phases, most illustrations emerged during the 1880s (stage two) and from 1911 to 1919 (stage four). The scorn and censure that characterized the popular art of the first two stages differed dramatically from the esteem and commendation that typified the final phases.

First published in *Utah Historical Quarterly* 59 (Winter 1991): 32–51. Reprinted by permission.

Enfranchisement

As early as 1856 William Hay saw the women's rights movements as an antidote to polygamy.[3] By 1869 linking woman suffrage and Mormonism as natural adversaries had become political reality because Rep. George W. Julian had proposed a bill "to discourage polygamy in Utah by granting the right of suffrage to the women of that territory."[4] But Julian, like many others, had underestimated the religious convictions of Mormon women.

To Julian's surprise—perhaps even chagrin—political prognostication had missed the mark. By 1870 the women of Utah were voting by mandate of their own territorial legislature. Furthermore, Mormon women were voting contrary to Julian's expectations, namely, in support of polygamy.

Ironically, that same year, politicians then drafted legislation to disfranchise the new voters. To the dismay of these disciples of disfranchisement, opposition surfaced from an unexpected source—Susan B. Anthony and Elizabeth Cady Stanton's National Woman Suffrage Association (NWSA). The NWSA was not about to stand idly by as any women—even polygamous women from Utah—were threatened with losing their right to the ballot. Thus these unforeseen circumstances forged the bond, tenuous at first, between Utah and the suffrage movement.[5]

The earliest editorial cartoon showing the potential association between Utah and woman suffrage appeared in an October 1869 issue of *Frank Leslie's Illustrated Newspaper*.[6] In the cartoon Brigham Young leads a formidable parade of ballot-and baby-carrying women to the polling booth. A banner held aloft, labeled "Straight Democratic Ticket," humorously conveys the impression that the Democratic party will gain the new votes. But the rhetorical question posed by the caption drives home the real meaning: "Wouldn't it [female suffrage] put just a little too much power into the hands of Brigham Young, and his tribe?" While the caricature may have been spawned by skepticism of Representative Julian's proposal to grant Utah women the vote, it also exhibited the powerful and popular stereotype of Mormon women: gullible, docile, and hoodwinked disciples of their faith.[7] In part, this degrading imagery accelerated the adoption of woman suffrage in Utah because the Mormons resolved to counter the offensive stereotype.[8]

Just four months later, February 1870, the hypothetical situation of woman suffrage in the territory of Utah had become political fact. Utah women would vote for the next seventeen years, but the reality of suffrage stimulated the political thrust for disfranchisement. Between 1870 and 1887 popular art was an effective agent in the campaign to take the ballot away from Utah women.

FEMALE SUFFRAGE.

Wouldn't it put just a little too much power into the hands of Brigham Young, and his tribe?

Frank Leslie's Illustrated Newspaper, October 2, 1869. *Courtesy of Library of Congress.*

Disfranchisement

As noted earlier, the threat of disfranchisement mobilized the national women's organization for suffrage in behalf of their Utah sisters. For example, in 1870 the NWSA remonstrated "against the proposition now pending in the Senate of the United States to disfranchise the women of Utah, as a movement in aid of polygamy, against justice, and a flagrant violation of a vested right."[9] The NWSA also commended the Utah and Wyoming territories as "the friends of woman suffrage." Not to be outdone, Lucy Stone's Boston-based American Woman Suffrage Association (AWSA) followed suit.[10]

In addition, Utah women vigorously denounced the threatening legislation. An 1871 cartoon captured the spirit, though not the essence, of resistance by Mormon women. Joseph Keppler, cartoonist for the German-language *Puck* magazine, depicted a chorus of Mormon women in bloomers militantly defending themselves.[11] At that time the bloomer was a telltale symbol of women's rights and advocacy usually reserved by the caricaturist for eastern suffragists. Here, however, Keppler cleverly and subtly links Utah women with the suffrage cause by means of the bloomer.

Five years later, in 1876, the NWSA claimed that the social experiment of woman suffrage in Wyoming and Utah territories was alive and well. "We have not learned that households have been broken up or that babies have ceased to be rocked," noted a chronicler of suffrage history.[12] And the constant effort to disfranchise Utah women continued to nettle the proponents of women's rights. Resolutions passed in 1876 and 1879 expressed frustration over the matter: "We denounce the proposition about to be again presented to Congress for the disfranchisement for the women of that territory, as an outrage on the freedom of thousands of legal voters."[13] The 1879 version took the issue one step further. After asking the Congress once again to "forbear to exercise federal power to disfranchise women of Utah," the resolution needled the male legislators by suggesting that the women of Utah "have had a more just and liberal spirit shown them by Mormon men than gentile women in the states have yet perceived in their rulers."[14]

But the agitation for disfranchisement was just warming up as the 1880s emerged. No sooner had the new decade dawned than the sweeping Edmunds legislation, which banned polygamists from voting, was enacted into law. J. A. Wales, artist for *Judge* magazine, portrayed the suffrage implications of the bill: "One Wife Or No Ballot" and "No Ballot For Slaveowners" were the featured captions.[15] True to the popular image, Wales drew degraded and dejected women, shackled by handcuffs and encircled by the bonds of polygamy. Eastern suffragists did not object to the disfranchisement of polygamous males, but they did continue to take exception to the constant legislative pressure to disfranchise Utah women. For example, Phoebe Cousins, a member of the NWSA, gave an impassioned argument against Sen. John T. Morgan's 1882 resolution to ban Utah women from voting. She could speak about the situation in Utah from firsthand experience. She had been admitted to the Utah bar in 1872, a right then denied by some states.[16] To buttress her case that "suffrage for women in Utah has accomplished great good," she drew on her one-week stay in the territory. "Outside of their religious convictions," she remarked, "the women are emphatic in condemnation of wrong." She ascribed the banishment of "liquor saloons" and the absence of "poison tobacco smoke" to the votes of women. The litmus test of morality, however, came when she walked the streets of Salt Lake City at midnight.

> No bacchanalian shout rent the air; no man was seen reeling in maudlin imbecility to his home. . . . no sound awoke the stillness but the purring of the mountain brooks which washed the streets in cleanliness and beauty. What other city on this continent can present such a showing?[17]

Despite such rhetoric the disfranchisement crusade escalated.

By 1884 the Edmunds-Tucker bill was gathering momentum. Yet eastern proponents of women's rights were undaunted by the opposition. In a speech to the annual NWSA convention, Belva Lockwood, an inveterate defender of the underdog and candidate for the presidency of the United States that year, severely criticized the latest effort to disfranchise Utah women.[18] Later, when Lockwood visited Salt Lake City in 1885, she was warmly welcomed as "champion of the oppressed." She modestly "said she had simply done her duty in speaking in defense of the women in Utah."[19] But there were risks of guilt by association affixed to helping Mormon women. In the aftermath of Lockwood's visit and in the midst of the growing controversy over polygamy, the San Francisco *Wasp* cartooned Belva Lockwood, Dr. Mary Walker, and Marietta Stow (Belva Lockwood's vice-presidential running mate) in a caricature of a Mormon home.[20] Walter, the creator of the scene, poked fun at Mormon women in "The Wives' Gallery," which consisted of sixteen portraits of ugly wives. This parody of the Mormon family also showed over thirty children stuffed into one bed. While the major intent of sardonic caricature was to defame Mormonism, the editorial commentary simultaneously misrepresented these "philanthropic women's-rights women" as well. The editorial pictured them recommending "that the men are to be hung or imprisoned and the wives sequestered."[21] Such exaggeration and distortion were simply part of the generous license accorded humorous illustrated weeklies.[22]

By the mid—1880s the practice of polygamy was under siege. As more and more prominent Mormon leaders were convicted and taken to prison, the women of Mormonism came to their defense.[23] Earlier, but to no avail, the leadership of Mormonism had protested, on constitutional grounds, their treatment under provisions of the Edmunds law. But the plea to the president of the United States and the Congress fell upon deaf ears.[24] As incarceration and harassment escalated, Mormon women took it upon themselves to formulate their own petition. An integral part of the women's resolutions dealt with the jeopardized franchise to women.

> *Resolved*, By the women of Utah in mass meeting assembled, that the suffrage, originally conferred upon us as a political privilege, has become a vested right by possession and usage for fifteen years, and that we protest against being deprived of that right without process of law, and for no other reason than that we do not vote to suit our political opponents.
>
> *Resolved*, That we emphatically deny the charge that we vote otherwise than according to our own free choice, and point to the fact that the ballot is absolutely secret in Utah as proof that we are protected in voting for whom and what we chose with perfect liberty.
>
> *Resolved*, That as no wife of a polygamist, legal or plural, is permitted to vote under the laws of the United States, to deprive non-polygamous women of suffrage, is high-hand oppression for which no valid excuse can be offered.[25]

Other resolutions expressed appreciation for the "moral courage" of certain senators, Belva Lockwood, and the AWSA "who in the face of almost overwhelming prejudice, have defended the constitutional rights of the people of Utah."[26]

Not only was the petition rejected, but its source was questioned by the *Washington Evening Star*: "It is understood that the petition was written by a well-known Mormon attorney, and is a device to gain sympathy for the 'Saints.'"[27] Emmeline B. Wells shot off a protest letter to the editor of the *Evening Star*. "The memorial was drafted by a committee of 'Mormon' women," she said, "whose signatures were attached to each . . . copy."[28]

Still, voices like Emmeline B. Wells were muted by the roar of derision. For example, Dalrymple, cartoonist for the New York *Daily*

Graphic, embellished and perpetuated the stereotype of Mormon women as inconsequential pawns in the hands of their male leaders.[29] The cartoonist depicted male church representatives, disguised in female attire, delivering the women's petition. A sign next to the White House gate emphatically declares "Notice: The Mormons Must Go." And the caption distills the cartoon message: "The Last Strategem of the Mormon Church—The 'Women of Utah' Protest Against the Laws of the United States." To be sure, the image of males masquerading as females was a clever artistic device and perhaps a powerful persuader of public opinion, yet no image was more repugnant to the Mormon women.[30] Nevertheless, the die was cast: the political crusade to disfranchise Utah women was rolling inexorably toward victory.

In 1887, when the Edmunds-Tucker Act finally passed, the NWSA expressed its disapproval "for the disfranchisement of the non-polygamous women of Utah," labeling the action "a disregard of individual rights which is dangerous to the liberties of all."[31] That neither women's rights nor Mormonism, protests and petitions notwithstanding, had the kind of credibility to wield sufficient influence to restore the ballot to Utah women was shown by a color lithograph drawn by F. Victor Gillam in *Judge* magazine. Susan B. Anthony, Belva Lockwood, and representatives of Mormonism, prohibition, communism, socialism, anarchism, and dynamitism were depicted as tailors trying to mend Uncle Sam's coat—a symbol of the United States Constitution.[32] The "Chorus of Tailors" queried: "Hadn't you better let us repair that coat? It's too old-fashioned for these go-ahead times." To which Uncle Sam replied, "The Coat is Good Enough for Me, and Will last at least Another Hundred Years!"

By the end of the 1880s the legal strictures imposed by the Edmunds-Tucker Act were taking their toll. Nothing short of substantial accommodation by leaders of the Mormon church would placate a resolute Congress. Phillip Cusachs, artist for the New York *Daily Graphic*, expressed the grim reality of the situation.[33] Although Uncle Sam would leave the door of statehood for Utah wide open, "Knocking for Admission" without substantial concessions from the Mormon leaders would be futile. Those concessions began with the church Manifesto that abolished polygamy in 1890 and were fully in place when statehood was sought in 1895 and bestowed in 1896.

Statehood and Reenfranchisement

The year 1896 was a good one for woman suffrage. Utah and Idaho joined Wyoming and Colorado as suffrage states, and the vote for suffrage in California, though not victorious, was encouraging.[34] Because of the tangible progress, members of the now consolidated National American Woman Suffrage Association (NAWSA) were in a festive mood at their 28th annual convention. Artist George Y. Coffin was commissioned to create the program cover which he entitled "The Apotheosis of Liberty."[35] Flanking George Washington were the trumpet-blowing Susan B. Anthony and Elizabeth Cady Stanton wielding "The Woman's Bible."[36] On each end of the print the states of Wyoming and Utah proudly waved their banners of suffrage under the NAWSA convention logo.

Utah was given special honor at the NAWSA convention. Sen. and Mrs. Frank J. Cannon and Rep. and Mrs. C. E. Allen of Utah were seated on the platform. Both Susan B. Anthony and Anna Howard Shaw paid tribute to Utah. The latter noted:

> We expected it of the men of Utah. No man there could have stood by the side of his mother and heard her tell of all that the pioneers endured, and then have refused to grant her the same right of liberty he wanted for himself, without being unworthy of such a mother. They are the crown of our Union, those three States [Wyoming, Colorado and Utah] on the crest of the Rockies, above all the others. In the name of the NAWSA we extend our welcome, our thanks, and our congratulations to Utah as one of the three so dear to the heart of every woman who loves liberty in these United States.[37]

Senator Cannon, the Allens, Sarah A. Boyer, and Emily S. Richards all responded to the tributes. "Our women had furnished courage, patience, and heroism to our men," observed Senator Cannon, "and so we said: Utah shall take another forty-nine years of wandering in the wilderness as a Territory before coming in as a State without her women."[38]

Once Utah women regained the ballot artists ceased to associate Utah with the suffrage cause until the final stage began. By 1911 the suffrage movement was gathering momentum for the decisive surge toward the full enfranchisement of women. The constituency for woman suffrage was growing and achieving a broader political base. New suffrage states were joining the cause each year, adding to the critical mass so essential for a real breakthrough. A new woman suffrage organization, the Congressional Union, spurred the drive for a federal amendment. And in 1915 new leadership in the NAWSA invigorated the movement. In short, the tide of public opinion was beginning to turn against the antisuffrage stance. Thus all these factors combined to place Utah in a favored position. Now, artists began to picture Utah in the vanguard of advancing women's rights.

"The Apotheosis of Liberty," pen and ink drawing by G. Y. Coffin, 1896, Prints Division, Library of Congress. *Courtesy of Library of Congress.*

Cover, *Woman's Journal*, November 30, 1912. *Courtesy of University of Wyoming.*

The Quest For National Suffrage

Between 1911 and 1913 virtually all cartoons involving Utah depicted Utah and the handful of other suffrage states as models worthy of emulation. In the *Woman's Journal* a trio of unimaginative cartoons by J. W. Beecroft exploited this idea. In 1911, when Washington adopted the vote for women, Beecroft saw the suffrage crusade "Cleaning Up the West."[39] Next, he used a lopsided Uncle Sam emblem to expose the disparity between those states that granted female suffrage, now including California, and the majority that did not.[40] The final Beecroft cartoon showed some ambivalence toward women's rights. While he portrayed Uncle Sam blaming John Bull for stoking the furnace of female suffrage, he also featured the six western suffrage states as stars in the national firmament.[41] In each case the people of Utah could savor their inclusion in the Beecroft cartoons since they were now receiving applause for their suffrage position. In the same vein, Ralph Silder placed Utah, California, Wyoming, Colorado, Idaho, and Washington in a reception line greeting suffrage aspirants Oregon, Michigan, Kansas, and Arizona. Rounding out the cartoons from the *Woman's Journal*, Harriet Park progressively magnified a woman's image to create the impression of concrete gain from 1869 to 1912.[43] Finally, *Judge* magazine, an early foe of suffrage, was now unabashedly portraying the suffrage states as intrepid "Conquerors" of "Conservatism," "Prejudice," and "Anti-Suffrage" forces.[44]

Yet not everything from the artist's palette was complimentary to Utah's citizens. *Life's* A. B. Walker could not resist showing his rendition of feminism's effects in Utah.[45] He drew an intimidated Mormon male fleeing from four attacking feminists who used a rolling pin, broom, frying pan, and eggs as weapons. The caption summarized the alleged effects of extending woman's sphere: "Mormonism is on the wane in Utah." And Harriet M. Olcott for *Puck*, drawing tongue-in-cheek, saw "Woman's Rights in Utah" tipping the scales of power in favor of polyandry.[46] Such lighthearted cartoons chided both Mormonism and woman suffrage with good-natured humor.

Another artistic artifice that publicized Utah was the map of suffrage haves and have nots. In 1913, when Illinois became the first suffrage state east of the Mississippi, John T. McCutcheon, cartoonist for the *Chicago Tribune*, acclaimed the breakthrough in the eastern block of states by recognizing the solid support from the West.[47] Two years later the noted illustrator Hy Mayer designed for *Puck* "The Awakening."[48] Although Mayer somehow excluded Illinois from the suffrage states, the moral of the cartoon was obvious: Women yearn for suffrage, and it is only a matter of time before the final conquest. The *Woman's Journal* rendered a more accurate map that included Illinois.

Cover, *The Suffragist*, September 4, 1915. *Courtesy of University of Illinois, Urbana.*

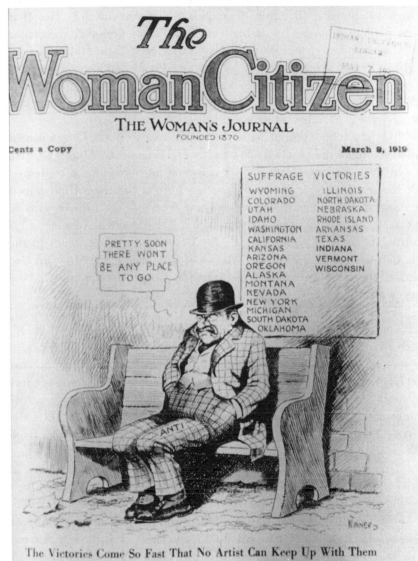

Cover, *The Woman Citizen*, March 8, 1919. *Courtesy of University of Indiana, Bloomington.*

The cartoonist depicted the suffrage blossoms growing in the soil of liberty and equality, watered by justice, pruned by education and truth, and sprayed by logic to eliminate the antisuffrage pest.[49] (The antisuffrage caterpillar teeters perilously on the tip of Maine.) "Prune away prejudice," exclaims Uncle Sam, "and these four states [Pennsylvania, New York, Massachusetts, and New Jersey] will blossom in November." Finally, a "Victory Map" in the 1917 *The Woman Citizen* graphically shows the erosion of antisuffrage backing.[50] Although Utah was only a part of the whole in these images, it was, nevertheless, lauded for its view.

In 1915 more specific notice for Utah came as the Congressional Union, the more militant women's rights organization and competitor to the NAWSA, promoted support for a federal amendment. Discontented with the snail's pace of the state-by-state suffrage strategy, Utah joined the constitutional amendment bandwagon. *The Suffragist*, media arm of the Congressional Union, photographed Sen. Reed Smoot and "some of his constituents" under a sign reading, "We Demand An Amendment to the U. S. Constitution Enfranchising Women."[51] Ultimately, the NAWSA also embraced the federal amendment tactic, and both organizations escalated the pressure on a reluctant Congress.

In addition to the federal effort, women seeking the vote in individual states continued to petition their own legislatures for enfranchisement. By March 1919 an impressive array of states had opted for suffrage. Winner, in a cartoon for *The Woman Citizen*, observed that "The Victories Come So Fast That No Artist Can Keep Up With Them."[52] Now the list contained twenty-five suffrage states, with Utah comfortably entrenched in the venerable position of third on the honor roll. Consistent with the balloon caption in the cartoon, "Pretty soon there won't be anyplace [for us] to go," the antisuffrage position was becoming increasingly difficult to defend.

That same year Utah figured in two other front cover illustrations in *The Woman Citizen*. Both attested to the impending passage of the Nineteenth Amendment. The first was an informal tally of the projected senatorial vote on the question.[53] Utah's two senators, Smoot and King, were shown in favor of the amendment. The "Sixty-Six To Thirty-Three" margin was not too far off the June 4, 1919, Senate vote (56–25) which sent the constitutional amendment to the states for ratification.

Six months later, as Utah was about to ratify the amendment, Winner drew the final cartoon linking the state to woman suffrage.[54] He illustrated "The Modern Betsy Ross" sewing the star of the state of Utah on the flag representing ratification. Thus ended fifty years of popular artistic representation of Utah associated with woman suffrage.

Conclusion

All the artistic images served multiple functions of entertainment, norm preservation, and the facilitation of social change. Entertainment, the heart and soul of caricature, was the constant intent of art during all four periods. The norms preserved and social change fostered varied with the times. For the first two decades, social and political satire sought to force accommodation— especially with respect to monogamy. Also, during this period artists did little to encourage the suffrage movement. In contrast to the later period, the cartoons had more venom and sting, were more partial and punitive, indulged in more misrepresentation, and pictured woman suffrage and Mormonism as fundamentally regressive social movements that undermined cherished moral values. The early illustrations also tended to come from a different set of periodicals: the New York *Daily Graphic, Puck, Judge,* San Francisco *Wasp,* and *Frank Leslie's Illustrated Newspaper.*

After 1910 the dominant source for Utah-woman suffrage connection came from the suffrage periodicals—the *Woman's Journal, The Woman Citizen,* and *The Suffragist.* During this period Utah, along with the other early suffrage states, was complimented as progressive. The cartoons began espousing new social norms and shaping a very different kind of social change. The anti-suffragists were now on the run, a posture they were unaccustomed to after so many years of artistic approbation. But equally unaccustomed were Utahns who, after a steady diet of contemptuous caricature for the better part of a century, were finally enjoying artistic respectability. For one brief moment in early state history, Utah found itself promoting values for which there was growing social consensus, normative reinforcement, and public recognition.

If, as historian Beverly Beeton has argued, one motive for the early alliance between Utah and suffrage was to counter the overwhelmingly negative image of Mormon women, then one might conclude that in the short run that function was not achieved. However, when evaluated from the long-term perspective the historic tie between Utah and woman suffrage enhanced the view of all of Utah's women and the state they served so well.

Notes

1. This is part of a larger project on "The Popular Print and Woman Suffrage." The research is funded by the Woman's Research Institute and the College of Family, Home, and Social Sciences at Brigham Young University.

2. For the history of caricature and Mormonism see Gary L. Bunker and Davis Bitton, *The Mormon Graphic Image, 1834–1914* (Salt Lake City: University of Utah Press, 1983). For the beginnings of a history of caricature and women suffrage see Gary L. Bunker, "Antebellum Caricature and Woman's Sphere," a paper presented to the Utah Academy of Sciences, Arts, and Letters, Dixie College, St. George, Utah, May 13, 1987.

3. Hay's argument follows: "Your convention is most opportune, for this continent is threatened with permanent and peculiar danger, produced by the feudal condition of women. I allude to the increasing curse of Mormonism, a consequence of woman's legalized inferiority or non-entity." Elizabeth Cady Stanton, Susan B. Anthony, Matilda J. Gage, and Ida H. Harper, *History of Woman Suffrage*, 6 vols. (Rochester, N. Y.: Charles Mann, 1881–1922), 1:656.

4. Ibid., 2:325.

5. For alternate explanations of the adoption of woman suffrage in Utah Territory see Beverly Beeton, "Woman Suffrage in Territorial Utah," *Utah Historical Quarterly* 46 (1978): 100–120, or Beverly Beeton, *Women in the West: The Woman Suffrage Movement, 1869–1896* (New York: Garland Publishing Co., 1986); Thomas G. Alexander, "An Experiment in Progressive Legislation: The Granting of Woman Suffrage in Utah in 1870," *Utah Historical Quarterly* 38 (1970): 20–30; and Alan P. Grimes, *The Puritan Ethic and Woman Suffrage* (New York: Oxford, 1967).

6. *Frank Leslie's Illustrated Newspaper,* October 2, 1869: 56. Although the initials of the artist appear to be W. D., we have not been able to establish identity. Mormonism and woman suffrage themes were juxtaposed in art as early as 1860. Then they were independently rendered as two unpopular groups. See the Currier and Ives lithograph "The Republican Party Going to the Right House," 1860, in the graphic arts collection of the American Antiquarian Society, Worcester, Massachusetts.

7. For an analysis of popular stereotypes regarding Mormon women, see Bunker and Bitton, *The Mormon Graphic Image*, 123–36.

8. On the heels of such negative publicity, the *Woman's Exponent* emerged (1872) in Utah to challenge the way Mormon women were depicted.

9. Stanton el al., *History of Woman Suffrage*, 2:780.

10. For evidence of comparable support from the American Woman Suffrage Association (AWSA) see *Woman's Exponent*, December 15, 1873: 108, and February 15, 1874: 137.

11. *Puck*, 1871, No. 34:12. The last line of the German caption was missing on our print. Full caption may be translated: "Chorus of the Mormon Women: We defend ourselves to the last man." In contrast, an earlier Utah publication, *KeepAPitchinin*, poked fun at senators and congressmen sponsoring bills inimical to the Mormon cause, see *KeepAPitchinin*, July 1, 1870: 33.

12. Stanton et al., *History of Woman Suffrage*, 3:6.

13. Ibid., 3:5.

14. Ibid., 3:128.

15. *Judge*, March 4, 1882: 8–9. "Disfranchise the Mormons. Let no man who has more than one wife have the right of suffrage, and much will be done towards purifying the moral atmosphere of Utah." Ibid., 2. Technically, those women practicing polygamy were also disfranchised.

16. See *Woman's Exponent*, October 1, 1872: 68. The *Missouri Republican* went out of its way to applaud Utah's progressive stance on women when Phoebe Cousins was admitted to the Utah bar. *Woman's Exponent*, October 15, 1872: 73.

17. Stanton et al., *History of Woman Suffrage*, 3:223–25.

18. Ibid., 4:18. The NWSA convention also passed a resolution protesting against the suffrage portion of the Edmunds-Tucker bill (4:26).

19. *Woman's Exponent*, July 15, 1885: 29.

20. San Francisco *Wasp*, August 29, 1885: 16. Neither Marietta Stow nor Dr. Mary Walker had accompanied Belva Lockwood on her trip to the West, but their potential for controversy and easy recognition kept them in the public eye.

21. Ibid., 3.

22. For Belva Lockwood's views on Mormon morals, Mormon women, the Edmunds bill, and Mormon children see "Belva A. Lockwood and 'Mormon' Mothers," *Woman's Exponent*, March 1, 1886: 150.

23. For a caricature of G. Q. Cannon and other Mormons being taken to prison see the New York *Daily Graphic*, February 19, 1886, front cover.

24. A cartoon in the New York *Daily Graphic*, June 16, 1885, front cover, portrayed Uncle Sam throwing a Mormon representative, bearing the petition, out of his presence. John T. Caine delivered the petition to President Grover Cleveland, accompanied by George Q. Cannon and John W. Taylor. For the origin and gist of the declaration of grievances see "We Have the Right to Protest," *Woman's Exponent*, May 15, 1885, 188.

25. *Woman's Exponent*, March 1, 1886: 148–49. Since the mass meetings were held on March 6, 1886, the March 1, 1886, issue was obviously published late. For other articles on the mass meetings speeches and resolutions see ibid., March 15, 1886: 157–60, and April 1, 1886: 165–67.

26. For an example of the AWSA's support see "The Utah Women," *Woman's Exponent*, February 15, 1886: 138, which reprints an article found in the *Woman's Journal*, January 16, 1886.

27. *Washington Evening Star*, April 7, 1886.

28. *Woman's Exponent*, April 15, 1886, p. 175.

29. New York *Daily Graphic*, March 9, 1886, front cover.

30. "The statement that the women of Utah—and particularly the Mormon women are coerced, terrorized or in any manner compelled to vote contrary to their inclination or conviction, is a gross calumny; and as a woman speaking for the women of the territory, we so denounce it." *Woman's Exponent*, January 31, 1873: 132.

31. Stanton et al., *History of Woman Suffrage*, 4:122.

32. *Judge*, September 3, 1887, front cover. One of the ironies of the illustration is that Mormon theology reveres the Constitution as a sacred document.

33. New York *Daily Graphic*, July 8, 1887 front cover.

34. For background on the inclusion of woman suffrage in the Utah constitution, see Jean B. White, "Woman's Place Is in the Constitution: The Struggle for Equal Rights in Utah in 1895," *Utah Historical Quarterly* 42 (1974): 344–69, and Carol Cornwall Madsen, "Schism in the Sisterhood: Mormon Women and Partisan Politics, 1890–1900," In Davis Bitton and Maureen Ursenbach Beecher, *New Views of Mormon History* (Salt Lake City: University of Utah Press, 1987): 212–41.

35. Pen and ink drawing by G. Y. Coffin, "The Apotheosis of Liberty," 1896, Prints Division, Library of Congress, Washington, D.C.

36. Elizabeth Cady Stanton's edited version of the "The Woman's Bible" deleted or revised passages offensive to women's rights. It was repudiated at the NAWSA convention.

37. Stanton et al., *History of Woman Suffrage*, 4:261.

38. Ibid. Emmeline B. Wells was "heartily applauded" in absentia, and a congratulatory telegram was sent to her.

39. *Woman's Journal*, September 30, 1911, front cover.

40. Ibid., January 27, 1912, front cover.

41. Ibid., April 13, 1912, front cover.

42. Ibid., November 30, 1912, front cover.

43. Ibid., May 3, 1913, front cover.

44. *Judge*, November 1, 1913: 12–13. Foster was the artist.

45. *Life*, June 25, 1914: 1162.

46. *Puck*, September 2, 1916: 14.

47. *Cartoons Magazine*, August 1913: 129.

48. *Puck*, February 20, 1915: 14–15.

49. *Woman's Journal*, May 22, 1915, front page. The name of the cartoonist is illegible.

50. *The Woman Citizen*, November 24, 1917: 494–95.

51. *The Suffragist*, September 4, 1915, front cover. Although the history of Utah's involvement in the Congressional Union and National Woman's Party has not been written, some attention to the issue is contained in Christine A. Lunardini, *From Equal Suffrage to Equal Rights* (New York: New York University Press, 1986).

52. *The Woman Citizen*, March 8, 1919, front cover.

53. Ibid., March 22, 1919, front cover.

54. Ibid., September 27, 1919, front cover. Additional accolades came in subsequent issues of the *The Woman Citizen* when Utah supported the League of Woman Voters; see December 6, 1919: 506.

12

A Fresh Perspective

The Woman Suffrage Associations of Beaver and Farmington, Utah

LISA BRYNER BOHMAN

While the battle for woman suffrage was brewing throughout many parts of the world, the foundation of women's rights in Utah Territory was firmly anchored in tradition and heritage. The Church of Jesus Christ of Latter-day Saints had traditionally voiced its support for giving women the right to vote.[1] Moreover, women had participated in church voting and decision-making since the establishment of Mormonism.[2] This background in religious matters naturally carried over into the realm of politics and support for woman suffrage. The cause of female voting rights was pursued by the People's party, which represented the Mormons in the territory.

The Liberal party members, usually non-Mormons or apostates, supported woman suffrage as well since they believed Mormon women were unwilling participants in polygamy. They maintained that if Mormon women were allowed to vote Mormon men would face certain political defeat at the hands of vengeful wives who detested polygamy as much as the rest of the nation. This strategy proved to be futile.

The virtually unanimous support from Utah's main parties aided the cause of woman suffrage. In 1870 when an act to grant women the franchise

First published in *Utah Historical Quarterly* 59 (Winter 1991): 4–21. Reprinted by permission.

came before the territorial government, the measure passed with the support of both the People's party and the Liberal party. However, the latter party's expectations of political victory after unification with Mormon women never came to fruition. Rather than turning against the men, Mormon women remained staunch political supporters of their husbands, the Mormon church, and the People's party.[3]

Together, Mormon men and women created an unbeatable block of voters. Because of this, the non-Mormons turned their backs on woman suffrage. The *Salt Lake Tribune*, the voice of the Liberal party, reported, "It [woman suffrage] originated with the church and the latter must father, or mother it, as the case may be."[4] The opinions on the franchise for women were divided along political and religious lines. For the next seventeen years the Liberal party cursed woman suffrage as a tool to keep the Mormons in political power while the People's party supported and defended it.[5]

Because of the conflicts between non-Mormons and Mormons over the practice of polygamy, Utah drew the attention of federal politicians. In response to the polygamy problem, Congress passed the Edmunds-Tucker Act in 1887 which repealed women's right to vote in Utah and confiscated church property. Almost immediately, suffrage organizations formed throughout the territory. Mormon women tried to align themselves with non-Mormon women in an effort to establish a territorial branch of the Woman Suffrage Association. Prominent non-Mormon woman refused to participate, however, because they believed that woman suffrage would turn the political reins of the territory back to the Mormon church.[6]

The leadership for the woman suffrage movement was centered in Salt Lake City. Dynamic women such as Zina D. H. Young and Emmeline B. Wells not only participated in the national suffrage movement but also organized the territorial association and encouraged women throughout Utah to form branches of the Woman Suffrage Associations (WSA) in their own counties and towns. Eventually nineteen Utah counties had branches of the association within their boundaries.[7]

These smaller branches supplied the grass-roots support for the movement. They were just as vital to woman suffrage as the more publicized branches in Salt Lake City and helped the development of the movement in many ways. Financial support of the territorial leaders was only one small, but important, result. The women in these outlying areas paid dues to join the WSA. The dues helped Utah's territorial suffrage leaders attend national meetings in New York and Washington, D. C.[8] Financial assistance was not the only service that these women rendered to the suffrage movement, however.

Perhaps more important than financial support, these county and town associations served to promote education, improve attitudes, and influence politicians concerning the suffrage movement throughout the territory. Women in towns and counties all over Utah held meetings to inform other women of the purpose of the suffrage movement. They improved public relations by participating in parades and other community events. They published details about the movement in local newspapers and monthly publications.[9] Finally, the women influenced local politicians participating in the territorial legislature and the constitutional convention to vote in favor of granting women the vote.[10]

Although this grass-roots support for the movement was important, few records survive that indicate what the women in these smaller towns and counties specifically said and did to promote the cause of suffrage. Both Beaver County's and Farmington City's Woman Suffrage Association Minutes have survived. A comparison of these records, which were kept from 1892 to 1896, provides information on the nature of the associations outside Salt Lake, the type of women who participated in the suffrage movement, their devotion to suffrage, the influence of the Mormon church, and the personal effects of the movement on the women involved in it.

During the 1890s Beaver County was different from other areas in Utah because of the large number of apostates and non-Mormons who gathered there. One reason for the attraction of non-Mormons was the trial of John D. Lee which took place in Beaver. Testimony in 1877 about his part in the Mountain Meadow Massacre focused national attention on the town and stirred animosity towards the Mormon church.[11] Beaver also had a large population of non-Mormons because the U. S. Army's Eighth Infantry, stationed two miles from Beaver, provided a steady influx of non-Mormons into the community.[12] In addition, Mormon Apostle Amasa Lyman, who resided in Beaver, apostatized. This lowered the morale of the Saints in the city. The faith and dedication of church members had already been tried as they practiced the United Order. Because of differences among its members the order was forced into dissolution. Many of the Saints became bitter toward each other and particularly toward those who had held positions of leadership in the order. John Riggs Murdock, who served as LDS bishop of Beaver in 1872, wrote that his biggest challenge was dealing with the factions of Saints within the city.[13] Joseph Fish, a Mormon resident of Beaver, described the situation:

> Beaver is full of apostates and the feeling against the Mormons bitter.
> Nothing but the Mormon question is talked of on the streets. Oaths

are uttered against them on every corner and it is a common saying
that they ought to be hung. The apostates are the most bitter. . . .
Things look as if a Mormon will not stand a chance of living here,
and one would not be allowed to if the apostates had their way.[14]

Beaver City was the county seat of Beaver County and the center of
political, religious, and social matters. In an environment with such overt
social tensions and religious divisions, the Woman Suffrage Association
survived but did not thrive. The women in the area made an effort to attract
new members but with little success. The Beaver women advertised their
association in the *Southern Utonian*, a local newspaper. They invited all women
in the city to join their society. Even this publicity did not seem to have much
of an effect. In a town with a population of 1,752 people in 1900, only 18
members were enrolled in the association, and the average attendance was 9.[15]

In Farmington, the county seat of Davis County, more favorable
conditions greeted the women as they created their own branch of the WSA.
Farmington was originally founded in 1848, not because church leaders called
families to settle there but as a natural extension of settlements around the
Salt Lake Valley. The city was named Farmington because of ample yields of
produce and grain that were harvested in this primarily agricultural town.
Wheat, corn, vegetables, and fruit were all grown in the area. The United
Order was practiced in this town as well; however, its dissolution did not have
such an adverse effect on the people of Farmington as it did on the residents
of Beaver. Apostates and non-Mormons also lived in Farmington but in much
smaller numbers. Under these more stable and less contentious conditions the
WSA flourished. The Farmington group had 49 members on its roll in 1892,
over twice as many as Beaver's organization. Farmington's population in 1900
was 1,036 people, approximately 700 fewer than Beaver's population for the
same year.[16] Farmington's location may also have influenced the number of
women who participated in the movement. Salt Lake City, the nucleus of
the woman suffrage movement in Utah, was a short distance away. News of
the movement's progress, territorial leaders, and suffrage conventions came
to Farmington much sooner than to Beaver.

Despite the communities' differences, the role of the Mormon church
was central to the development of the association in both cities. The
Farmington branch was originally founded on April 13, 1892, in the
Farmington meetinghouse during a combined meeting of the church's Relief
Society and its Young Ladies' Mutual Improvement Association. The purpose
of the meeting was to organize a WSA in the ward. Meetings continued to be
held in the local meetinghouse and members' homes until the dissolution of

the association. Unlike Farmington, the origin of the Beaver WSA is unclear. However, the meetings in Beaver were also held in the Relief Society Hall of the local meetinghouse.[17]

Although the organizations were founded around existing Mormon organizations, each association used its religious influences differently. The Farmington branch emphasized the importance of the Mormon church in the woman suffrage movement while Beaver downplayed the Mormon influence. The Beaver minutes do not include any discussion about the Mormon church's approval or disapproval of woman suffrage.[18]

In January 1894 Emmeline B. Wells, later general president of the Mormon Relief Society and prominent suffrage leader, wrote a letter to Mary A. White, president of the Beaver WSA. Wells stated that she had asked the Mormon church presidency for advice concerning woman suffrage; however, she requested that White not make this information public, even to her fellow association members. Wells explained, ". . . you must not make this public—not even in the Association, as I find some in the various associations call that union of church and state. . . ."[19] She went on to say that she hoped she would be allowed to attend the National Council, since the First Presidency was in favor of several Utah women attending.[20] Thus, one of the reasons for not addressing the topic in Beaver may have been a lack of knowledge about church support. Other reasons could include indifference towards the matter or deliberate silence regarding the issue.

The Farmington branch confronted this subject in a totally different manner. Zina D. H. Young, president of the Relief Society and another distinguished territorial suffrage leader, was a guest speaker at the first Farmington suffrage meetings. She spoke openly of the First Presidency's support for woman suffrage. Young said that she was present when the topic was initially considered by this select group of Mormon leaders. She knew that the First Presidency approved of suffrage for women and could see no reason not to join the movement herself.[21] Apostle Francis M. Lyman, who spoke following Young, provided further information on the topic. He contended that President Brigham Young had always believed that women were just as reliable in government participation as men were. Lyman added that President Wilford Woodruff also held this same viewpoint. The apostle continued, saying that if President Woodruff had been against woman suffrage, then Zina Young and others would have never supported the movement. Lyman gave a final endorsement when he said, "I desire to say here that it is according to the mind and will of the Lord, as manifested by the First Presidency, that the women take hold of this woman suffrage movement as they do in the Relief Society."[22]

Beaver Relief Society Hall. *Utah State Historical
Society. All rights reserved. Used by permission.*

The large number of women involved in Farmington's association can be partially attributed to Lyman's strong recommendation. During the meeting at which Lyman and Young spoke, at least two women declared that their opinion on woman suffrage had changed. Athelia Steed said that "she did not understand it [woman suffrage] at one time but now looked upon it in a different light." A Sister Leonard also stated that the movement was new to her, but she had decided it was a good thing. Furthermore, on the day the Farmington branch was organized, 22 women had their names on the roll.[23] Less than six months later the group's membership had grown to 49 members.[24] Official church sanction, as expressed by Apostle Lyman, might have changed some women's opinions about the movement and might have convinced some to participate who would have otherwise ignored it.

Although these two associations differed in the direct discussion of church approval, their goals were similar and were aligned with those of the territorial association. The local associations primarily intended women to receive the right to vote, but along with this central goal came other commitments and questions. Women were to use the suffrage movement to become more educated about politics, to use this knowledge to improve their family lives, and to transmit womanly virtues into the realm of government.[25] Yet within these worthwhile goals were inherent conflicts. How politically involved should women be? When did political interests interfere with family interests? If a woman were to extend her virtue into the vice of the political world, then would she not risk becoming contaminated herself? How were women to preserve their "natural virtue"? The Beaver WSA secretary recorded the following remarks, concerning one of the goals of the association:

> Let no man or woman be mistaken as to what this movement for suffrage really means. None of us want to turn the world upside down, or to convert women into men. We want women, on the contrary, above all things to continue womanly womanly in the highest and best sense—and to bring their true, honest, just, pure, lovely and of good report to bear upon conduct of public affairs.[26]

An edition of the *Equal Rights Banner*, a monthly, hand-written newsletter produced by the Beaver County women, reinforced this idea and referred women to their previous voting record in Utah. The *Banner* claimed that prior to 1870 women had exercised a "purifying influence" on government in the territory and encouraged this practice to begin again.[27] The editors of the *Banner* continually referred to superior womanly virtues. On April 16, 1894, an editor wrote that those men controlling the nation had been described as lacking sympathy, mercy, charity, and all "ennobling virtues." The editor concluded that women should be allowed to vote since women, not men, had dominion over all those characteristics.[28]

The question of virtue was used not only by Utah suffragists but also by national suffragists. Antisuffragists had also used "virtue" in their arguments against granting women the right to vote. Supporters of the suffrage movement usurped this discussion of virtue from antisuffragists, however, and used it to stress the purifying results women would have on politics. The National American Woman Suffrage Association frequently referred to the social evils that women had combatted and defeated in the past. The organization stressed that confronting these evils had not caused a decrease in morality, virtue, or femininity.[29] How women could remain virtuous when active in "evil" politics was not explained by the local or national suffrage leaders.

The incongruence continued. Home and religion, not politics, were clearly of ultimate importance, but suffrage was a political question. What combination of interests was acceptable and preferable for women? The members in Farmington were reminded that they were not to become so involved in politics that it interfered with their religious duties and beliefs.[30] Emmeline B. Wells addressed this topic in her letter to Mary A. White. Wells wrote, "I never wish family duties neglected—they are *first*, after that other things."[31] Louissa Jones, editor of the *Equal Rights Banner*, in September 1893 agreed with Wells and wrote a description of what she believed was the proper woman's sphere. A woman was "to conduct her home in such a manner that she gathers happiness and contentment around herself and others, to advance the race on the path to civilization and progress by teaching her children. . . ."[32] The suffrage leaders continually urged women to use the knowledge gained at meetings to improve their families. The women in both Farmington and Beaver constantly expressed the belief that the right to vote would make every woman a better mother, since a child's education would be enhanced by a mother who participated in politics. Zina Young encouraged women in Farmington to disseminate information in their association that would make them better wives and mothers.[33] The content of the *Equal Rights Banner* is indicative of this tangle of family, religion, and politics, since scattered among articles addressing the progress of woman suffrage are recipes and hints for raising children and improving spirituality. Exactly how women were to juggle these differing goals and admonitions was left up to them.

Despite the confusing designs the associations had for women, instructions relating to political parties on the territorial and local level were quite clear. Both branches were explicitly politically neutral. The Utah suffragists' goal was to create a coalition of political parties to support woman suffrage in elections and the constitutional convention in 1895.

Emmeline B. Wells's letter to Mary White addressed this issue. Wells suggested that women exert themselves in areas that were traditional strongholds of womanly influence, such as at social gatherings and school meetings. She warned that there were "unwise" women who threatened to antagonize the men in the territory by politically uniting with one party. These same alienated men would ultimately decide whether or not women would vote. Wells urged White's branch not to unite with either political party, even after the People's and Liberal parties had disbanded to form the national Democratic and Republican parties.[31] Marriage to one political party had denied women the right to vote in the past, and the Mormon women did not intend to cause the same divisions a second time. Political affiliation is never mentioned in the Beaver minutes or the Farmington minutes.

Despite certain similarities, many notable distinctions, besides their different populations, existed between the two organizations. The topics discussed in the meetings and the ardor for the movement varied a great deal in Farmington and Beaver. Farmington women were quick to participate and to fulfill their responsibilities in the association. Beaver women placed less emphasis on the importance of their association. This conclusion is suggested by the minutes of the meetings in both towns. For instance, in Beaver in the May 16, 1892, meeting, hymnbooks were discussed as well as the purchase of a book for the executive board. One woman who had been assigned a part on the program was not present, and another was not prepared. The women heard a lecture on the free coinage of silver, sang a song, listened to a reading, and then adjourned. On July 18, 1892, there was no program, and the women just had a short discussion. Again on September 18, 1892, there was no organized program. The president of the association "thought we [the Beaver members] ought to take an interest in our meetings and try and get others to attend." The nadir of the Beaver WSA came on January 16, 1894, when the secretary recorded the following:

> Programme next in order. Musick Instrumental by W. G. Bickley. Civil Government Class omitted, Prest. Farnsworth not prepared. Song by Mrs. Fernley, "The Pardon come too late" next Reading from Womans Suffrage History by Louissa Jones lady not present. Speech by W. G. Bickley. . . . The Gentlemen, not being prepared with a lecture, he read a selection from W. Tribune[*sic*].

At the next meeting, on March 16, the women established a ten-cent fine for members who did not fulfill their parts on the program. The only appropriate way to escape the fine was the excuse of illness.

These problems indicate that some of the participants may not have been suffrage enthusiasts. Indeed, an analysis of the duties performed verifies this observation. Louissa Jones, S. C. Maeser, and M. E. Murdock appear to have done most of the work to support the activities of the Beaver association. These women served on more committees, wrote more articles, and participated in more association programs than any of the other women.[35] Some women may have used the WSA as a type of social organization and an excuse to meet with other women. Mary Fernley, an editor for the *Banner*, worried that some women did not care about the political consequences, only the social benefits of the association. She wrote, "In fact, it has been stated that one of our own members when asked what was the object of our meeting together, answered that she did not know, that she attended because she liked the meetings, and enjoyed the society of the members."[36]

The members of the WSA in Farmington, however, were very active in most of their meetings. Rarely did a person not fulfill her responsibility on the scheduled program. Only once was the program deemed a total failure because the week had been unusually busy.[37] These women usually met twice a month, rather than once a month as the Beaver women did. The minutes reveal many interesting discussions on a variety of topics and many women who were dedicated to the cause of woman suffrage.

On May 8, 1893, the Farmington women heard lectures on the queen of Italy and the U. S. Constitution and then debated the question of what constituted a just war. On June 14 they heard Lucy A. Clark's description of the World's Fair. Later, on June 26, a lecturer addressed the silver question. In August the life of a Scottish countess was recited, and a report on the Woman Suffrage Festival in Salt Lake was given. Soon after, the members began to study prominent women of the Bible, such as Sarah, Hagar, Queen Esther, Abigail, and Judith. The Farmington association was very well organized and appears to have enjoyed a great deal of support from a number of its members.

One of the characteristics shared by both Farmington and Beaver was the type of women involved in the movement. Both Woman Suffrage Associations appear to have consisted of a select segment of the population. Generally the women who participated were members of a political and religious elite who were involved in many other groups and causes in addition to woman suffrage. The private motivations of most of these women are unclear. Some may have participated to further their husbands' or their own social interests. Others surely must have been dedicated to achieving the right to vote for all women in the territory. Despite their motivations, the women involved formed a small network connected by family, social, and religious ties. An examination of the Beaver City WSA roll for 1892 shows that the women and men involved in this association were very influential in their community.

W. G. Bickley was a very active member of the Beaver branch of the suffrage movement, even serving as chaplain for a time.[38] His wife Jane was also a member. Professor Bickley taught music at the local school and was well known throughout Beaver City for being an accomplished musician. He led the acclaimed Beaver City Choir that toured southern Utah. Because of its fine reputation, the choir was invited to join in the service dedicating the St. George Temple and performed a song composed by Bickley for the occasion. Jane Bickley was the first Relief Society president in the East Ward.[39]

William and Matilda Fotheringham were another husband and wife team of suffragists. William was voted an honorary member of the Beaver County WSA.[40] He was elected as county clerk and served in that position from 1866 to 1884. He was also known in the religious circles of the town since he had served as bishop in Beaver in 1877.[41]

Daniel and Ruth W. Tyler were honorary members as well.[42] He had been president of the Switzerland mission prior to settling in Beaver. His writing abilities were reputed to be among the best in the county. He displayed his talents in a book entitled *The Mormon Battalion*. He also published the *Beaver Chronicle*, the town newspaper, during 1879.[43]

Lucinda Howd joined the Tylers as an honorary member of the association. In 1890 she served as president of the Relief Society. Her husband, S. G. Howd, was one of the original settlers in Beaver and was selected as the first presiding elder of the newly founded town. He later served as a town councilman from 1894 to 1895. Howd was succeeded by Edward Fernley who served in the same position from 1896 to 1897. His wife, Mary Fernley, was another member of the association.[44]

Sarah Caroline Maeser, whose name also appears on the 1892 roll, was the wife of the one of the prominent educators in Beaver City, Reinhard Maeser, the first school principal in the town. In addition, he, along with other important citizens, is given the credit for convincing Mormon officials to establish the Beaver Stake Academy, which was the first such church school south of Provo.[45] Reinhard Maeser's father, Karl G. Maeser, was famous for his association with the Brigham Young Academy (now Brigham Young University) in Provo, Utah.

The WSA roll also contains J. R. Murdock's name. In 1870 Murdock was reported to have a personal wealth of $15,000. In 1898 he bought part of the abandoned military post near Beaver and donated it to the LDS church for the establishment of a branch of the Brigham Young Academy at Provo. For this generous donation the school was named the Murdock Academy. Murdock was involved in town and county political matters as well and held numerous offices. For example, in 1882 he served as selectman and was voted county commissioner in 1903. In 1890 he was selected to be the president of the Beaver LDS Stake. His wife, Mary, and his daughters-in-law, Caddie and Clara, were members of the suffrage association as well.[46]

Mary A. White was a very prominent member of the association and served as its president. She was invited to give a speech to the citizens of Beaver when Utah became a state in 1896. Charles D. White, her husband, was the second president of the Beaver LDS Stake. He was also involved in community affairs and was a selectman in 1895–96.[47]

An examination of the Farmington roll shows great similarities. In this town as well the cause of suffrage appears to have been supported by a group of social, political, and economic elites. Nettie Abbott was the first name on the roll for the Farmington WSA in 1892. She taught at the local school and in August 1892 became president of the Primary in the ward. Her husband, Thomas M. Abbott, was reputed to have been the first to herd cattle up Ogden Canyon. Brigham Young had requested Abbott to carry a letter from him to Joseph Morris during the Morrisite War.[48] Clara Leonard, also a member, was another schoolteacher involved in the suffrage movement. Leonard served as an organist and treasurer in the first LDS Primary in Farmington. Mary Millard was another WSA member involved in the Primary organization. She was second counselor to Nettie Abbott and became president in 1896.[49]

The record also contains the name of Emmeline Hess Bourne, wife of John A. Bourne who served two terms in the Farmington City Council. He later served as mayor of Farmington from 1920 to 1922, twenty-four years after Utah women received the vote.

Amasa Lyman Clark was also well known politically in the city of Farmington. He served two years as county treasurer and in 1882 began an eighteen-year career as city treasurer. He eventually served as mayor during 1908–11 and as bishop of the Farmington Ward from 1915 to 1930. Mary S. Clark, wife of Ezra Thompson Clark and mother of Amasa Lyman Clark, participated in the suffrage movement, as did her daughter Mary Elizabeth Clark. Mary S. Clark's daughter-in-law, Lucy A. Clark, was also prominent in the community and a suffragist. She was the first president of the LDS Young Women's Association in Farmington, which was organized in 1873, and later served in the Davis Stake Primary.[50]

Lizzie Coombs, a president of the suffrage association, and her husband were part of the economic backbone of Farmington. Together they operated the first telephone office, the first molasses mill, and the second store in Farmington.[51]

One of Coombs's fellow members, Julia Hess, was very prominent in the community. Hess served with Aurelia Rogers in the Davis Stake Primary. She was the third wife to John W. Hess who was called on March 4, 1894, to be president of the Davis Stake.[52]

Arthur Stayner was a counselor to Bishop Hess and known for raising the first sugar cane in Utah. Stayner's wife, Clara, was a member of the WSA.

The Miller family was another suffrage family. Two wives of Jacob Miller, Helen Mar Cheney and Annie Christenson Miller, were members of the Farmington WSA. Helen was first counselor to Aurelia Rogers in the Primary. Jacob Miller was superintendent of the Davis County School District and an assistant editor for the *Farmington Journal*. He was also first counselor to Bishops Hess and Secrist.[53]

Although she spent most of her life in poverty, Aurelia Rogers was one of the most beloved women in the city of Farmington and in the WSA. The community's appreciation was demonstrated when she and Eliza R. Snow received the first silk dresses manufactured in Utah. Rogers is given credit for founding the Mormon Primary and served as the president of the Davis Stake Primary for seven years. She accompanied Emmeline B. Wells, and others to Washington, D. C., in 1895 to attend a suffrage convention. Rogers also served for twenty-two years as secretary of Farmington's first Relief Society. In 1935 a plaque in her honor was placed in the southwest corner of the Farmington Chapel. Her daughter, Leone, was also a WSA member.[54]

Monica Secrist, another president of the Farmington WSA branch, was the wife of Bishop Jacob Secrist. He was the president of the Farmington Commercial and Mercantile Company and a director of the Davis County Bank. In 1890 he was nominated for a county commissioner and later ran for office in the legislature.[55]

Harriet Staniforth, although not politically or religiously prominent, was still well known in the community. She was one of the first midwives in Farmington and aided in the delivery of hundreds of babies.[56]

The members of the Farmington WSA and their husbands included four prominent educators, two Relief Society presidents, ten civil servants, three bishops, one stake president, one mission president, five Primary presidents or counselors, and two economic leaders. Based on Farmington's 1892 roll, 56 percent of the women could be considered social, religious, economic, or political elites. In addition, sixteen of the twenty-four Beaver women on the 1894 roll could be considered prominent in their community. This is 66 percent of the women involved in the WSA in that city. These women were the strength of their communities and the suffrage movement. Through their social connections they wielded a great deal of influence in political and religious circles. They helped garner support for the cause of woman suffrage and convinced many of their political leaders, who were often their husbands or friends, to embrace the cause as well.

The associations in Beaver and Farmington had many of the same characteristics. They shared similar goals and presented their members with similar challenges as the women sought to discover what degree of political activity was acceptable. The women in both associations were forced to confront other questions that the suffrage movement presented to Mormon women. The women and the associations differed according to the degree of involvement in and dedication to the suffrage movement. Yet for all their similarities and differences these two associations did their unique parts to expand awareness of the existence and importance of the woman suffrage movement.

As the women sought to extend support for woman suffrage, those suffragists who truly took hold of the cause experienced a transformation in themselves. Their political awareness increased. They became curious and informed themselves about the development of woman suffrage outside Utah. They avidly awaited news concerning the progress of the suffrage movement in Wyoming, Colorado, and elsewhere. They read the *Woman's Exponent* and the *Woman's Tribune*, newspapers that provided coverage of the activities of suffragists everywhere.

The women also learned about great women, both in current events and biblical times. With this knowledge they were able to develop female role models who were socially, politically, and religiously active. The women also used the movement as an opportunity to prepare themselves for the time when they would be allowed to vote. They accomplished this through lectures on civil government and current topics, such as the silver and tariff controversies.

In addition, the suffrage movement improved the national reputation of Mormon women, which had been severely damaged by the practice of polygamy. Through work in the suffrage movement women discovered common bonds of sisterhood between themselves and women throughout the nation and the world. The women in Beaver and Farmington supported this common cause of women's rights. For example, when the women of Farmington donated an apron and bonnet to the Woman's Bazaar held in Florida, the Farmington members received a warm thank you from their fellow suffragists.[57] Mormon women and the suffrage organizations in the territory were, at times, even held up as examples to other women in the United States. George Catt, a national suffragist leader, complimented the work of Utah women saying, "Utah was twelve times as organized as Massachusetts, fourteen times as well as Iowa, and nineteen times as well as New York."[58] This statement must have provided a feeling of accomplishment for many suffragists whatever their personal motivations for joining the movement were.

The Beaver and Farmington women involved in the grass-roots support of woman suffrage helped Utah women to receive the right to vote. The movement also helped the women themselves. Those involved in the movement faced questions about themselves and how they were to enter a new sphere of politics while balancing traditional roles. Although both the Beaver and Farmington WSA groups appear to have gone out of existence after the adoption of woman suffrage in Utah, the associations had helped women to become more politically aware and better prepared to take on a portion of the new mantle of political participation.

Notes

1. Thomas G. Alexander, "An Experiment in Progressive Legislation: The Granting of Woman Suffrage in Utah in 1870," *Utah Historical Quarterly* 38 (1970): 25.

2. Joseph Smith, *History of the Church of Jesus Christ of Latter-day Saints*, 2d ed., 7 vols. (Salt Lake City: Deseret Book Co., 1978), 4:604–7.

3. Alexander, "An Experiment," 29.

4. "Our Lying Old Grandmothers," *Salt Lake Tribune*, November 14, 1877: 3.

5. B. H. Roberts, *A Comprehensive History of the Church of Jesus Christ of Latter-day Saints*, 6 vols. (Provo, Ut: Brigham Young University Press, 1965), 6:7.

6. Richard D. Poll et al., eds., *Utah's History* (Provo, Ut.: Brigham Young University Press, 1978): 352.

7. League of Women Voters, *The Voice of Womankind* (Salt Lake City: League of Women Voters of Utah, 1987): 3.

8. Minutes of Farmington City Woman Suffrage Association Meetings, 1892–1896: 17, LDS Church Library-Archives, Salt Lake City. Hereinafter referred to as Farmington Minutes.

9. Minutes of the Beaver County Woman Suffrage Association Meetings, 1892–1896, August 16, 1894: 17, and March 16, 1894: 12, Special Collections, Lee Library, Brigham Young University, Provo. Hereinafter referred to as Beaver Minutes.

10. Emmeline B. Wells to Mary A. White, January 14, 1894, in Beaver Minutes.

11. Wayne Stout, *History of Utah*, vol. 1, 1870–96 (Salt Lake City: Author, 1967): 68.

12. J. M. Tanner, *A Biographical Sketch of John Riggs Murdock* (Salt Lake City: Deseret News, 1909): 171.

13. Ibid., 172.

14. Joseph Fish, *The Pioneers of the Southwest and Rocky Mountain Regions* (Salt Lake City: J. F. Smith and Seymour P. Fish, 1968): 65.

15. "Equal Suffrage," *Southern Utonian*, January 17, 1896: 4; U. S., Department of the Interior, *Census Bulletin 50 of the 12th Census of the U. S.* (Washington, D.C.: GPO, 1902): 3; Beaver Minutes, October 16, 1893: 8.

16. Farmington Minutes, no meeting date, 1892: 17; *Census Bulletin 50*, 3.

17. Farmington Minutes, no meeting date, 1892: 17; *Beaver Minutes*, May 16, 1892: 1.

18. Beaver Minutes, 1–23 *passim.*

19. Wells to White.

20. Ibid.

21. Farmington Minutes, April 13, 1892: 4.

22. Ibid., 7–8.

23. Ibid., 5,6–7, 1.

24. Ibid., no meeting date, 1892: 17.

25. Ibid., April 13, 1892: 4.

26. Beaver Minutes, January 16, 1895: 22.

27. *Equal Rights Banner*, undated, 8, in Beaver Minutes.

28. Ibid., Henrietta Gentry, ed., April 16, 1894: 4.

29. National American Woman Suffrage Association, *Woman Suffrage Arguments and Results, 1910–11* (New York: Kraus Reprint Co., 1971): 47.

30. Farmington Minutes, June 15, 1892: 15.

31. Wells to White.

32. *Equal Rights Banner*, Louissa Jones, ed., September 16, 1894: 19.

33. Farmington Minutes, April 13, 1892: 4.

34. Wells to White.

35. Beaver Minutes, 1–23 passim.

36. *Equal Rights Banner*, Mary Fernley, ed., August 16, 1894: 18.

37. Farmington Minutes, June 1, 1892: 12.

38. Beaver Minutes, June 16, 1892: 2.

39. Aird G. Merkley, ed., *Monuments to Courage: A History of Beaver* (Beaver, Ut: Daughters of the Utah Pioneers, 1948): 136, 116.

40. Beaver Minutes, May 16, 1894: 15.

41. Susan Easton Black, ed., *Membership of the Church of Jesus Christ of Latter-day Saints: 1830–1848*, 50 vols. (Provo, Ut: Religious Studies Center, Department of Church History and Doctrine, Brigham Young University, 1989), 16:943.

42. Beaver Minutes, October 16, 1893: 8.

43. Merkley, *Monuments to Courage*, 116, 97.

44. Beaver Minutes, October 16, 1893: 8; *Southern Utonian*, February 27, 1890: 10; Black, *Membership of the Church*, 14:166; Merkley, *Monuments to Courage*:180.

45. Merkley, *Monuments to Courage*, 76.
46. Black, *Membership of the Church*, 32:36; Merkley, *Monuments to Courage*, 82, 177; *Southern Utonian*, September 9, 1890: 4.
47. *Southern Utonian*, January 17, 1896: 1; Merkley, *Monuments to Courage*, 113, 177.
48. Margaret Steed Hess, *My Farmington, 1847–1976* (Salt Lake City, 1976): 295; George Quincy Knowlton, *A History of Farmington, Utah*, ed. Janetta K. Robinson (Farmington, Ut, 1965): 40.
49. Hess, *My Farmington*, 346, 295.
50. Knowlton, *A History of Farmington*, 67; Black, *Membership of the Church*, 10:2; Hess, *My Farmington*, 291, 297.
51. Hess, *My Farmington*, 6, 305, 47.
52. Ibid., 295, 509.
53. Ibid., 295; Jacob Miller, *Journal of Jacob Miller: Pioneer, 1835–1911*, ed. Joseph Royal Miller and Elna Miller (n.p., 1968): 75.
54. Hess, *My Farmington*, 6, 295, 297, 260.
55. Ibid., 154.
56. Ibid., 9, 17.
57. Farmington Minutes, October 14, 1894: 36.
58. "How Women's Suffrage Won," *Woman's Exponent*, January 31, 1896: 9.

Salt Lake City and County Building, c. 1895. *Utah State Historical Society. All rights reserved. Used by permission.*

13

Woman's Place Is in the Constitution.

The Struggle for Equal Rights in Utah in 1895

JEAN BICKMORE WHITE

In July of 1894 the nation's leading advocate of woman suffrage, Susan B. Anthony, voiced a hope and a warning to the officers and members of the Woman Suffrage Association of Utah. "My dear friends," she wrote, "I am delighted that you are now to be in the Union of States, as you have been for many years in the union of the dear old National Woman Suffrage Association! I congratulate you not only because Utah is to be a state, but because I hope and trust that her men, in Constitutional Convention assembled, will, like the noble men of Wyoming, ordain political equality to her women."

Noting that Utah's women had once had the right to vote, Miss Anthony said: "And I am sure that you, my dear sisters, who have not only tasted the sweets of liberty, but also the bitterness, the humiliation of the loss of the blessed symbol, will not allow the organic law of your state to be framed on the barbarism that makes women the political slaves of men."[1]

Miss Anthony was a political realist, and it seems that she could foresee the struggle ahead for Utah's women. She urged them to fight to get their right to vote in the state's new constitution and not to leave it to future legislatures or to separate vote of the electorate. She warned:

First published in *Utah Historical Quarterly* 42 (Fall 1974): 344–69. Reprinted by permission.

Now in the formative period of your constitution is the time to establish justice and equality to all the people. That adjective "male" once admitted into your organic law, will remain there. Don't be cajoled into believing otherwise! Look how the women of New York toiled and toiled over forty years to get "male" out of our constitution. . . . No, no! Don't be deluded by any specious reasoning, but demand justice now. Once ignored in your constitution—you'll be as powerless to secure recognition as are we in the older states. . . .[2]

She went on to warn against leaving the vote for women out of the constitution and submitting it for a separate vote of the electorate, pointing out that Colorado was the only state in which the male voters had agreed to extend the franchise to women.[3] By 1894 only Wyoming and Colorado granted full political rights to women; some other states permitted them to vote in school or municipal elections.

Miss Anthony's letter had arrived at a crucial time, on the eve of statehood for Utah. Earlier in 1894 Congress had passed the Enabling Act, providing for a constitutional convention to be held in 1895. If the constitution conformed to the provisions of the Enabling Act, and if it were approved by the voters at a subsequent election, President Grover Cleveland would proclaim Utah a state, and the dream of most citizens of the territory of Utah would be fulfilled. Utah would at last be a state on an equal footing with the other states of the union, free of territorial laws enacted by Congress and free to elect her own state officials.

It was particularly crucial time for advocates of equal political rights for women. Ahead of them lay a unique opportunity to secure these rights. Utah women had once had the right to vote, as a result of an act of the territorial legislature, from 1870 until 1887, when it was taken away by Congress with the passage of the Edmunds-Tucker Act.[4] In the meantime, several of the prominent women in the Mormon church (Church of Jesus Christ of Latter-day Saints) had become active in the national woman suffrage movement, and in 1889 they had founded the Woman Suffrage Association of Utah.[5] Many of these same women were leaders in the Mormon Relief Society, the women's auxiliary of the church, and had promoted lessons in government, parliamentary law, history, and other subjects that would stimulate women's interest in public affairs.[6] They had also moved out into the territory, organizing suffrage associations in the outlying counties, to make sure that there was widespread support for the movement. They had stayed in close touch with the leaders of the Mormon church, obtaining their blessings and support for their activities in the national women's organizations. By the time Miss Anthony's advice arrived, the leading Utah suffragists were already getting well prepared for the struggle ahead, continuing to organize at the grass-roots as well as cultivating support at the top of the religious hierarchy.

In September of 1894, both of the national political parties held territorial conventions, and it became evident that the women's efforts were beginning to bear fruit. The Republicans met first, at the Opera House in Provo on September 11. The party platform included a list of twenty-one items, starting with the need for a protective tariff and free coinage of silver. The eighteenth item stated simply: "We favor the granting of equal suffrage to women."[7] There is no indication in the *Tribune* account of the convention that there was any controversy over this provision, although there was to be considerable debate later about its exact meaning. It would be argued later that the provision was hastily placed in the platform by a minority and that it was not the sense of the Provo convention that Republicans be committed to placing woman suffrage in the new constitution. This was denied by the resolutions chairman, former governor A. L. Thomas, who said he felt a majority of his committee and of the convention delegates "strongly supported" the provision.[8]

The Democrats met on September 15 in Salt Lake City, and again the question of woman suffrage was placed near the end of the platform. However, it received a much stronger endorsement than it had from the Republican convention. The Democratic platform stated:

> The Democrats of Utah are unequivocally in favor of woman suffrage, and the political rights and privileges of women equal with those of men, including eligibility to office, and we demand that such guarantees shall be provided in the Constitution of the State of Utah as will secure to the women of Utah these inestimable rights.[9]

A lone voice, that of Scipio Africanus Kenner, asked to have the platform adopted by sections in order to permit objections to sections that some delegates could not endorse. After his objection died for lack of a second, he is quoted as saying, in a hoarse whisper, "Well I'll never vote for woman suffrage, anyway."[10] Two prominent suffragists, Emily S. Richards and Electa Bullock, rose to thank the convention for its actions on behalf of women's political rights, pointed out the difference in the two platforms, and promised that women never would abuse their political privileges.[11]

During the weeks following the conventions the political parties held precinct and county conventions at which candidates were selected to run for seats in the constitutional convention. It is important to note this sequence of events, for some convention delegates were to argue later that they had not attended their party's territorial convention, that they had not had a voice in its territorial platform, and that they had not made any pledges on the suffrage question in their own campaigns.

After the election was held in November, the president of the Woman Suffrage Association of Salt Lake County, Dr. Ellen B. Ferguson, urged members to visit the newly elected constitutional convention delegates to see if they intended to put woman suffrage in the constitution. She warned that some of the delegates were now wavering and noted that "many are inclined to hang back, saying wait till we are a State then we will give to women Suffrage."[12]

The editor of the *Woman's Exponent*, an unofficial journal reflecting the interest of the Mormon Relief Society and dedicated to promotion of woman suffrage, warned also that the vote for women faced some opposition—from women. Emmeline B. Wells, editor of the *Exponent*, observed that some women in the territory felt no need of extending the political rights to their sex because they were sitting in "luxury and ease." These same women, she commented, might someday need political rights "for their own defence and protection, or mayhap for their little ones. . . ."[13]

The women favoring suffrage continued their organizing efforts and were able to report in mid-February that nineteen of Utah's twenty-seven counties had suffrage organizations.[14]

As the constitutional convention opened on March 4, 1895, the restoration of the franchise for women looked fairly certain. True, there was some opposition, but the suffragists had done their work well and had every right to hope for success. The *Tribune* reported that "a strong sentiment in favor of giving women the right to vote is manifested by the delegates."[15]

Yet within a month the political rights of women in the new state became the most bitterly fought issue of the convention, raising anew the old charges of Mormon church domination in politics and bringing forth the most eloquent oratory the delegates could muster.

Why did this issue, which had seemed non-controversial only a few months before at the parties' territorial conventions, consume so much time at the constitutional convention? Was it a sham battle with the outcome never in doubt? And why did the suffrage supporters finally win their fight? These are the questions to be explored in this paper.

II

The men who assembled at the constitutional convention in March of 1895 were in many ways a remarkable group. The 107 delegates included 28 non-Mormons, among them Charles S. Varian, a former district attorney in charge of the prosecution of polygamists; C. C. Goodwin, editor of the *Salt Lake Tribune*; and George P. Miller, a Methodist Episcopal minister. The Mormon members included the president of the convention, Apostle John Henry Smith, Apostle Moses Thatcher (who was absent much of the time), Presiding Bishop William B. Preston, and Brigham H. Roberts, member of the First Council of Seventy. Heber M. Wells, who would become the state's first governor, and President Karl G. Maeser of Brigham Young University were among the many other prominent men attending. Approximately two-thirds of the delegates were farmers and ranchers, and the rest were businessmen, lawyers, or mining men. There were 59 Republicans and 48 Democrats.[16] Only 29 of the delegates had been born in the Utah Territory.[17] There seemed to be a determined effort to keep the old religious animosities from dividing the convention, and partisan politics played a smaller role than might have been expected. There were several excellent orators who could be counted on to display their knowledge of constitutional history and classical literature at the slightest provocation. Although some of the speeches went on for seemingly endless hours, it must be admitted that the quality of the rhetoric was considerably above that generally found in legislative bodies today.

On March 11 the subject of equal rights for women was taken up before eight of the fifteen members of the Committee on Elections and Suffrage, and the ensuing debate proved to be a preview of the problems that lay ahead. Seven of the eight members present approved a provision taken from the Wyoming constitution. It read:

> The rights of citizens of the State of Utah to vote and hold office shall not be denied or abridged on account of sex. Both male and female citizens of this State shall equally enjoy all civil, political and religious rights and privileges [18]

The *Tribune* reported that "the discussion was quite animated between Mr. Kiesel [a non-Mormon businessman from Ogden], who is stoutly opposed to woman suffrage, and the seven other delegates present, but the latter were not won over by Mr. Kiesel's arguments, nor did Kiesel succumb to theirs, and the vote stood seven to one." A *Tribune* editorial the same day condemned the committee's action as hasty and ill-advised and voiced the main argument that would be used against woman suffrage in the weeks of debate ahead. The merits of this or such other controversial topics as prohibition were not at issue at this time, the editorial writer argued; the question was one of expediency. The constitution would be sure to draw some negative votes, he reasoned. Why ask for more?

> Now, we submit to the convention whether it is wise to put in the Constitution woman suffrage, prohibition, etc., and thus add to the hostility that must inevitably be drawn upon it. It is not likely that any of the voters will oppose the Constitution merely because woman suffrage and prohibition are left out of it. It is certain that a good many will oppose it merely because they (or either of them) are put in. Even to submit them as separate propositions will be sure to draw adverse votes to hundreds, perhaps thousands. We put it to the convention, whether it can afford to take the risk of putting these propositions or either of them, in the Constitution, and so perhaps put their whole work in jeopardy.[19]

While the committee was continuing its deliberations, Emmeline B. Wells, president of the Woman Suffrage Association of Utah, returned from the National American Woman Suffrage Association meeting in Atlanta. In an interview published in the *Tribune*, Mrs. Wells voiced the arguments that were to be heard often in the weeks ahead. Rather than making broad, general appeals for the franchise as a matter of fundamental rights and equality between the sexes, she referred to practical matters and to the unique history of the territory. Women of Utah, she said, should have the vote because it was given to them by the territorial legislature, was used without abuse for seventeen years, and was taken away only as a "political measure." Another reason cited was that "there are undoubtedly more women in Utah who own their own homes and pay taxes (if in a small way) than in any other State with the same number of inhabitants, and Congress has, by its enactments in the past, virtually made many of these women heads of families." This was a reminder of the fact that women had been left to support families while their husbands were imprisoned for unlawful cohabitation. She concluded with the statement that educational equality had always existed in the territory, in keeping with the sentiment of its founders, and added that she was glad to be back to work for suffrage in the convention.[20] There was much work waiting for her to do.

A few days later, on March 18, both the Salt Lake and the Utah suffrage associations presented memorials to the convention summarizing the reasons why they felt women should have political equality with men. They touched on the "taxation without representation" theme and quoted Abraham Lincoln as believing that "women would someday wield the ballot to purify and ennoble politics." Reminding the delegates that both political parties were on record pledged to woman suffrage, the women engaged in transparent flattery, designed to persuade the men to take a historic step and make Utah the third state to grant full suffrage in its constitution. They wrote:

> We believe that now the time clock of American destiny has struck the hour to inaugurate a larger and truer civil life, and the future writers of Utah history will immortalize the names of those men who, in this Constitutional Convention, define the injustice and prejudice of the past, strike off the bonds that have heretofore enthralled woman, and open the doors that will usher her into free and full emancipation.[21]

Under the heading, "God Bless the Ladies," the *Tribune* reported that the presentation of the memorials by the seventy-five women who crowded into the convention hall was made before a convention that was already strongly in favor of woman suffrage. "Under the circumstances," the *Tribune* reported, "it was but a pleasing method of conveying to the delegates an assurance of the regard in which they are held by their sisters, with incidental arguments designed to keep the convention steadfast in devotion."[22]

The women were conceded to be in a good position to gain their objectives, but they were taking no chances. They knew there were those who were not ready to open the doors into "free and full emancipation," including some members of the committee drafting the elections and suffrage article—and the publisher of the *Tribune*.

The majority report of the committee was presented on March 22, with the explanation that most members of the committee had found it difficult to find a reason why women should *not* have political equality. They had, therefore, adopted literally the language of the Wyoming constitution, since woman suffrage in that state had for twenty-five years been demonstrated to be a "pronounced success."[23]

The following day the *Tribune* editorial maintained that by adopting the equal suffrage article, "Utah will join the small group of freak states. Its insertion in the body of the Constitution as proposed, will invite many votes adverse to statehood." If proposed at all, woman suffrage should be submitted separately, the editorial stated, in order to find out how the people at large really felt about the issue.[24]

A few days later the report of the minority members of the committee came before the convention, and the battle lines began to be drawn. Signed by F. J. Kiesel, Richard Mackintosh, and Robert McFarland (Kiesel and

Mackintosh were non-Mormons), the report began by agreeing that women were intellectually qualified to vote as intelligently as men. It went on to suggest that women are, in fact, better than men but are ruled more readily by "their sympathies, impulses and religious convictions. . . ." In the carefully worded passages that followed, the minority report played upon a number of fears that still underlay Utah politics. It recalled the period, only a few years before, when Mormons had belonged to one party—the large and predominating People's party—and the badly outnumbered non-Mormons had belonged to the Liberal party. Both parties had dissolved by 1894 in the interest of gaining statehood, and their members had gone into the national parties of their choice.

The report asserted that during the period of political division along religious lines women had been taught "sincere allegiance to a local government and in that allegiance has been woven an absorbing affection and pious devotion" which they would find difficult to change. The vote had been taken away by Congress, it continued, because the sympathies and devotion of the women were "all bending in one direction," and it was feared that with the voting privilege restored "the old overwhelming force would destroy the present equality of parties. . . ." There would be "a terrible temptation on the part of those who ruled before, to resume their sway by working upon the generous impulses and religious instincts of women, which would result in political, if not social and business, ostracism of the minority."[25]

The careful wording did not obscure the message. The minority report raised the fear that Mormon church leaders could achieve political and economic domination of the new state through their control of the women's vote. This possibility was so repugnant to the nation at large, the report asserted, that it might result in the withholding of statehood and keep away eastern capital which was badly needed for the development of the area. As for party platform pledges, the minority members observed that platforms are changed from year to year and suggested that there had been a change of heart in the territory since people began to consider seriously the consequences of granting woman suffrage. Leave this vital question to the state legislature, the report concluded.[26]

The *Salt Lake Herald*, a newspaper with pronounced Democratic sympathies, undertook to refute the minority views point by point:

> The fear that conditions have not actually changed in Utah is a buried bugaboo, pulled out of its grave to do duty for this occasion. If there is not a sincere division on party lines, then the whole contention between parties—which every sane man recognizes as a vigorous

reality—is a sickening sham. . . . The assertion that this alleged fear is felt throughout the nation, is a straight undiluted falsehood without any semblance of fact. . . .[27]

Kiesel later attempted to explain his position by acknowledging that the process of assimilating Mormons and non-Mormons into the national parties was going on; however, he feared that the addition of thirty thousand or more women—four-fifths of them Mormons—would concentrate in the hands of the Mormon clergy a power that they would be unable to resist. "I know we Gentiles would use it," he said.[28]

On Thursday, March 28, the majority report of the committee, calling for equal political rights for women, was placed before the convention for debate. Kiesel quickly offered a substitute limiting the vote to males of the age of twenty-one or over. The issue was now before the convention, and one of the outstanding orators of the Mormon church, Brigham H. Roberts, a Davis County Democrat, rose to speak against extending suffrage to women. He conceded that the overwhelming sentiment of the convention was to place political equality for women in the new constitution; therefore, he would not deliver the part of his speech devoted to discussing the merits of the question. Nor would he discuss the arguments contained in the minority report—which he had had no hand in preparing. He would only advance the argument that adoption of woman suffrage would be dangerous to the acquiring of statehood.[29] Advance it he did, in a lengthy speech before a rapt audience. The *Salt Lake Herald* provided a vivid description of the scene:

He spoke to an audience composed of the leading women suffragists of this city, the delegates of the convention and the packed lobby, in which there was not an inch of standing room. From the beginning of his speech until the last word was uttered, fully an hour and a half, the interest never flagged. All eyes were fixed on the orator as he stood in front of the desk, towering over those who were ready to oppose him the most, as he one moment rose to a climax thrilling in its intensity, and the next checked himself and allowed his voice to become slow and pleading. It took him sometime to gather himself, but once he did he was an oratorical avalanche. A stream of language, potent and pleasing, flowed from his lips and caught his listeners until even those who were most bitterly opposed to him were compelled to pay compliment to his power with rapturous applause. As he stood alone, disclaiming any desire for charity and fully recognizing the consequences of his action, the suffragists themselves could not but admire his courage, and when he had finished they crowded around him and shook his hand enthusiastically.[30]

The content of the speech can be summarized briefly. He argued that there were already many grounds for rejection of the constitution and for a vote against statehood—fear of high taxes, fear of prohibition, fear of a return to church domination. Why add to these negative votes those of the men opposed to woman suffrage? And why tempt a rejection in Washington by easterners opposed to the West's strong stand for silver? He pleaded with women to give up their struggle for enfranchisement in order to further the cause of statehood—a cause that had been lost by the territory so many times before. He concluded by warning the convention delegates that in their desire to gain immortal fame by granting women the vote, they might be digging a grave for statehood.[31]

Delegate Andrew Anderson undertook to answer Roberts, not on the basis of expediency but on the merits of the issue. He argued that it was unjust to tax women without representation, contended that women were morally superior and would help to purify politics and government, pointed to the lack of bad effects from women having the vote in Wyoming, and denied that equal suffrage would cause the defeat of the constitution. Failure to keep their party platform pledges would be more likely to do so, he asserted. He also voiced this appeal to ethnocentric instincts:

> Millions of ignorant slaves have been admitted to the right of suffrage, and thousands of ignorant foreigners are admitted yearly, and yet why hesitate to grant our mothers, our wives and our sisters the rights of suffrage, most of whom are native born, many are property owners and well educated, and all are most vitally interested in the welfare of the government, in the principles of liberty and the perpetuation of the same.[32]

These were themes that would be embellished almost endlessly in the debates ahead by supporters of woman suffrage.

One of the most scholarly speeches of the convention was delivered on the same day by Franklin S. Richards, son of Apostle Franklin D. Richards and an early suffrage leader, Jane S. Richards. He was the LDS church attorney and a party to some of the most delicate negotiations between church leaders and government officials in Washington, D.C., during the later territorial period. He was also the husband of a tireless organizer of many suffrage association chapters in Utah, Emily S. Richards. He stood squarely for statehood *and* suffrage and felt there should not be conflict between the two. Quoting prominent jurists, constitutional experts, and sociologists, Richards asserted that the vote for women was the next necessary step in the march of human progress. Richards said he had never known a woman who felt complimented by the statement that she was too good to exercise the same rights and privileges as a man. "My experience and observation lead me to believe that while men admit the superiority of women in many respects, the latter do not care so much for this admission as they do for an acknowledgement of their equality, and that equality we are bound in honor to concede. . . ."[33]

Several speakers challenged the contention of the minority report that giving women the vote would cause a return to the old political divisions along religious lines or threaten church domination. A Utah County Democrat, Samuel Thurman, asserted vigorously: "I have this confidence in the Mormon Church, that if political parties will let them alone, they will let political parties alone."[34]

During the next two days the debate continued, despite an effort by Washington County Democrat Anthony W. Ivins to cut off debate and advance the suffrage article to third reading. Again the star performer was the eloquent Roberts, but at this point he moved from the low ground of expediency to the higher ground of merit. He contended that the franchise should be given only to individuals who could act independently, free from dictation. Since most women over twenty-one were married, they could not act feely but would—and should—be ruled over by their husbands. As for the argument advanced by the suffragists that it was unfair to expect women property owners to pay taxes without representation at the ballot box, Roberts maintained that voting was a privilege, not a right. Historically, he pointed out, there had been qualifications of age, property ownership, and literacy imposed as a condition for voting. Women gained their representation through their husbands, whose votes represented not only themselves but their families. Most demands for the franchise in the past were made to provide a protection against tyranny, Roberts said, but men were not the enemies of women and there was no need to give them the vote on this account.

Turning to the question of equality, Roberts said men and women were no doubt equal as to abilities and mentality, but they were different in their dispositions, tastes, and constitutions. Men needed women as a civilizing influence, he said, and without them would soon sink into a state of barbarism.

> I place the values of woman upon a higher pinnacle, and there is not
> a suffragist among you all that has a higher opinion of her and of her
> influence than I myself entertain. But let me say that the influence

of woman as it operates upon me never came from the rostrum, it never came from the pulpit, with woman in it, it never came from the lecturer's platform, with woman speaking; it comes from the fireside, it comes from the blessed association with mothers, of sisters, of wives, of daughters, not as democrats or republicans. [Applause.][35]

He warned women that if they permitted themselves to be dragged into the political arena they would fall from their high pinnacle, and quoted Cardinal James Gibbons on the dangers involved:

Christian wives and mothers, I have said you are the queens of the domestic kingdom. If you would retain that empire, shun the political arena, avoid the rostrum, beware of unsexing yourselves. If you become embroiled in political agitation the queenly aureola that encircles your brow will fade away and the reverence that is paid you will disappear. If you have the vain ambition of reigning in public life, your domestic empire will be at an end.[36]

As for the argument that women would purify politics, Roberts asserted that the sensibility and delicacy of good women would keep them away from the polls, "while the brazen, the element that is under control of the managers and runners of saloons, will be the ones to brave the ward politicians, wade through the smoke and cast their ballot. The refined wife and mother will not so much as put her foot in the filthy stream."[37] Instead of purifying politics, women involved in public affairs would destroy the peace and harmony in their homes. He pleaded for the delegates to leave a refuge for man to come out of the strife and bitterness often engendered in business, professional, and political life.

Perhaps the most persuasive pleader for equal political rights was the Mormon author and historian, Orson F. Whitney. He challenged Roberts's major arguments concerning the effect of political activity on women and the possible effect of women upon political life:

I believe that politics can be and will be something more than a filthy pool in which depraved men love to wallow. It is a noble science—the science of government—and it has a glorious future. And I believe in a future for woman, commensurate with the progress thereby indicated. I do not believe that she was made merely for a wife, a mother, a cook, and a housekeeper. These callings, however honorable—and no one doubts that they are so—are not the sum of her capabilities. While I agree with all that is true and beautiful in the portrayals that have been made of woman's domestic virtues in the home sphere, and would be as loath as anyone to have her lose that delicacy and refinement, that femininity which has been so deservedly lauded, I do not agree that this would necessarily follow, that she could not engage in politics and still retain those loveable traits which we so much admire. . . .[38]

On the contrary, Whitney maintained, the elevating and ennobling influence of women would "someday help to burn and purge away all that is base and unclean in politics." The woman suffrage movement was in tune with the march of human advancement:

This great social upheaval, this woman's movement that is making itself heard and felt, means something more than that certain women are ambitious to vote and hold office. I regard it as one of the great levers by which the Almighty is lifting up this fallen world, lifting it nearer to the throne of its Creator. . . .[39]

By the time the convention adjourned for a Sunday break, the same arguments for and against woman suffrage, for and against holding fast to party platform pledges, and for and against submitting woman suffrage for a separate vote had been repeated dozens of times. Weary of the oratory and cognizant of the cost of the convention, Utah County Democrat Edward Partridge, Jr., remarked in his diary:

The whole day was taken up in discussion of the suffrage question. Bishop O. F. Whitney in a very forcible speech of over an hour demolished B. H. Roberts' efforts. . . . Thus the time is used to no purpose and some $600 a day of the public money used up to no purpose only to gratify the vanity of man.[40]

Although many delegates were beginning to tire of the debate and to resent its cost in time and money, the suffrage discussions wore on into the following week. By this time delegates who had had no intention of speaking rose to put their positions on the record. The opponents of suffrage began to concentrate their efforts on a new strategy.

On Saturday, March 30, an editorial in the *Ogden Standard* urged delegates to forget their party platforms and extricate themselves from the question by leaving it to the people to decide. This proved to be a tempting position to take when pressures from outside the convention began to be felt during the following week.

On Monday, April 1, a motion was made to submit the woman suffrage question to the voters as an issue separate from the body of the new constitution. This was discussed during the day but not acted upon, and it was agreed that the debate would close the following day with a speech by B. H. Roberts.

The prospect of hearing the summation of the debate by Roberts attracted crowds so great that a move to the Salt Lake Theatre was briefly considered. By 8:00 A.M. the crowd started to gather; by 9:30 the entrance was so tightly jammed that the services of a squad of police were necessary before members could take their seats. The *Herald* reported on April 3 that "the hall and lobby, with every approach, was fairly packed and some very prominent ladies even stood on the tables in the cloak room in order to see and hear." Roberts held his audience for two hours, the *Herald* report stated, "and hardly one stirred from the uncomfortable positions in which the great majority of the listeners had to stand or sit."

Despite this dramatic appearance, in which Roberts offered little that he had not said before, the antisuffrage forces failed to pass the motion for separate submission of a suffrage article. Only 28 votes could be mustered for separate submission—but this was substantial enough to encourage suffrage foes outside the convention to increase their pressure. Public meetings in Ogden on April 2, 3, and 5 culminated with a vote of 424 to 28 for separate submission of an article on woman suffrage.[41] The Salt Lake Chamber of Commerce went on record favoring separate submission.[42]

The delegates returned to the suffrage issue on Thursday, April 4, to learn that petitions were being sent all over the territory to be signed by those who wanted woman suffrage submitted as a separate article. Antisuffrage delegates urged that further consideration of the article be postponed until the people could be heard from. What harm could there be in waiting for the petitions to be circulated if the people favored the women's vote overwhelmingly—as the suffragists claimed they did?

The next day a group of prominent non-Mormon women called an open meeting in the Opera House. Oddly enough, they suggested in a resolution to the convention that the new constitution provide for women to vote in school elections and hold school district offices. However, they advised that the question of granting further political rights to women be postponed until a special election to be called by the first legislature. And they resolved that women should be able to vote in this election. They explained that they were not opposed to the vote for women as a matter of principle, but they felt its inclusion under pressure in the state constitution might endanger statehood.[43]

In an effort to see that the non-Mormon women's meeting did not produce a unanimous vote against suffrage in the constitution, Mormon suffrage supporters also attended the meeting. Mary A. Freeze notes in her diary that she was asked to attend the meeting, even though she had to miss a session of the Mormon General Conference:

> At noon I learned that it was desired that a lot of the sisters should go down to the Opera House and attend an Anti-suffrage Mass Meeting, so I went there instead of Conference, much against my natural inclinations, but soon learned that it was necessary.[44]

The same afternoon, Varian moved that the suffrage article be sent back to committee with instructions to frame an article providing for a separate vote of the people on the question of woman suffrage. A substantial number of delegates—42—voted for the motion, showing that the separate submission forces were gaining strength. But there still were not enough votes for the motion to carry. A few minutes later the equal suffrage section was passed by a vote of 75 to 14, with 12 absent and 5 excused from voting, most of them on the grounds that they were in favor of woman suffrage but against having it put in the constitution.

Despite the fact that woman suffrage was now a part of the main article on elections and suffrage to be voted on later, the controversy was not over. The Mormon church's General Conference was being held on April 5, 6, and 7, and the convention was adjourned for two days because of the Arbor Day holiday. Although the subject was studiously avoided by conference speakers, the church leadership was very much aware of the issue. Church President Wilford Woodruff noted in his journal on April 2 that he was "visited by a Company of Sisters upon Womans Suffrage" [*sic*].[45] He did not disclose what they said to him or what he said to them. On April 4 at a meeting of the First Presidency and the apostles, John Henry Smith, an apostle and president of the convention, said that all the Gentiles in the constitutional convention were united in their opposition to the suffrage provision, and many Mormons were also opposed to it. According to Apostle Abraham H. Cannon's account of the meeting, President Woodruff said he feared the constitution would be defeated if woman suffrage was not a part of it, and he said he had advised B. H. Roberts not to oppose it. Joseph F. Smith, a counselor in the First Presidency, spoke in favor of including it in the constitution, as did several others. George Q. Cannon, another counselor and a former territorial delegate to Congress, urged that the suffrage question wait rather than threaten the achievement of statehood:

> I believe we can better wait for a time to get Suffrage for the women, than to force the matter now, and thus array against us the opposition of the Gentiles. It gives the opponents of Statehood the opportunity to work strongly against the Constitution. Things which are right in themselves it is not always wise to attempt. . . .

Since there was no unity of opinion of the subject, the matter was left for the members to do as they desired, Abraham Cannon reported.[46] It is obvious that there was little the church leadership could have done without arousing fears of church interference in the affairs of state.

On Monday, April 8, a large number of petitions asking for separate submission of the woman suffrage section arrived at the convention. Nevertheless, the entire article containing the woman suffrage section was passed with a vote of 75 for, 16 against, 13 absent and 2 paired. But it was agreed that the article could be recalled for further consideration later if a simple majority, rather than the two-thirds majority usually required for reconsideration, should desire to do so.[47]

At this point the delegates were faced with the fact that their $30,000 appropriation was rapidly running out, and they needed to move on to other subjects. It was one thing to spend time listening to overblown oratory in the early days of the convention; it was quite another to face the prospect of working on into the summer without their four-dollar-a-day salary.

Although the issue seemed settled, the petitions calling for separate submission of the woman suffrage section continued to pour into the convention from all corners of the territory. Recognizing the need for a counterforce against this tide, the well-organized suffragists swung into action with their own petitions calling for equal political rights to be embedded in the constitution.[48] The petition game was one that both sides could play.

On April 18 a motion to reconsider the suffrage and election article was offered by Varian. After a brief flurry of debate centering on fears for passage of the constitution by the people, the motion was lost on a vote of 32 for, 69 against, 3 absent, and 2 paired.[49] The petitions obviously had helped to keep the opposition alive, but the supporters of political equality generally had held firm throughout the controversy. The *Tribune*, which had kept up a steady opposition to woman suffrage, reported on April 19 that the tally on petitions as of April 18 stood at 15,366 signatures for separate submission and 24,801 signatures for including the vote for women in the constitution. Ultimately both the *Tribune* and the *Ogden Standard*, which had favored separate submission, urged Utahns to "gracefully accept" the new constitution.[50]

Although the long-sought prize was now nearly within their grasp, the woman suffragists were warned in October by *Woman's Exponent* editor Emmeline B. Wells to keep on working hard for passage of the constitution. She urged women to see that no vote was lost because of neglect or indifference and to remember that "one vote more or less might turn the scale for or against."[51]

After the election on November 5, 1895, it was clear that there had been opposition to the constitution in some parts of the state, for nearly one-fifth of the voters had opposed its adoption. The largest percentage of the "no" votes came from Weber, Salt Lake, Summit, and other counties where there was a substantial non-Mormon vote.[52] On the other hand, more than four-fifths of the voters—all male—apparently had found it possible to accept the new constitution with political equality in it, despite the threats to their happy homes and the fear of adding Utah to the small list of "freak" states.[53]

III

It seems strange that a proposal which started out with the strong support of a majority of delegates could have generated so much heat and consumed so much time. It is one of the theses of this paper that much of the argument over woman suffrage had little to do with the issue of women's political rights. The Mormon-Gentile political and economic conflicts of the past, supposedly forgotten in the struggle for statehood, were lying just below the surface. The fear of domination by the Mormon majority was a real one to the non-Mormons in the convention. These fears probably had to be aired, and this was one of the issues to which the fear of Mormon domination became attached. There was also a deep concern that statehood, which seemed so near, might once again slip away if the convention produced a document that displeased Congress or President Cleveland. The memories of several past constitutional conventions which had failed to bring statehood were still fresh in many minds. These fears, together with the excitement produced by a charismatic orator, were enough to keep the question alive for such a long period of time. Although the oratory made good newspaper copy, and makes interesting reading even today, it probably did not change many votes. It simply took time to air the question thoroughly and give everyone a chance to be heard.

After reading through so many pages of debate and knowing that in the end nothing was changed, it is tempting to view this entire struggle as a sham battle, staged for political glory by ambitious politicians. One would have to impugn the integrity of B. H. Roberts, among others, to reach this conclusion. The author believes that Roberts was sincere in his actions, as were the others who worked so hard to keep the suffrage article out of the constitution. For his efforts Roberts earned the ill-concealed scorn of many of his colleagues in the convention, was bitterly assailed and urged to resign by members of his own party in Davis County, became estranged from the top church leadership, and gained the hearty disapproval of many future women voters. The battle was real to Roberts and to the outnumbered minority who opposed woman suffrage for various reasons.

The one strategy that might have kept the woman suffrage section out of the constitution was the movement to submit it for a separate vote. This proposal offered a tempting haven to those who felt committed to the cause of woman suffrage but did not want to risk the rejection of the constitution. It was a kind of "half-way house" for those who wanted to keep their party platform pledges but who were concerned about the flood of petitions indicating strong opposition to putting equal rights in the constitution. Supporters of separate submission could argue, with some logic, that if woman suffrage were so clearly preferred by the people they would certainly vote for it separately. Those who wanted it nailed down in the constitution generally replied that all the bad elements in the state—saloon keepers, gamblers, prostitutes, and the like—would use their evil money to sway the election and keep the purifying influence of women out of politics.[54] Moreover, the Democrats were continually reminded that their platform had promised to put woman suffrage in the constitution—not to shift the question to the voters. The strength of this appeal for a separate vote can be seen on April 4 when forty-two delegates tried to send the suffrage section back to the committee for rewriting into a separate article. When casting their votes, many affirmed their devotion to woman suffrage but argued that no harm would be done by a separate vote.

Given more time to raise doubts, the minority probably could have won a few more converts to the separate submission proposal. But the convention was tired of the subject; the appropriation was rapidly running out; there was a strong core of suffrage supporters who wanted the issue decided without further delay. By the time the subject came up for reconsideration, the delegates were in no mood to open again such an emotion-clouded issue. So it seems that the real battle was over separate submission. This strategy offered a ground of compromise that is always tempting to politicians who do not want to displease anyone and who are usually happy to shift emotional issues to the voters for decision. However, even on this issue, the suffrage supporters won.

Why did women find a place in the constitution in 1895? There are several reasons. First, although the vote for women was something of a radical proposal at the time—since only two states then granted full suffrage— it was not identified with radicals in Utah. There was no militancy; there were no public spectacles. The suffragists concentrated on winning equal political rights and did not espouse other controversial reform measures that might have alienated their supporters. The women supporting suffrage were predominantly from the respectable Mormon establishment, women who were wives and daughters of church leaders. Among them were Zina D. H. Young, a wife of Brigham Young; Jane S. Richards, wife of Apostle Franklin D. Richards; Dr. Martha Hughes Cannon, a wife of Angus M. Cannon; Margaret Caine, wife of Delegate to Congress John T. Caine; Susa Young Gates, editor of the *Young Woman's Journal*; and, of course, the tireless editor of the *Woman's Exponent*, a wife of Daniel H. Wells, Emmeline B. Wells. These women were prominent in the Young Ladies Mutual Improvement Association or in the Relief Society and frequently promoted suffrage through the Relief Society.[55]

The suffrage movement leaders had enjoyed the support of the church's First Presidency in attending national meetings for many years, ostensibly to show the women of the rest of the nation that they were not ignorant, down-trodden victims of a peculiar marriage system. Apostles openly promoted suffrage in the early 1890s.[56]

Support from the top, however, was not enough. The woman suffrage leaders had carried their educational efforts throughout the territory, and there was no question that they had developed broad support. A movement so widespread, so completely dominated by the "respectable" women of the territory, could hardly be laughed off as the pet cause of a few radicals.

A second reason may be found in the fact that woman suffrage had already been tried in Utah for seventeen years and the territory had survived the experience. So the new state would not be taking a plunge into the unknown. As a *Herald* writer asked rhetorically at the height of the suffrage debate: "Where are its terrible consequences? Where is the degradation of women as its effect? Where are the discordant and wifeless and motherless homes as the result?"[57]

A third reason lay in the careful cultivation of grass-roots, bipartisan support throughout the territory. As a result, the women were able to obtain a minimal commitment to the cause of equal political rights in party platforms, a commitment that some delegates felt unhappy about but still felt obliged to keep. Those who wanted to cast platform promises aside were charged with a lack of honor and with creating a low opinion of politicians among citizens who had elected them on those platforms. This proved to have been an important part of the preconvention strategy of the suffragists and a result of their excellent groundwork in the years before 1895. The value of these platform commitments may be seen in the statements of two of the strongest non-Mormon members of the convention, former U.S. attorney Varian and *Tribune* editor Goodwin, on March 29, that they were against putting suffrage in the constitution but felt bound to keep faith with the people who had expressed their will in the party platforms.

A fourth reason why women won their fight in the 1895 convention was because they had a solid core of supporters in the convention—supporters who parried the oratorical thrusts, who made sure they were not outwitted in parliamentary maneuvering, and who stood fast when the compromise move for separate submission threatened to postpone the achievement of their aims. Anyone who has ever lobbied a bill through a legislature knows that there are supporters who will vote for your cause when there is little controversy over it and there are supporters who will put up a real fight for your bill, using their influence to convince others and holding firm to the end.

Most people today who know anything about the woman suffrage fight in the constitutional convention recall only that B. H. Roberts led the oratorical fight against it. A few may recall that Orson F. Whitney made a stirring speech in rebuttal. But few know of the many men who fought the wearying fight day after day, the men who firmly believed that women had rights that should be clearly expressed in the new state constitution, the men who had faith that putting women in the constitution did not mean driving them out of the home. Among the strongest of these was the son of one prominent suffragist and husband of another, Franklin S. Richards. Permit me to close with just one more bit of convention oratory, a paragraph from a speech made by Richards on April 1, 1895, when many feared that the inclusion of woman suffrage in the constitution might mean the loss of statehood:

> So I say that if the price of statehood is the disfranchisement of one half of the people; if our wives, and mothers, and daughters, are to be accounted either unworthy or incapacitated to exercise the rights and privileges of citizenship, then, however precious the boon may be, it is not worth the price demanded, and I am content to share with them the disabilities of territorial vassalage till the time shall come, as it will come in the providence of God, when all can stand

side on the broad platform of human equality, of equal rights, and equal capacity.[58]

Notes

1. *Woman's Exponent*, 23 (August 1 and 15, 1894), 169.
2. Ibid.
3. Ibid. For a discussion of the attempts to gain woman suffrage by constitutional amendment see T. A. Larson, "Woman Suffrage in Western America," *Utah Historical Quarterly*, 38 (Winter 1970), 7–19.
4. The 1870 law and its consequences are discussed by Thomas G. Alexander in "An Experiment in Progressive Legislation: The Granting of Woman Suffrage in Utah in 1870," *Utah Historical Quarterly*, 38 (Winter 1970), 20–30. See also Ralph Lorenzo Jack, "Woman Suffrage in Utah as an Issue in the Mormon and Non-Mormon Press of the Territory, 1870–1887" (M. A. thesis, Brigham Young University, 1954).
5. *Woman's Exponent*, 17 (January 15, 1889), 121–22.
6. Alexander, "Progressive Legislation," 27.
7. *Salt Lake Tribune*, September 17, 1894.
8. *Woman's Exponent*, 23 (May 11, 1895), 261.
9. *Tribune*, September 16, 1894.
10. Ibid.
11. Ibid.
12. *Woman's Exponent*, 23 (December 1, 1894), 211.
13. Ibid., 23 (November 1 and 15, 1894), 204.
14. Ibid., 23 (February 1 and 15, 1895), 233.
15. Ibid., 23 (February 1 and 15, 1895), 233.
16. This is the convention profile given in Stanley S. Ivins, "A Constitution for Utah," *Utah Historical Quarterly*, 25 (April 1957), 100–101. This article gives a concise, readable account of the main business of the convention.
17. *Tribune*, March 18, 1895.
18. Ibid., March 12, 1895. Fred J. Kiesel cast the dissenting vote.
19. Ibid.
20. Ibid., March 15, 1895.
21. Utah, Constitutional Convention, 1895, *Official Report of the Proceedings and Debates*, 2 vols. (Salt Lake City, 1898) 1:197–99. Hereinafter referred to as *Proceedings*.
22. *Tribune*, March 19, 1895.
23. *Proceedings*, 1:265.
24. *Tribune*, March 23, 1895.

25. *Proceedings*, 1:407.
26. Ibid., 1:408.
27. March 29, 1895.
28. *Proceedings*, 1:531.
29. Ibid., 1:421.
30. *Salt Lake Herald*, March 29, 1895.
31. See *Proceedings*, 1:420–28, for complete text of Robert's speech.
32. *Proceedings*, 1:433. For text of Andersons's speech see 431–33.
33. Ibid., 1:444. For text of Richards's speech see 437–52.
34. Ibid., 1:436.
35. Ibid., 469. For text of Roberts's March 29 speech see 459–73.
36. Ibid.
37. Ibid., 1:473.
38. Ibid., 1:508.
39. Ibid.
40. Edward F. Partridge, Jr., Diaries, March 30, 1895, Harold B. Lee Library, Brigham Young University, Provo.
41. *Ogden Standard*, April 6, 1895.
42. *Tribune*, April 6, 1895.
43. *Proceedings*, 1:754–55.
44. Mary A. Burnham Freeze Diaries, April 5, 1895, Lee Library.
45. Wilford Woodruff Journal, Archives Division, Historical Department, Church of Jesus Christ of Latter-day Saints, Salt Lake City.
46. Abraham H. Cannon Journal, April 4, 1895, Lee Library.
47. *Proceedings*, 1:804.
48. Mary A. Freeze reported in her diary on April 9 that she had copied headings for petitions and helped to get them circulated.
49. *Proceedings*, 2:1150.
50. *Standard* editorial, April 19, 1895; *Tribune* editorial, May 8, 1895.
51. *Woman's Exponent*, 24 (October 15, 1895), 68.
52. Results of the 1895 election are found in Utah Commission, Minute Book G, 413, Utah State Archives, State Capitol, Salt Lake City. Out of a total vote of 38,992, the "yes" votes numbered 31,305 and the "no" votes 7,687.
53. Susan B. Anthony reported in May 1895 that only two states, Wyoming and Colorado, granted full political equality to women, while one state permitted them to vote in municipal elections and 25 permitted them to vote in school elections. *Woman's Exponent*, 23 (May 15, 1895), 268.
54. See speech of Lorin Farr, *Proceedings*, 1:701.
55. F. J. Kiesel acknowledged the role of the Relief Society during a convention debate: "I admit that there is a society existing in Utah—a very estimable body of ladies—the Female Relief Society, an adjunct of the Church of Jesus Christ of Latter-day Saints, and those are the ladies that have worked up sentiment,

while on the other side there is a large body of ladies that do not want, and are not in favor of, woman's suffrage." *Proceedings*, 1:734.

56. For example see speech of Apostle Franklin D. Richards on March 19, 1891, reported in "Woman Suffrage in the West," in *Heart Throbs of the West*, Kate B. Carter, comp., 12 vols. (Salt Lake City, 1939–51), 5:311. This article traces the history of Utah's suffrage fight, including the relationships between the territorial and national suffrage organizations and the role of the Relief Society in organizing suffrage association chapters in Utah. See especially 291–94, 299–301, and 310–14.

57. April 7, 1895.

58. *Proceedings*, 1:444.

Rocky Mountain Woman Suffrage Convention (1895). Susan B. Anthony is seated third from right. *Courtesy of Archives, Historical Department, Church of Jesus Christ of Latter-day Saints.*

14

Schism in the Sisterhood

Mormon Women and Partisan Politics, 1890–1900

CAROL CORNWALL MADSEN

Utah's long struggle to become the forty-fifth state in the Union featured conflict, concession, and eventual conciliation, a process which has been characterized as "the Americanization of Utah."[1] Objection to Utah's entry focused on the Mormon political hegemony, inherent in the numerical dominance of Mormons in the territory, and the more sensational Mormon practice of plural marriage. The resolution of both of these controversial impediments to statehood bore heavily on the political, legal, and social status of women in the future state. The Woodruff Manifesto of 1890, which disestablished plural marriage as a religious practice, disrupted the family and social order of its adherents and required extensive legal and social adjustment for plural wives and their children extending well into this century. But the implementation of a national two-party political system, which broke the Mormon political unity, also altered the topography of Mormon life by generating dramatic new configurations of political and social alignments among Mormon and Gentile women, as well as among men.

Gentile (non-Mormon) women had long been antagonistic toward

First published in Davis Bitton and Maureen Ursenbach Beecher, eds., *New Views of Mormon History: Essays in Honor of Leonard J. Arrington* (Salt Lake City: University of Utah Press, 1987), 211–41. Reprinted by permission.

Mormon women over the issue of polygamy, and passage of a woman suffrage bill by the Utah legislature in 1870 only exacerbated the discord.[2] It was clear to Gentiles in Utah that contrary to the supposition of easterners, Mormon women would not use their new voting power to eliminate polygamy. Rather, local non-Mormons regarded this extension of political power as a means of sustaining Mormon religious domination and thus perpetuating the practice of plural marriage. To counter this situation, Gentile women organized the Anti-Polygamy Society in 1878, which sought local and federal means to eradicate polygamy, beginning with the disfranchisement of Mormon women, even at the expense of losing their own political rights.[3]

The first major legal challenge to the statute occurred in 1880 when members of the Gentile Liberal party filed suit for a writ of mandamus compelling the voting registrar in Salt Lake County to strike from the registration list the names of all women. Their challenge was based on the claim that the law granting the vote to women was discriminatory because the 1859 statute on elections provided that only men who were taxpayers could vote while the 1870 law extending the vote to women contained no such requirement. The writ of mandamus was denied and in a test case the following year the court found the taxpayer distinction neither illegal nor unconstitutional but against the "policy of the law" and ordered it struck from the statute.[4] Several other unsuccessful local attempts to disfranchise women followed. When local efforts failed, the Anti-Polygamy Society enlisted the help of militant Protestant reform women who were equally anxious to abolish polygamy, which they considered an affront to Christian womanhood. In October 1884, more than two hundred and fifty thousand signatures were gathered from all over the country memorializing Congress to withdraw the vote from the women of Utah. Whatever their own antipathy to polygamy, eastern suffragists deplored this move to disfranchise such a large body of voting women and did not join in the anti-polygamy movements.[5]

Congressional approval of the Edmunds Bill in 1882, which disfranchised all polygamists, reflected the growing national concern over affairs in Utah. While not solely responsible for passage of the Edmunds Bill, the Anti-Polygamy Society had been instrumental in creating enough agitation and public sympathy to its cause to require some kind of congressional response. More stringent anti-polygamy legislation was proposed thereafter, most of which included the disfranchisement of all Utah women, and in March 1886, responding to the latest congressional proposals, Mormon women held a mass rally in Salt Lake City to protest the imprisonment of polygamists, removal of the legal immunity of plural wives to testify against their husbands, and the proposed repeal of woman suffrage. Suffragists Emmeline B. Wells, editor of the Mormon woman's newspaper, the *Woman's Exponent*, and Dr. Ellen B. Ferguson carried a memorial to Congress soliciting reconsideration of the Mormon question. A more convincing voice was heard, however, that of Angie Newman of Lincoln, Nebraska, a Methodist social reformer who had joined the cause of the anti-polygamists. She carried her own memorial to Congress, endorsed by organizations representing three hundred thousand women. Passage of the Edmunds-Tucker Bill the following year, which disfranchised all Utah women, vindicated her efforts.[6] With a diminished Mormon electorate, the non-Mormon Liberal party began winning local elections for the first time.

In the meantime, Mormon women were gaining political experience by serving as members of the central committee of the Mormon People's party and as delegates to the 1882 and 1887 constitutional conventions. Some of these women, Emmeline B. Wells, Emily S. Richards, Isabella M. Horne, and Sarah M. Kimball, later played significant roles in public politics until after statehood was achieved in 1896.[7]

With a view toward eventual statehood, Mormon suffragists made plans, with the encouragement of church leaders, to organize suffrage associations throughout the territory.[8] A preliminary meeting was held early in January 1889, attended by several church authorities and the general presidency of the Relief Society, Zina D. H. Young, Jane Richards and Bathsheba Smith, the two general secretaries, Sarah M. Kimball and Emmeline B. Wells, and board member Emily S. Richards. An organizing meeting was scheduled for the following week. President Woodruff then appointed Emily S. Richards to attend the annual National American Woman Suffrage Association convention later that month since she was "posted in these matters and had previously reported the labors of the Ladies of this Territory at Washington." An effort to enlist the support of Gentile women proved ineffectual when Wells and Richards called on Jennie Froiseth, author of the anti-polygamy volume, *Women of Mormonism*, and also first vice-president of the National American Woman Suffrage Association for Utah. Not surprisingly, she refused to assist and the work of organization was left almost exclusively to Mormon women.[9]

At the organizing meeting, Margaret N. Caine, wife of Utah's congressional delegate, John T. Caine, was elected president. Most of the major officers were monogamous Mormons in an effort to avoid associating the nascent franchise movement with polygamy. Several Gentile suffragists joined the association: Corinne Allen, wife of C. E. Allen, who became Utah's first congressman; Emma J. McVicker, coworker of Emmeline Wells in the territorial kindergarten association; Isabella E. Bennett, wife of Judge Charles W. Bennett and member of the territorial silk committee; and Mrs. Lillie R. Pardee, a prominent Utah educator.[10] Seventeen county associations were organized that same year. Territorial conventions were to be held annually in Salt Lake City. The next year, 1890, veteran suffragist Sarah M. Kimball was elected president with Emmeline B. Wells, who would ascend to the presidency in 1893, as vice-president.

Meanwhile, Utah demonstrated its willingness to concede to public demand in its sixth attempt at statehood, following the Edmunds-Tucker Act in 1887. The proposed constitution included sections prohibiting polygamy, restricting suffrage to male citizens, and insuring political separation of church and state. Its failure to receive a favorable hearing in Congress, even with these provisions, coupled with the punitive measure of the Edmunds-Tucker Act, led inevitably to the more dramatic conciliatory gesture by the church, the Woodruff Manifesto of 1890, advising Church members to abide by the law of the land. This major religious capitulation, followed by the termination of Utah's local political parties, opened the way to statehood.

Efforts to dissolve the People's party and realign church members with the national political parties began early in 1891.[11] Throughout this early transformation period, the major thrust of church counsel was directed not toward political doctrine but toward numerical balance of the parties. It was essential to create political symmetry in the new state, not only to reassure non-Mormons but to meet the political imperatives of securing statehood. Since virtually all repressive measures against the church had been initiated by Republicans, beginning with their 1856 vow to obliterate the "twin relics of barbarism"—slavery and polygamy, Mormon sympathy had largely been with the Democratic party. Southern Democrats, remembering their own experience with Republican-directed reconstruction, had empathized with what they saw as a parallel infringement on state and territorial rights during the anti-polygamy "raids" of the 1880s. Southern congressional Democrats had thus resisted some of the more stringent legislation proposed against the Mormons. However, when Utah's attempt at statehood failed during Grover Cleveland's first administration, the first Democratic administration since pre-Civil War days, there was a natural disillusionment among many Mormons.[12] In the meantime, an active campaign by the Republicans to win favor with Utahns by promising support for their statehood efforts, a gesture successful in bringing in several other territories under the Republican banner, bore fruit when President Woodruff, Counselor Joseph F. Smith, and several apostles privately affirmed their Republican preference. Because of the predominant Mormon allegiance to the Democratic party, those who espoused Republicanism were urged by church leaders to solicit converts to their party.[13]

By May 1891 both Democrats and Republicans had effected organizations in Salt Lake City, and in June the People's party formally disbanded.[14] A large faction of the Gentile Liberal party, supported by the *Salt Lake Tribune*, continued as a third party, unable to accept the "good faith" of the Mormons. It finally disbanded in 1893 after a heavy election defeat, many of its members moving into the Republican party. The *Tribune* followed them into the Republican camp.

The new political divisions among a heretofore politically united Mormon electorate created "considerable feeling and some pettiness," Emmeline B. Wells observed. L. John Nuttall, secretary to the First Presidency of the church, noted the anxiety felt by many: "I fear the results of these measures of uniting on party lines as some of our people will carry their party feelings into their church membership."[15]

These new alignments, which teamed Mormons and Gentiles in the same political parties, created an ambiguous future for woman suffrage. "Which party will recognize women?" Emmeline B. Wells queried in a *Woman's Exponent* editorial in June 1891. Perhaps neither, she feared, for "wherever suffrage for woman is spoken of in public gatherings," she wrote, "there are only a few who dare speak for Utah upon this question."[16] It was still too soon to determine which if either party would favor the vote for women or whether woman suffrage would be expedient or even possible for Utah. "It does not yet appear to be the time of women's choosing in political issues," Wells wrote, "until further developments of difficult questions now pending are made in this Territory."[17] Women's exclusion from a federal amnesty act in July 1893, restoring the vote to disfranchised male polygamists, intensified her resolve to regain the vote for women with statehood.

At this time, most women had not publicly declared a party preference, keeping woman suffrage a bipartisan issue, as they had been advised by national suffrage leaders. Moreover, most women, like Ruth May Fox, who later became an active Republican, preferred to do "further study of the parties" to determine their choice.[18] At a meeting of the Utah Women's Press Club to which many Mormon suffragists belonged, President Emmeline Wells, anticipating the divisive influence of partisan politics, set the limits of political expression. "These meetings," she said, "are simply for literary improvement and devoted to the press and similar things, and not for the discussion of religion or politics as we can secure these things in other places. No subject should be presented here upon which we are likely to conflict or that will create unpleasantness."[19]

Occasional infractions occurred, however. Shortly before the ratification election of 1895 Ruth May Fox, giving a paper on current political affairs to the Reaper's Club, another popular literary association, criticized a statement of prominent Democratic Judge Orlando Powers. She "immediately withdrew it," as the club was "divided in politics and some of the ladies thought we should take no note of it on that account." At the next meeting, however, a Democratic member of the club found opportunity to defend Judge Powers, before she was presumably silenced also.[20]

The surface unity of the suffrage association, like other women's groups, also rippled with waves of dissension created by a growing acknowledgement of basic political differences and individual ambitions. A predictable rivalry developed early between Ellen Ferguson, able president of the influential Salt Lake County Suffrage Association, and Emmeline Wells, president of the territorial association. Wells unsuccessfully sought to block Ferguson's nomination for chairman of the organizational meeting of the Salt Lake County Suffrage Association, preferring Ruth May Fox to have the position.[21] Marshalling the force of her county organization, Ferguson retaliated by drafting a letter objecting to unfair treatment by the territorial officers and questioning the legality of the recent territorial elections that had given Wells a second term as president. The effort failed, but among other names, the letter carried the concurring signature of Emily S. Richards, Wells's vice-president.[22] Though these three women had not yet publicly announced their party preferences, their political rivalries were already generating differences within the otherwise unified suffrage effort. The political contest between Emmeline Wells and Emily Richards intensified in the following months when these two capable leaders chose opposing political parties.

Concerned about a movement within the suffrage ranks to establish independent women's political leagues, President Wells warned Mary A. White, president of the Beaver County Suffrage Association, about these "unwise women who would push the Association to the extreme and antagonize all the men in the country." Referring to three or four unnamed women who were "trying to form a League—and go ahead and have said to me they would write to the County Associations and get them to join in this League," she advised White not to ally herself with either political party, though there were many suffragists who were beginning to do so. These are "smart women," she wrote, "who are very dangerous and have to be guided if they will submit, and if not then one must be on the watch for breakers."[23] Throughout the letter her major fear was of those women whose zeal and aggressiveness might jeopardize five years of careful spadework for the restoration of the ballot to women. Confident in the men who controlled the political future of the women in the state, she wrote, "I rather trust men than *distrust* them by far . . . most of our leading brethren I believe think the woman element in politics at this present crisis will be a *saving* power." Nevertheless, the letter conveyed an apprehension as she suggested strategies in case of defeat.

Despite internal squabbles, the diligent efforts of the suffragists resulted in the inclusion of woman suffrage in both party's platforms, though not all of the individual delegates were enthusiastic.[24] Enough declared their support that on the eve of the constitutional convention in March 1895, the suffragists, the press, and the general public acknowledged confidence that woman suffrage would be part of the new state constitution.[25] Favorable reports from the governors of Colorado and Wyoming of its effectiveness in their states reassured many doubters.[26]

A warning note from Susan B. Anthony, which accompanied her letter of congratulations on impending statehood, proved to be timely: "I am sure that you, my dear sisters, who have not only tasted the sweets of liberty, but also the bitterness, the humiliation of the loss of the blessed symbol, will not allow the organic law of your state to be framed on the barbarism that makes women the political slaves of men. . . . Demand justice now. Once ignored in your constitution you'll be as powerless to secure recognition as are we in the older states. And more, the men of your convention should not allow the question to be separately voted upon, either."[27] These became the very issues on which the suffragists would wage their unexpected battle for the vote in the weeks ahead.

Soon after the convention began, the territorial and several county suffrage associations submitted memorials. Their rather perfunctory reception by the delegates seemed to verify the general confidence in the measure's passing. Thus Democratic delegate B. H. Roberts's unexpected challenge caught both delegates and suffragists off guard and prolonged what had been thought to be a "rubber-stamp" measure into a two-week debate.[28] Arguing that a suffrage clause might jeopardize congressional approval of the constitution, Roberts ignored the intent of the Democratic platform on which he ran, garnering widespread disapproval from many of his constituents. He was countered in the convention not only by those Republicans who, regardless of their private convictions, held firmly to their party platform, but also by fellow Democrats Orson F. Whitney and Franklin S. Richards, whose persuasive oratory was equal to his.[29] But Roberts managed to create doubts about the advisability of including woman suffrage in the constitution, and a proposal to submit the articles on woman suffrage separately to the voters in November was made in the convention, as Susan B. Anthony had anticipated. Two informal straw polls indicating a majority of women against equal suffrage added momentum to a *Salt Lake Tribune* campaign to urge separate submission of the woman suffrage section.[30]

On 2 April, a mass political meeting was held in Ogden that concluded with a recommendation for separate submission and a call for petitions favoring it. Three days later a similar meeting, called by Gentile women for "those who do not hold suffrage above statehood" was held in the Grand Opera House in Salt Lake City. Several LDS women were called out of the general church conference to observe the proceedings.[31] A resolution in favor of separate submission was drawn up and signed by twenty-nine women, many of them suffragists such as Jennie Froiseth. Conspicuously absent were the names of Gentile members of the Utah Woman Suffrage Association, Corinne Allen, Emma McVicker, Isabella Bennett, Lillie Pardee, and Margaret Salisbury.[32] While both parties were split over this measure, suffragists were more visibly divided along the old Mormon-Gentile lines.

At the request of Emmeline Wells, Relief Society President Zina Young turned the morning session of the general Relief Society conference to a consideration of the separate submission proposal. Both Emmeline Wells and Emily Richards spoke. To Emily Richards's request for a standing vote of those in opposition to a separate proposal, the entire congregation of women in the assembly hall stood.[33] Armed with this support Mormon women mobilized to counter the growing tide of separate submission sympathy.[34] On 5 April the Utah Women's Press Club abandoned its planned program in order to talk about suffrage and voted to aid the cause by circulating petitions against separate submission. County suffrage associations joined in the effort.[35]

In the midst of the deluge of petitions both for and against separate submission, the proposed section on woman suffrage was suddenly called up for vote in the convention and passed with a large majority.[36] According to a *Tribune* report, the petitions ultimately tallied 15,366 signatures for separate submission and 24,801 signatures for inclusion of woman suffrage in the constitution.[37] Both the delegates and the people had given their endorsement to the principle of equal suffrage. With ratification of the constitution, the women of Utah would once again be voters.

The success of the suffragists infused the Rocky Mountain Woman Suffrage Convention, held in Salt Lake City just a few days after the close of the constitutional convention in May, with jubilance. The presence of Susan B. Anthony and the Reverend Anna Shaw heightened the joy of success. But the constitutional convention proved to be only a preamble to the political attention women would continue to engender in the following months. It began with a proposition submitted by convention delegate Franklin S.

Richards to allow women to vote in the November ratification election. It was defeated in the convention, but the issue had already been addressed by the papers in several articles that reviewed the legality of women exercising their newly acquired franchise before statehood. The controversy centered on the legal interpretation of an ambiguous phrase in the Enabling Act providing that "the qualified voters of said proposed state" should vote in November for or against the constitution. While the act seemed to be clear that only males could vote on the constitution, there seemed to be a legal possibility that women could at least vote for the new state officers. Opinions were divided on the intent of the Enabling Act regarding women.[38]

Recognizing the political potential of a female electorate in this important election, the Democrats issued a formal call to women to join their party. Their invitation was appealing: "The party now leads out in welcoming the women of Utah into their political organizations as full members, entitled to a voice in choosing delegates to the county and territorial conventions, and also to act as delegates themselves. . . . Whether they can vote or not in November, they have an interest in the choice of the proper persons for office in the new state."[39]

The propriety of publicly affiliating with the political parties became a topic of much concern to both the leading sisters and church leaders. Early in the morning of 15 June, Relief Society general president Zina Young visited her counselor Jane Richards and her husband at the home of Franklin S. and Emily Richards, Jane's son and daughter-in-law. Democrat Franklin S. explained to them the party's plan to have women join with men in the political societies, caucuses, and conventions and to become involved with the party on the precinct, city, county, and territorial levels. The Democrats wanted women to be part of the nominating process as well as to vote in the election. Later that day the three women attended the quarterly woman's conference of the Salt Lake Stake where discussion centered on steps to be taken toward dividing on party lines. At the conference, Zina Young, Jane Richards, and Salt Lake Stake Relief Society president Isabella Horne all declared for the Democratic party.[40]

Before the month was over, five women had been appointed to the Salt Lake County Democratic executive committee and a move to add women to executive committees in all the counties was well under way. When Bathsheba W. Smith, second counselor in the general Relief Society presidency also joined the Democrats, along with three prominent women doctors and suffragists, Martha Hughes Cannon, Ellen Ferguson, and Romania Pratt Penrose, the Democrats had reason to feel secure in the woman's vote.[41]

The political activity of these respected women and the assurance of the

Democratic *Salt Lake Herald* that political participation would not require anything that would be "offensive to their true womanhood," that, indeed, government was a "great household and women [could] do much to keep it clean," helped assuage the fears of many women that their womanliness would be compromised by an interest in politics.[42]

Through most of the month of June, the Democratic *Herald* chided the Republican *Tribune* for failing to take the initiative in bringing women into its party's ranks. To the question, "What to do with the ladies?" the *Herald* claimed that the Republicans would wait until the courts decided whether the women could vote. The Democrats, on the other hand, the *Herald* was quick to point out, had wanted them in the party ever since they had been given the right to vote by the constitution. Moreover, it claimed, there were many "leading and influential" women who were desirous of aiding the party to carry the state elections in November. It concluded its recital of the party's program to include women with a challenge to the Republicans to copy them.[43]

The conservative *Tribune* countered with the question, "Who will care for mother now?" But the *Herald* had an answer: "The Democratic societies; so long as she has a vote and they a chance to get it." The *Herald* reminded the *Tribune* of the Republican opposition to woman suffrage but thought the party would be quite willing to change its position if there were any possibility that women would be able to vote in the fall.[44]

Though the *Tribune* had frequently expressed its opinion that women would lose some of their womanliness if they joined in political activities, it noted, for the *Herald's* benefit, that a woman was a delegate to the national Republican convention and that Republican women had organized their own Republican league. The *Herald* merely pointed out the party's inconsistency, suggesting that it had added one more change to its "chameleon journalistic colors."[45]

As the Democratic drive to enlist women gathered momentum, the Republicans recognized the political necessity to follow suit. Being reminded by the persistent *Herald* that the Republican-controlled convention had caused the problem by defeating the Richards amendment to the constitution that would have entitled the women to vote by legislative decree, the Republicans reiterated their view that women were not eligible before the constitution was ratified. They did, however, acknowledge that political expedience necessitated the inclusion of women in the party. At bottom, the *Herald* rightly asserted, was the fear of Republicans that if women were somehow permitted to vote in November, their party would be "swamped" and the Democrats would carry the day.[46]

Determined to "fight the thing out on the lines proposed by the

Democrats," the Republicans urged the organization of women's Republican clubs, modeled after the national Woman's Republican League. The greatest advantage of the Republicans in this effort was the decision of Emmeline B. Wells to join their party in early July. Except for the aged Sarah Kimball she was initially the only prominent Mormon woman to declare for Republicanism. Many Mormon women were reluctant to join the party because of its large Gentile membership. As Ruth May Fox rationalized, "When the women who had been ardently working for suffrage arrayed themselves for the political battle, most of them [Mormons] seemed to be Democrats while Aunt Em Wells stood almost alone, a Republican. To even things up a bit, I joined hands with that great leader."[47]

Wells's decision to separate herself politically from most of her Mormon associates and join with her Gentile friends is not immediately apparent. The male political influence in her family, on which most women depended, was varied. Without a living husband or son, she did not have the natural persuasion toward a political affiliation that the Richards women did. One son-in-law, John Q. Cannon, son of George Q. Cannon, was a Democrat.[48] But another son-in-law, Septimus Sears, was a Republican. Her close confidante, friend, and relative, and champion of woman suffrage, Orson F. Whitney, was a popular Democrat.[49] Daniel H. Wells, her third and last husband, who had died four years earlier, was considered the "father of Republicanism" in Utah and his political influence may have lingered. Her family loyalties were thus divided. But Emmeline Wells was fiercely independent and undoubtedly made her decision for her own purposes. Though she indicated in a political speech that she had "turned from a Democrat to a Republican," she did not articulate her reasons, which were undoubtedly based on her own appraisal of the parties and her personal aspirations. Even her daughter Annie's disapproval did not dissuade her.[50]

Just days after joining the party, Emmeline Wells was chosen permanent chairperson of the territorial Republican Women's League. Though both men and women of the party deliberated at some length before deciding on a separate organization for women, the *Herald* quickly ridiculed the plan:

> While the Democratic women are thus enjoying equal political privileges, . . . a handful of Republican women will be endeavoring to devise some means of carrying on a sort of afternoon tea and sewing circle style of politics separate from the regular organization, which does not want them and is content that they shall get off in one corner and do what they like, so long as they do not interfere with the plans of the men. What a spectacle for gods and men.[51]

In reality, women were included in both the party organizations as well as their own clubs, Emmeline Wells and Corinne Allen having been appointed to the territorial executive committee, and Lillie Pardee elected as permanent secretary. The party sent a letter signed by Wells, Pardee, and Allen to Republican women throughout the territory, announcing its intention to organize individual clubs and advising the women to prepare "at once for the possible exercise of your franchise in November." The *Tribune* was less hopeful. While supporting the move to organize women's clubs, it asserted its opinion that "under the law women have no more rights to vote this year than have boys of twenty years of age."[52] But the work of organizing went on. Besides the help of two young Mormon women, not yet prominent in community or church affairs, Ruth May Fox and Clarissa Williams, Wells was assisted in organizing Republican clubs by her Gentile suffrage associates, Corinne Allen, Emma J. McVicker, Isabella Bennett, and Lillie Pardee.

Throughout the summer of 1895 the *Herald* continued to attack the Republicans for their hesitancy to admit women, their reluctance to endorse a favorable position toward woman's vote in November, and their decision to organize independent women's clubs. The Republican *Tribune* continued to justify the party's caution and its separate organizations. As membership grew in the Republican women's league, the *Herald* warned of the impending contest: "Now the Democratic women have a foe in sight," the *Herald* declared. "They see that the game of politics for them has begun in real earnest."[53] If the women themselves did not yet perceive the political schism in military terms, the warring "morning contemporaries" as the newspapers were known, would keep the battle cry ringing from their paper columns throughout the campaign.

The extent to which women had been rapidly absorbed into the Democratic party was evident in the third annual convention of the Democratic societies held in the Salt Lake Theatre on 13 July 1895. Three days before, the *Herald* trumpeted the news that women would be a part of all its deliberations. Many of the delegates were leading ladies of the community, it commented, and others would attend "to see how their sisters comport themselves in a public political meeting." Some of these "leading ladies" were from the Fourteenth (political) Ward in Salt Lake City, which elected Amelia Folsom Young and seven other women as delegates, forming a majority of the fifteen-member delegation from that ward. Four women were named to the executive committee of the ward, also comprising a majority. Other wards and precincts had also elected women to various party committees. "The ladies are better hustlers," than the men, one Democrat reported, and he wanted them "on all the committees."[54]

At the Democratic convention it was estimated that one-third of the delegates were women. Featured on the stage beside Governor Caleb West, congressional delegate J. L. Rawlins, former delegate John T. Caine, and other prominent Democrats, were Zina D. H. Young, Jane S. Richards, Bathsheba W. Smith, Mary Isabella Horne, Martha Hughes Cannon, and "others not known to the Newsman." Judge Henderson, who presided, congratulated the convention on the fact that "women had been taken in as an auxiliary aid, to mingle their wisdom and advice with the men." He opined that if they were allowed to vote in November, they "would aid in giving party principles clearness and strength." At the convention Zina D. H. Young was elected first vice president of the party's executive committee and Euretha LaBarthe and Electa Bullock were elected secretaries. Several women were appointed to the committee on resolutions, and Zina Young, Euretha LaBarthe, and Isabella Horne were invited to address the twelve hundred delegates. The convention endorsed the right of women to vote in November if the Enabling Act permitted.[55]

However much the *Herald* ridiculed the organization of Republican women's clubs, Democratic women were not above forming their own separate organizations. A number of Salt Lake City women, under the chairmanship of Euretha LaBarthe, combined into "a special political education and work society" with the intention of meeting regularly for their own political edification and assistance to the party. Other groups followed that eventually included most of the prominent women Democrats in the city.[56]

The expanding political activity of Mormon leaders, particularly women, became a matter of concern. The problem was aired at a meeting on 30 July attended by the First Presidency of the church, five apostles, the Salt Lake Stake presidency, and John T. Caine, Samuel R. Thurman, Judge William King, and clerk George F. Gibbs. Caine voiced the fear of some Gentiles that "the Church was using the women to help it accomplish things they desired in a political way," and that the Democrats had capitalized on the leading sisters who had joined their party with the result that Salt Lake Stake president Angus Cannon, a Republican, had asked them "to resign their [church] positions or cease mixing in politics." Such church interference, he felt, would create "discord and bitterness on the part of Gentiles." After a lengthy discussion in which all viewpoints were aired, from nonparticipation to total political freedom, President Woodruff expressed regret as to "the course the sisters had taken, but now that they have gone so far," he concluded, "it will be better to let them finish this campaign on the lines which have been marked out for them."[57] In the future both men and women in high church positions would be counselled not to take "a very active part" in political affairs. George Q. Cannon further suggested that the sisters and all others should be restrained from declaring the politics of "our dead leaders," an obvious allusion to Isabella Horne's and Amelia Folsom Young's impassioned speeches invoking the "democratic political beliefs" of Joseph Smith and to some political literature circulated by both parties making similar assertions in support of their own political philosophies.[58]

Afterwards, the general Relief Society presidency, Isabella Horne, and Emily S. Richards were called before the First Presidency and counselled "as to the course they should pursue in their political relations and labors as suffragists and as Democrats. Very clear, pointed & energetic instructions as to political principles and as to practice," were given to them, according to Apostle Franklin D. Richards. Republican Emmeline B. Wells was pleased with the outcome of the meeting, when she heard about it, and was confident that "Sister Young, Smith and Horne will be more moderate."[59]

In August, the voting eligibility of women was finally decided by the territorial supreme court. A test case had been brought in Ogden by Sarah E. Nelson Anderson, who was refused when she applied for registration on 6 August. Anderson sought a writ of mandate to compel Deputy Registrar Charles Tyree to register her. Judge H. W. Smith of the Ogden district court found for the plaintiff and ruled that women were eligible to vote not only for state officers at the next election but also on adoption or rejection of the state constitution. Tyree immediately appealed to the territorial supreme court.[60]

On 22 August, while the case was being deliberated, Republicans held their Salt Lake County convention. Emmeline Wells was named temporary chairman of the convention and applauded the delegates for the honor conferred upon the "women of Utah" through that gesture.[61] When Charles S. Varian was elected permanent chairman, she was elected one of the permanent vice-chairmen. On the second day of the convention nominations were made for the new state legislature, twenty-nine persons nominated for ten seats. Emmeline Wells was nominated for the house and Lillie A. Pardee for the senate by Ruth May Fox. Both became official candidates of their party along with Emma J. McVicker, nominated for state superintendent of schools a week later at the territorial convention.[62]

The Democratic county convention assembled on 31 August. At the same time, the supreme court delivered its ruling on Anderson vs. Tyree, reversing the judgment of the lower court. Democratic convention chairman James H. Moyle concluded that the decision denying women the right to vote in the coming election also denied them the right to run for office, though the ruling was not explicit. Thus, no women were nominated by the Democrats. The Republicans, however, already had three women candidates

Emma J. McVicker, Utah's first woman state superintendent of education. *Utah State Historical Society. All rights reserved. Used by permission.*

on their ballot. At their ratifying meeting on 2 September, speaker Arthur Brown, who had successfully represented Tyree in the supreme court case, interpreted the ruling differently from Moyle. "The right of women to vote has been questioned," he said. "Her right to hold office after the adoption of the constitution has never been questioned. I have never questioned that. The whole question is one of time. After the proclamation is issued women may hold office. . . . If you believe in woman suffrage, here is the only ticket with women upon it."[63]

In a curious reversal of positions, the Republicans were now defending the right of women to run for office. Though women were not entitled to vote in the election, a decision Brown had helped obtain, there was nothing to prevent them from being elected to office, he reasoned, as they would be qualified voters and legal officeholders before they took their seats. In an overtly hostile attack, the *Herald* now lambasted the Republicans for favoring women:

> Of course now that the supreme court has decided that women cannot vote this fall, the ambition of Mrs. Emmeline B. Wells and Lillie Pardee must be nipped in the bud. They must be taken down from their high pedestals, the salaries of $100 per month which they have been receiving as the prices for relinquishing their previous Democratic ideas, and carrying on the evangelical and organization work of the Republicans, will be stopped and they will be relegated to a condition of innocuous desuetude into which the hum of ambition will penetrate but weakly.
>
> It is truly a mournful spectacle. Here were two distinguished women who have always been understood to be Democrats until the time for organization of the Democratic women. Then neither happened to be invited to take a very high position in the Democratic ranks. The Republicans held out promises of honor and emolument, and they followed.[64]

Public pressure mounted against the Republican women candidates, and doubts about their eligibility were raised in a Republican planning meeting. Republican lawyers could not agree, but while they were conferring Emma McVicker declared her own ineligibility. By the end of September Lillie Pardee, while still holding that women had the right to run for election, acknowledged lack of support from members of her own party and thus felt the necessity to withdraw.[65]

Emmeline Wells held back on principle. "I suppose there is really no alternative but to withdraw," she reflected. But "I believe it is wrong. . . . I do not believe it would really affect the party or statehood or cut any figure in the matter whatever, and I think moreover I have a right to be elected to the legislature—as also other women—I yield unwillingly to the pressure brought to bear against the name of women on the Ticket."[66]

While she deliberated, the issue developed into another political confrontation with Emily Richards. On 7 October, the *Herald* began printing Richards's four-part reply to *The Republican Catechism*, a pamphlet Wells prepared for distribution to women explaining the Republican platform. In her reply, Richards made a pointed reference to Wells's assertion that Governor West, a Democrat, did not favor equal privileges for women because he failed to appoint any to territorial boards. His refusal, Richards pointed out, resulted from the restrictions of the Edmunds-Tucker Act (prohibiting women from voting or holding office). That he was correct in his conclusion, she continued "is demonstrated fully for Republicans in the resignations of Mrs. Pardee and Mrs. McVicker . . . for the reason that the decision of the court withholding from the women the right to vote disqualified them for holding office."[67] The implication was clear that Emmeline Wells should also resign. On the day the first installment of the Richards criticism was published, Wells and Richards met together in a woman suffrage meeting. Emmeline Wells found it "a very unpleasant affair with Mrs. Richards, who made up her mind to have some changes made."[68] While not detailing the difficulties, Wells recorded that at the afternoon meeting "came the struggle with the faction from the county" (meaning the Salt Lake County association), another manifestation of the ongoing conflict between the county and territorial suffrage leaders with Emily Richards, territorial vice president, supporting Ellen Ferguson, Salt Lake County president. "I suffered very much in my feelings," Emmeline Wells recorded. It is not known how Emily Richards responded to the situation. This incident had followed on the heels of a similar unpleasant episode in a Relief Society board meeting a week earlier.[69]

As the pressure for her resignation continued to mount, Wells's resolve to remain firm weakened. On 17 October she decided to resign against her own "better and best judgment." Convinced that her name on the ballot would not adversely affect either her party or statehood, or make any difference, except to "make a test of the principle of woman's equality," she unwillingly submitted a letter of resignation. While acknowledging the legal doubts of women's eligibility to run for office, she did not relinquish her own opinion on the matter. She gave credit to the Republican party for "expressing their appreciation of this new element in politics . . . by placing the names of women in nomination for offices of emolument and trust, expecting them to take an active part in the affairs of the new State."[70]

Despite her resignation, she continued to campaign for her party, as did her Democratic counterparts. The overwhelming acceptance of the constitution in November pleased them all. That the Republicans made a sweep of state offices was especially satisfying to Emmeline. After writing to Susan B. Anthony and Carrie Chapman Catt, national officers of the suffrage association, she expressed to her diary her personal feelings about the election: "It seems almost too good to be true that we have equal suffrage . . . Junius [a nephew] has been in and several others of my friends, and all seems secure and no permanent ill feelings I trust."[71]

Her hopes that this first experiment in partisan politics would not produce an enduring schism among the politically active women of the church at first seemed to be premature. A Leap Year Ball, planned by the suffrage association as a fund-raising event in connection with the statehood celebration in January 1896, created another opportunity for disagreement with Emily Richards. After much preparation, the event turned out to be "a fine affair" though inexplicably none of the Richards family attended. The next day, however, as Wells noted in her diary, "Mrs. Richards [Emily] was on hand to know all about the party—and was very disagreeable when she learned that no more [money] had been made." She then suggested that if Emmeline Wells, who had supervised the affair, had not been so involved in planning the annual birthday celebration for Relief Society President Zina Young, set for a few days later, she "might have succeeded better," a curious criticism from a sister Relief Society worker.[72]

But Emily Richards's diasppointment did not last long. On 18 December 1895, the suffrage association nominated a delegation of twelve to attend the celebration of Utah's statehood and the achievement of woman suffrage at the National American Woman Suffrage Association convention in Washington the next January.[73] As president of the territorial suffrage association, Wells was naturally expected to attend. In fact, Margherita Hamm, correspondent of the *New York Mail and Express*, described the coming celebration: "From far-off Utah will appear Mrs. Emmeline B. Wells, who has toiled thirty years for her principles, and now sees them triumphant in her own home. She will receive an ovation because long ago she foresaw and foretold what happened in the Great Basin last November. In fact, five years ago she laughingly said: 'Women will vote and hold office in my poor little mountain State before they do in the rich and powerful states of the seaboard.'"[74]

Only two of the nominees, however, actually attended as official delegates, Emily Richards and Sarah Boyer. Unable to raise the funds for her own expenses and evidently unable to obtain church or Relief Society financial support, as she had done in the past, Emmeline Wells found it necessary to forgo the grand celebration. "I can scarcely believe I am not going to Washington," she wrote on the day Richards and Boyer left for Washington. She may have been somewhat mollified by the expressions of regret proffered by many church leaders. President Woodruff indicated that his preference had been for Relief Society President Zina Young and Emmeline Wells to represent the suffrage association, but since President Young would not go without her and she was unable to go without financial assistance, the honor fell to Richards and Boyer.[75] Despite her own keen disappointment, she enthusiastically reported in the *Woman's Exponent* the details of the festivities in Washington, including the victory speech of Emily Richards.

In Washington, both Anna Shaw and Susan Anthony paid tribute to Utah, which had joined Wyoming and Colorado as "the crown of our Union, those three states on the crest of the Rockies." Corinne Allen, wife of Utah's new congressional representative, Sarah Boyer, and Emily Richards all responded to the speeches of congratulations. A special tribute to Emmeline Wells, "whose influence had been paramount in securing the franchise for the women of Utah," was heartily applauded and a telegram of congratulations sent to her.[76]

In the following months both of these leaders repeatedly appealed to women to maintain the best of feelings toward each other, despite party difference, and to put aside "intense partisanship" in the interest of the public good. As evidence of the sincerity of her own appeal, Emmeline Wells, on the last day of December 1896, recommended Emily Richards as a new member of the Reaper's Club, a conciliatory conclusion to their political conflicts.[77]

It is not improbable that most Mormon women shared the sentiments of Ruth May Fox as they encountered the divisive experiences of partisan politics. "I do hope they will not engender bad feelings in their divisions on party lines," she wrote. "As for my part I care nothing for politics. It is Mormonism or nothing for me."[78]

Capitalizing on her shared political affiliation (and family relationship) with the new governor, Heber M. Wells, son of Emmeline's sister-wife, Martha, Emmeline immediately lobbied to create opportunities for women in the new state government. A week after the election, at the suggestion of a party member, she wrote to each member of the senate and house proposing that they elect a woman as chief clerk of the senate, nominating Lillie R. Pardee for the position. Her efforts were successful, and she felt well pleased to think "that the Certificate of the new senators had to be signed by a *woman* as well as a man." Nor was she slow to complain to the inauguration committee that "it was noticeable women were not considered in the proceedings or in any way recognized as a part of the new state."[79] She lobbied for a state-sponsored silk commission, passage of a kindergarten bill, the building of a public library, and the appointment of women to various state boards. She was determined that woman's voice would be heard in the affairs of the new state.

By summer of that first year of statehood, interest was again focused on the coming election, the first one to include women since 1887. Both Emmeline Wells and Emily Richards had maintained active association with their respective parties. Both were nominated for the state senate, although Richards declined to run. Republican state chairman George M. Cannon claimed that Wells's name on the ticket "would strengthen the ticket to the extent of 6000 votes."[80] Alas, it proved to be empty rhetoric. From a field of ten candidates for the senate, five were elected. Emmeline Wells came in last. It was a clear-cut Democratic victory. Dr. Martha Hughes Cannon trailed the Democrats on the ticket for state senator but she garnered more votes than any of the Republicans, including her husband, Salt Lake Stake president Angus Cannon, who had decided to enter the political field himself, after advising the women who held church office in his stake to withdraw the year before.[81]

After their first success, the Republicans went down to defeat. How decisive a factor the women's vote was in the election was suggested by a Republican appraisal from the year before. "The Gentile women don't register," the pollster complained, "the Mormon women do. That hurts us. The majority of Mormon women are Democrats. The majority of Gentile women are Republicans." Another Republican observed that "far from being converts to Republicanism, women are flocking to the Democrats."[82] Though only impressionistic appraisals, they suggest that the woman's vote may well have been a factor in the 1896 election.

Three women, all Democrats, won legislative seats that year and eleven throughout the state were elected to the position of county recorder. While congratulating the women who won, Emmeline Wells expressed her own very personal disappointment that "all the women [who were candidates] were not elected, for it would have been a much truer test of women's power had there been some women from each party." Her fighting spirit not entirely extinguished, she concluded, "women as well as men must content themselves as best they can until another election, when things may be different."[83]

Though women had established a foothold in the political affairs of the new state, they had not been given a clear mandate for continued widespread involvement. Only two years after statehood the active Utah County Woman Suffrage Association denounced the "informal understanding" between the two political parties "eliminating women from the state and county tickets at the next election" and refuted the charge that women were "a weakness upon the ticket" because they lacked executive ability and could not draw the votes of other women. While the charge may not have been universally supported, it indicated the association's awareness of the persistence of social and psychological barriers to women's full political participation: the reluctance of men to integrate women into the political system, and the ambivalence of women toward the propriety and capability of women entering politics. Utah would never replicate the events of 1895 or 1896 when women were at center stage in the political drama.[84]

In their transition from the Woman Suffrage Association to the political parties, women lost both power and autonomy. The year 1895 was an exceptional year for Utah women, not a portent of a continued pattern of political attention and involvement. The campaign to put woman suffrage in the Utah state constitution had been a woman's campaign, planned and executed by women who had to convince the majority of 104 men that woman suffrage, which the legislatures of forty-two other states opposed, was good for Utah. In leaving their suffrage association and moving into the political parties, these same women, capable, experienced, energetic, moved back into traditional organizational relationships with men. They were often vice-chairpersons, but seldom permanent chairpersons. They were delegates but not strategists. Their experience and ability were useful in the parties but not to lead them, conduct the campaigns, or develop political philosophies. And in that one exceptional year, 1895, it is not difficult to appraise the attention they received from both the press and the parties as exploitive.

Ultimately, while still participating in party organizations and continuing in small numbers to hold public office, they organized separate women's Republican and Democratic clubs. Separatism, they discovered, proved to be the most reliable strategy for achieving authority and recognition. But for one year, at least, the women of Utah commanded the political spotlight. It was a year that produced a unique chapter in Utah's political history.

Notes

1. See for example, S. George Ellsworth, "Utah's Struggle for Statehood," *Utah Historical Quarterly* 32 (Winter 1963): 60–69; Richard D. Poll, "A State is Born," *Utah Historical Quarterly* 32 (Winter 1964): 9–31; Gustive O. Larson, *The Americanization of Utah for Statehood* (San Marino, Calif.: The Huntington Library, 1971); Howard R. Lamar, "Statehood for Utah: A Different Path," *Utah Historical Quarterly* 39 (Fall 1971): 307–27. Grant Underwood, in his paper "Mormonism as a Historical Concept," presented at the annual

meeting of the Western History Association in Salt Lake City, 13 October 1983, challenges the prevailing conceptual framework of this period that insists that statehood necessitated major shifts in Mormon life. Arguing that only a minority of Mormons practiced polygamy, that the communal economic systems were short-lived and ineffective, and that the majority of Mormons were basically "mainstream" Americans, he suggests that the "Americanization" view is too narrow a perspective. It focuses on religious, social, and economic concepts and principles rather than on actual practice, he maintains, and posits that for the majority of Mormons statehood necessitated no significant accommodation or adjustment.

2.   Woman suffrage in Utah has been the subject of a number of historical studies. See T. A. Larson, "Woman Suffrage in Western America," *Utah Historical Quarterly* 38 (Winter 1970): 8–19; Beverly Beeton, "Woman Suffrage in the American West, 1869–1896," (Ph.D. diss., University of Utah, 1976); Thomas G. Alexander, "An Experiment in Progressive Legislation: The Granting of Women Suffrage in Utah in 1870," *Utah Historical Quarterly* 38 (Winter 1970): 20–30; Ralph L. Jack, "Woman Suffrage as an Issue in the Mormon and Non-Mormon Press of the Territory, 1876–1877," (M. S. thesis, Brigham Young University, 1954); Carol Cornwall Madsen, " 'Remember the Women of Zion': A Study of the Editorial Content of the *Woman's Exponent*, A Mormon Woman's Journal," (M.A. thesis, University of Utah, 1977).

3.   A full discussion of the organization and activities of the Anti-Polygamy Society can be found in Robert Joseph Dwyer, "The Gentile Ladies Hoist Their Standard," *The Gentile Comes to Utah: A Study in Religious and Social Conflict, 1862–1890* (Salt Lake City: Publishers Press, 1971), 190–214.

4.   Another issue in the case concerned differing citizenship requirements for men and women, the 1870 law allowing alien women who were married to citizens the right to vote. A federal statute granted such women citizenship on the basis of their relationship to a citizen, but in the case of Utah the legality of alien plural wives obtaining citizenship in this manner created another Mormon-Gentile friction point until 1882 and the disfranchisement of all polygamists and their wives by the Edmunds Bill.

5.   Dwyer, *Gentile Comes to Utah*, 201. Lucy Stone, editor of the Boston suffrage paper, the *Woman's Journal*, responded for many suffragists to these attempts at disfranchisement: "It is hardly possible that so bold an attempt to disfranchise citizens who have exercised the right to vote for ten years can be accomplished. It would certainly never have been attempted if these citizens had not been Mormons." (9 October 1880), in Dwyer, *Gentile Comes to Utah*, 201–2.

6.   See Orson F. Whitney, *History of Utah*, 4 vols. (Salt Lake City: George Q. Cannon and Sons Company, Publishers, 1893), 3:60–61. For a full account of the proceedings see "Mormon Women's Protest, An Appeal for Freedom, Justice and Equal Rights," Salt Lake City, Utah, 6 March 1886, Utah

State Historical Society, Salt Lake City, Utah, hereafter cited as USHS. The Woman's Christian Temperance Union, the Woman's Home Missionary Society, and the Presbyterian Missionary Society, all prestigious and large women's associations, were among the organizations endorsing the memorial. The Newman memorial to Congress can be found in "Woman Suffrage in Utah," Misc. Doc. #122, 49th Congress, 1st Session, United States Senate, USHS.

7. Susa Young Gates Papers, USHS. See also *Woman's Exponent* 17 (15 June 1888): 10. The 1870 statute allowing Utah women to vote did not include a corresponding right to hold public office. A move in 1880 to amend the statute failed when the governor refused to sign the bill, which had passed both houses of the legislature.

8. General Relief Society President Zina D. H. Young, her counselor Jane Richards, and Jane's daughter-in-law and board member, Emily S. Richards, met first with L. John Nuttall, secretary to the First Presidency, in November 1888 and arranged a meeting for the following January. In attendance at the January meeting were President Wilford Woodruff, Apostles Franklin D. Richards, Brigham Young Jr., John Henry Smith, Heber J. Grant, and Secretary Nuttall, along with the Relief Society President Zina Young, Jane Richards, and Bathsheba W. Smith, Secretaries Sarah M. Kimball and Emmeline B. Wells, and board member Emily S. Richards. For details of the meeting see Emmeline B. Wells, Diary, 2 January 1889, Special Collections, H. B. Lee Library, Brigham Young University, Provo, Utah, hereafter cited as BYU Library; Zina D. H. Young, Diary, 2 January 1889, Archives, Historical Department of the Church of Jesus Christ of Latter-day Saints, Salt Lake City, Utah, hereafter cited as LDS Church Archives; L. John Nuttall, Journal, 2 January 1889, also 14 November and 31 December 1888, LDS Church Archives; and Franklin D. Richards, Journal, 2, 10, and 24 January 1889, LDS Church Archives.

9. *Woman's Exponent* 17 (15 February 1889): 138; *Salt Lake Tribune*, 11 January 1889.

10. Wells, Diary, 8 January 1899. These women signed the memorial to the constitutional convention in behalf of woman's suffrage along with a number of Mormon suffragists. See *Woman's Exponent* 23 (1 April 1895): 241.

11. L. John Nuttall, Journal, 25 February 1891.

12. Lamar, "Statehood for Utah: A Different Path." For other factors in a diminishing Democratic preference see Davis Bitton, "The B. H. Roberts Case of 1898–1900," *Utah Historical Quarterly* 25 (January 1957): 27; Richard D. Poll, "A State is Born," *Utah Historical Quarterly* 32 (Winter 1964): 9–31; Lamar, "Statehood for Utah: A Different Path"; Leo Lyman, "The Mormon Quest for Statehood," (Ph.D. Diss., University of California at Riverside, 1981); and Larson, *The Americanization of Utah for Statehood*.

13. See Lyman, "Mormon Quest for Statehood," 323–83. See Jean Bickmore White, "The Making of the Convention President: The Political Education of John Henry Smith," *Utah Historical Quarterly* 39 (Fall 1971): 350–69.

14. *Deseret Evening News*, 7 May 1891; B. H. Roberts, *A Comprehensive History of the Church*, 6 vols. (Provo, Utah: Brigham Young University Press, 1965), 6:299–301.

15. Wells, Diary, 9 June 1891; Nuttall, Journal, 21 May 1891.

16. *Woman's Exponent* 20 (15 June 1891): 188.

17. "Women in Politics," *Woman's Exponent* 20 (15 August 1891): 28.

18. *Woman's Exponent* 23 (1 and 15 November 1895): 201.

19. *Woman's Exponent* 22 (15 August 1893): 21.

20. Ruth May Fox, Diary, 12 and 28 October 1895, Ruth May Fox Papers, USHS.

21. Ruth May Fox, "My Story," Ruth May Fox Papers, USHS.

22. Fox, Diary, 30 December 1894 and 9 January 1895.

23. Minutes of the Beaver County Woman's Suffrage Association, 14 January 1895, BYU Library.

24. *Woman's Exponent* 23 (1 and 15 February 1895): 233; Fox, Diary, 19 February 1895.

25. *Salt Lake Tribune*, 15 March 1895. The *Young Woman's Journal* ran a series of statements by prominent Utahns, Mormon and Gentile, men and women, expressing their views on the topic. All were, to varying degrees, favorable. See *Young Woman's Journal* 6 (February and March 1895): 224–37 and 279–86.

26. Journal History of the Church (hereafter cited as JH), 21 February, 19 March, and 5 April 1895, LDS Church Archives.

27. *Women's Exponent* 23 (1 and 15 August 1894): 169.

28. For details of this debate, see Jean Bickmore White, "Woman's Place Is in the Constitution, The Struggle for Equal Rights in Utah in 1895," *Utah Historical Quarterly* 42 (Fall 1974): 344–69.

29. Orson F. Whitney, Diary, 6 April 1895; White, "Woman's Place Is in the Constitution."

30. *Salt Lake Tribune*, 31 March and 1, 2, and 3 April 1895. Orson F. Whitney explained to the convention the invalidity of one poll taken at the Opera House in Salt Lake City. Tickets in favor and against woman's suffrage were issued to children who were told to deposit only those against the measure. JH, 5 April 1895.

31. Mary Ann Burnham Freeze, Diary, 5 April 1895, Mary Ann Burnham Freeze Papers, Special Collections, BYU Library.

32. Proceedings of the Constitutional Convention, 1:754–55, as quoted in White, "Woman's Place Is in the Constitution." See also *Salt Lake Tribune*, 7 April 1895. Charlotte Kirby, former corresponding secretary of the Utah Woman Suffrage Association, submitted an article to the *Tribune* supporting both woman suffrage and separate submission. While disclaiming the validity

of Roberts's arguments against suffrage on its merits, she supported his arguments on expedience.

33. Wells, Diary, 4 April 1895; *Woman's Exponent* 23 (1 May 1895): 262. Church leaders were divided on this issue. Wilford Woodruff expressed a fear that the constitution would not pass if woman's suffrage were not part of it. He was supported in that view by Counselor Joseph F. Smith. Second Counselor George Q. Cannon, however, favored separate submission and argued so strongly for it that he succeeded in changing the mind of President Woodruff, though not that of Joseph F. Smith. See Abraham H. Cannon, Journal, 4 and 12 April 1895, Ms., USHS.

34. Fox, Diary, 3, 4, and 9 April 1895; Freeze, Diary, 4, 5, and 9 April 1895. An interesting sidelight involves suffragist Margaret Roberts, wife of B. H. Roberts. Before the debate on suffrage began, she frequently attended the convention with Mary Ann Freeze. After Roberts's speeches on 28 and 29 March, however, she no longer attended nor was she visibly present in the political campaigns that followed.

35. Utah Women's Press Club Minutes, 5 April 1895, USHS. For a humorous account of the name-gathering effort, see Cactus [pseud.], "Cactus Papers No. 2," *Woman's Exponent* 23 (15 May 1895): 267, 271–72.

36. Final tally was 75 for, 14 against, 13 absent, and 5 excused from voting. See White, "Woman's Place Is in the Constitution," 362. A later motion to reconsider was defeated, Ibid., 363.

37. *Salt Lake Tribune*, 19 April 1895.

38. Jean Bickmore White, "Gentle Persuaders, Utah's First Woman Legislators," *Utah Historical Quarterly* 38 (Winter 1970): 40–41; *Salt Lake Tribune*, 1 April 1895.

39. *Salt Lake Daily Herald*, 2 June 1895.

40. Franklin D. Richards, Journal, 15 June 1895; Wells, Diary, 15 June 1895.

41. *Salt Lake Daily Herald*, 15–18 and 25–28 June 1895.

42. Ibid., 19 June 1895.

43. Ibid., 16 June 1895.

44. Ibid., 19 June 1895.

45. Ibid., 21 June 1895.

46. Ibid., 11 July 1895.

47. *Salt Lake Tribune*, 15 June and 2 July 1895; *Salt Lake Daily Herald*, 3 July 1895; Wells, Diary, 2, 3, 5, and 6 July 1895; Fox, "My Story," 26.

48. Her daughter, Annie Wells Cannon, was appalled when Wells became a Republican though she herself joined the party a few years later. Wells, Diary, 25 August 1895.

49. Whitney's grandfather, Newel K. Whitney, was Emmeline's second husband, but as a plural wife Emmeline was not Orson's grandmother. Whitney's support of suffrage in the constitutional convention endeared him to all the suffragists.

His speeches in behalf of suffrage were printed in a separate pamphlet by the Utah Woman's Suffrage Association.

50. *Salt Lake Tribune*, 7 January 1896; *Salt Lake Daily Herald*, 28 July 1895; Wells, Diary, 25 August 1895.

51. *Salt Lake Daily Herald*, 13 July 1895.

52. Wells, Diary, 9 September 1895; Fox, Diary, 30 August and 15 and 23 September 1895; Wells, Diary, 6 and 9 July 1895; *Salt Lake Tribune*, 2 July 1895.

53. *Salt Lake Daily Herald*, 18 July 1895.

54. Ibid., editorial, 10 July 1895; *Salt Lake Tribune*, 9 July 1895.

55. JH, 13 July 1895: 6.

56. *Salt Lake Daily Herald*, 18 July 1895.

57. Abraham H. Cannon, Journal, 30 July 1895. See also Jean Bickmore White, "Utah State Elections, 1895–1899," (Ph.D. diss., University of Utah, 1968), 81–85; Wells, Diary, 30 July 1895.

58. *Salt Lake Tribune*, 9 July 1895; see also "Nuggets of Truth" and "Nuggets of Truth, Hear Ye the Whole Truth," pamphlets, USHS.

59. Franklin D. Richards, Journal, 30 July 1895. See also White, "Utah State Elections, 1895–1899," 81–85; Wells, Diary, 30 July 1895.

60. The Utah Commission had been approached to issue a directive to registrars concerning the eligibility of women to register, but the members had left the decision to the individual registrars initially. However, they later decided to instruct the registrars to register women in case they could vote in November. Since the legislature had not ruled, the issue would ultimately have to be decided judicially. Sarah Anderson's suit against Tyree was a deliberate effort to have the issue resolved. See *Salt Lake Daily Herald*, 14 and 20 July and 7, 9, and 11 August 1895. See also White, "Gentle Persuaders," 40–42.

61. *Deseret Evening News*, 22 August 1895.

62. Emmeline Wells had hoped for a senate nomination but a miscue in nominations gave that honor to Lillie Pardee. See *Salt Lake Daily Herald*, 24 August 1895.

63. *Salt Lake Daily Herald*, 3 September 1895; *Salt Lake Tribune*, 3 September 1895.

64. *Salt Lake Daily Herald*, 2 September 1895.

65. *Salt Lake Tribune*, 12 and 15 September 1895. See letter in *Salt Lake Tribune*, 29 September 1895.

66. Wells, Diary, 16 and 17 October 1895.

67. Emily S. Richards, *The Republican Catechism Criticized and Amended for the Benefit of the Women of Utah*, pamphlet, USHS, 40, reprinted from the *Salt Lake Daily Herald*, 30 August and 1, 6, and 21 September 1895.

68. Wells, Diary, 7 October 1895.

69. Ibid., 1 October 1895. The two women were also active members of the newly organized Federation of Women's Clubs, which provided another setting for

their power struggles. As a member of the nominating committee in May 1895, even before the heated campaign of that election year began, Emmeline Wells and Emily Richards displayed their competitiveness. Discovering that the Ogden delegates "had been coached and were primed ready to vote for Mrs. F. S. [Emily] Richards" as the new president, Wells was "very determined" that she would not be and succeeded in making Emma McVicker's nomination to replace retiring president Corinne Allen unanimous (Wells, Diary, 22 May 1895).

70. Wells, Diary, 17 and 20 October 1895. See also *Salt Lake Tribune*, 20 October 1895.

71. Wells, Diary, 7 November 1895.

72. Ibid., 16 and 17 January 1896.

73. *Woman's Exponent* 24 (1 February 1896): 108; Wells, Diary, 18 December 1895.

74. JH, 23 January 1896: 8.

75. Wells, Diary, 11, 15, 19, 21, and 23 January 1896.

76. Susan B. Anthony et al., *The History of Woman Suffrage*, 6 vols. (New York: Fowler and Wells, 1881–1922), 4:260–62; JH, 27 January 1896: 5; *Woman's Exponent* 24 (1 March 1896): 122; 25 (1 and 15 November 1896): 68; Minutes, Utah Women's Press Club, 30 December 1896, USHS.

77. *Woman's Exponent* 24 (1 March 1896): 122; 25 (1 and 15 November 1896): 68; Minutes, Utah Women's Press Club, 30 December 1896 USHS.

78. Ruth May Fox, Diary, 14 July 1895.

79. Wells, Diary, 13 and 17 November 1895 and 1 and 22 January 1896.

80. Annie Wells Cannon, "In Memoriam: Emily Sophia Tanner Richards," Utah State Historical Society, 25; *Salt Lake Daily Herald*, 8 October 1896.

81. *Salt Lake Tribune*, 14 November 1896 and White, "Gentle Persuaders," 31–49.

82. *Salt Lake Daily Herald*, 11 July and 25 August 1895.

83. "Woman's Work and Duty," *Woman's Exponent* 25 (1 and 15 November 1896): 69.

84. "The Women Resolve," *Woman's Exponent* 27 (1 September 1898): 33.

Ruth May Fox. *Utah State Historical Society. All rights reserved. Used permission.*

15

"I Care Nothing for Politics"

Ruth May Fox, Forgotten Suffragist

EDITED BY LINDA THATCHER

In Utah's history there have been many important women of whom little has been written; one such person is Ruth May Fox. Besides raising twelve children she was active in the Utah Woman's Press Club (president), the Reaper's Club, the Utah Woman Suffrage Association (treasurer), the Salt Lake County Republican Committee, the Second Precinct Ladies' Republican Club (chairman), the Deseret Agricultural and Manufacturing Society (board member), and the Traveler's Aid Society (board member). She also served on the general board and as general president of the Young Ladies' Mutual Improvement Association of the Church of Jesus Christ of Latter-day Saints (Mormons).

She was born November 16, 1853, in Westbury, Wiltshire, England, the daughter of Mary Ann Harding and James May. When Ruth was five months old her parents joined the Mormon church. Her mother died in March 1855 after giving birth to a second child, who also died. After her mother's death her father was called to be a traveling elder for the church. Ruth lived

First published in *Utah Historical Quarterly* 49 (Summer 1981): 239–53, with the following acknowledgment: "Leonard Grant Fox gave his kind permission to publish here a portion of the Ruth May Fox diary, later donated to the LDS church." Reprinted by permission.

with various Mormon families and relatives until she was around eight years old and her father took her to Yorkshire where he was employed. There they boarded with a Mrs. Saxton who had a daughter named Clara, five months younger than Ruth. While living with the Saxtons Ruth attended the Church of England Sunday School where she learned about deathbed repentance. This concept appealed to her as she was fun loving and occasionally did things like take a bite out of a china saucer, skip school, or give her grandmother's possessions away. When her father went to her grandmother's house to pick her up to take her to Yorkshire, her grandmother exclaimed: "She's a bad maid, she's a bad maid."

In 1865 Ruth's father journeyed to America. A few months later he sent for Mrs. Saxton, Clara, and Ruth. Soon after arriving, Mrs. Saxton and James May were married. They lived in Manayunk, a manufacturing district a few miles out of Philadelphia, where at the age of twelve Ruth and Clara were put to work in a factory to help earn money for the journey to Utah. Later, the family moved into Philadelphia where Ruth and Clara worked in another factory, but eventually the girls found jobs doing housework. In July 1867 the Mays started for Utah, first traveling to North Platte, Nebraska, where they purchased supplies for their trip. After doing so they found that they had only enough money left to purchase "one yoke of cattle," so they shared a wagon with another family and ended up walking most of the way. Upon arriving in the valley Ruth experienced a sense of disillusionment:

> At last the long journey was ended. We had pulled up the hill out of Parley's Canyon just as twilight shrouded the valley. We could still catch a glimpse of the city below, but I confessed to some disappointment as I asked, "Did we come all this way for this?" This, however, was my first and last disappointment.[1]

Her father soon found work as a carder in the Deseret Woolen Mill at the mouth of Parley's Canyon. Ruth and Clara worked in the factory as well in order to help the family accumulate enough money to purchase a home. James May worked in this mill for two years before moving to Ogden to work in the Ogden Woolen Mills, started by Alfred Randall, near the mouth of Ogden Canyon. Ruth remained in Salt Lake for a short time, but her father soon sent for her to work in the mill. After seven months she returned to Salt Lake and attended John Morgan's College for four months, ending her formal education.

Her father returned to Salt Lake City at that time, purchased some used carding machines, and started his own business. Ruth worked in the mill, operating equipment meant to be run by a man. She had strong feelings about equality and felt that since she was doing a man's work she should receive a man's pay. Of the incident she later wrote:

> Here I reeled yarn and wove cloth and finally undertook a man's job running the Jack, a machine for spinning scores of threads at a time. I should have had a man's wages for this, but Father thought that his partner would object since I was a girl. Although I did quite as well as a man, I was given only $10.00 a week; but that was very good for a girl at the time.[2]

After working at this job for four months she quit to prepare for her wedding to Jesse Williams Fox, Jr. They were married May 8, 1873; she was nineteen, he twenty years old. On April 14, 1874, their first child, Jesse May, was born. The following year her husband was called to serve a mission in New York but stayed only three months before being called home to help his father, Jesse Williams Fox, Sr., survey for the Utah Southern Railway.

Ruth and her husband prospered financially the first twenty years of their married life, building in 1880 a large home at 261 West Second South in Salt Lake. Most of her time was consumed with household duties, but later in life she looked back on her experiences and noted the changes in her attitude toward raising children:

> There was mischief always in process, and at times tempers flared. I can't blame my children too much for their quarrels, as I was myself quick with sharp words and could not always count ten when provoked. I had been brought up in the English tradition of family discipline and applied the flat of my hand or a switch when I thought it necessary. I improved in self-restraint through the years, or else grew weary of the continued and fruitless effort to impose on my children my own standards of conduct. Though my first children got more whippings, I don't see that they are any nearer perfection than those that came later and escaped with fewer and lighter punishments.[3]

At the height of their prosperity in the late 1880s they made plans to build a three-story mansion on South Fifth East. Everything seemed to be going well in Ruth's life when, in 1888, her husband decided to take a second wife, Rosemary Johnson. He did not ask Ruth's permission. Obviously hurt by his action she wrote about it later:

At this peak of our prosperity my husband was prompted to take a second wife. It seemed a noble thing for him to do; especially when it was almost certain to result in a term in the State Prison. He did not ask my advice, but if he had, I am sure that my convictions of the soundness of the principle would have enabled me to suppress every urge to jealousy and to bear my cross as did every other good L.D.S. woman under similar circumstances.[4]

About this time financial disaster hit the Foxes. Jesse lost his business and accumulated large debts, and they eventually lost their home. He took his financial collapse extremely hard, even staying in bed for a few days. Ruth was also upset but responded by doing what needed to be done; she let domestic help go and eventually took in roomers. Her husband retained possession of his farm, so they were able to eat. During the year 1900 Ruth and her children ran the Saint Omer Boarding House to help supplement their income.

In 1896 her last child, Emmeline Blanche, was born; and two months later her oldest child, Jesse May, was married. Emmeline Blanche contracted scarlet fever and never recovered, dying in February 1914. Afterward, Ruth moved in with her son Feramorz Y. Fox, who was living at 124 North State Street, to be near her ailing father and to work as a typist for the Young Ladies' Mutual Improvement Association. She lived with her children the rest of her life and resumed housekeeping only to nurse her husband through illnesses in 1921 and from 1927 until his death in 1928.

Always interested in writing, she joined the Utah Woman's Press Club and the Reaper's Club, both groups emphasizing literary pursuits. Thus, she became better acquainted with such women leaders of the day as Dr. Ellis R. Shipp, Dr. Ellen B. Ferguson, Emma McVicker, and the person who was the most influential in her life, Emmeline B. Wells. It seems likely that Ruth became involved in the clubs and causes that she did because Emmeline B. Wells was also involved in them. Emmeline had a profound influence on Ruth's life, so much so that she later wrote:

> No other woman had so great an influence as she in shaping my life. I became her devoted disciple and she in turn loved me as a daughter. I named after her my last child, Emmeline Blanche, born September 14, 1896, when Sister Wells was the center of my orbit of public activities. For many years subsequently she had much to do with my progress.[5]

Ruth always had strong beliefs, though, and chief was suffrage for women. She was not particularly interested in politics but became active in the Utah Woman Suffrage Association and the Republican party to further the suffrage cause. She actively worked for the inclusion of the woman suffrage clause during the 1895 Utah Constitutional Convention, helping draft the suffrage memorial to the convention. Later, she worked for the election of candidates who would support women's issues and for the approval of the new constitution.

Viewing politics as merely a means to an end, she was never again as active in politics as during the year 1895. A great deal of her later life was devoted to the Young Ladies' Mutual Improvement Association, and she eventually served as the general president of the organization. She lived to be 104 years old, for which achievement she seemed to be the most remembered at her death on April 12, 1958. The significant contributions she had made to woman suffrage in Utah were mostly forgotten.

The portion of Ruth May Fox's diary selected for publication covers the final time period in Utah's struggle for statehood and women's fight for the franchise. The diary covers one person's life during those hectic days and illustrates how the women worked within the already established structures to promote their causes. Left out are the maneuverings to get men elected to the constitutional convention who were willing to include suffrage within the constitution. Ruth does comment a great deal about working for the Republican party and traveling around the state to speak. Noticeably absent are extensive comments about her own daily life, her husband, and children.

The extract from her diary is printed exactly as it was written, with spelling, punctuation, and capitalization errors. Footnotes have been added to help explain events.

Diary
December 29, 1894, to November 5, 1895.

Dec 1894

29 Went to Press Club in the evening had a pleasant time Club entertained Phebe Cousins[7] who spoke to us on the sufferage and currency questions.[8]

Sun 30 was invited to Dr E. Firrgusons[9] where some ladies met to complain of the way they had been treated by the Ter. Board of U.W.S.A.[10] Questioned the legality of the elections of officers etc I gained some experience at that time. Made a mistake in signing letter requesting the calling of a another [constitutional] convention. Although I did it with the best of feelings towards Sister Wells.[11] Went to meeting in the evening Bro Stevenson occupied the entire evening.

31 Miss Cousins was at the Reaper's to day. Mrs. F.[ranklin] S. Richards and I delevered letter to Mrs. E. B. Wells. Was interviewed in the evening by Margaret Caine[12] who thought the letter was wrong Jet[13] and I sat up with some of the children to see the old year out.

Jan 1, 1895 snowing Jet and I called on Mrs. W. C. Morris, Father, Uncle Gid, went in cutter, [fine] sleighing.

Jan 2 Met E. B. Wells had a long talk on the sufferage question paid my yearly fee. *3d.* Very busy making dresses for S. School party. Clera[14] was here and spent the afternoon

Fri 4th Got children off to party Went late to Emily Clawsons to Primary O.[15] meeting to arrange about Miss Chapins class which was imediately afterward I remained and enjoyed it.

Sat 5 In the afternoon went to Mrs. Beatty's tea she gave to help raise funds to send delegate to Atlanta[16] 6 Remained at home Jet being poorly. *Mon 7* Went to R. C.[17] in the afternoon and Y. L.[18] meeting in the eve. which met at S. Rockwells was asked to write for their paper called at Georgie's going home to see Lylie about taking part in a Primary entertainment *Wed.* 9 very busy Peral. E.[19] left. Daisy[20] and I did work attended Ter.[ritorial] S.[uffrage] executive meeting I refused to withdraw my name from letter because the ladies I signed with were not present with the exception of Mr. F. S. Richards It was quite late when I returned home being to late for supper *Thur.* 11 Frank was sick to day, did not go to Primary Borrowed $10.00 from Mrs Wimley for Jette[21] to get his glasses.

Fri 12 Worked hard at 4 o'clock went to Miss Chapins class[22] came home in time to get supper 4 of the children have gone to a party at Mrs Pollocks.

Sat 13 hurryed all day to get to the club and found it was not to be untill the 15th

Sunday Went to hear Miss Phebe Cousins lecture on the silver conspiracy.[23] Which she did in a very able manner, Jet went also.

Tues Went to sufferage meeting in the afternoon and P[ress] Club in the evening.

Fri 18 Miss Chapin class was dismissed as the members were all falling off

Sat worked very hard all day in the evening finished writing the Ten Virgins.[24]

Feb 9th Have been to busy to remember my journal when I might have taken time to write in it *Jan 29th* went to Relief Society.[25] Sister E S Taylor[26] spoke to us asking our faith and prayers as she was going to Washington to represent the Young ladie *Tues Feb 5th.* Went to S.A. heard Prof [W. M.]

Stewert and [Dr.] S. B. Young also a Mr Adams from N Da [North Dakota][27] on sufferage tried to vote down petition but failed *Feb 8th* Went to Sister E. Stevenson's birthday party had a glorious time Sister B.[athsheba] Smith and Helen [M.] Whitney were present. Sister Sarah Phelps spoke in toungs[28] with great power insomuch that the floor and the chairs and our limbs trembled, she blessed Sister Whiting, who was an invalid for years said we should know a year hence wether God spoke or not, the Sisters laid hands on Sister W. and prayed for her speedy recovery Sister N C. Taylor being mouth.[29]

Fri 15 Went to Weiler Horne's funeral. In the evening tended S.L.Co. Sufferage Ass.[30] entertainment to celebrate Susan B. Anthony's birthday.

Sat eve Went to P. Club Sister Shipp[31] had gone to Washington[32] I was chosen to represent the club at the Federation[33]

Sun 17 I have been to evening meeting Bro Eli Pierce told us that General Carter of Industrial Army fame on the day of his departure made these remark. That slaves were or words to that effect rising up against their masters and would shortly plunge the U.S. in blood that it was but the sequal to the Civil War. Being a fulfillment of J. Smith's prophecy.[34]

Fri. 22 Last Monday at the Reapers Club we voted to send 50ct a piece as a birthday present to Sister E. B. Wells who is now in Washington.[35]

Tue Went to suffrage meeting we decided to interview the delegates to the Constitutional Convention[36] Sister Ebba Hyde and myself were appointed to see Samuel [H.] Hill. Richard [G.] Lambert and Mr [William G.] Vanhorne[37] On thursday attended Primary and changed my name so that it would go on the minutes from Polly to Ruth M. I thought it would prevent confusion in the future. To-day the children are out of school and I want to do some sewing if I can get time

24th Sunday Sick had cramps

Mon 24 I interview delegates Mr Hill was favorable Mr Vanhorn did not think the constitution was the place for sufferage to come up[38] Went to see Mrs. McVicker[39] about the federation. I forgot to write that last Friday night Jet told me he was going to the store and he did not come home till next day I was quite worried was afraid something had happened to him I don't like to be treated that way.[40]

I am afraid their are many little incidents my journal will not get. I am so busy I do not get time to attend to it but to day the *6th of March* I attended the Federation business meeting, this morning and this afternoon a reception given to the delegates, both at the Women's industrial home[41] everything went along nicely I was appointed one of a committee to organize womans clubs throughout the territory, but declined my home duties are too pressing. Two subjects of the Press Clubs were accepted for discussion at the May meeting in Ogden. Yesterday attended Suff. Meeting.

Mon. gave my paper Herbert Spencer and Frances Hodgson Burnett[42] at the Reapers.

Sat 2nd Called at Georgie's, the sewing class met there had refreshments then went to Dr. R. [illegible] about the Federation.

Fri attended Mrs C E. Dye's Funeral.

Mar 11 Was called to a meeting on the suffrage question at S.[arah] M. Kimballs but could not remain it being to near the dinner hour.

12 Attended Relief Socity.

13 Went to W Coop[43] Directors meeting

14 Saw Dr E R Shipp and decided to pospone Press and Reapers meeting in her and Sister E B Wells honor till Saturday night on account of Bro Hornes party

Sat 16th Had a pleasant time at the Club Mrs E B. Wells and Dr. Shipp gave interesting accounts of their visit to the East.[44]

17th Bro Brigham Young [Jr.] spoke this evening his theme was to not mix to much with outsiders[45]

Mon 18 Met with S. A in convention at City and County building drafted memorial being one of the committee[46]

18 Presented memorial to committee on suffrage was very courteously treated we all felt it a great day in the history of Utah.[47] the Committee informed us they had passed on W. S. being ten to five in favor. Friday am invited to meet the committee in the Probate Court room. When I hope to see inside of State convention Hall.[48]

Fri. 22 Met with committee and decided to ask for a room not now in use for the purpose of holding public meetings for, ladies, of course,

Thur 28. A very rainy day but I attended the convention to hear the debate on the Sufferage question Mr B. H. Roberts was very eloquant but his only argument was that he thought it would defer statehood.[49]

31 It is grand-pa Fox's[50] birthday. We had all the members of his family to dinner.

April 1st. O dear I have worn myself out to-day. Have been to the convention all day and stood up all the time with the exception of a little while that I sat on the tabble Mr Roberts was to give his oration but did not have time so it went over till next day. What a shame he does not use his eloquience in a better cause *2nd* attended W. S. meeting Dr Fergusen thought if we had petitioned it would have been a benefit but we shall see.

Wed 3d Was called out suddenly to circulate petions[51] met with good success *Thurs 4* went with petitions a little while again but did so dislake to visit the business block.

Fri. Press Club met in the evening had a pleasant time adjourned early to discuss the suffrage question every one present and there was some gentlemen, expressed themselves as being in favor of its being adobted and put in the Constitution[52] The article giving women the Franchise passed in the convention to day 75 to 13[53] but it is expected to be brought up again So I am afraid the fight is not over

Sat afternoon attended conference. Bro Snow and Bro Talmage addressed us. *Sun 7* went to conference both meetings The First Presidency occupied the time.

Tue. Went to mutual

Wed 9 Have been arround a gain with petitions to find out who are willing the Sufferage Clause should remain in the Constitution met with very good success.

Apr 14 Sunday. Jette is 21 to-day should like to have remembered him but did not feel able. *15th* Clara's birthday made her a call after Reapers Club also attended P. C. called for the purpose of considering wether we should entertain officers of Federation *Tues.* attended S Ass. *Thurs.* As usual went to Primary

May 1st have been very busy housecleaning with that exception nothing of importance has happened to me personally although the air seems full of misfortune, excepting the entertaining of the Federation officers. We had a very pleasant time but was greatly disappointed on account of Sister E. B. Wells being unable to attend also Dr Ellis Shipp so we had to do the best we could. I was chosin to preside.

Sun. May 19th So many things have happened since I wrote last, in fact I have been too busy to write. There was the reception given to the delegates to Constitutional Convention, at the [Hotel] Templeton. which I attended and enjoyed very much. Then the visit of Susan B. Anthony[54] and the Rev. Anna Shaw[55] whom we met at the depot last Sunday morning on the 12th We had breakfast at the Templeton, about 40 of us and Thurs had a nice ride around the City using the Utah and other carriages then it was *meeting meeting* meeting which I enjoyed very much[56] and now comes the meeting of the Federation of Clubs in Ogden to which I am a delegate from the Reapers. We go on the 22nd.

May 27 The meeting of the Federation was a success in every way The topics were particularly fine. The one by Anna K. Hardy's and Lizzie Wilcox being very creditable to our clubs'[57] I was made a director of the Federation our Press Club met Fri. 24th I was chosen on a debate "Is the double standard of money the one for America." For the sake of argument I am to take the negative side.[58]

Sat June 15 The Press club was entertained by Mrs. I Cameron Brown we had a pleasant time I wrote for the occasion Two sides of a question which I read and they seemed to enjoy. *16th* we visited Aunt Purdie her son Gid being very sick.

18 Went to R. Society in the evening attended a surprise party given in honor of Sister Mary Freeze[59] in 14 wd. it was unusually fine but oh! the dressing down Mr B H. Roberts got from Joseph F. Smith I really felt sorry for him[60]

Sat 22 Went to both meetings of primary conference.

Mon June 24 started to the summer school at the university am taking grammar and English Literature do hope I shall make a success of it shall have to work very hard to keep up in Grammar.

28 Went to the Temple to do some sealing with Jette.

July Sun 14 nothing of importance has happened excepting that the Republican women are forming Legues[61] I have been made Treasurer of the Ter State Organization. I do hope they will not engender bad feelings in their division on party lines for my part I care nothing for politics It is Mormonism or nothing for me. *Wed.* I am to recite at Saltair for the R. S. I do hope I shall do it creditably.

July 21 Well I went on the excursion gave one of my own pieces I guess I did allright as so many people wanted a copy. *Sat the 20* I was invited with some other ladies to meet with the gentlemen's Co. Republican Committee we had a very nice meeting. In the evening the ladies Republican League called a meeting which I attended *This afternoon Sun.* I went to the Tabernacle.

24 July pioneer day went with Jet to the Lake had a bath *Fri 26th* I was notified that I was one of the ladies chosen on the S. L. Co. R. Committee.[62]

Aug 23 Since last writing I have been chosen one of the ladies to act on the reception Committee Republican day at Saltair which meets

Mon. 26. Yestreday 22 attended Salt Lake Co. [Republican] Convention was there till 3 o clock in the morning I nominated Mrs Wells for the [illegible] *House* which was carried Mrs Lillie Pardee carried for the Senate.[63] Today Emma Empey and myself went to Farmington to a Rep. Convention.

Sept 1st I am so busy that I almost forget my journal Bro Fox and I went to the Lake Republican day had a very pleasant time. *Tues. 27 of Aug.* I went to speak in the sixth ward on registration.

Fri. 30th I went to Brigham City with Sister E B Wells to organize a R. Womens club.

1895

We returned home with Jet who had been to Preston the following day. We had a meeting in the opera house staid with Bro. Rich and had a very pleasant time. To day I have been home all day there was no one to stay with the children so did not go to meeting. I have been invited to speak at the Re. Ratification to morrow eve my speeches as yet are very short not being accustomed to it[64] *Sept 12* the Y. Ladies M. held there annl [illegible] this eve. here

Sept 15 Since I last wrote I have been to Payson Spanish Fork and to American Fork to attend Republican meetings I also went to speak in the 1 [illegible] Ward tues the 10th but did not do very well. I felt very timid. I forgot to state that I was made chairman of the 2nd precent ladies' republican club I did not want it but because I was a Mormon they wanted me to take it we were organized Aug 8th 1895

Sept 17 Gave report of 2nd Precent in the Grand Opera house today where the Republican lady's held a meeting

Sept 23 went to South Cottonwood Ward with Mrs E B Wells to talk Republicanism

24 Was chosen President of the young ladies of the 14 ward

27 went to sugar house to the house of Sister Mary Young to speak on politics

30 spoke in the 1st precint to the woman of the Rep. Club

Oct 8 held a very successful meeting in the 2nd precint serving refreshments at the close.

Oct 12 Attended Reapers Club. I happened to give in as a current event, Powers play against the Priesthood for the democratic party, but withdrew it as our club is divided in politics and some of the ladies thought we should take no note of it on that account. But I think it quite serious.[65]

Sun. 20 Mrs Evan's has come to pay me a visit she is 86 yrs old and nearly blind.

21 went to south jordan with Mrs Edna Smith[66] to speak at a political meeting. Pres Smith came to Depot to meet his wife with his whiskers tied back with a handkerchief.[67] *25* Went with the young Ladies to take a party of Aggie and Annie Campbells house as a recognition of their efficint labors in the M.I. Ass *Sat 26* took part in the ladies Republican parade which was a great success.

Mon 28 Attended Reapers Club again a democratic member had a chance to defend Judge Powers

Oct Tues 29 Discontinued the meetings of the Womans R League at the meeting Bo Roberts posed as a blacksmith being [illegible]

Nov

Fri 1st The republican ladies met at my home to day to see what we could do about a lunch for the workers on election day And this evening I have been to the theatre to hear B. H. Roberts speak on democracy some of his remarks I enjoyed some I could have wept over. Day before yestreday Bro George Q Cannon was accused of saying a certain thing in Box Elder in a sermon he preached there which he promptly denied and afterward he was told that he did say it by some of the brethren though he could not remember it he accepted their statement and made a public acknowledgement and withdrawal[68] I feel very sorry for him and I felt sorry for Roberts when he said the church had meddled in politics and he cared not who the meddler was he should be branded as an enemy to the church and a traitor to the State.

Sat 2 Went to Young ladies in the morning, officers meeting, In the afternoon went to the Walker Pavillion settled the affairs of the precint Rep. Club and found we did not have to serve lunch as the candidates wives were going to attend to it. In the evening went to East Bountiful to speak at a Republican meeting, but did not make myself know[n], Mrs Clark who should have been there not being forth comming. I staid all night with Elisabeth Fox and visited Jessie Stephen and Eva Grant returning in the afternoon. *Mon eve 4* went to Rep. Rally in the theatre *Tus eve.* It is election day, have been to the Y.L.M.I.A., do not know as yet how it will turn out but do not care much. beleive we have got Statehood assured so far as the vote is concerned and that means suffrage for women.[69]

Notes

1. Ruth May Fox, "My Story," MS, Utah State Historical Society, Salt Lake City.
2. Ibid.
3. Ibid.
4. Ibid.
5. Ibid.
6. The Utah Woman's Press Club was organized October 31, 1891, by Emmeline B. Wells. The club was open to women writers with published works. Furtherance of literary development and women's interests were two of the club's objectives. Meetings were held in the *Woman's Exponent* offices, Dr. Ellis R. Shipp's office in the Constitution Building, or in members' homes. Ruth May Fox served in all offices of the club from its first treasurer to president.
7. Phoebe Wilson Couzins, 1839?–1913, was the first woman law graduate from Washington University in Saint Louis, Missouri, in 1871. A prominent

figure in the national suffrage movement, she traveled extensively lecturing on suffrage. At odds with the national suffrage organization, she started lecturing on her own in the early 1890s, supporting temperance and other reforms. Turning against her former causes in later years, she denounced woman suffrage and became a Washington lobbyist for the United Brewer's Association.

8. See *Salt Lake Tribune*. December 30, 1894, for text of speech.

9. Dr. Ellen Brooke Ferguson, 1844–1920, was a physician who was widowed a few years after moving to Salt Lake City. Active in the woman's suffrage movement, she received a call along with Zina Young from Mormon church authorities in 1881—shortly before she left for New York for further education—to be an advocate of woman suffrage and defend polygamy. For these causes she gave many lectures during her stay in the East and developed significant contacts with important suffrage leaders. She remained an active supporter of the Mormon church until around 1896 when she became associated with Theosophy, which she embraced. She severed her relations with the Mormon church and moved to New York where she died at the age of seventy-six.

10. Territorial Board of the Utah Woman Suffrage Association, formed in 1889 and affiliated with the National Woman Suffrage Association. For further information see Beverly Beeton, "Woman Suffrage in the American West, 1869–1896" (Ph.D. diss., University of Utah, 1976): 128–31.

11. Emmeline Blanche Woodward Wells, 1828–1921. She joined the Mormon church in 1842 and eventually emigrated to Utah. She married Daniel H. Wells, a prominent Mormon, and devoted a great deal of time to church work, the suffrage movement, and journalism. She served as president of the Relief Society as well as editor of the *Woman's Exponent*, organ to the Relief Society. She also served as president of the Utah Woman Suffrage Association during the period when full suffrage was secured.

12. There were two Margaret Caines, Margaret N. Caine, wife of John T. Caine, Utah's delegate to Congress, and Margaret A. Caine, a widow. This diary entry most likely refers to Margaret A. due to her somewhat meek attitude toward the constitutional convention.

13. Jesse Williams Fox, Jr., 1852–1928, her husband.

14. Clara. Most likely the daughter of Mrs. Saxton, whom Ruth's father married shortly after they arrived in America.

15. The Primary organization is for Mormon children.

16. In January 1895 Emmeline B. Wells, accompanied by Marilla M. Daniels from Provo and Aurelia S. Rogers from Farmington, attended the National Woman Suffrage Association convention in Atlanta.

17. The Reaper's Club was organized in 1892, mainly for those women who could not qualify for the Press Club but were interested in the same pursuits. Ruth May Fox was never as active in this club as in the Press Club mainly because it met during the day when it was more difficult for her to attend.

18. Young Ladies' Mutual Improvement Association. Organized in 1869 as the Retrenchment Society by Brigham Young for the benefit of his daughters to help them better cope in the "worldly" world, it soon became a churchwide organization for young women, and eventually its name was changed to Young Ladies' Mutual Improvement Association. Ruth May Fox was most active in this organization, serving as its general president from 1929 to 1937.

19. Most likely someone who helped with the housework.

20. Her daughter Ruth Clare Fox, 1879–1961.

21. Son Jesse May Fox, 1874–1947.

22. Ending her formal education at an early age, Ruth occasionally took correspondence classes and summer classes from the University of Utah in such subjects as English.

23. Popularly known as the "silver question," it involved a complex set of issues related to the country's economic situation. For further information see Robert Harkness, "The Silver Question," *The Utah Monthly Magazine* 9 (March 1893): 201–16, and C. C. Goodwin, "Another View of the Silver Question," *The Utah Monthly Magazine* 9 (April 1893): 249–60.

24. She wrote many poems during her lifetime and published one volume of verses: Ruth May Fox, *May Blossoms* (Salt Lake City: General Board of the Young Ladies' Mutual Improvement Association, 1923).

25. The Relief Society was organized for the women of the Mormon church.

26. Elmina Shepard Taylor, 1830–1904, president of the YLMIA during 1880–1904.

27. For summary of meeting see *Woman's Exponent*, April 15, 1895.

28. Called the "Gift of Tongues," it was common, during religious occasions, especially among the women of the early Mormon church, to speak in another language, usually the "Adamic tongue" or some contemporary language. Afterward, someone would interpret what had been said. Claudia L. Bushman, ed., *Mormon Sisters: Women in Early Utah* (Cambridge, Mass.: Emmeline Press Limited, 1976): 7.

29. It was also common until 1914 for women in the Mormon church to administer to sick women and children. Ibid., 17.

30. Following the formation of the Utah Woman Suffrage Association, county chapters were organized as well. Beeton, "Woman Suffrage in the American West, 1869–1896," 131.

31. Dr. Ellis Reynolds Shipp, 1847–1939. Besides having a medical practice she served on the general board of the Relief Society and belonged to both the Reaper's and the Utah Woman's Press Club.

32. President Ellis R. Shipp and Emmeline B. Wells were in Washington, D.C., as representatives to the National Council of Women. Utah Woman's Press Club, "Minutes, 1894–1898," MS, Utah State Historical Society.

33. She was chosen, being first vice-president of the Press Club, to represent it at

the Federation of Women's Clubs on February 12, 1895. Utah Woman's Press Club, "Minutes, 1894–1898."

34. First printed in 1851, this entry refers to part of what is known as Joseph Smith's "Great Prophecy on War" in Doctrine and Covenants, sec. 87:4— "And it shall come to pass, after many days, slaves shall rise up against their masters, who shall be marshaled and disciplined for war."

35. See note 32.

36. The main interest of the Utah Woman Suffrage Association during this period was to persuade the delegates to the constitutional convention to frame a constitution which would include equal rights for women as well as men, rather than be submitted as a separate proposal.

37. All were delegates to the constitutional convention from the Salt Lake City Second Precinct. Utah, Constitutional Convention, 1895, *Official Report of the Proceedings and Debates*, 2 vols. (Salt Lake City, 1898), 2:1942, 1957, 1999.

38. Both eventually submitted motions to petition for a separate submission of suffrage. Ibid., 1:850.

39. Emma J. McVicker, 1846-. Little is known about her except that she was a non-Mormon community leader. She was the only woman superintendent of public schools in Utah, for three months in 1900.

40. Apparently her husband kept irregular hours, as in her autobiography she wrote: "My English training had fitted me to be a conscientious wife. Three meals a day, on time, was always the rule in my Father's home. My husband, however, was not quite so particular as to the time or place. I had to discipline myself, which was not always easy as I had a quick temper and a strong sense of justice." Fox, "My Story."

41. Located at 145 South Fifth East, today housing the Ambassador Athletic Club, the building was erected by the federal government around 1889 for the purpose of housing polygamous wives deserted by their husbands as a result of the enforcement of the Edmunds law. In its ten years of existence only ten women connected with polygamy sought shelter, and the building was sold at auction in 1899 for a fraction of its original cost.

42. Herbert Spencer, 1820–1903, a philosopher and author who attempted to explain Darwinism and other popular thought of the day. Frances Eliza Hodgson Burnett, 1849–1924, a noted author whose most remembered work is *Little Lord Fauntleroy*.

43. Woman's Co-operative Mercantile and Manufacturing Institution, established in 1890 to sell locally produced goods. Shares in the organization were sold by Relief Societies for five dollars each.

44. This was a combined meeting of the Utah Woman's Press and Reaper's clubs.

45. Brigham Young, Jr., 1836–1903, was ordained an apostle in the Mormon church in 1864. For summary of speech see *Deseret News*, March 18, 1895.

46. Ruth May Fox, along with fourteen other women, was chosen by the UWSA

to prepare the memorial on woman suffrage for the constitutional convention.

47. Franklin S. Richards presented their memorial to the convention.

48. The majority of this committee, on March 22, reported that they could not find any good reasons why women of Utah should not have equal rights.

49. On March 28 the majority report of the committee was placed before the convention for debate. B. H. Roberts spoke against the inclusion of woman suffrage as he felt that it would endanger statehood: "It is a sacrifice that I believe the women of this Territory are capable of making." *Proceedings*, 1:426.

50. Jesse Williams Fox, Sr., 1819–94, was the surveyor general of Utah, 1852–84, and Salt Lake City surveyor, 1851–76.

51. Opponents of the suffrage issue wanted it submitted separately; and even though the issue of woman suffrage seemed settled in the convention, petitions for separate submission of woman suffrage continued to flow into the convention. The suffragists organized petition drives for equal political rights to remain in the body of the constitution and submitted them to the convention.

52. Emmeline B. Wells made a motion that the club meeting be resolved into a meeting for the consideration of woman suffrage, each person giving "the strongest reason she has for desiring suffrage." According to the minutes, "Mrs. R. M. Fox said that personally she felt equal to any emergency. In reading her Bible she found that man and women were created equal. Quoted a sentiment from Luther and made remarks thereon. Thought most emphatically the article should be in the constitution." Utah Woman's Press Club, "Minutes, 1894–1898."

53. The vote was actually: Ayes, 75; Noes, 14; Absent, 12. *Proceedings*, 1:767.

54. Susan Brownell Anthony, 1820–1900, was the president of the National Woman Suffrage Association during 1892–1900. Besides working for a federal suffrage amendment she also spent a great deal of time helping with state campaigns for suffrage.

55. Anna Howard Shaw, 1847–1919, besides being a minister, was active in the suffrage movement as vice-president of the National Woman Suffrage Association during 1892–1904.

56. The conference held in Salt Lake City was one of four planned for different places in the country during that year by the National Woman Suffrage Association to promote woman suffrage. At the time it was planned it was not known that the issue of woman suffrage would already be settled. For text of speeches see *Salt Lake Tribune*, May 13, 14, and 15, 1895.

57. Lizzie S. Wilcox of the Utah Woman's Press Club gave a talk entitled "Women in Journalism." Annie Kay Hardy of the Reaper's Club gave an address on the subject "Training Schools for Girls." For full report of convention, see *Ogden Standard*, May 23 and 24, 1895.

58. The affirmative side was assigned to Mrs. Phoebe C. Young. Utah Woman's Press Club, "Minutes, 1894–1898."

59. Mary A. Burnham Freeze, 1837–1912, served on the general board of the Young Ladies' Mutual Improvement Association from 1898 until her death in 1912. She was also a member of the Press Club and active in the suffrage movement.

60. She elaborated on the incident in her autobiography "My Story" as she wrote: "Evidently President Joseph F. Smith did not approve of the course taken by Brother Roberts, for at an evening entertainment he spoke earnestly on what he considered the unwisdom of some of the members of the Constitutional Convention."

61. Ruth May Fox's husband joined the Democratic party. After attending a meeting in Logan, Utah, where John Henry Smith and John Morgan spoke on Republicanism, she joined the Republican party as she believed "in protection and centralization of power." The fact that Emmeline B. Wells had joined the Republican party may have influenced her also.

62. She felt that she had been appointed because she was a woman, as she later wrote in "My Story": "On July 25, I was invited to meet with the men's Republican County Committee. Anticipating suffrage for women, the men were vying with each other in consideration for the ladies. The next day I was informed that I had been chosen a member of the Salt Lake County Committee."

63. After the constitutional convention the women of the state continued in politics by joining political parties and working to get candidates in office who were sympathetic to their causes. During the Republican convention Mrs. Emma McVicker was also nominated for superintendent of public instruction. It was declared that although women could not vote yet, it was possible for men to vote for women. But finally the women's names were withdrawn from the ticket for fear that the ticket might be voted down.

64. She evidently attended the meeting but lost her nerve and did not speak, as in her autobiography she wrote: "In September I was scheduled to speak at the ratification meeting in the Salt Lake Theatre. Though I had prepared what I thought was a wonderful speech, and though I attended the meeting, I lost my nerve and hid away in the crowd."

65. Political issues entered in everywhere at the time, as she later wrote in "My Story": "How deeply party lines were cutting across and through non-political groups may be illustrated by occurrences at successive meetings of the Reapers' Club. At the October 12 meeting in speaking by assignment on 'Current Events,' I referred to a dramatic speech against the Priesthood by O. W. Powers, a non-Mormon and a Democrat. I was asked to withdraw my comment because the Club members were divided on political questions. Partisanship was revealed again at the next meeting when one of the members talked in defense of Judge Powers."

66. Wife of Mormon President Joseph F. Smith.

67. Afraid of being arrested for cohabitation he wore the disguise.

68. George Q. Cannon attended the Box Elder Stake conference on October 27 and 28, 1895, without being called but volunteering to be present. He apparently stayed after the conference was over to make additional speeches.

69. On November 5, 1895, the Republican party carried the election by a large majority, and the constitution, containing the suffrage memorial, was approved 28,618 to 2,687 by the voters of Utah. President Cleveland proclaimed Utah Statehood on January 4, 1896, and ceremonies were held January 6, 1896, in Utah.

16

Gentle Persuaders

Utah's First Women Legislators

JEAN BICKMORE WHITE

The night of November 3, 1896, marked the end of an election that is probably unsurpassed in the state's history for intense interest and bitter division over a major issue. It also marked the end of a race that attracted national attention—a contest for a state Senate seat that involved a prominent Mormon polygamist and his fourth wife.

The major issue in the election was silver, one that split Utah Republicans into two rival camps and badly hampered their campaign efforts.

Adding a note of human interest to the election, Utah's first since statehood, was a contest in the Sixth Senatorial District in Salt Lake County, where Angus M. Cannon, Sr., and his physician wife, Dr. Martha Hughes Cannon, were competing.

Ten candidates were running "at large" for the district's five seats, five nominated by the Republicans and five on a Democratic-Populist fusion ticket. Voters were free to vote for *any* five—all Democrats, all Republicans, or any mixture they might choose. It was not true, as has often been stated, that Dr. Cannon and her husband were running *directly* against each other. Both could have won seats, or both could have lost. But they were in a

First published in *Utah Historical Quarterly* 38 (Winter 1970): 31–49. Reprinted by permission.

lively contest, with Democrats benefiting from strong sentiment for William Jennings Bryan at the head of their ticket. It is small wonder, as the daughter of Angus M. and Martha Hughes Cannon has recalled, that her father was "sweating blood" on election night as he waited for the returns.[1] Two proud and strong-willed individuals were in contest where someone's pride was likely to be hurt.

When the returns were in, Dr. Cannon was one of the five Democrats elected in the district, having polled 11,413 votes. Her husband, who was expected to benefit by his prominence as president of the Salt Lake Stake of the Church of Jesus Christ of Latter-day Saints, drew only 8,742 votes. Dr. Cannon ran behind the rest of the Democratic-Populist ticket, while her husband ran ahead of all but one of the five Republican candidates. Also running on the Republican ticket was one of Dr. Cannon's personal friends and co-worker for many years in the woman suffrage movement, Emmeline B. Wells.[2]

Dr. Cannon had become the first woman state senator in the United States in a contest with both her husband and her close friend—a dramatic beginning for a legislative career.

During the campaign this contest had attracted considerable attention, with two daily newspapers lining up on opposite sides. The *Salt Lake Tribune*, which was Republican oriented, supported Angus M. Cannon, while the Democratic *Salt Lake Herald* supported his wife. The public followed the contest with some amusement through the pages of the newspapers. In response to a *Herald* writer's suggestion that Dr. Cannon would be the better choice as a legislator, the *Tribune* offered some advice to her husband: "We do not see anything for Angus M. to do but to either go home and break a bouquet over Mrs. Cannon's head, to show his superiority, or to go up to the *Herald* office and break a chair over the head of the man who wrote that disturber of domestic peace."[3]

Women also won other legislative contests in Utah. In elections for the state House of Representatives, two women competed in Salt Lake County, one in Weber County, and one in Utah County. Two Democratic candidates won: Mrs. Sarah E. Anderson of Ogden and Mrs. Eurithe K. LaBarthe of Salt Lake City.

In the Third Senatorial District, which included Davis, Rich, and Morgan counties, a prominent Republican woman, Mrs. Lucy A. Clark, was defeated by Aquila Nebeker, a Democratic rancher, for the district's only Senate seat. During the campaign, Nebeker was candid about the agony he would suffer if he should happen to lose to a woman. "I am in an awkward position," he told a *Tribune* reporter. "If I don't get out, people will say I

Martha Hughes Cannon, first woman state senator in the
United States. *Courtesy of Archives, Historical Department,
Church of Jesus Christ of Latter-day Saints.*

am frightened. If I do make a struggle for the place, the same people will declare that I am fighting a woman. Then if I win, no one will concede that any credit is due me, while defeat would make me the laughing stock of the whole state."[4]

It seems that the presence of women in Utah's first statewide election was not accepted with complete equanimity, despite the fact that three women were elected to the legislature and eleven women were elected to the position of county recorder. All of the women legislative candidates ran behind their tickets, which may indicate that many Utah voters were not yet willing to accept women in legislative halls.

By the time Utah gained statehood, women had some practical experience as party workers and voters. Utah women had voted in territorial days, from 1870 until they were deprived of the vote by the Edmunds-Tucker Act in 1887. Women had served on party committees, had formed political clubs, and had been wooed with promises of suffrage by both major parties when delegates to the 1895 constitutional convention were chosen.

During the convention, delegates were often reminded of those pledges, not only by the speakers but by the determined suffragists who crowded around the convention hall and listened to the debates with intense interest. One of the most vocal champions of woman suffrage was Orson F. Whitney, a prominent Mormon leader and historian, who pictured women's participation in politics as a giant leap toward purification of government and society. Denying that women were meant only to be mothers and housekeepers, Whitney went on to say:

> I believe the day will come when through that very refinement, the elevating and ennobling influence which woman exerts, in conjunction with other agencies that are at work for the betterment of the world, all that is base and unclean in politics . . . will be "burnt and purged away," and the great result will justify woman's present participation in the cause of reform. . . . It is woman's destiny to have a voice in the affairs of government. She was designed for it. She has a right to it. This great social upheaval, this woman's movement that is making itself heard and felt, means something more than that certain women are ambitious to vote and hold office. I regard it as one of the great levers by which the Almighty is lifting up this fallen world, lifting it nearer to the throne of its Creator. . . .[5]

Whitney was answering the arguments of many who opposed placing the woman suffrage clause in the new constitution—most notably the popular

Mormon official and orator, B. H. Roberts. During the course of the debates over this issue, some of the misgivings about women in politics were voiced, and some of the problems of woman suffrage peculiar to Utah were brought into the open.

It should be realized that the woman suffrage issue was interwoven with the long Mormon-Gentile struggle for electoral strength during the territorial period. The law granting women the vote in territorial elections was passed in 1870 with the active support of Brigham Young. It was opposed by non-Mormons generally in the territory and was challenged in territorial courts on at least two occasions. The provision of the Edmunds-Tucker Act in 1887 withdrawing the right of woman suffrage seems to have sprung from a desire to reduce the number of Mormon voters and to add the weight of non-Mormons (particularly that of such single men as miners and railroad workers) in Utah politics. Through the years, the woman suffrage movement in Utah had the blessing of the First Presidency of the Mormon church; the wives of apostles had been among its leaders. By 1895 the issue of woman suffrage was one that divided many—but by no means all—Mormons and non-Mormons. One of the main arguments of B. H. Roberts against the inclusion of woman suffrage in the constitution was that it would cause non-Mormons (as well as those Mormons who were not enthusiastic about having women vote) to vote against the new constitution and end Utah's hopes for statehood.

According to Apostle Abraham H. Cannon, members of the church First Presidency and Quorum of Twelve Apostles were divided over the question of including a woman suffrage article in the state constitution, fearing that "agitation" of the issue would open old Mormon-Gentile political wounds and lead to the rejection of the constitution and statehood.[6]

There could be little fear that women would "take over" political life by sheer numbers. In 1890 United States Census reports showed that males in the territory outnumbered females by a substantial margin, 110,463 to 97,442. By 1895 the territorial census showed a population of 126,803 males and 120,521 females, still a comfortable edge for the masculine population in the unlikely event that a political issue should sharply divide the sexes.[7]

Instead, delegates to the convention voiced fears that women would not act independently in political life but would obey the dictation of husbands and fathers. It was also asserted that women were of a "higher" nature, not suited to enter the political jungle. Some predicted that women would lose their finer virtues and be "unsexed" in the process of gaining political rights, becoming deeply involved in political life and destroying the tranquility of their homes. No less a personage than Cardinal Gibbons was quoted by Roberts, warning against the extension of political rights to women:

Christian wives and mothers, I have said you are the queens of the domestic kingdom. If you would retain that empire, shun the political arena, avoid the rostrum, beware of unsexing yourselves. If you become embroiled in the political agitation the queenly aureola that encircles your brow will fade away and the reverence that is paid you will disappear. If you have the vain ambition of reigning in public life, your domestic empire will be at an end.[8]

Cardinal Gibbons's remarks seem to be directed beyond the question of woman suffrage to the question of women seeking the power of political office. In 1895 no one knew how many would seek office—or what they would try to accomplish if they won. Would they, as some predicted, lose their femininity and destroy their homes? Would they act independently or obey their husbands' wishes? Would they be militant reformers, trying to impose "radical" programs on the state? Or would they simply fail to do anything constructive if they gained political office?[9]

Some observations relating to these questions were made after less than two decades of statehood by a prominent Utah woman, Mrs. Susa Young Gates. In an appraisal of the effects of woman suffrage in the state, she wrote that the proportion of women in office in the state at that time (1913) was small, "as most women in office in the state are domestic in their habits and lives; they prize the franchise and use it independently, but their attention to politics consists chiefly in their desire, nay their determination, to see that good and honorable men are put in office."[10]

Mrs. Gates held no illusions that women would behave very differently in political life than men did, except perhaps to make political parties "extremely cautious as to the moral qualifications of their candidates," particularly where "liquor and other moral affiliations of the candidates" were concerned.[11]

"Women themselves too often made the mistake of urging that the vote will enable them to purify politics, and to reform the world," she wrote. "What nonsense!" Women would do as much good as men would with the same rights, she said, and would do no more harm than men would.

As for the disruptive effects of equal political rights upon domestic life, Mrs. Gates denied that giving women the franchise had any ill effects. "On the contrary," she observed, "it tends to increase woman's poise, for she has nothing left to ask for, and so turns with delight to giving her best self, her fuller attention in the usual channels of domestic and social life, with the added zest of vital interest in civic affairs."[12]

With the constitutional convention debates and the observations of

Mrs. Gates in mind, the careers of the first three women elected to Utah's legislature will be examined in this article. It should be pointed out that effectiveness in a legislative body rarely can be determined by examining the official records, for they tell us little about personal influence patterns or about all-important committee work on bills. Journals of the House and Senate give little of the flavor of the debates and none of the "behind-the-scenes" activity; fortunately, some of this is brought out in newspaper reports and personal reminiscences. Evaluations must be made on the basis of records and reports now available—after the passage of nearly three-quarters of a century. Within these limitations, the kinds of bills sponsored by Utah's first three women legislators will be shown, as well as the success they had in getting their measures passed and the importance of some of their efforts.

Utah's two women members of the House in the Second Legislature, Eurithe K. LaBarthe of Salt Lake City and Sarah E. Anderson of Ogden, did not capture as much attention as did the more colorful state senator. However, each made her own contribution to Utah political history.

Eurithe K. LaBarthe was a prominent clubwoman in Salt Lake City and the wife of an express company official. She was particularly active in the Ladies' Literary Club and was president of that group at the time she served in the legislature. Under her direction plans were made for building a clubhouse, a structure that was opened January 1, 1898. The clubhouse, located between First South and South Temple, is said to be the first clubhouse built and owned by women west of the Mississippi River.[13]

Although she is usually referred to as a clubwoman—which is sometimes a pejorative term—Eurithe LaBarthe was also a teacher and a former principal of a school in Colorado. Perhaps because of this experience, she served as chairman of the Education Committee in the House. A native of Peoria, Illinois, she came to Utah with her husband in 1892 and became active in Democratic politics.[14]

After her legislative service, Mrs. LaBarthe moved to Denver, where she continued to be active in women's club work. She returned to Utah for a visit, became ill, and died in Salt Lake City on November 22, 1910, at the age of sixty-five.[15]

The so-called "High Hat Law" was Mrs. LaBarthe's most memorable contribution to Utah legislative history. Often cited as an example of the trivial interests women pursue in politics, the bill provided that "any person attending a theater, opera-house or an indoor place of amusement as a spectator shall remove headwear tending to obstruct the view of any other person." A fine of from one to ten dollars was provided for persons convicted of violating provisions of the act.[16]

The "High Hat Law" was vigorously defended by the Ladies Literary Club historian a quarter of a century after its passage:

> Only those who can recollect the high hats, the broad hats, the waving plumes and nodding flower gardens that women carried about on their heads thirty years ago, and who remember how utterly impossible it was to enjoy a performance at the theatre if you happened to sit directly behind one of these monstrosities, can fully appreciate how great a public benefactor Mrs. LaBarthe really was at the time. Although the "High Hat Law" was regarded at first as "freak legislation" by women who were averse to removing their decorative headgear in public places, it was from the first looked upon with favor by men, and it was not a great while before it received universal approval.[17]

Mrs. LaBarthe introduced *H.B.* 50 establishing a curfew ordinance to keep children off the streets at night. The House rejected the bill, upon recommendation of its Committee on Municipal Corporations, on the grounds that such regulations should be within the province of the governing body of cities and towns.[18]

She also introduced a memorial to Congress that was passed in substitute form by both houses and approved by Governor Heber M. Wells. The memorial asked that the Industrial Home on Fifth East, built by the federal government as a refuge for women and children fleeing from polygamous marriages, be granted to the State of Utah to be used for educational or charitable purposes. The memorial pointed out that the building had stood idle for several years because of "changed conditions" in the state and was badly needed by the state for educational and charitable purposes.[19] Apparently Congress turned a deaf ear to the prayers of this memorial, for the building was sold a few years later.

Sarah Elizabeth Nelson Anderson of Ogden, Utah's other woman House member in the Second Legislature, was described by a writer for the Ogden *Standard* as "naturally a strong woman, mentally and physically," and as "one of the most prominent and popular women in Ogden city and Weber county."[20] A legislative colleague, S. A. Kenner, wrote that she was a staunch advocate of equality of man and woman. Her political views were not marked with wavering indecision, he noted, but were thoroughly formed and remained firm. "Yet she did not lose her sweet, womanly repose," he added— perhaps for the benefit of those who felt that women politicians inevitably would lose their feminine charm.[21]

A *Tribune* writer took pains to point out that she was "not what might be termed a clubwoman, her large property interests and her home life with her children occupying the greater portion of her time." The writer added that she took time for reading and study and was "remarkably well posted on matters of current interest and public concern."[22]

Born in 1853, Sarah married an Ogden physician, Dr. Porter L. Anderson, at the age of seventeen. He died in 1888, leaving her with five children. She died on December 22, 1900. Her major contribution to Utah political history was not her legislative record but her part in a lawsuit that threw Utah's registration procedures into turmoil briefly in 1895.

As has been noted, Utah women were deprived of the franchise in 1887 by the Edmunds-Tucker Act. The Enabling Act passed by Congress in 1894 provided for the election of delegates for a constitutional convention by "all male citizens over the age of twenty-one years, who have resided in said Territory for one year next prior to such election. . . ." Delegates to the convention were required to have the same qualifications.[23]

The Enabling Act seemed to make it clear in Section 2 that voting on the ratification or rejection of the new constitution should be confined to "persons possessing the qualifications entitling them to vote for delegates under this act," or male voters only. However, the Act stated in Section 4 that the "qualified voters of said proposed State" should vote in November for or against the constitution, and women were clearly part of the "qualified voters" of the new state under the new constitution. The act further provided in Section 19 that officers for a state government might be elected during the ratification election, but gave no instructions as to eligible voters.[24] The Utah Commission, a federally appointed board that had conducted elections in Utah since the Edmunds Act of 1882, was to make up the registration list for the election of 1895, in which voters would accept or reject the new constitution and choose a slate of state officers. The provisions of the Enabling Act soon came into question, for some women were asking to be registered, and the often-unpopular federal commissioners apparently did not want to have to interpret the law. They suggested that all female electors be registered in alphabetical order on separate pages, so as to be readily distinguished.[25] The commission was relieved of its unhappy burden of decision when Sarah Anderson appeared at the office of Deputy Register Charles Tyree in Ogden's Second Precinct on August 6. Mrs. Anderson asked to be registered to vote both on the ratification of the constitution and on the election of a slate of officers for the new state; Tyree refused to register her on the ground that she was a female. The next day, Mrs. Anderson went to court, seeking a writ of mandate to compel Tyree to register her. The battery of lawyers acting on Mrs. Anderson's behalf—or perhaps using her as part of a scheme to show Democratic sympathy for woman suffrage (as the Republican Ogden *Standard* asserted)—included a number of prominent Democrats. Attorneys bringing the action included both Mormons and non-Mormons, notably Franklin S. Richards, Samuel R. Thurman, and H. P. Henderson.[26]

Sarah Anderson won the first round. Judge H. W. Smith of the District Court in Ogden ruled that women were qualified not only to vote for state officers but on adoption or rejection of the constitution as well, and he ordered Tyree to register Mrs. Anderson.[27] The case was promptly appealed to the territorial Supreme Court by Tyree's equally prominent attorneys, which included Attorney Arthur Brown, later to be a Republican United States senator from Utah. Two of the three justices agreed with Brown that Mrs. Anderson had not been enfranchised by the Enabling Act. The Mormon member of the court, Associate Justice William H. King (later a Democratic congressman and senator from Utah) offered a dissenting opinion.[28] Utah's women had to wait until after statehood to vote—although their hopes had been raised while the case was being appealed. During this time the Republicans in their state convention had nominated a woman to run for state superintendent of public instruction in case women should receive the franchise.[29]

Sarah Anderson served as chairman of the House Committee on Public Health, which handled a number of important bills. However, she does not seem to have been active in introducing and getting her own bills passed. She introduced one bill (*H.B.* 39) regarding police and fire commissioners that was killed by an unfavorable committee report. She also introduced *H.B.* 26 to provide for teaching the effects of alcoholic drink and narcotics in schools. A substitute bill with these provisions was incorporated in the state's revised statutes.[30]

Dr. Martha Hughes Cannon is the best known and most colorful of Utah's women politicians of her era.[31] Born on July 1, 1857, in Llandudno, Wales, she came to Utah with her parents as a young child. Her father died only three days after the family's arrival in Salt Lake City, and her mother married a widower, James P. Paul. Despite the family's limited means, she dreamed of studying to become a physician. To realize this goal she saved as much as she could from her salary as a school teacher and later as a typesetter for the *Deseret Evening News* and the *Woman's Exponent*. She had been "called" by the First Presidency of the L.D.S. Church for the typesetting position and had learned to set Scandinavian type in order to earn higher wages.

In 1876 she enrolled in the pre-medical department of the University of Deseret. Two years later she was blessed and "set apart" by L.D.S. church President John Taylor for medical studies. Arriving at the University of

Michigan in the fall of 1878 with slender financial resources, she began her studies, washing dishes and making beds at a boarding house to help defray costs. She graduated with the M.D. degree on her twenty-third birthday, July 1, 1880. Feeling that training in oratory would enable her to be more effective as a lecturer on public health, she went to Philadelphia and enrolled in both the University of Pennsylvania and the National School of Elocution and Oratory. In 1882 she received a Bachelor of Science degree from the university, the only woman in a class of seventy-five. She also received a Bachelor of Oratory degree from the school of elocution.

After returning to Utah she built a private medical practice and served as resident physician at Deseret Hospital. On October 6, 1884, she became the fourth wife of Angus M. Cannon, a man who was twenty-three years her senior and a member of the board of the hospital. After the birth of her first child, she left the state in an effort to permit her husband to avoid imprisonment by federal authorities. She went to Europe, where she visited leading hospitals; after returning to Utah she established the first training school for nurses in the state. When her second child was born she again left her medical practice to live in San Francisco. On her return she resumed her practice, specializing in the diseases of women and children.

Mattie Cannon, as she was usually known, became an ardent Democrat and also played an active role in the woman suffrage movement. Before her election to the Senate she was active in suffrage groups in Utah and spoke at a national suffrage meeting at the Columbian Exposition in Chicago in 1893. In 1898 she went to Washington D.C., to speak at a convention marking the fiftieth anniversary of the Seneca Falls declaration of women's rights and appeared before a congressional committee urging the lawmakers to give women the vote. Of this convention Dr. Cannon wrote to her friend, Emmeline B. Wells, that "Utah received her full share of honor and recognition, and was acknowledged to be in the vanguard of progress. On every occasion was her representative treated in the most courteous and considerate manner."[32] Dr. Cannon's strong Democratic party loyalties were evident in the same letter when she described President William McKinley as "a great man, notwithstanding he is not a Democrat."[33]

Because of her unique position as a physician, state senator, and plural wife, Mattie Cannon was the subject of several interviews by writers for leading publications. She was described by the English socialist, Beatrice Webb, as a "vivacious frank little Senator. . . ." Mrs. Webb's appraisal continued:

She was such a self-respectful vigourous pure-minded little soul:

sensitive yet unself-conscious, indiscreet yet loyal. She had no training for the political career she had chosen, and I suspect her medical knowledge was as fragmentary as her economics. As a citizen I should doubt her wisdom as a legislator—and as a patient I certainly should not trust her skill in diagnosing my case. But as a friend I should rely on her warm sympathy and freedom from the meaner motives of life.[34]

As usual, Dr. Cannon strongly defended polygamy in the Webb interview. She also offered a firm defense of plural marriage when she was interviewed a few days after her election by a writer for the *San Francisco Examiner*. Dr. Cannon maintained that a plural wife was not as much a slave as a single woman. She noted that "If her husband has four wives, she has three weeks of freedom every single month." She was firm in her defense of women working and engaging in worthwhile activities outside of the home:

Somehow I know that women who stay home all the time have the most unpleasant homes there are. You give me a woman who thinks about something besides cook stoves and wash tubs and baby flannels, and I'll show you, nine times out of ten, a successful mother.

She said she felt women should run for political offices, except perhaps for such offices as governor—they were too "mannish."[35]

It is unlikely that Mattie Cannon was ever described as "mannish." She was frequently described by her contemporaries as attractive, charming, and completely feminine. With the charm went an independent spirit; she had a mind of her own and interests of her own to pursue in her legislative career. Not even the redoubtable Angus M. Cannon could control her vote.

When she took her seat in the Senate at the opening of the Second Legislature on January 11, 1897, it was noted in the *Tribune* that she was a little late arriving, and that a handsome bouquet of roses adorned her desk.[36] Within a month she had introduced three bills, including "An Act to Protect the Health of Women and Girl Employees" (*S.B.* 31), "An Act Providing for the Compulsory Education of Deaf, Dumb and Blind Children" (*S.B.* 27). The first made it mandatory for employers to provide "chairs, stools, or other contrivances" where women or girls employed as clerks might rest when not working.[37] The second made education of deaf, dumb, or blind children at the state school mandatory (with certain exceptions).[38]

The third measure was the one in which Dr. Cannon was most vitally involved, since her interest in sanitation and public health had provided much of the motivation for her entry into politics. The act became part of the revised statutes that were compiled by a special commission and provided the basis for a statewide attack on problems of sanitation and contagious disease.[39] The act established a seven-member State Board of Health to stimulate and encourage establishment of local boards of health and to carry out a number of other functions designed to improve sanitary conditions, water supply, and disease control. Dr. Cannon was one of the first members appointed by Governor Wells to the board, all unpaid except the secretary.

The annual report of the new health board makes it clear that Dr. Cannon and other members had a difficult and frustrating first year in 1898 trying to get apathetic local officials to organize boards of health and to get public support for enforcement of a law prohibiting school attendance of children with contagious diseases.[40] It was also clear that more legislation, with "teeth" for enforcement, was needed. During the second half of her four-year Senate term, in the Third Legislature in 1899, Dr. Cannon introduced an act that contained much needed rules and regulations in a number of public health areas. The act (*S.B.* 40) provided for the suppression of nuisances and contagious diseases, prescribed quarantine rules and regulations, provided for burial permits, promoted protection of water supplies, and established rules for inspection of school buildings and exclusion of persons with contagious or infectious diseases from schools.[41]

Another measure relating to health introduced by Dr. Cannon in the Third Legislature (*S.B.* 1) authorized the erection of a hospital building for the Utah State School for the Deaf and Dumb. A member of the board of the school until she resigned to serve on a newly created State Board of Health, Dr. Cannon was a sympathetic supporter of the school.[42] Another bill she introduced in 1899 providing for the teaching in the public schools of the effects of alcoholic drinks and narcotics (*S.B.* 37) was passed by the Senate but defeated in the House. She spent considerable time studying narcotics problems; perhaps her suggestions for extensive education on drug problems would meet with a more favorable response today.

Mattie Cannon was expecting her third child during the 1899 session. She was sometimes absent from roll-call votes during the long balloting for United States senator but generally seems to have been present to pursue her interests and to serve as chairman of the Public Health Committee.

Any fears that women legislators would accept the dictation of their husbands were unfounded in the case of Mattie Cannon. Her daughter reports that in 1897 Angus M. Cannon was upset because she had voted for the excommunicated Mormon apostle, Moses Thatcher, for United States senator against his wishes and in the face of strong opposition by Mormon church leaders.[43] His annoyance may have been compounded by the publicity his wife received when she switched her vote to Thatcher. During the first part of the prolonged balloting for senator by the two houses in joint session, Mattie Cannon appeared to be staying out of the battle, voting first for Senate President Aquila Nebeker, and later for a Democratic attorney, Orlando W. Powers. On the forty-third ballot on February 1, she suddenly switched her vote to Moses Thatcher, explaining that she feared a prolonged deadlock might mean the entrance of "an inferior dark horse, backed by Republican influence and gold . . . who might be elected."[44] The *Tribune* the next day ran a large front-page story with a two-column drawing of Dr. Cannon. "Senator Cannon prefaced her vote with an address so eloquent that despite parliamentary decorum and the rigid rules against demonstrations she was cheered and cheered again at its conclusion," the *Tribune* reported on February 2. She stayed with Thatcher through the fifty-third and final ballot, when Joseph L. Rawlins was elected by a bare majority of thirty-two.

Another United States senator was to be elected in 1899 during the Third Legislature. Again, according to her daughter, she defied her husband's wishes as well as the pleas of her charming and persuasive nephew, Senator Frank J. Cannon. Elected as a Republican in 1896, Frank J. Cannon faced an uphill fight for re-election in 1899 by an overwhelmingly Democratic state legislature. Needing every possible vote, he visited his Democratic aunt and asked her to support him. She refused, telling him that she could not vote for a Republican since she had been elected on the Democratic ticket. He left Dr. Mattie's home by the back door, feeling "quite depressed" by her refusal.[45]

The Senate and House members struggled unsuccessfully through 164 ballots trying to find a candidate on whom 32 members could agree. Near the end, Angus M. Cannon's brother, George Q. Cannon, counselor in the First Presidency of the Mormon church and father of Frank J., entered the race. He did not receive Mattie Cannon's vote, either. She voted from the beginning to the end of the balloting for the millionaire mining man, Alfred W. McCune, apparently unimpressed by charges (investigated by a special committee but not proved) that he tried to bribe a House member. She proved to be a highly independent woman in a body full of legislators too independent to reach a common decision in 1899. The end result of all this independence was that one of Utah's seats in the United States Senate remained vacant.

Mattie Cannon did not run for office after her term expired. She continued to serve on the State Board of Health and to practice medicine. During the last years of her life, she lived in Los Angeles, where she worked in the Graves Clinic. She died in Los Angeles July 10, 1932, and was buried in Salt Lake City. The main funeral speaker was none other than B. H. Roberts, who had predicted dire consequences if women were given the vote—to say nothing of entering office. Both faithful Democrats, Mattie Cannon and Roberts had become good friends over the years since the constitutional convention.

Utah's first three women legislators did not reform the state over night; they did not even attempt to do so. They were typical of the earnest suffragists of their times, with political aims not markedly different from those of their male colleagues. They showed, perhaps, a greater concern for women, children, and the physically handicapped. However, they left to the Populists the introduction of most of the labor and "progressive" legislation, apparently having little inclination to sponsor sweeping reforms.

Dr. Cannon was able, because of her professional training, to help the state move forward in the area of public health. But even in this area, the approach was one of "gradualism," moving at a moderate rate and seeking to build public support.

Except for the memorial asking for the Industrial Home, the three women legislators did not sponsor any of the many pieces of legislation that sought favors or funds from the federal government. If some of their bills seem trivial—notably the "High Hat Law"—a day-by-day reading of the legislative journals shows that their colleagues also introduced much legislation that was equally trivial and catered to parochial interests. In short, their legislative records need neither a contrived defense nor unwarranted praise. They were about the same as those of their fellow legislators, containing both the significant and the relatively unimportant.

Governor Wells was reported by Beatrice Webb to have said that the women in the Senate and House in 1897 had not accomplished anything except a law prohibiting large hats at places of amusement. And this law, he added, had been passed "out of courtesy" by the men.[46] Perhaps he signed it for the same reason. If the governor ignored the more substantial victories of the women legislators, he inadvertently made a vital point about women in politics before the turn of the century—and perhaps today as well. They were always reliant upon the "courtesy" of the men. With militant tactics they would have accomplished nothing. With quiet charm and gentle persuasion they contributed much to Utah's Second Legislature.

> Give us the power and we'll dispel,
> The reign of tyrants born of hell:
> From men's unblushing demon deeds,
> Her earnest soul for freedom pleads.
> (*Woman's Exponent*, 22 [January 15, 1894], 81.)

Notes

1. Interview by the author with Mrs. Elizabeth Cannon McCrimmon, August 4, 1969, in Alhambra, California.
2. Election returns from Salt Lake County, *Salt Lake Tribune*, November 14, 1896.
3. *Salt Lake Tribune*, November 1, 1896.
4. Ibid., October 30, 1896.
5. Utah, Constitutional Convention, 1895, *Official Report of the Proceedings and Debates* (2 vols., Salt Lake City, 1898), I, 508. Hereafter referred to as *Convention Proceedings*.
6. Abraham H. Cannon Journal (Utah State Historical Society), April 4, 1895.
7. Results of both enumerations reported in the *Salt Lake Tribune Almanac*, 1896 (Salt Lake City, 1897), xii. For more detailed information on sex and marital status in 1890 see U. S. Department of the Interior, Census Division, *Abstract of the Eleventh Census: 1890* (2nd ed., Washington, D.C., 1896), 10 and 56.
8. *Convention Proceedings*, I, 469.
9. According to the *Tribune Almanac*, women wasted little time before voting and seeking office after the new state constitution was adopted. The *Almanac* for 1899 reported that Mrs. M. J. Atwood was elected school trustee in Kamas, Summit County, on January 9, 1896—just a few days after statehood day. The same source listed the first woman to vote in Utah statehood as Mrs. George Mullins, who cast a ballot in the municipal election at Mercur on April 21, 1896. *Salt Lake Tribune Almanac*, 1899, 36.
10. Letter from Susa Young Gates to Arthur W. Page of *Women's Work*, answering the inquiries of a number of prominent English women as to the effects of woman suffrage, 1913. Reprinted in Kate B. Carter, comp., *Woman Suffrage in the West* ([Salt Lake City], 1943), 304.
11. Ibid., 305.
12. Ibid., 306–7.
13. Katherine B. Parsons, *History of Fifty Years — Ladies' Literary Club* (Salt Lake City, 1927), 93.
14. *Salt Lake Tribune*, January 10, 1897.
15. *Deseret Evening News* (Salt Lake City), November 23, 1910.
16. Original and substitute H. B. 13 in file of House Bills, 1897 (Utah State Archives, State Capitol).
17. Parsons, *Ladies' Literary Club*, 95.
18. Utah, Second Legislature, *Journal of the House of Representatives*, 1897, 145.
19. See Senate Joint Memorial 9, incorporating Mrs. LaBarthe's House Joint Memorial 6 in file of Memorials, 1897 (Utah State Archives).
20. *Standard* (Ogden, Utah), December 22, 1900.
21. S. A. Kenner, *Utah As It Is. With a Comprehensive Statement of Utah As It Was* (Salt Lake City, 1904), 451.
22. *Salt Lake Tribune*, January 10, 1897.

23. *Convention Proceedings*, I, 3. The text of the Enabling Act is contained therein, I, 3–8.

24. Ibid., 4, 5, 8.

25. *Deseret Evening News*, July 23, 1895.

26. *Standard*, August 7, 1895.

27. *Deseret Evening News*, July 23, 1895.

28. Anderson V. Tyree, 12 Utah Reports 129 (1895).

29. *Deseret Evening News*, August 29, 1895, Mrs. Emma J. McVicker was nominated, with Dr. John R. Park as a substitute to run if women were denied the right to vote and run for office. Dr. Park's name was placed on the ballot after the Supreme Court ruled in the Anderson case, and he was elected.

30. See file of House Bills, 1897 (Utah State Archives).

31. Several biographical articles on Dr. Cannon have been published. Data herein, unless otherwise cited, is from an unpublished manuscript by her daughter, Mrs. Elizabeth C. McCrimmon, in the Utah State Historical Society library, and from Andrew Jenson, *Latter-day Saint Biographical Encyclopedia* (4 vols., Salt Lake City, 1901–1936), IV, 86–88.

32. McCrimmon MS, 17.

33. Ibid.

34. David A. Shannon, ed., *Beatrice Webb's American Diary, 1898* (Madison, Wisconsin, 1963), 134–35.

35. Interview published in the *San Francisco Examiner*, November 8, 1896, reprinted in the *Salt Lake Herald*, November 11, 1896.

36. *Salt Lake Tribune*, January 12, 1897.

37. Utah, *Laws of Utah*, 1897, Ch. XI, 24–25.

38. Ibid., Ch. XX, 36.

39. Utah, *Revised Statutes*, 1898, Title 24, 315–18.

40. See Utah, *Public Documents*, 1897–98, Sec. 22, "Report of the State Board of Health."

41. Utah, *Public Documents*, 1899–1900, Sec. 22, "Report of the State Board of Health."

42. Bill as amended in file of Senate Bills, 1899 (Utah State Archives).

43. Interview with Mrs. Elizabeth C. McCrimmon.

44. *Salt Lake Tribune*, February 2, 1899.

45. McCrimmon interview. Dr. Cannon received several "courtesy votes" for United States senator from her colleagues in 1897 and one vote for senator in 1899.

46. Shannon, *American Diary*, 130.

Heber M. Wells, first governor of the state of Utah. *Courtesy of Archives, Historical Department, Church of Jesus Christ of Latter-day Saints.*

Epilogue

Woman Suffrage in Utah (1902)

HEBER M. WELLS, GOVERNOR OF UTAH

The lawmakers seem to be afraid of enfranchising women because of the deteriorating effect which politics might have on womankind. If this be true let the experience of Utah speak. For six years women in this State have had the right to vote and hold office. Have the wheels of progress stopped? Instead we have bounded forward with seven-league boots. Have the fears and predictions of the local opponents of woman suffrage been verified? Have women degenerated into low politicians, neglecting their homes and stifling the noblest emotions of womanhood? On the contrary women are respected quite as much as they were before Statehood; loved as rapturously as ever, and are led to the altar with the same beatific strains of music and the same unspeakable joy that invested ceremonials before their enfranchisement.

The plain facts are that in this State the influence of woman in politics has been distinctly elevating. In the primary, in the convention and at the polls her very presence inspires respect for law and order. Few men are so base that they will not be gentlemen in the presence of ladies. Experience has shown that women have voted their intelligent convictions. They understand the questions at issue and they vote conscientiously and fearlessly. While

---

First published in Susan B. Anthony and Ida Husted Harper, eds., *The History of Woman Suffrage*, vol. 4 (New York: Fowler & Wells, 1902): 1089.

we do not claim to have the purest politics in the world in Utah, it will be readily conceded that the woman-vote is a terror to evil-doers, and our course is, therefore, upward and onward.

One of the bugaboos of the opposition was that women would be compelled to sit on juries. Not a single instance of the kind has happened in the State, for the reason that women are never summoned; the law simply exempts them, but does not exclude them. Another favorite idiocy of the anti-suffragists is that if the women vote they ought to be compelled to fight. In the same manner the law exempts them from military service.

For one I am proud of Utah's record in dealing with her female citizens. I take the same pride in it that a good husband would who had treated his wife well, and I look forward with eager hope to the day when woman suffrage shall become universal.

Chronology of Woman Suffrage in Utah

COMPILED BY KATHRYN L. MACKAY

1848

In Seneca Falls, New York, Elizabeth Cady Stanton and Lucretia Mott organize a convention to consider: "The social, civil and religious condition and rights of woman." 100 men and women sign a Declaration of Sentiments which calls for women to secure "the sacred right to the elective franchise."

1866

After several annual "rights" conventions, women help form the American Equal Rights Association, dedicated to human rights, which works for passage of the 14th Amendment—"No State shall . . . abridge the privileges . . . of citizens."

1868

Congress considers legislation to enfranchise the women of the western territories. "Female suffrage might perhaps be tried with novel effect in the territory of Utah—the State of Deseret. There the 'better half' of humanity is such a strong numerical majority that even if all the other half should vote the other way, they would carry the election. Perhaps it would result in casting out polygamy and Mormonism in general. . . . Here would be a capital field of woman suffrage to make a start, and we presume nobody would object to the experiment" (*New York Times* editorial).

1869

Elizabeth Cady Stanton and Susan B. Anthony form the National Woman Suffrage Association (NWSA), an all-female organization, advocating a variety of women's rights reforms. This group fights for constitutional recognition of woman suffrage.

Lucy Stone and others organize the American Woman Suffrage Association (AWSA), which includes men in leadership roles and becomes a place for women who value the appearance of respectability. Because of the polygamy issue, Mormon "leading sisters" are not accepted by this group. AWSA focuses on woman suffrage in the territories and in state constitutions. (The *Woman's Journal* was the publication of the AWSA, becoming in 1917 *The Woman Citizen*.)

William Godbe and other Mormon dissidents initiate the New Movement, part of which is a Ladies Improvement Society, headed by writer Fanny Stenhouse. The Society sends Godbe wives to the NWSA to represent Utah.

December 10: Wyoming women petition for the ballot; the Wyoming territorial legislature establishes woman suffrage, including the right to hold office.

1870s

NWSA encourages women to test 14th Amendment by attempting to register and vote, which shifts suffrage focus from benefits that would supposedly accrue from women voting to the legal right of the franchise.

1870

January 13: A "great indignation meeting" is held on Temple Square, Salt Lake City; nearly 6,000 women rally to express opposition to the Cullom anti-polygamy bill.

February 12: The Utah territorial legislature passes a law "That every woman of the age of twenty-one years who has resided in this Territory six months next preceding any general or special election, born or naturalized citizen of the United States, shall be entitled to vote at any election in this Territory."

The act enfranchises 17,179 women, many times the number in Wyoming, but does not allow women to hold office.

February 14: Twenty-five Utah women vote.

Sarah M. Kimball, an LDS "leading sister," begins a program of civil education. Relief Society meetings become classes in government, mock trials, and symposia on parliamentary law.

August 14: Two thousand women enter polling places through separate women's entrances and cast their votes.

The Liberal Party organizes to oppose Mormon Church–nominated candidates for elected territorial offices. The Mormon Church counters by organizing the People's Party. Women participate in the conventions and mass rallies held by both parties.

Woman suffrage is under legislative consideration in most states outside the South; no state legislature is convinced.

1871

June: Elizabeth Cady Stanton and Susan B. Anthony, while touring the western United States on behalf of woman suffrage, visit Salt Lake City and meet with New Movement women and LDS women.

1872

Utah makes fourth bid for statehood. Women help select delegates to a constitutional convention and vote to ratify a proposed state constitution that contains a woman suffrage clause.

Cornelia Paddock, Sarah Ann Cooke, and other Utah women, fearing statehood will strengthen the power of the LDS leadership, initiate a petition drive against statehood and the proposed state constitution.

Georgiana Snow and non-Utahn Phoebe W. Couzins are admitted to the Utah Bar. (Couzins is active in national suffrage efforts until 1897, when she declares herself opposed to suffrage. She explains that she has come to realize that women are no better than men in finding cures for the nation's many ills. This unmarried career woman urges women to fulfill their "natural" destinies by being good "home-keepers" and wives.)

April 3: United States Congress considers Wheeler bill "to promote purity of elections" in Utah. It includes measure to disfranchise Utah women.

June: *Woman's Exponent* begins publication in Utah to encourage in women an interest in political issues and to rebut attacks against Mormon women and polygamy. (Louisa Greene Richards is first editor.)

1877

Emmeline B. Woodword Wells assumes full editorial and publishing responsibilities for the *Woman's Exponent* (which continues until 1914). She challenges Charlotte Cobb Godbe in representing Utah women. This year she becomes the first "leading sister" to be recognized by NWSA as representing Utah women.

Woman suffrage fails by popular vote in the new state of Colorado. Not until 1893 does a woman suffrage referendum pass there.

1878

An anti-polygamy mass meeting is held in Salt Lake City. The Ladies Anti-Polygamy Society is organized with Sarah Ann Sutton Cooke (who in 1877 had helped found the Ladies Literary Club) as president. In its publication *The Anti-Polygamy Standard*, the society maintains that woman suffrage in Utah Territory is simply a tool LDS Church leaders use to overwhelm the "gentiles." The society networks with the Women's Christian Temperance Union and other "social purity" movements.

A federal woman suffrage amendment is first introduced in Congress, to be reintroduced in each successive session through 1887.

1879

Utah Mormon women rally to protest pending federal anti-polygamy legislation. That same year, delegates sent by the LDS Relief Society (Zina Young Williams and Emmeline B. Woodword Wells) are officially recognized as representing Utah women at the NWSA Convention.

U.S. Supreme Court upholds the constitutionality of anti-polygamy legislation.

1882

Congress passes the Edmunds Act which disfranchises all polygamous men and women.

1886

March: Mormon women conduct additional mass meetings and draw up a resolution entitled "Appeal for Freedom, Justice and Equal Rights": "Resolved, By the women of Utah in mass meetings assembled, that the suffrage originally conferred upon us as a political privilege, has become a vested right by possession and usage for 16 years and that we protest against being deprived of that right without process of law, and for no other reason than that we do not vote to suit our political opponents."

1887

Congress passes the Edmunds-Tucker bill which disfranchises all women in Utah Territory. (Women in Washington Territory also lose, in a court decision, the franchise they had exercised since 1883.)

1888

Emily S. Richards proposes to LDS church officials and to NWSA leaders that a Utah suffrage association be formed. Anti-polygamist leader Jennie Froiseth opposes Emily because she does not think "woman suffrage is good for Utah." The next year, Richards helps create the Utah Woman Suffrage Association (UWSA), and she forms nineteen suffrage associations in twenty-seven Utah counties by 1894.

1890

LDS President Woodruff issues a manifesto advising Mormons to submit to the laws of the land, including those outlawing polygamy.

At its Washington, D.C., convention the NWSA merges with the AWSA to become the National American Woman Suffrage Association (NAWSA).

Wyoming enters the union with a state constitution that includes woman suffrage.

1891

LDS Church dissolves its own political party and encourages members to affiliate with national political parties. Two years later, the opposition Liberal Party disbands.

1894

July: Congress passes the Enabling Act for Utah statehood.

September: Utah Republican and Democratic Parties hold conventions, and both ratify platforms supporting woman suffrage.

1895

March 4–May 8: Utah's state constitutional convention is held. UWSA presents memorials to the convention summarizing the reasons Utah women should have political equality with men. Women's political rights become the most bitterly fought issue of the convention. Arguments against woman suffrage include concerns that Congress will not accept a state constitution allowing woman suffrage, fears that woman suffrage will only increase the political domination of the LDS church, and warnings that suffrage will lessen women's "domestic virtues."

April 18: Delegates vote in favor of including in the proposed Utah state constitution an article based on the Wyoming constitution: "The rights of citizens of the State of Utah to vote and hold office shall not be denied or abridged on account of sex. Both male and female citizens of this State shall equally enjoy all civil, political, and religious rights and privileges."

May 12: Susan B. Anthony and Rev. Anna Howard Shaw visit Utah to share in the celebration of Utah woman suffrage. They hold a NAWSA meeting.

August 6: Sarah E. Nelson Anderson of Ogden tries to register to vote both on the ratification of the constitution and on the election of a slate of officers for the new state. Eventually the territorial Supreme Court rules that women have not been enfranchised by the Enabling Act. Women (Emma McVicker, Lilie Pardee, Emmeline B. Wells) who had been nominated to offices withdraw.

November 5: More than four fifths of the male voters vote in favor of the new state constitution.

1896

January 4: President Cleveland signs the act admitting Utah as a state.

November 3: Sarah E. Nelson Anderson (a major property owner in Ogden) and Eurithe K. LaBarthe (prominent in SLC women's clubs) are elected to the Utah House of Representatives. Dr. Martha Hughes Cannon (SLC physician) is elected the first woman state senator.

The state of Idaho enfranchises women through a constitutional amendment.

1899

Carrie Chapman Catt, chair of the NAWSA, visits Utah to assist in forming a Utah Council of Women to support the suffrage efforts in other states. Emily S. Richards is elected president.

1901

The Socialist Party is organized nationally and in Utah. Kate S. Hilliard, who had been active in the UWSA, is one of the organizing leaders. Until 1912, when the Progressive and Prohibition parties endorse suffrage, the Socialists are the only national political party unequivocally supporting full voting rights for women. In every election from 1902 to 1920, Utah Socialist state and county tickets include women candidates.

1911

The National Association Opposed to Woman Suffrage (NAOWS) organizes out of a number of state and local anti-suffrage groups. The next year it begins publishing *The Woman's Protest*. Articles deriding woman suffrage in the West appear regularly.

1914

A federal woman suffrage amendment is again introduced to Congress.

1915

The U.S. Senate Committee on Woman Suffrage holds hearings. Alice George, one of the leaders of the NAOWS, testifies that the western states that have woman suffrage are influenced by the LDS Church, which uses women's votes to augment its political power.

Carrie Chapman Catt resumes presidency of NAWSA. The Utah state chapter endorses her "Winning Plan," a unified campaign to get the suffrage amendment passed.

1916

Alice Paul creates the National Woman's Party which begins using more radical tactics, leading to the arrests of hundreds of women picketing the White House. The Utah chapter of the party protests these arrests. (In 1923 the NWP will sponsor the introduction in congress of an Equal Rights Amendment. The U.S. Senate will not pass this amendment until 1972; it will fail ratification.)

1917

Utah State Senator Elizabeth A. Pugsley Hayward sponsors a memorial from Utah to the U.S. Congress urging passage of a federal suffrage amendment.

1919

June: The U.S. Senate passes a woman suffrage amendment. Carrie Chapman Catt begins organizing in various suffrage states a new association—The League of Women Voters.

1920

February: The National League of Women Voters is organized at Chicago. Susa Young Gates is one of the Utah delegates.

August: The Nineteenth Amendment is ratified by Tennessee, the thirty-sixth and final state needed. It states that "The right of citizens of the United States to vote shall not be denied or abridged by the United States or by any State on account of sex."